KINtop Studies in Early Cinema – volume 2
series editors: Frank Kessler, Sabine Lenk, Martin Loiperdinger

Importing Asta Nielsen:
The International Film Star
in the Making 1910–1914

KINtop. Studies in Early Cinema
KINtop Studies in Early Cinema expands the efforts to promote historical research and theoretical reflection on the emergence of moving pictures undertaken by the internationally acclaimed *KINtop* yearbook (published in German from 1992–2006). It brings a new collection of anthologies and monographs in English by internationally renowned authors as well as young scholars. The scope of the series ranges from studies on the formative years of the emerging medium of animated photographs to research on the institutionalisation of cinema in the years up to the First World War. Books in this series will also explore the many facets of 19th and early 20th century visual culture as well as initiatives to preserve and present this cinematographic heritage. Early cinema has become one of the most dynamic fields of scholarly research in cinema studies worldwide, and this series aims to provide an international platform for new insights and fresh discoveries in this thriving area.
Series editors: Frank Kessler, Sabine Lenk and Martin Loiperdinger

Importing Asta Nielsen:
The International Film Star
in the Making 1910–1914

Edited by
Martin Loiperdinger and Uli Jung

British Library Cataloguing in Publication Data

Importing Asta Nielsen:
The International Film Star in the Making 1910–1914

Series: KINtop Studies in Early Cinema – volume 2

A catalogue entry for this book is available from the British Library

ISBN: 9780 86196 708 7 (Paperback)

Cover: Cut-out of a poster from Det Danske Filminstitut.

Published by
John Libbey Publishing Ltd, 3 Leicester Road, New Barnet, Herts EN5 5EW, United Kingdom

e-mail: john.libbey@orange.fr; web site: www.johnlibbey.com
Direct orders (UK and Europe): direct.orders@marston.co.uk

Distributed in N. America by **Indiana University Press**, 601 North Morton St, Bloomington, IN 47404, USA. www.iupress.indiana.edu

© 2013 Copyright John Libbey Publishing Ltd. All rights reserved.
Unauthorized duplication contravenes applicable laws.

Printed and bound in China by 1010 Printing International Ltd.

Contents

Acknowledgements ix

Uli Jung and Martin Loiperdinger
Introduction 1

PART I ASTA NIELSEN IN DENMARK

Casper Tybjerg
Presenting AFGRUNDEN in Copenhagen and Skive 15

Isak Thorsen
Nordisk Films Kompagni and Asta Nielsen 25

Julie K. Allen
Ambivalent Admiration. Asta Nielsen's Conflicted Reception in Denmark, 1911–14 39

Agnes Schindler
"Aðalhlutverkið leikur: Frú Asta Nielsen Gad".
Asta Nielsen Films in Reykjavík, 1912–1915 53

PART II AFGRUNDEN – DEBUT FILM OF AN UNKNOWN ACTRESS

Outi Hupaniittu
AFGRUNDEN aka KUILU in Finland.
Nordiska Biograf, Exclusive Distribution and Newly Established Censorship 65

Andrzej Dębski
AFGRUNDEN in Warsaw and Asta Nielsen's Popularity in Polish territories 77

Ouissal Mejri
AFGRUNDEN and Professor Ehrlich's Magic Bullet in Alexandria 87

PART III THE MAKING OF THE FILM STAR IN GERMANY

Martin Loiperdinger
"Die Duse der Kino-Kunst". Asta Nielsen's Berlin Made Brand 93

Pierre Stotzky
Screening Asta Nielsen Films in Metz before the First World War 113

Andrea Haller
Advertising Asta Nielsen and the Long-Feature Film – the Case of Mannheim 123

Contents

PART IV ASTA NIELSEN FILMS IN LOCAL EXHIBITION

Patric Blaser
Asta Nielsen Films in Innsbruck before the First World War — 142

Mattia Lento
Asta Nielsen in Zurich – Film Exhibition and Reviews — 153

Adrian Gerber
Advertising Asta Nielsen. Traces of Local Trade Rivalry in Zurich and Transnational Circulation — 163

Pierre-Emmanuel Jaques
Asta Nielsen in the Cinema Theatres of Lausanne, 1911–1913 — 169

Paul Lesch
"Earning the Audience's Unbridled Applause" – Asta Nielsen Films in Luxembourg — 179

María Antonia Paz and Julio Montero
"Celebrada artista de fama mundial". Asta Nielsen in Barcelona, 1910–1914 — 187

PART V CENSORSHIP VERSUS ART DISCOURSE

Jon Burrows
"The Great Asta Nielsen", "The Shady Exclusive" and the Birth of Film Censorship in Britain, 1911–1914 — 203

Anne Bachmann
Vindicating THE GREAT MOMENT against Swedish Censorship. Asta Nielsen's Soulful Eyes as On-Screen Pantomime — 215

PART VI THE INTERNATIONAL CINEMA CELEBRITY

Giovanni Lasi
Italy's First Film Star – Asta Nielsen, 'Polaris' — 235

Lauri Piispa
Asta Nielsen and the Russian Film Trade — 247

Ansje van Beusekom
Distributing, Programming and Recycling Asta Nielsen films in the Netherlands, 1911–1920 — 259

Valdo Kneubühler
Opportunities Gone By – Asta Nielsen Films in France before the First World War — 273

Richard Abel
Asta Nielsen's Flickering Stardom in the USA, 1912–1914 — 279

PART VII OUTSIDE THE WESTERN WORLD

Rielle Navitski
Asta Nielsen as Import Commodity. International Stardom and Local Film Distribution in Brazil, 1911–1915 — 291

Dafna Ruppin
Asta Nielsen, Cinema-going and Film Censorship in the Netherlands Indies, 1912–1918 — 299

Stephen Bottomore
"The Great Favorite, Miss Asta Neilson". Asta Nielsen on Australasian Screens   309

Sawako Ogawa
Asta Nielsen and Shimpa Films in Japan   321

PART VIII   ASTA NIELSEN – POSITIONING HER STATUS

Caroline Henkes
Asta Nielsen and Her Destitute Female Characters   329

Annemone Ligensa
Asta Nielsen in Germany: A Reception-Oriented Approach   343

Ian Christie
From Screen Personalities to Stars: Analysing Early Film Fame in Europe   367

Asta Nielsen – International Filmography, 1910–1914   367

The Contributors   379

Acknowledgements

This book collects the proceedings of the international conference "Importing Asta Nielsen: cinema-going and the making of the star system in the early 1910s" which took place at the German Film Museum in Frankfurt, 27 to 29 September 2011, hosted by Deutsches Filminstitut. We wish to thank all participants for their willingness to submit their contributions. We were lucky to be able to invite since yet another number of researchers who did fine and original research on Asta Nielsen's significance in countries which could not be covered during the conference. Their contributions are an invaluable addition to the scope of this book.

We are grateful to Det Danske Filminstitut, Copenhagen; Nordisk Film Archive, Valby; Icelandic Film Archive, Reykjavík; National Library of Sweden, Stockholm; National Archive of Finland, Helsinki; Deutsche Kinemathek, Berlin; Renate Seydel Collection, Berlin; Stadtarchiv Mannheim; Stadtarchäologie, Zurich; Archiv Tram-Museum, Zurich; Musée historique de Lausanne; Archives Départementales de la Moselle, Saint-Julien-lès-Metz; Médiathèque de Metz for giving us permission to use photographs from their collections. We also owe thanks to Scott Merrillees and Equinox Publishing, Jakarta, for making available to us picture post cards from the book *Greetings from Jakarta*.

Filmarchiv Austria, Vienna, permitted us to translate and print two articles from Heide Schlüpmann et al. (eds): *Unheimliche Liebe. Asta Nielsen, ihr Kino*. They also gave us access to frame enlargements made from Asta Nielsen film prints of the Bundesarchiv-Filmarchiv, Berlin, and of Det Danske Filminstitut, Copenhagen. Moreover, Pyotr Bagrov and Anna Kovalova, St. Peterburg; Marlis Schmidt, Filmarchiv Austria; Ian O'Sullivan, British Film Institute; Thorsten Kretzer, University of Trier, helped us with the provisioning and production of illustrations. Frankie Kann, Trier, proof-read, corrected, and oftentimes translated into English all manuscripts by non-anglophone authors. Her fine and vigorous contribution to this book cannot be underestimated.

This volume was made possible through the generous grant of the Deutsche Forschungsgemeinschaft (German Research Foundation, DFG) for the conference, and through funds provided by Deutsches Filminstitut, Frankfurt, and the University of Trier for the proceedings of the conference.

Supplementary to conference and book alike there is the online database *Importing Asta Nielsen* which collects adverts and articles of the trade press and local press from all over the world to provide sources for further research on the distribution and exhibition of Asta Nielsen films before the First World War. This database will be expanded by and by once new findings will turn up. The database *Importing Asta Nielsen* was generously supported by Freundeskreis Universität Trier.

Uli Jung and Martin Loiperdinger

Introduction

The beginning of Asta Nielsen's film career is breathtaking: After the unknown actress of the Copenhagen New Theatre had appeared in the lead role of her debut film AFGRUNDEN (DK 1910), she became a well-known and popular actress in many countries all over Europe and beyond, within only one year. AFGRUNDEN (THE ABYSS) was premiered on 12 September 1910 in Copenhagen and distributed widely in many countries of the continent in the 1910/11 season. In this very same season two 'white slave' films produced by the Danish company Nordisk Film caused a furore alongside AFGRUNDEN. They were shown in many cities, be it shortly before, shortly after, or at the same time as AFGRUNDEN. In some places, e.g. in Warsaw, it was promoted as part of a 'white slave series'.[1]

In 1910 the European film market had gone through a crisis of overproduction of short film programmes for two years. New economic impulses were urgently needed: a new kind of film which could be produced, distributed and exhibited profitably. Long-feature films, which could have long running periods in the cinemas, promised to be the lifesaver. While short film programmes were usually exchanged after only three or four days, AFGRUNDEN played at the film theatre Kosmorama in Copenhagen, belonging to the producer, for several weeks on end. The producer sold the exhibition rights to AFGRUNDEN to various countries where the film was usually distributed and exhibited as an exclusive – as was the case in Germany. In Paris it ran as an exclusive for four weeks.[2] In a short period of time, in the spring of 1911, two more films with Asta Nielsen in the lead role were also released in Germany and distributed abroad. And as of August and September 1911 the first 'Asta Nielsen series' made in Berlin started in many European countries.

Asta Nielsen had not only proven herself a convincing actress, but she had entered the cinema business in Germany's first exclusive long-feature at exactly the right time. She was also embraced by audiences as a new actress whose acting skills convinced not only the general public, but also the cultural elite. A German trade paper reports from Düsseldorf:

Facing page: Danish poster for TOD IN SEVILLA (SPANISH BLOOD). [Det Danske Filminstitut].

> Up to now, it was assumed that all film dramas were 'kitsch'. But ABGRÜNDE, showing at the Palast-Theater, has all of a sudden made artists enthusiastic fans of cinema pantomime. The audience was delighted by everything about this film, not the least by the gaucho dance. (...) I have met almost no artist or actor there who had not seen ABGRÜNDE [AFGRUNDEN] for the third, fourth, fifth or even the eighth time. (...) At any rate, ABGRÜNDE has contributed a great deal, if not the most, to turning the conversation in society more than usual to film theatre and to leading people whom you would never expect to go to the cinema.[3]

It follows that the art circuit of Düsseldorf, at the time the Western German centre of high art and highbrow entertainment, shaped the tastes of the city's 'better circles' and selected AFGRUNDEN (and thus Asta Nielsen) as an example of a new attraction for the educated. This is an example of how the audience thus laid the ground work of her success in Germany[4] – a popular success that quickly spread internationally. This earned Asta Nielsen and Urban Gad, the writer-director, an exclusive contract for three 'Asta Nielsen series'. In her autobiography the actress reminisces:

> Out there in the world outside, ABGRÜNDE ran in triumph across the white screen, and outside sat a few men who could both see and calculate. And, when everything was all totalled up, the quills scratched a thick line drawn under the sum. The noise became a brief squeak with which the door to the world opened for me.[5]

With her acting skills she had created the necessary prerequisites to acquire the status of a star. Most commentators and historiographers, starting with Béla Balázs, and also the later academic research literature, have focussed on Asta Nielsen's proficiencies as an actress. But only a few publications have focussed on the role of the film trade in the transition from short film programmes to multiple-reel films. In her ground-breaking standard work *Frühe deutsche Kinematographie*, Corinna Müller has explored the economic changes that shaped the German film market before the First World War by analysing the trade journals of the time.[6] In his dissertation, Ivo Blom has more or less done the same for the Netherlands by studying the commercial correspondence of the Amsterdam cinema owner and film distributor Jean Desmet.[7] Some articles in the magnificent two-volume homage to Asta Nielsen, edited by Heide Schlüpmann, Karola Gramann et al., *Unmögliche Liebe* and *Nachtfalter*, cover the international distribution, exhibition and allotment of Asta Nielsen films in different countries.[8]

From this, the international conference "Importing Asta Nielsen: Cinema-Going and the Making of the Star System in the Early 1910s", held at the Deutsches Filmmuseum in Frankfurt in late September 2011, took its point of departure. More than two dozen film scholars scrutinized the role Asta Nielsen films played in different film markets of various countries, in distribution and exhibition practices, in the competition between local cinemas, in the innovation in film marketing and film advertising, in short, in the establishment of a new basis for the film markets in many countries around the world. This book collects the presentations given at the conference; even more contributors were invited to enlarge the number of national, regional, and local case studies. Thus we acquired quite an overview of the various strategies applied in different countries to establish Asta Nielsen as a film star within an environment of film marketing which at the same time launched a new film commodity requiring new modes of film trading and film exhibition: the exclusive long-feature changed the film programmes profoundly and subsequently also the habit of cinema-going.

As a consequence of an overproduction of short films, which made up the programmes of the store front cinemas as well as the cinema theatres and cinema palaces,[9] the film industry resorted to the production of long-feature films to overcome the economic crisis. At the same time a rental system was introduced that guaranteed cinema owners the exclusive rights to exhibit films for a defined territory for a specified period of time.

To achieve this structural change in cinema programming, the long-feature film alone was not sufficient because the markets were not unified. Small towns which had seen travelling cinemas at their fairgrounds and which were now met with a single fixed-site cinema cannot be compared with sizeable cities which boasted, early on, the competition of several cinema enterprises at the same time. Whereas the short film programmes were more or less indistinguishable from one another, the long-feature film – especially under the conditions of the exclusive rental system – set apart the offer by one cinema in town from those of all other venues. Still, the long-feature was no guarantee of success. Sizeable segments of the audience continued to fancy the diversity of the short film programme, which catered to all kinds of individual predilections; hence, some audiences preferred the short films stubbornly to the *Kilometer-Films*, as they were ironically called in Germany during this period. This induced producers and distributors in various countries to take new measures to draw cinema-goers to the shows. In Germany and Denmark, for example, reputable literary artists were hired (and duly advertised) as scriptwriters; in Italy grandiose historical or mythical epics were produced and proved very successful. Also biographical films on great figures of history and culture were made in many countries. Yet another measure which was most promising was the branding of films by linking them to the name of an actor. This is where Asta Nielsen comes in.

The crucial point in most countries was to establish Asta Nielsen as a star. The offer that the distributor Internationale Films-Vertrieb-Gesellschaft (IFVG) made was accepted by distributors, exhibitors and audiences in many countries. For distributors and exhibitors this was a result of promising perspectives to make money by speculating on mostly rising box-office earnings. For audiences, this was a result of their desire for entertainment and their craving to see Asta Nielsen. Once in the cinema theatre, they felt confirmed by the innovative adverts. These, on the other hand, looked very much the same nearly all over the world. In many local newspapers theatre owners started advertising Asta Nielsen in adverts ever increasing in size, embellished with portrait sketches or even photographs of the actress, as can be seen in

Mannheim, Innsbruck, Lausanne etc. On the other hand, when the *Innsbrucker Nachrichten* introduced a regular film column to the paper, adverts for films became rather standardised, and special adverts in larger size and print became rare. In Barcelona, film adverts were treated like those for stage plays. They had the same size, the same layout – they did not look like commercial adverts but rather like announcements.

Many of the adverts for Asta Nielsen films conspicuously look alike to a degree that it seems more than probable that they were being orchestrated by the German companies: highlighting Asta Nielsen's name, many times over in even larger print than the title of the film, graphic portraits of the leading lady, embellishing her name with epithets that suggest a comparison with the most culturally acclaimed theatrical actresses, Eleonora Duse and Sarah Bernhardt, etc. Moreover, Asta Nielsen is very often referred to as a member of the Royal Dutch Theatre, which was actually not the case. This clearly indicates that alongside the strategies to implement the exclusive rental system, yet another goal of the film industries was to attract a target audience which as yet was not likely to be interested in the cinema, namely the educated middle class who were hitherto accustomed to going to the legitimate theatre. This is furthermore evidenced by the fact that many of Asta Nielsen's films were labelled in terms of theatrical genres – as melodramas, dramas, tragedies, comedies, etc., on the screen.

This aspect must be seen in combination with the introduction of the exclusive rental system which made film exhibition more expensive for exhibitors but gave them an opportunity to lure more patrons into their cinema theatres. One of the crucial questions is to what extent it was the innovation in film exhibition or the screen personality of Asta Nielsen that made the new mode a success. These questions are furthermore complicated by the fact that the strategies did not seem to work the same in different countries. For instance, the exclusive system was not easily imposed in all local markets. Barcelona is an especially clear case in point here.[10] It is very likely that other local studies will bring to light similar developments in other major cities.

This, at the same time, makes it obvious that information gathered from the study of local newspapers not only grants an insight into local film (and media) history, but also gives us evidence on how differences in the overall national distribution system are reflected in local exhibition; by extension, we can learn about large scale changes on the national level by looking at the local form of exhibition. Thus it can be said that alongside the research in the trade press, which has given us quite a good insight into the marketing strategies of producers and distributors, as Corinna Müller has demonstrated convincingly in her work on the transition from short film programmes to multiple-reel feature films and the *Monopolfilm*, the German exclusive film distribution system,[11] the local daily press will provide us with abundant information on exhibition practices of film theatres. Hence, beyond the scope of local media historiography, a closer and more systematic scrutiny of local newspapers will give us a better idea of how films were presented to audiences, how they were being advertised and reviewed.

The local level is where we can see Asta Nielsen's star status most clearly. First of all, we find adverts in the daily press which refer directly to bookings of her films at local film theatres – often speaking of an 'Asta Nielsen Festival' or of a 'guest appearance', yet another reference to cultural practices of the legitimate stage. Moreover, as early as in November 1911, a newly purpose-built cinema theatre opened in Düsseldorf and was named after Asta Nielsen.[12] She and her husband Urban Gad were present at the festive opening and the *Asta Nielsen Waltz*, especially written for the occasion, was performed.[13] And quite naturally an Asta Nielsen film was shown, DER FREMDE VOGEL (THE COURSE OF TRUE LOVE). This may gain even greater significance when one remembers that the grandiose opening of the Mozartsaal, which was to become one of the most preferred venues for lavish film premieres in Berlin, was launched in September 1910 with a special programme consisting of only the most select films showing Emperor Wilhelm II.[14] Since films of the Kaiser were usually not distributed exclusively, they were available to any cinema owner. What could be organised in Germany's capital as a special ceremonial programme became a celebration of Asta Nielsen once she had been established as one of the most popular celebrities in the film world. Her public standing in the popular culture of her time apparently equalled that of Wilhelm II: She was expected to be able to bestow as much glamour to a cinema opening as the Kaiser could – at least outside of the capital. Also outside of Germany, she had that appeal: In Lausanne, for instance, the gala re-opening of the Royal Biograph in 1911 was celebrated with Asta Nielsen's latest film, DEN SORTE DRØM (THE CIRCUS GIRL). And the Nýja Bíó (new cinema), the second cinema in Reykjavík, started its showings on 29 June 1912 with NACHTFALTER (RETRIBUTION).

The exclusive system was a marketing measure that was meant to secure a smooth exhibition of films without direct local competition by another cinema offering the same film in the same week. Thus audiences no longer had to decide which cinema to go to in their leisure time – as had been the case with the short film programme – but rather which film to select. This system applies especially to Asta Nielsen because her name functioned as a brand linked to all those films which were part of the 'Asta Nielsen series' and were advertised as such. This marks her star status as something unique and sets her apart from all other film stars who were coming up in a short period of time. Moreover, every four to six weeks, a new film of hers appeared on the market, and the adverts placing her name above the title, oftentimes printing it even larger than the film title, indicated that Asta Nielsen had become the figurehead of a commodity that was automatically labelled by the use of her name.

Asta Nielsen and her star status were obviously very instrumental in this process, as can be seen in the example of Innsbruck, where in 1911 two cinemas competed with each another with exclusively programmed long-feature films. The exclusive exhibition of Asta Nielsen's films was so attractive for audiences that a new film theatre which opened in April 1912 in Innsbruck secured the exclusive rights to her films, apparently hoping to make a major sweep of the local cinema-goers. One of the competing cinemas responded by announcing an exclusive Ida Nielsen series, obviously hoping that the clients would confuse the two names.[15]

What is most remarkable is that the marketing innovation of the exclusive rental system had not only recuperations in the local exhibition practices in Germany but that it was rather established across the world within a short time. In many countries the exclusive system was introduced as a most promising attraction for audiences and thus became the regular market policy of distributors and cinema owners. The attraction consisted, on the one hand, in the introduction of long-features which made it possible to tell more complex, psychologically more 'realistic' stories. On the other hand – and this is most significant for the purpose of this book –, it was Asta Nielsen whose screen personality was so closely linked to the establishment of the long-feature programme that it is easy to identify the one with the other. It can thus be said that, on an international scale, Asta Nielsen was very instrumental in the transformation of film marketing. Accordingly, in the 1911/12 and 1912/13 seasons, she became increasingly not only a popular film actress but rather a commodity, a brand name that was acknowledged by film exhibitors and audiences alike as guarantors of commercial success and good entertainment.

The contract that bound Asta Nielsen and Urban Gad to the Deutsche Bioscop stipulated an hitherto unheard-of salary of 85,000 marks for five months of shooting the ten films of the first 'Asta-Nielsen series', plus a percentage of the profits. What Urban Gad was being paid is not known. To obtain a return on this expense, the company had of necessity to export these films. German producers had already cooperated with international distributors. In this case, this was obviously part of the calculation to make Asta Nielsen the brand name of a new film commodity, the German 'Asta-Nielsen series'. The first series was offered as early as September 1911 in France, Sweden, the Netherlands, Great Britain, etc. Thus, in a short period of time Asta Nielsen had become a trademark. By making her films available to the international markets in short succession – a new film was released every four to six weeks during the season – the combination of the long-feature programme, Asta Nielsen as a leading actress with star qualities and new ways of advertising which by and by included the spreading of human interest stories about her in daily papers and the gradually emerging fan magazines, the concept eventually proved very lucrative commercially. As early as the 1911/12 season, the international marketing of German films was quite common, as the example of SÜNDIGE LIEBE, a film produced by Deutsche Bioscop shows – a film that became a success in Great Britain (titled FOOLS OF SOCIETY) although it could not boast of a star in the leading role.[16]

On the other hand, this mode of distribution and exhibition did not work everywhere. In the USA, for instance, Asta Nielsen's stardom was quite limited. Although adverts constantly compared her to Sarah Bernhardt, reviewers, while lauding her films for their complex stories, often found fault with her films because they perceived them as 'jumpy' and lacking logic, probably due to cuts by "over-scrupulous authorities". Her films were also cut for purely commercial reasons. Since the German long-feature format running up to one hour screening time did not fit the American programme standards, some Asta Nielsen films were cut down from three to two reels. In the 1912/13 season, some Asta Nielsen films were brought to the USA through the American outlet of Pathé Frères, who at the same time, however, specialized in the supply of those theatres which were hanging on to the traditional short-feature programme. Moreover, they invested intensely in the production of serials, which in many American theatres posed a serious competition for the long features. What is more, although Pathé initially banked on Asta Nielsen's name, as in the cross-dressing comedy of LADY MADCAP'S WAY (JUGEND UND TOLLHEIT) – beginning with THE DEVIL'S ASSISTANT (DIE SÜNDEN DER VÄTER), trade press adverts made no mention of her. One advert for A ROMANY SPY (DAS MÄDCHEN OHNE VATERLAND) quoted three trade press reviews without including her name. Others for A MILITANT SUFFRAGETTE (DIE SUFFRAGETTE) were illustrated with production stills of Asta Nielsen's recognizable face yet made no reference to her name at all.[17]

In Australia and New Zealand there was no necessity for an exclusive system, since Asta Nielsen films entered these markets usually with only one or two prints which circulated in these countries. Moreover, the long-feature film had been long established in Australia and New Zealand, so that audiences were already accustomed to long-running films. Not everywhere was Asta Nielsen the first film star in a modern sense. Australasian audiences, for example, had already had an opportunity to see recognizable stars before Asta Nielsen entered the market. Likewise in Great Britain, she was faced with the competition of other very successful actors. To be sure, she acquired quite a popular following, but an 'Asta craze' that could be seen in countries like Russia or Italy did not materialise. Although Asta Nielsen's popularity in distant countries – Brazil, the Netherlands Indies, Australasia, Japan etc. – was more likely limited, yet her presence in these countries as part of the world market which had already been in place from the days of Georges Méliès and early Pathé is proof that this market was quite suitable to be used for the commercial turnover of films branded by the main actor, and Asta Nielsen was very functional in its construction. This was a result of very deliberate planning. For Arthur Mellini, editor-in-chief of the German trade journal *Lichtbild-Bühne* and, at the same time, in charge of the public relations campaign for the first 'Asta Nielsen series', the development of the film industry proceeded as follows:

> In the very earliest period, we simply took the *film* and had interest only in the length. Later, we filled the programme according to the genre (...). Then came the period of the *plot*, a situation which continues to this day, and now we have the personality who, with her all-encompassing dramatic mimic artistry in the leading role, is to draw in the public.[18]

He describes this development not in terms of a natural progression, but rather as a succession of marketing modes that reflected different business activities in the various stages of the development of film into an internationally active industry. Therefore, the focus on the 'personality' of actors and actresses is, from Mellini's point of view, a logical consequence of the previous stages. His last remark, of course, refers to Asta Nielsen, whose DEN SORTE DRØM (DER SCHWARZE TRAUM, THE CIRCUS GIRL) is reviewed in this article.

Moreover, she became an international film star who was not only advertised in connection with her films but who also became the focal point of a fan community which was interested in her persona. As a consequence, cinema owners published articles on Asta Nielsen to either promote a forthcoming film of hers or to keep the readers' interest in her person alive. For instance, a cinema owner in Trier had told the readers of the local daily paper that Nielsen was paid 85,000 marks for the ten films of the 1911/12 season – a shooting period of five months.[19] The press also carried reports on Asta Nielsen's private life in Copenhagen – or rather what was staged to pass for her private life. Even more significant is a report in the *Union-Theater-Zeitung*, founded by the Union-Theater cinema chain in 1912 and distributed in Berlin where the chain boasted of five film palaces. In its 12th issue, the paper reported that the Danish actress had moved to Berlin and had thus become a "Berlin compatriot" who was by now not only shooting films in the streets of the German capital but could also be seen at location-shootings in the Mark Brandenburg.[20] In addition, Asta Nielsen was also photographed in poses that suggested the privacy of her Berlin home; these images were distributed on fan picture postcards as of 1913 at the latest. They were meant to propose to the consumers that Asta Nielsen, although a famous movie star, was yet not withdrawn from the realm of reality. She had become a 'Berliner' like all the readers of the paper: she goes to the Mark Brandenburg and brings in her films the comforts of the countryside back to those cinema-goers who cannot afford spending their leisure time outside the metropolis. Yet, Mellini, in his aforementioned article, also points to the commercial aspect of Asta Nielsen's popularity:

> At the moment, we may consider Asta Nielsen as the *Fortuna* of cinematic art. It is, of course, regrettable that dramatic, mimic art is linked so brutally to profit, but even the best royal court actor works, after all, for hard cash, whereby, even here despite all idealism, pure materialism has gained the upper hand.[21]

The theatre owners can live with the gratifying fact that the famous Asta Nielsen has fled into the wide-open arms of a capitalistic society. She wishes to transform her art into money; thus the enterprising theatre managers can convert the Nielsen films into tinkling hard cash. A practical transformation that profits everyone.

Although the production of films had become more expensive, and, although the distributors bought their prints from the producers at a higher price, and, even though they rented these prints to the exhibitors at higher fees – while it was not at all clear whether the cinema owners could easily raise their admission fees – Mellini describes the new marketing strategies in terms of a win-win situation.

Whereas the short film programmes of the century's first decade had already provoked very negative responses from educators and the clergy – ultimately leading to the formation of the cinema reform movement in Germany as of about 1907 – now it was the local authorities who eyed the new medium quite suspiciously. The venues for film screenings in fairground tents or the backrooms of pubs and dance halls did not seem fit for the entertainment of the masses. Police in many places enforced regulations that called for special previews to prove the decency of the programmes. When long-feature films took centre stage, a new debate emerged. Especially among the educated strata of society, film started to be acknowledged as an art form which did not have to fear comparison with the legitimate stage. The strategies distributors and exhibitors had applied to promote their films, namely, to link actors to the theatres and screenplay authors to highbrow literature, did not necessarily initiate intellectual debate, but the short-lived correspondence of the two tendencies gives us a clear idea that the point of reference on both sides was the theatre or highbrow culture at large. This was applied at first to Asta Nielsen who was – as already mentioned – advertised as the 'Duse of the art of cinema' or the '*Fortuna* of the art of cinema'. But beyond that there is also mention of her versatility as an actress. Before Asta Nielsen appeared on film, all the actors who were known by name – Max Linder, Prince, André Deed etc. – were more or less fixed to the genre of comedy shorts. They stuck in the memory of audiences just because they kept appearing in ever new variations of the same. Arthur Mellini supports this point of view: "Actually, we already have the popular figure within the humorous genre".[22] With the advent of Asta Nielsen the dramatic genre saw now for the first time an established film celebrity who was cherished by an ever growing fan community. But something else must be mentioned here. Asta Nielsen is perceived as a very versatile actress. On the occasion of TOD IN SEVILLA (SPANISH BLOOD) Paul Ehren, editor in chief of the promotional journal of the Union-Theater cinema chain, wrote:

> Up to now, she has surprised us again and again. She has appeared to us as a flirtatious female, as a fighter for her beloved husband; we have seen a humiliated woman, then, in turn, a proud, domineering temperament – always someone else and yet always herself, always unmistakable – Asta Nielsen.[23]

Although Ehren does not refer to it explicitly, it is clear that he suggests Asta Nielsen's art to be comparable to the artistic capacities theatre-goers would expect from stage actors. What is even more: Asta Nielsen was seen throughout her early career in even a much wider variety of roles than Ehren enumerates. She appeared not only in social dramas, but also in comedies, in cross dressing roles, in historical epics, etc. This once again, must be seen as an innovation that was part of the industry's marketing strategies.

On the other hand – regardless of the growing cultural reputation of the new medium – Asta Nielsen's roles, their frequent connection to the demi-monde

– the circus, variety theatres and the like – her repeated representation of motherhood out of wedlock, her often depicted social decline as a consequence of her falling victim to aristocratic suitors etc., – all in all, the many roles she played, which were perceived as being risqué in the conservative educated middle class, called the censors to the fore in many different countries. Thus, the growing complexity of the stories told in films was answered by state and local authorities by calling into question whether the complex structure of meaning was in line with official and officious demands political and clerical circles made on society. In some countries it was the Asta Nielsen films which gave reason for establishing formally or informally working censorship boards.[24] Apparently, in most cases, her films were not outright banned from public screening, but many times over children and youth up to 14 or even 16 were not admitted, or the films were restricted to evening screenings when children and youth were not allowed to attend cinema shows, anyhow.

Asta Nielsen's stardom has – as can be seen in this volume – many different aspects. One can read her films in terms of marketing strategies, ideological responses, aesthetic innovation and, last but not least, unifying audiences. To be sure, by the beginning of the First World War other actors and actresses had come forward and overshadowed her star status. But when these entered the screen Asta Nielsen was already established as the first transnational European film star.[25]

Notes

1. Cf. Andrzej Dębsky's article in this volume.
2. Cf. Valdo Kneubühler's article in this volume.
3. Nico, "Düsseldorf im Januar 1911", *Der Kinematograph*, no. 213 (25 January 1911).
4. Cf. Annemone Lingensa's article in this volume.
5. Asta Nielsen, *Die schweigende Muse* (Berlin, GDR: Henschelverlag Kunst und Gesellschaft, 1977), 127.
6. Corinna Müller, *Frühe deutsche Kinematographie. Formale, wirtschaftliche und kulturelle Entwicklungen* (Stuttgart and Weimar: Metzler, 1994).
7. Ivo Blom, *Jean Desmet and the Early Dutch Film Trade* (Amsterdam: Amsterdam University Press, 2003).
8. Heide Schlüpmann et al. (eds), *Unmögliche Liebe. Asta Nielsen, ihr Kino*, (2nd edn) (Vienna: filmarchiv austria, 2010); Karola Gramann and Heide Schlüpmann (eds), *Nachtfalter. Asta Nielsen, ihre Filme* (2nd edn) (Vienna: filmarchiv austria, 2010).
9. Cf. for a distinction of different types of fixed-site cinemas Joseph Garncarz, *Maßlose Unterhaltung. Zur Etablierug des Films in Deutschland 1896–1914* (Frankfurt and Basel: Stroemfeld, 2010).
10. Cf. the article by María Antonia Paz and Julio Montero in this volume.
11. Cf. Müller, *Frühe deutsche Kinematographie* , 105–158.
12. Cf. Sabine Lenk, "Das Asta-Nielsen-Theater in Düsseldorf (1911–1986)", in Schlüpmann, *Unmögliche Liebe*, 308–312.
13. Cf. Jeanpaul Goergen, "Drei Walzer für A.N.", in Schlüpmann, *Unmögliche Liebe*, 281–286.
14. Cf. O.A., " Lichtspiele", *Vossische Zeitung* (5 September1910), as quoted in: Dominik Petzold, *Der Kaiser und das Kino: Herrschaftsinszenierung, Populärkultur und Filmpropaganda im Wilhelminischen Zeitalter* (Paderborn: Ferdinand Schöningh, 2012), 153.
15. Ida Nielsen was the married name of Ida Kier (1887–1918), a Danish operetta actress who appeared

Introduction

as the leading lady in Swedish long-feature films in 1911 and 1912. Cf. Jan Olsson, *Sensationer från en bakgård. Frans Lundberg som biografägare och filmproducent i Malmö och Köpenhamm* (Stockholm: Symposion, 1988). Cf. also Patrick Blaser's article in this volume.

16. Cf. Jon Burrows' article in this volume.
17. Cf. Richard Abel's article in this volume.
18. [Arthur Mellini], "Asta Nielsen – die populäre Kino-Schauspielerin", *Lichtbild-Bühne*, no. 35 (2 September 1911).
19. *Trierischer Volksfreund* (31 October 1911). Cf. Martin Loiperdinger's article in this volume.
20. "Asta Nielsen als Berliner Bürgerin", *Union-Theater-Zeitung* 1:19 (20–26 July 1912): 15. Cf. Martin Loiperdinger's article in this volume.
21. [Mellini], "Asta Nielsen".
22. Ibid.
23. P.E. [Paul Ehren], "Die spanische Asta Nielsen. Ein neues Kinodrama", *Union-Theater-Zeitung* 2:8 (21–27 February 1913): 1.
24. Cf. the articles by Outi Hupaniittu, María Antonia Paz and Julio Montero, and especially by Jon Burrows and Anne Bachmann in this volume.
25. Cf. Ian Christie's article in this volume.

PART I

ASTA NIELSEN IN DENMARK

Casper Tybjerg

Presenting AFGRUNDEN in Copenhagen and Skive

The following article will try to give a sense of how Asta Nielsen's breakthrough film AFGRUNDEN was presented in Denmark on its initial release, focusing on its premiere run in Copenhagen and its presentation in Skive, a provincial town.

The cinema where AFGRUNDEN (THE ABYSS) first opened on 12 September had also financed it. It was not made by a major film company; it was a one-off experiment by the proprietor of Kosmorama, an important Copenhagen cinema. Kosmorama was founded in 1904 by cinema entrepreneur Constantin Philipsen on Strøget, Copenhagen's main shopping street, and it was the first viable cinema in Denmark. Kosmorama was not located directly on Strøget itself, but in rooms off of a courtyard that had been built as the first part of City-Passagen, a never-completed project to construct an elaborate arcade. To attract spectators, a uniformed barker, a so-called 'Swiss guardsman', would pace back and forth on Strøget's pavement and attract attention to the show inside. The Swiss guardsman is pictured on the cover of Kosmorama's programme booklets: like more traditional theatres, Kosmorama printed booklets describing its programme. The cover picture (drawn by the painter Paul Fischer) also shows a pair of well-dressed ladies; one is urging her friend to go inside and visit the picture-show. These ladies, I think, we can assume are the cinema proprietor's own image of what his ideal audience looks like.

Constantin Philipsen did not stay to run Kosmorama for very long. He left to found a whole series of Kosmoramas across Denmark, 26 in all, or about one-quarter of all picture-houses in Denmark, selling Kosmorama to Hjalmar Davidsen in May 1908. Davidsen was the son of a wholesale dealer in dried fish; he had seen films in Paris and become fascinated. His father advanced him part of his inheritance, allowing him to take over Kosmorama. Davidsen soon had a great success with L'ASSASSINAT DU DUC DE GUISE (THE ASSASSINATION OF THE DUKE DE GUISE) and other French film d'art productions. Davidsen

Facing page: Cover for Kosmorama programme booklet, c. 1910. For each new film, a printed programme booklet with a cast list and a detailed plot description was stapled inside this cover. The picture is signed by the celebrated artist Paul Fischer. [Det Danske Filminstitut.]

Newspaper advert for the opening run of AFGRUNDEN at the Kosmorama Cinema in Copenhagen. September 1910.

had been a friend of the Gad family from childhood.[1] It was therefore him that Urban Gad approached with the idea of making a film with Asta Nielsen, for which he had written a script. In an interview from 1954, Davidsen said: "We agreed that I, who had a bit more experience with films, would rework it".[2] The film took three weeks to shoot, according to the interview. It had apparently been completed by 21 June 1910, when a newspaper item described it as "ready to roll".[3] According to Davidsen's reminiscences, however, the results had initially looked very discouraging:

> But although Urban Gad denied all responsibility because I had changed the script, I did not give up. I recut the film completely, putting the scenes in a different order, and at the premiere it turned out that the film gave a completely different impression. The success was assured, and Gad and I became friends again.[4]

This claim seems rather unlikely – AFGRUNDEN's plot is very straightforwardly structured, and it is hard to imagine how it might have been structured differently. But even if Davidsen's contribution may not have been quite as extensive as he recalled it many years later, the film was certainly a hit from the start and played for many weeks at Kosmorama, with performances from early afternoon and almost until midnight. Davidsen was not involved in the wider distribution of the film. In a 1919 interview, he claims that he had travelled "all over Germany" to sell it, "but nobody wanted it. It was thought to be too big. Back then, you only had films that ran for fifteen or twenty minutes and couldn't imagine people could stand having them bigger."[5] After the film's success in Copenhagen, he sold the German distribution rights to Ludwig Gottschalk.[6] But what about Denmark?

In her book on Asta Nielsen, Marguerite Engberg writes that the film company Skandinavisk-Russisk Handelshus (SRH) acquired the distribution rights for

Interior of Biograf-Teatret, Skive. Photograph from 1910–1920. [Det Danske Filminstitut.]

AFGRUNDEN.[7] SRH later changed its name to Filmsfabriken Danmark and became one of the most significant Danish production companies, and it has been the subject of a massive, voluminous study by Jan Nielsen. Nielsen quotes Engberg's original 1955 taped interview with Johan Christensen, one of the company's managers: "The first one we sold was, as it happens, the very well-known film AFGRUNDEN, shot by Alfred Lind and Hjalmar Davidsen with Asta Nielsen and Poul Reumert".[8] Jan Nielsen points out that this is not supported by the first and then only Danish film trade paper, *Nordisk Biograf-Tidende*, which was closely connected with SRH but makes no mention of AFGRUNDEN. Nielsen also quotes an unpublished manuscript, probably from the mid-1930s, describing the early history of another company, Fotorama, based in Aarhus and initially named Th. Hermansen, Ltd. Here, we read: "Of other purchases may be mentioned Hjalmar Davidsen's 'mimic drama' AFGRUNDEN owned exclusively for Denmark – except for Strøget in Copenhagen – for 3600 crowns for two prints".[9]

Jan Nielsen does not try to resolve these discrepancies, but I think a brief newspaper item may help. Three days after the premiere, we can read the following brief announcement in the newspaper *Politiken*: "The exclusive rights for Kosmorama's new art film AFGRUNDEN have been sold for Norway and Sweden by Mr. Hjalmar Davidsen to Skandinavisk-Russisk Handelshus (…). The latest stage triumph of Mr. Reumert and Miss Asta Nielsen will be repeated throughout Scandinavia."[10] I think it is likely that this purchase of rights is what Johan Christensen of SRH recalled in 1955, and that Fotorama did indeed control AFGRUNDEN's distribution in Denmark as indicated in the unpublished company history quoted by Jan Nielsen.

What of local exhibition? The Irish sociologist Richard Jenkins picked the town of Skive, in Jutland, when carrying out his extensive field study about Danish national identity because it seemed a good example of "a very ordinary town in most respects".[11] I chose to focus on Skive because of some particularly interesting source material. In 1911, Skive had a population of 5,500 inhabitants.[12] Unusually for a town of its size, it had two cinemas, Kosmorama and Biograf-Teatret. Constantin Philipsen opened the first in 1906 and soon sold it to a local entrepreneur; the second was opened the following year. The chief of police refused to grant a license, because he saw no need for more than one theatre, but the proprietor appealed directly to the minister of justice and was allowed to continue; but "sparks frequently flew between the two", according to the pioneering historian of Danish cinemas, Gunnar Sandfeld.[13]

Biograf-Teatret showed AFGRUNDEN in April 1911 and printed an elaborate promotional folder for the occasion – large in size, between A3 and A4, four pages, printed on thin orange newsprint. I knew of its existence from earlier research at the Danish Film Institute, but when I went back to examine it, it had unfortunately disappeared from the files. Luckily, I still had photocopies I took of it fifteen years ago. The first two pages consist of extended excerpts from the uniformly enthusiastic reviews of the film in the Copenhagen newspapers. We only get to Skive on page 3, where we get the following text, set in large type:

> Biograf-Teatret, Skive, has at great expense purchased the performance rights for this piece for Skive and the surrounding area, and hopes that the audience will appreciate this sacrifice by showing interest in the shows.
>
> AFGRUNDEN's character is something like the great French play *Pangs of Conscience* which was so tremendously popular a couple of years ago. The Copenhagen artists show here that they are in every way equal to the most illustrious artistes of France.
>
> *The ticket prices are, despite the great costs of the acquisition, only the usual 25 øre.*
>
> *Children are definitely not admitted.*[14]

The French film mentioned can be identified as L'EMPREINTE OU LA MAIN ROUGE, a Film d'art production directed by Paul Henry Burguet and released in France in 1908. It is a showcase for the famous mime Gaston Séverin and does not have a story similar to AFGRUNDEN, but it does feature a striking apache dance, a 'dance chaloupée', performed by Mistinguette and Max Dearly. Moreover, this film was imported to Denmark by none other than Hjalmar Davidsen, so it seems quite likely that it served as a source of inspiration.

The same page of the promotional folder includes another section, set in somewhat smaller type, entitled: "The audience's verdict on AFGRUNDEN". It starts out by describing how audiences in Copenhagen have braved long lines to see the film: "People stood like fish in a barrel outside and waited patiently

Presenting AFGRUNDEN in Copenhagen and Skive

Page 3 of the tabloid-sized four-page programme Biograf-Teatret in Skive printed to promote AFGRUNDEN. [Det Danske Filminstitut.]

for the packed auditorium to empty and a new show to start." If this description is accurate, it means that the film was not shown in continuous performance, and that the cinema had to be emptied after each show. We can see from the newspaper adverts that the show times were just 45 minutes apart.[15] This would not have left much time for emptying and filling the auditorium. The film lasts 37 minutes in the 2005 DVD version produced by the Danish Film Institute, which was transferred at 16 frames per second, and it may originally have been slightly longer: the only extant print of the film seems largely complete (if badly damaged in many places), but the original titles are missing, and certain descriptions indicate that there may have been an additional shot at the end, showing the police putting the Asta Nielsen character into a car and driving off with her. Still, there may have been just enough time to allow audiences to enter and leave without running the film at a noticeably higher speed.[16]

In Skive, the folder suggests (in a hopeful tone), the cinema will be similarly mobbed:

> The coming days, therefore, will see a broad and dense stream of people coming to *"Biograf-Teatret"*; they will secure their tickets and programme booklets and wait patiently to be let in if they are not so fortunate as to arrive just when a show is starting. In short, the lively Copenhagen spectacle will repeat itself every hour of the evening for the time *"Biograf-Teatret"* keeps AFGRUNDEN on the programme.[17]

This suggests that Biograf-Teatret would usually show films in continuous performance, but shifted to fixed show times for AFGRUNDEN. I looked through the newspaper adverts from September 1910 through April 1911, and in most cases, they do not include show times. One advert includes the text: "In order that people from the countryside may get the chance to watch this excellent program, there will be *continuous performance on market day*".[18] This may possibly mean that continuous performance was not the norm, but it may also just mean that there would be film shows throughout the day, while the cinemas normally ran only in the evenings, judging from the few cases where show times were listed.[19]

The existence of the elaborate promotional flyer agrees with Sandfeld's description of Skive as a rather competitive film market, and a study of newspaper advertisements also bears this out. *Skive Folkeblad*, the largest newspaper in town, would carry advertisements for both cinemas. They both usually changed their programmes twice a week: one programme would play Monday through Thursday, another from Friday to Sunday. Kosmorama had two musicians to accompany the films, a pianist and a violinist.[20]

Apart from the two permanent cinemas, the area was also regularly visited by travelling film showmen. An advert from 20 January 1911 reads:

> *Moving pictures* shown at Højslev Inn Saturday the 21st at 8 o'clock.
>
> At Stoholm Temperance Hall Sunday the 22nd at 8 o'clock.
>
> In particular, the programme includes:
>
> DEN HVIDE SLAVEHANDEL
>
> See the posters!
>
> THE PASGAARD BROTHERS.[21]

White Slavery films were very popular at the time. In the first week of April 1911, both of Skive's cinemas showed DEN HVIDE SLAVEHANDELSE SIDSTE OFFER (IN THE HANDS OF IMPOSTORS), a brand-new Nordisk production.[22] The two cinemas seem to have competed intensely, although they usually did not both show the same film at the same time. In December 1910, Kosmorama ran Nordisk's DEN HVIDE SLAVEHANDEL (THE WHITE SLAVE) whereas Biograf-Teatret ran UNCLE TOM'S CABIN and gave it the subtitle "The Black Slave Trade", possibly to make it appear a direct competitor to the 'white slave' film.[23] UNCLE TOM'S CABIN is probably the Vitagraph version; Biograf-Teatret showed a number of Vitagraph films, identified as such in the adverts: WHISKY-SMUGLERNE I KENTUCKYS BJÆRGE (probably IN THE MOUNTAINS OF KENTUCKY) was called a "Grandiose, exciting American Vitagraph art film".[24]

Kosmorama and Biograf-Teatret would often advertise different films with the same title, however. In late November 1910, for instance, Kosmorama showed a film called ANSIGTSTYVEN (The Face-Thief).[25] A month or so later, Biograf-Teatret showed a film of the same title. A closer study of the adverts, however, shows that two different films are involved. Biograf-Teatret's advert dismissed the competition: "Note: ANSIGTSTYVEN must not be confused with a picture which was previously shown under the same title to deceive the audience. This is one of the usual big all-evening plays, performed by the ensemble of Aarhus Theater."[26] "All-evening" is certainly an exaggeration; a fragment of 100 meters survives, but the film may have been a two-reeler. The film was produced by Fotorama, an Aarhus based distribution and exhibition company which had launched an ambitious production programme in 1909. In the spring of 1910, they had released the first Danish feature-length film, DEN HVIDE SLAVEHANDEL, with a number of respected actors from Aarhus Teater, the most important stage of the country outside Copenhagen, in the leading roles. In the fall, it was plagiarised by Nordisk, leading to a confrontation between the two companies.[27] A mutually satisfying deal was struck, however; Fotorama received the distribution rights for Nordisk's films in Norway and Sweden and in return agreed to withdraw from film production, and leading figures from Fotorama were subsequently brought into management positions at Nordisk.[28]

Before this happened, however, the rivalry between the two companies made itself felt in places like Skive. As a rule, Kosmorama ran films from Nordisk, whereas Biograf-Teatret showed Fotorama's productions, and DEN HVIDE SLAVEHANDEL was far from being the only case where the offerings of the two companies were very similar. The film entitled ANSIGTSTYVEN which had been shown at Kosmorama, provoking accusations of "deceiving the audience" from the competition, is not easily identifiable; it does not appear in the Danish National Filmography.[29] The advert calls it a detective story and names three actors, [Agnes] Nyrop Christensen, [Otto] Lagoni, and [Einar] Zangenberg,[30] but the only film listed in the Danish National Filmography featuring all three is KEAN, from Dumas's play. Zangenberg and Lagoni were regular players at Nordisk, however, and made a number of detective films. One of these may have been retitled as an underhand tactic to draw audiences away from the Fotorama film.

In October 1910, both cinemas ran a film called I BONDEFANGERKLØER (In the Claws of Confidence Tricksters), but actually these were two different films. One (at Biograf-Teatret) was a Fotorama production of this very title, while the other one, better known under the title FRA DET MØRKE KØBENHAVN (FROM DARKEST COPENHAGEN), was produced by the smaller Copenhagen company Biorama.[31] Fotorama and Biorama also both made adaptations of *Elverhøj*, a romantic-nationalist Danish favourite and in Denmark possibly the best-known 19th-century stage play; both these film adaptations were also called ELVERHØJ, and later that October, they also played in Skive at the same time, one in each cinema.[32]

It is difficult to know if Fotorama was being ripped off by the Copenhagen film companies in all these cases or whether they gave as good as they got. The recurring head-to-head competition, however, shows that there was an intense struggle for predominance. In all cases mentioned, the films involved were labelled *kunstfilm* (art films). The term *kunstfilm* is of course a translation of the French *film d'art*", but while some later film historians have tended to associate the French term with costume pictures, in Denmark, at least, it generally means that the performers were artists, that is, established actors from the legitimate stage. Even DEN HVIDE SLAVEHANDEL was promoted as a *kunstfilm* for this reason. The term also laid claim to higher quality than regular picture-house fare, and many of the films mentioned ran longer than one reel.

If art films were the battleground, it would certainly make sense for Fotorama, which did not have the facilities to make a large number of films, to buy up the distribution rights for AFGRUNDEN, the most popular art film around. If it was distributed by Fotorama, it would also fit with the fact that it was shown at Biograf-Teatret like all the Fotorama productions. The proprietor of Kosmorama was probably aware several months before the premiere of AFGRUNDEN in Skive that the competition had locked it up: in December, Kosmorama presented a film called AFGRUNDEN, but the small print reveals that this was actually an American film: The Danish title might have been chosen to cash in on the success of Urban Gad's film, but the advertisement is at least honest enough to admit that this was "A uniquely exciting American art film".[33] In fact, this time AFGRUNDEN was a one-reeler, made by American Kinema, Pathé's subsidiary company in the US. It was released end of October 1910, before Urban Gad's and Asta Nielsen's AFGRUNDEN became famous in Europe, with the title THE INDIAN AND THE MAID. The film tells the story of a red indian who saves a white girl from falling into an abyss, then falls in love with her and commits suicide. The French title is LA GOUFFRE FATALE (THE FATAL ABYSS), and the German title is DER ABGRUND (THE ABYSS)[34] – maybe for the same reason it was called AFGRUNDEN in Denmark.

When the long-feature AFGRUNDEN appeared in Skive in April 1911, it too was promoted as an art film. The newspaper advert is more detailed than usual. Beneath the title, the film is described as "Drama in 2 acts (50 scenes) by Urban Gad". A cast list follows, naming all the six actors with roles of any size and the characters they play, and the scene of the action is described: "partly in Copenhagen and the surrounding area, partly in a Zealand vicarage, in the present day". Then the advert goes on:

> The *Gaucho-Dance* appearing in the drama is performed by Miss Asta Nielsen and Mr. Poul Reumert.
>
> With rare unanimity and in even rarer detail the press of the capital has discussed this great art film which is now playing at the leading picture-theatres the world over, and many are the words of praise that have been spoken of it.[35]

AFGRUNDEN opened on Tuesday, 18 April 1911; Monday the 17th was Easter Monday. It ran the whole week, until Sunday. The advert also includes show times: 8 and 9 o'clock every evening, with Sunday shows at 4, 5, 7, 8, 9, and 10 o'clock. On Wednesday, an extra show for Friday at 3 o'clock was added to give "people from the countryside the chance to see AFGRUNDEN".³⁶

Neither *Skive Folkeblad* nor the other newspaper, *Skive Social-Demokrat*, carried any film reviews in this period, and I found no news articles about the cinemas' programmes in *Skive Folkeblad* either. *Skive Social-Demokrat*, though, occasionally mentions film programmes in a listing of upcoming events. AFGRUNDEN is very briefly described: "This poignant picture will be held over by Mrs. Jensen of Biografen until the end of the week so that everyone may have the opportunity to see it. It is splendidly done but very frightening."³⁷

AFGRUNDEN was replaced by the 26-minute Italian epic LA CADUTA DI TROIA (THE FALL OF TROY), directed by Giovanni Pastrone and Luigi Borgnetto for Itala Film. With this film, "Itala was the first Italian film company to step beyond the 600-metre mark and to define two-reelers as feature films".³⁸ The adverts do not give any showtimes for LA CADUTA DI TROIA, suggesting that it did not bring the great crowds that flocked to AFGRUNDEN. On the other hand, it ran at both cinemas at the same time, and the notice in *Skive Social-Demokrat* was longer and more enthusiastic than the one for AFGRUNDEN:

> THE FALL OF TROY which is on the programme at both Kosmorama and Biograf-Teatret these evenings, is the newest of the new and the most magnificent yet seen.
>
> Everybody is familiar with the historical drama of the Greeks and the Trojans, and in this picture everything is shown, from the departure of King Menelaus to the death of Prince Paris.
>
> The picture itself has been magnificently staged; it is incredible that this could be done. In addition, both programmes include a couple of other interesting pictures.³⁹

We may conclude that while AFGRUNDEN was a one-off production for Hjalmar Davidsen and an unusually successful film, it was also part of a general trend where more ambitious productions with established actors and longer running times were used by film companies jockeying for position as a means of gaining a competitive edge.

Notes

1. For more information on the Gad family, cf. Julie Allen's essay in this book.
2. "Hvorfor er filmen ikke blevet bedre end den er", interview with Hjalmar Davidsen, *Politiken* (31 July 1954).
3. "Teater og Tribune", *Politiken* (21 June 1910).
4. "Hvorfor", interview with Davidsen (1954).
5. "Oplevelser omkring Optagelsesapparatet", part VIII, interview with Hjalmar Davidsen, *B.T.* (29 December 1919).
6. Cf. Martin Loiperdinger, "AFGRUNDEN in Germany: *monopolfilm*, cinemagoing and the emergence of the film star Asta Nielsen in Germany", in Daniel Biltereyst, Richard Maltby and Philippe Meers (eds), *Cinema, Audiences and Modernity. New perspectives on European cinema history* (London: Routledge, 2011), 142–153.
7. Marguerite Engberg, *Filmstjernen Asta Nielsen* (Aarhus: Klim, 1999), 53.
8. Johan Christensen interviewed by Marguerite Engberg, tape, Det Danske Filminstitut (DFI),

quoted in Jan Nielsen, *A/S Filmfabriken Danmark: SRH/Filmfabriken Danmarks historie og produktion* (Copenhagen: Multivers, 2003), 45.

9. "A/S Fotorama – Et Tilbageblik paa Selskabets første 25 Leveaar", unpublished manuscript, DFI, 6, quoted in Nielsen, *A/S Filmfabriken*, 46.
10. "Teater og Tribune", *Politiken* (15 September 1910).
11. Richard Jenkins, *Being Danish: Paradoxes of Identity in Everyday Life* (Copenhagen: Museum Tusculanum, 2011), 24.
12. "Skive", in *Salmonsens Konversationsleksikon* (2nd edn), vol. 21 (Copenhagen: J.H. Schultz, 1926), 576–578.
13. Gunnar Sandfeld, *Den stumme scene: dansk biografteater indtil lydfilmens gennembrud* (Copenhagen: Nyt Nordisk Forlag / Arnold Busck, 1966), 81–82.
14. "Afgrunden", undated folder, photocopy, DFI ([Skive: Biograf-Teatret]), 3.
15. *Politiken* (12 October 1910).
16. Thanks to Martin Loiperdinger for bringing up this question.
17. Afgrunden, undated folder, 3.
18. *Skive Folkeblad* (30 December 1910).
19. E.g. *Skive Folkeblad* (17 October 1910 and 24 March 1911).
20. *Skive Folkeblad* (3 April 1911).
21. *Skive Folkeblad* (20 January 1911).
22. *Skive Folkeblad* (3 April 1911).
23. *Skive Folkeblad* (5 December 1910).
24. *Skive Folkeblad* (27 March 1911); other films identified as Vitagraph productions are mentioned 19 December 1910, 6 February 1911, 10 February 1911, 27 February 1911.
25. *Skive Folkeblad* (25 November 1910).
26. *Skive Folkeblad* (30 December 1910).
27. Cf. Marguerite Engberg, "Plagiarism and the Birth of the Danish Multi-Reel Film", in Dan Nissen and Lisbeth Richter Larsen (eds), *100 Years of Nordisk Film* (Copenhagen: DFI, 2006), 72–79.
28. Isak Thorsen, *Isbjørnens anatomi: Nordisk Films Kompagni som erhvervsvirksomhed i perioden 1906–1928*, PhD thesis (Copenhagen: University of Copenhagen, 2009), 93–98.
29. http://www.dfi.dk/FaktaOmFilm/Nationalfilmografien.aspx
30. *Skive Folkeblad* (25 November 1910).
31. *Skive Folkeblad* (14 October 1910).
32. *Skive Folkeblad* (21 October 1910).
33. *Skive Folkeblad* (16 December 1910).
34. Cf. Herbert Birett, *Das Filmangebot in Deutschland 1895–1911* (München: Winterberg, 1991), 4.
35. *Skive Folkeblad* (18 April 1911).
36. *Skive Folkeblad* (19 April 1911).
37. *Skive Social-Demokrat* (22 April 1911).
38. Silvio Alovisio, "The 'Pastrone System': Itala Film from the Origins to World War I", *Film History* 12:3 (2000): 250–261, here 254.
39. *Skive Social-Demokrat* (25 April 1911).

Isak Thorsen

Nordisk Films Kompagni and Asta Nielsen

In September 1911, the founder and General Manager of Nordisk Films Kompagni, Ole Olsen, made the following pronouncement in a letter to the company's London branch: "I also noticed what you say about the Asta Nielsen films; we do not find her especially good, but this is a matter of taste (…)".[1]

Asta Nielsen made only four films in Denmark in the silent era: her film debut and breakthrough AFGRUNDEN (THE ABYSS, 1910), followed by DEN SORTE DRØM (THE BLACK DREAM, 1911), BALLETDANSERINDEN (THE BALLET DANCER, 1911) and finally MOD LYSET (TOWARDS THE LIGHT, 1919). Only the last two were produced by the leading Danish film company of the period, Nordisk Film. Letters from Nordisk Film suggest that the company was eager to get hold of the distribution rights to AFGRUNDEN in late 1910,[2] and perhaps Olsen's judgement of Asta Nielsen's early films was biased by the part they played in a struggle for power in the company, a struggle closely connected to the company's reorganisation in order to produce multi-reel films and make the transition to a limited company.

On the basis of research in the Nordisk Special Collection, Nordisk Film's surviving business archive, this article will take issue with the common interpretation of Nordisk Film's plagiarism of the Fotorama production DEN HVIDE SLAVEHANDEL (THE WHITE SLAVE TRADE, 1910) and analyse how Nielsen's contract with Fotorama and the sale of DEN SORTE DRØM and BALLETDANSERINDEN influenced the structure of the company's management.

The Crisis at Nordisk Film
Since its establishment in 1906, Nordisk Film had grown into a healthy and prosperous firm. But when the general crisis hit the international industry by the end of the decade – a crisis mainly due to an overproduction of film and the lack of organised distribution – Nordisk Film was hit as well. In 1907 the average sale of film copies was 67, the following year 48, and in 1909 it was 40.[3] Nordisk Film's management was sincerely in doubt about how to cope with the situation. One solution was sought in the actual topics and themes of the films, as a letter to a scriptwriter from January 1909 indicates:

Ole Olsen, around 1915. Det Danske Filminstitut.

> Since we have been doubtful as to the specific taste we should prefer in the upcoming season, we have not wanted to make a decision concerning your manuscript. We believe the adventurous genre has played itself out and that public taste now favours grandiose, realistic stories, yet without crime, and burlesque.[4]

Another possible solution was put forward in a letter from December 1909 by the manager of the company's copying laboratory, Wilhelm Stæhr, who suggested the possibility of making the films longer, but the company must have given up the idea.[5] Nordisk Film's production policy was that the films were not to exceed 300 metres,[6] which followed the international convention of the time. The multi-reel films eventually became part of the solution to the crisis, not only for Nordisk Film, but also for the international film industry at large. The company's first long film, DEN HVIDE SLAVEHANDEL (THE WHITE SLAVE), 603 metres long, from 1910, coincided with the beginning of the golden age of Danish silent cinema and brought Nordisk Film up among the leading European film companies.

DEN HVIDE SLAVEHANDEL

Nordisk Film was not the only film company in Denmark. Among the other companies was the Aarhus-based A/S Th. S. Hermansen, founded in 1908 by

Frede Skaarup.

the photographer Thomas S. Hermansen with the purpose of renting or selling films and running cinemas. The former merchant Frede Skaarup was hired as manager, and the following year his trusted employee Eduard Schnedler-Sørensen joined the company.

With Skaarup as manager, business grew fast in a sometimes aggressive way. Skaarup demanded 20 to 25 per cent of the cinema owners' profits from the films instead of a fixed rental fee. Many cinema owners felt threatened by Skaarup, and, as a reaction, Biograf Teater Foreningen for Provinsen (The Cinema Theatre Association of the Provinces) was founded in March 1910. But for fear of not getting access to the films from A/S Th. Hermansen, many cinema owners did not dare join the association. In a very short time the company had gained control of large parts of the cinema market in Denmark.[7]

The ties between Nordisk Film and Hermansen had existed for years. Olsen granted Hermansen the exclusive rights to his films in Aarhus in 1907,[8] and they had stood together when the Danish film industry succeeded in keeping the French company Pathé Frères out of the Danish market in late 1909.[9]

In 1909, A/S Th. S. Hermansen made its first film production, DEN LILLE HORNBLÆSER (THE LITTLE HORNBLOWER), directed by Schnedler-Sørensen. Because of the film's success, the company decided to continue the production of films and changed its name to Fotorama, and a branch with a cinema, Løvebiografen (The Lion Cinema), was established in Copenhagen.

On 11 April 1910, Fotorama's film DEN HVIDE SLAVEHANDEL premiered in

Løvebiografen and was an instant success. It was shown about 400 times, and what was extraordinary about the film was its length of 706 metres.[10] Olsen's reaction was to send his director August Blom to the cinema and note down every scene from Fotorama's film.[11] Less than four months later, on 2 August, Nordisk Film released their nearly identical version of DEN HVIDE SLAVEHANDEL with the exact same title, 603 metres long. Nordisk Film did not attempt to conceal the plagiarism in any way. To a Swedish cinema owner the company wrote: "By request, we open with DEN HVIDE SLAVEHANDEL on August the first, executed in the exact same way as the one that ran here at the Løvebiografen, but performed by better artists and with Miss Diedrich in the lead. It is a role she performs to perfection".[12] To a Norwegian business acquaintance, the film was described as: " a picture whose content is exactly the same as the film of Scandinavian fame from Hermansen in Aarhus".[13] Only the Nordisk Film version has survived, but Danish Film historian Marguerite Engberg has compared the Nordisk Film version with stills and fragments from the Fotorama version and convincingly confirmed that it was plagiarism. Not only the content, but also actual shots are framed nearly identically.[14]

Just three days after the premiere of the Nordisk Film version, on 5 August, Fotorama reacted by placing adverts in the Copenhagen newspapers with the headline "Warning to the public". Nordisk Film's version was called a bad copy, which should not be compared with the Fotorama version, and the advert stated: "This can only take place because the law as yet provides no protection against such things".[15]

Nordisk Film's plagiarism of DEN HVIDE SLAVEHANDEL is one of the most known incidents in early Danish film history, and Engberg's interpretation is the generally accepted one.[16] Engberg writes that Fotorama threatened to take Nordisk Film to court, and, to avoid any 'unpleasantness', Olsen entered into an agreement with Fotorama in which Fotorama, among other things, were granted the rights to distribute films from Nordisk Film in Denmark, Norway and later Sweden. Skaarup became manager in Nordisk Film and Schnedler-Sørensen was employed as film director.[17] According to Engberg, the agreement was "fatal" for Nordisk Film.[18] In early 1911, when the agreement was finally closed, only a small percentage of Nordisk Film's sales went to the Scandinavian countries. But, when the First World War broke out, the borders were closed and the export of film stopped, and it was Fotorama which made the money on the films from Nordisk Film, Engberg writes.[19] This version of the events can be challenged, though. The deal was hardly fatal for Nordisk Film. Denmark, Norway and later Sweden were small markets, e.g. the average sale to Denmark 1912–1914 was 2.6 per cent of total sales.[20] In 1915 Fotorama and Nordisk Film established the rental company Fotorama Films Bureau A/S, and it was here that Nordisk Film acquired half of the profits on its own and other films that Fotorama sold or rented in Denmark, Norway and Sweden.

However, it is important to keep separate two occurrences: (1) Nordisk Film's plagiarism of DEN HVIDE SLAVEHANDEL together with the ensuing distribution agreement, and (2) Skaarup and Schnedler-Sørensen's employment by Nordisk Film, which happened half a year later when the company became a limited company.

The question is whether Fotorama was able to create any 'unpleasantness' at all for Nordisk Film through a court trial or the threat of one. On the one hand, Fotorama's 'warning advert' states there were no copyright laws in Denmark, at least not for films. Had there been a copyright law in Denmark at the time, it would have been reckless of Nordisk Film to promote its version of DEN HVIDE SLAVEHANDEL in its correspondence as identical. The company was well aware that intellectual rights were a potential future problem that Nordisk Film had to deal with. As an example, Stæhr wrote to the Berlin branch in the beginning of 1910 in order to be updated on the copyright problems.[21] Germany had signed the Berne Convention on 22 May 1910,[22] and not until 1912 was film included in the copyright laws in Denmark.[23] There are no indications of a court trial or a threat of one in Nordisk Film's correspondence or in the regional archives.[24] On the other hand, as Danish film historian Jan Nielsen points out, the letters in the Nordisk Film Special Collection indicate that the negotiations between Nordisk Film and Fotorama were carried out at meetings and by telephone.[25] Although there were no copyright laws protecting film, and apparently no official records of a court trial involving the two companies, the law opened opportunities for Fotorama to create unpleasantness for Nordisk Film. *Lov om Forfatterret og Kunstnerret* (The Law on Copyright and Artistic Rights) from 1904 included a clause which protected authors from having their texts transferred to other media without the author's permission. It was actually used by the Danish author Johan Prægel against Fotorama in late 1910. Fotorama had to pay Johan Prægel 500 Danish crowns for adapting his stage play *Kapergasten* to film because the stage play and the text of the film's souvenir cinema programme of the film were too similar! In the case of DEN HVIDE SLAVEHANDEL, Nordisk Film copied the content of the Fotorama film, using the same settings and names, and in this context Louis Schmidt, who wrote the script for Fotorama's DEN HVIDE SLAVEHANDEL, could have taken Nordisk Film to court for transferring his script to the film's souvenir cinema programme. But in his memoirs Louis Schmidt writes: "In Aarhus, they tried to bring an injunction against the copy, but to no avail – living pictures were not yet copyrighted then".[26] One must assume that if Fotorama had been able to apply the Law of 1904 against Nordisk Film, Schmidt would have remembered it, on the strength of such a spectacular case as the plagiarism of DEN HVIDE SLAVEHANDEL. It is also worth noting that the actual case involving Johan Prægel and Fotorama was not settled until 1912,[27] which may indicate an uncertainty on the part of the courts on how to interpret the new copyright laws. In 1911 and 1912, a few other copyright cases evolved around Nordisk Film, most spectacularly when the company copied Oskar Messter's DAS GEFÄHRLICHE ALTER (THE DANGEROUS AGE) in 1911; and Nordisk Film and Kinografen struggled in 1912 over the film rights to the book on which the film DEN SORTE KANSLER (THE BLACK CHANCELLOR) was to be based.

What is certain is that Nordisk Film and Fotorama did close a distribution agreement on 3 December 1910, which was confirmed on 6 February 1911.[28] The agreement stipulated that Fotorama distribute films from Nordisk Film in Denmark, Norway and later Sweden. Furthermore, Nordisk Film was obligated to make twelve art films (another term for multi-reel films) which were to premiere at the Copenhagen cinema Panoptikonteatret, which Fotorama had invested heavily in.

It was in Nordisk Film's interest to hand over the distribution rights to Fotorama in Denmark, Norway and Sweden. Nordisk Film had tried to hand over the agency for Sweden and Norway in late 1910.[29] The deal with Fotorama is very similar to the distribution deals Nordisk Film had closed for other territories, with an agent who bought a fixed number of films and thus guaranteed Nordisk Film a steady sale of films. Fotorama was the obvious choice for the Scandinavian countries. In March 1911, M.P. Drescher, chairman of Fotorama's board, reported at the company's general assembly that Fotorama now had 100 customers as compared to 60 the previous year.[30] The Aarhus-based company controlled a solid share of the Danish and Scandinavian market to which Nordisk Film now had access. From Fotorama's perspective, the deal was favourable, because, as Casper Tybjerg writes: "(…) with the rights to the most attractive Danish films, [Fotorama] could impose their rental system by which the cinema owners had to pay a fixed share of the profit instead of a fixed price".[31] The deal secured Fotorama a steady supply of attractive and profitable films for the Danish market as well as for Norway, which at the time had no film production. The distribution deal was the first step in the bond between the two companies. The next step took place half a year later when Nordisk Film converted its base to a limited company on 8 May 1911.

Forced or voluntarily?

In his memoirs, the actor Olaf Fønss writes that Fotorama, with Skaarup in the lead, planned a large new Copenhagen-based film company, and because of this, "(…) Ole Olsen became anxious and suggested a collaboration resulting in the formation of the company 'Nordisk Film Co.' in 1911".[32] The author Arnold Hending similarly presents Fotorama as a threat to Nordisk Film which made "Ole Olsen so nervous that he hastened to sign up their leading men with Nordisk".[33] Olsen's own version of the events is very close to Fønss and Hending's. In his autobiography Olsen writes how more and more people became aware of the lucrative potential of the film industry: "As it was not to be too cumbersome for the new men, they preferred to deviously lure my staff – whom I had trained in the business for years – away from me".[34] Olsen does not reveal who 'the new men' were, but it can only be people from Fotorama, since Olsen recounts how he had to cut a deal with them, and Nordisk Film turned into a limited company. Olsen finishes his recollection with the following: "But I had never forgotten, and never will, their original plan to knock me to the ground if they could".[35]

However, it was actually Olsen, who on 22 April 1911 presented the idea to a few select gentlemen of establishing a limited company. Except for the Nordisk Film managers Stæhr and Olsen, the gentlemen attending the meeting all came from or were connected to the management and/or the board of Fotorama: chairman of Fotorama's board, M.P. Drescher; barrister O. Gulmann; merchant H. Gielstrup and consul E. Bergmann, who were all members of Fotorama's board; A.W. Mammen was Drescher's partner in the shipping company Mammen & Drescher; and Skaarup and Schnedler-Sørensen. During the meeting, Olsen outlined his plans for establishing a limited company.[36]

Two days later, on 24 April, M.P. Drescher reported the following to the board of Fotorama: Olsen had tried to sign up Skaarup to Nordisk Film with a generous offer, but Skaarup had refused because of his obligations to Fotorama. Drescher reported from the meeting with Olsen:

> Furthermore, Mr. Ole Olsen had contemplated launching a film rental business that would have been troublesome and harmful to Fotorama, just as one could expect that Mr. Ole Olsen, in case an understanding could not be reached, would be of much harm to Fotorama Film Factory, partly by contracting the best actors, partly by making agreements with the two existing raw stock factories so as to make it difficult for Fotorama to acquire raw film.[37]

Under these circumstances, Drescher recommended a continuation of the negotiations. In M.P. Drescher's account, it is Olsen who threatened Fotorama with starting a competing rental business and preventing Fotorama from access to raw stock, thereby forcing the people from Fotorama to put up the capital for the limited company quite contrary to Olsen's own recount.

On 8 May, the limited company was founded with a capital of kr. 450,000. All the share-holders, except for Olsen, had a connection to Fotorama.

E. Bergmann	Kr. 5000
H. Gielstrup	Kr. 5000
J. Ramm	Kr. 26,000
O. Gulmann	Kr. 24,000
A.W. Mammen	Kr. 20,000
E. Schnedler-Sørensen	Kr. 20,000
F. Skaarup	Kr. 25,000
O. Olsen	Kr. 125,000
-	Kr. 200,000 in preferred shares.[38]

Olsen still owned half of the voting shares and 72 per cent of the share capital. He was now chairman of the board and did not take part in the day-to-day business.[39] Stæhr and Skaarup became managers, and Skaarup retained his position as manager of Fotorama as well.

Why a limited company?

So why was Nordisk Film restructured into a limited company? And why did Olsen want to sign up the people from Fotorama to his company? The success of AFGRUNDEN, DEN HVIDE SLAVEHANDEL and other multi-reel films had

Contract between Frede Skaarup and Asta Nielsen, 2 May 1911. Nordisk Film Archive, Valby.

demonstrated that the audience was ready for the long films. A reorganisation of production in favour of the more demanding and expensive long films required capital for larger investments and a quicker return in profits. The film industry was still a young business, and it was probably hard for Olsen to find investors. In her study, Janet Wasko has shown how reluctant banks were to invest in the early American film industry. The banks looked down on the film industry as "a novelty or a fad that eventually would fade into obscurity".[40] The international film business had been through its first major crisis. In 1911, no one could know whether film was just a passing fad or a permanent entertainment offer. If the film industry was to face a new crisis, it would be wise for Olsen to have someone with whom to share the losses.

The idea of converting Nordisk Film into a limited company was not new to Olsen. In 1909, he and German film producer Oskar Messter planned to merge into a limited company, and in the spring of 1910 Olsen corresponded with the lawyer Heinrich A. Müller, who was negotiating on behalf of an unknown investor with the purpose of founding a limited company.[41] Neither of these plans was carried out. In the circle of people connected to Fotorama, Olsen saw the investors he needed, especially Mammen and Drescher, who were partners in a large shipping company and who had shown their willingness to invest in Fotorama.

There might also have been personal reasons. Olsen liquidated some of the capital he had acquired at Nordisk Film for himself. He was 48 years old; the average life span of a man living in Denmark was 55 years in 1911, and Olsen's wife was terminally ill with tuberculosis.

Finally, Olsen was searching for new directors and managers. Viggo Larsen, who had been in charge of Nordisk Film's studios and had directed nearly all of the company's fiction films from 1906 to 1909 – an average of 60 films a year – had left Nordisk Film to pursue a career in Germany. Viggo Larsen's replacement was Holger Rasmussen, who was hired on 1 January 1910 and given notice again in October, effective January 1911, because he was "incompetent in all areas".[42] With Skaarup and the director Schnedler-Sørensen, Olsen hired qualified staff members who had already shown their worth in the film business.

The Asta Nielsen and Urban Gad Contracts

Among the assets transferred from Fotorama to Nordisk Film were two contracts. One was between Asta Nielsen and Skaarup, signed on 2 May 1911, less than a week before establishing Nordisk Film as a limited company. In the contract Nielsen agreed to work for a newly established limited company based in Copenhagen in July and September. Asta Nielsen's engagement with Deutsche Bioscop in August 1911 is represented in the contract. It further stipulates that Nielsen had to play as many parts as possible in the period, and in case of breach of contract, a conventional fine of 10,000 Danish crowns was to be paid.[43]

The other contract was between the film company A/S København Kunstfilms Kompagni (Copenhagen Art Film, Ltd.) and the director Urban Gad, who was also Nielsen's partner. Gad agreed to direct and prepare films for the company. The contract allowed Gad to direct films abroad and permitted him to fulfil his contract with Deutsche Bioscop in August 1911, but with no salary from København Kunstfilms that month. Seen in the light of the events surrounding DEN HVIDE SLAVEHANDEL, a clause found in the contract is curious: "Mr. Gad retains the right to abstain from making films that copy previous films, as well as films that include royalties to Danish writers." The contract further stipulates that if København Kunstfilms should be taken over by a larger company, the contract will be transferred to the new company within three months, with the guarantee that Gad is not to direct more than twelve films. The signers for København Kunstfilms were Gulmann, Mammen and Ramm, all from the board of Fotorama.[44]

Both contracts took into consideration Gad and Nielsen's engagement with Deutsche Bioscop in August 1911 and included the possibility of transferring the contracts to a future limited company. It is intriguing that Fotorama and Skaarup signed contracts with Gad a month before and with Nielsen less than a week prior to finally establishing Nordisk Film as a limited company. The negotiations must have been going on for a while, and one can wonder whether Fotorama, with the two contracts with the attractive couple Gad & Nielsen, wished to raise the value of Fotorama's assets during the negotiations?

In their individual recollections of establishing Internationale Films-Vertrieb-Gesellschaft on 27 May in Frankfurt am Main, the German film producer Christoph Mülleneisen Sr. and Asta Nielsen both refer to the conventional fine in Nielsen's contract. In Mülleneisen and Nielsen's accounts, Mülleneisen hastened to Copenhagen to engage Nielsen in May 1911. Mülleneisen, Nielsen and Gad met at the fashionable Hotel d'Angleterre in the centre of the city.[45] Mülleneisen's stay is confirmed by a letter dated 15 May from Nordisk Film manager Stæhr to Mülleneisen's hotel. In the letter, Stæhr forwards a telegram received at Nordisk Film addressed to Mülleneisen together with an apology that an employee had opened the telegram by mistake.[46] The negotiations between Nordisk Film and Fotorama are mentioned in Mülleneisen's memoirs where he writes how, after meeting Gad and Nielsen, he travelled to Aarhus to annul Asta Nielsen's contract and pay Skaarup the conventional fine. According to Engberg and Nielsen's reports, the conventional fine was paid, and Asta Nielsen was free to travel to Germany and work.[47] However, Mülleneisen writes that he failed to make a compromise with Skaarup,[48] and, seen in the light of what happened in June 1911, Nielsen must have worked for Nordisk Film in either June or September that year as stated in her contract with Skaarup.

The Breitung & Mülleneisen Case

With Nordisk's transition to a limited company Olsen lost influence. Stæhr reported to the Berlin branch: "In short, it goes like this; Mr. Frede Skaarup and I are the managing directors. Director Ole Olsen is the chairman of the board and does not take part in the daily decisions, only when we ask him for advice".[49] Skaarup and Stæhr were now in charge. "Various manoeuvres had the result that Skaarup resigned as director after a few months. Olsen's control was thus established", writes Casper Tybjerg, without explaining what manoeuvres Olsen carried out to regain the power at Nordisk Film.[50] Only Olsen has given an account of what happened in his memoirs, which are not entirely to be trusted:

> Some time after the two directors started in office, I received a telephone call announcing that now they had made the biggest and best deal ever. They had signed a one-year contract with a German firm and had sold our entire production of the upcoming season for one million marks; and they were elated.[51]

Olsen rushed to the main office of Nordisk Film and saw two foreigners, "who I knew were the type of people who close deals of one million marks without owning anything".[52] Olsen demanded to see the contract and made sure that no other papers were signed in the deal and then tore up the contract. His argument was that such a big deal would influence the entire company and had to be discussed with the board of directors. But more papers were signed. In Germany, films from Nordisk were confiscated, and Olsen took off together with one of the managers and a member of the board to remedy the situation. In Germany they met the two foreigners, and after some negotiations Olsen bought back the confiscated films for 17,500 marks. The incident was not without consequences. The two directors left, and as early as the following meeting of the board of directors, Olsen was asked to re-enter the management.

On the whole, Olsen's memoirs concur with the Breitung & Mülleneisen case. As mentioned, Skaarup had engaged Asta Nielsen, and she had made DEN SORTE DRØM for Fotorama. Skaarup sold this film to German distributor Theodor Breitung and gave him the option to buy the next Asta Nielsen film, BALLETDANSERINDEN, which was to be shot at Nordisk Film beginning in June 1911. A few days later, Breitung returned to Copenhagen and signed a contract with Skaarup to buy 60 copies of twelve multi-reel films and 40 copies of the next Nielsen film as 'monopol' films. Skaarup signed the contract representing the company Skandinavien Kunstfilm Fabrik (Scandinavian Art Film Factory), which was about to be established, and Breitung signed for a limited company which also was not yet officially founded. As a guarantee for the deal, Breitung made a down payment of 50,000 marks, an amount which was to be paid back on the fulfilment of the contract by March 1912. The entire deal was worth between 800,000 and 900,000 marks.

On 27 June Skaarup then met with Breitung and his partner Christoph Mülleneisen Sr., who had signed Gad and Nielsen for Internationale Films-Vertrieb-Gesellschaft exactly a month before. The 50,000 marks had not yet been deposited and the German limited company was not yet established. A new contract was signed stipulating that Breitung and Mülleneisen deposit a bill of 10,000 marks, which was to go to Skandinavien Kunstfilm Fabrik in case the 50,000 marks had not been deposited by 3 July. Skandinavien Kunstfilm Fabrik was established on 1 July, and the contract with Breitung and Mülleneisen was passed on to Nordisk Film. By 3 July, Breitung had not deposited the 50,000 marks, and Nordisk Film collected the 10,000 marks bill.[53] A court trial now commenced, which ended in January 1913. Breitung and Mülleneisen adhered to the first contract from the beginning of June, the original of which they had and would not hand over to Nordisk Film. Nordisk Film adhered to the contract of 27 June. The dispute ended with Mülleneisen having to let Nordisk Film keep the 10,000 marks plus 6 per cent interest and 58 marks and 83 pfennig in exchange fee.⁵⁴

As it appears in Olsen's memoirs, Skaarup had agreed on a contract of nearly one million marks with two Germans, and there were two different signed contracts. The consequences of the Breitung-Mülleneisen case was a change in the procedures of decision making in Nordisk's management. During a meeting of the board in August 1911, one of the new clauses was:

> The board or at least the chairman is kept up to date concerning business, and neither the managing directors nor others may make decisions concerning anything outside daily business without consulting the chairman or the executive committee. The managing directors and others have a duty to comply with the instructions of the chairman and the executive committee and to do their best to execute these.⁵⁵

This clause makes it clear that Olsen now had regained his influence, except for the daily business. By negotiating such a large contract without the board's or Olsen's approval, Skaarup had outmanoeuvred himself. His authority to bind the company was withdrawn on 28 December 1911.⁵⁶ He went on to become the uncrowned king of the Copenhagen Theatre life, and he and Olsen later collaborated closely on several business ideas.

In the common interpretation of the events concerning Nordisk Film's plagiarism of DEN HVIDE SLAVEHANDEL, Fotorama is seen as having been able to cause 'unpleasantness' for Nordisk Film, and in this manner Fotorama gained the distribution rights to films from Nordisk Film in Denmark, Norway and Sweden, and Frede Skaarup and Eduard Schnedler-Sørensen became members of the management of the Copenhagen company. It is not certain whether Fotorama was able to put pressure on Nordisk Film, since the copyright laws in Denmark were not yet introduced in 1912. The early Danish copyright laws opened possibilities, but it was in Nordisk Film's interest to use Fotorama as agent for the company's films and later to attach people from Fotorama's management and board in the transition of Nordisk Film to a limited company. Though Asta Nielsen was only briefly attached to the largest Danish film company in the silent era, her two early Danish films – the Fotorama production DEN SORTE DRØM and the Nordisk Film production BALLETDANSERINDEN – came to play an important part in the struggle for power in the newly established limited company. Perhaps this lay behind Olsen's negative judgement of Asta Nielsen's film in September 1911.

Acknowledgements: I am grateful for discussing parts of the article with Stephan Michael Schröder and Lars Kaaber for helping with the translations of the Danish quotes and improving the English in the article.

Notes

1. Nordisk Special Collection (NFS): II, 16. Det Danske Filminstitut (DFI). 822.
2. NFS: II, 14, DFI. 401.
3. The figures are based on the distribution protocols of the Nordisk Special Collection: NFS: XI, 7 a+b and XXII, 33–39. DFI. No distribution protocols have survived from approximately 1908 to the spring of 1912. Data from this period is taken from NFS: XI,1. DFI., which has information about the films with negative numbers, sometimes the length of the films and how many copies sold.
4. NFS: II, 9. DFI. 156.
5. NFS:II, 11. DFI. 717.
6. NFS: II, 12. DFI. 746.
7. Casper Tybjerg: "Teltholdernes verdensteater", "Spekulanter og Himmelstormere", in Peter Schepelern (ed.), *100 års dansk film* (Copenhagen: Rosinante, 2001), 27.
8. NFS: II, 6. DFI. 427.
9. NFS: II, 11. DFI. 203 and 807.
10. "Hvor man morer sig.", *Politiken* (10 May 1910). Quoted from Marguerite Engberg, *Dansk Stumfilm* (Copenhagen: Rhodos, 1977), 222.
11. Interview with cameraman Axel Graatkjær undated. The tape is held at DFI.
12. NFS: II, 13. DFI. 305.
13. NFS: II, 13. DFI. 345.
14. For a detailed analysis cf. Marguerite Engberg, "Plagiarism and the Birth of the Danish Multi-reel Film", in Dan Nissen and Lisbeth Richter Larsen (eds), *100 Years of Nordisk Film* (Copenhagen, Det Danske Filminstitut, 2006), 73–79.
15. *Politiken* (5 August 1910). Quoted from Jan Nielsen, *A/S Filmfabriken Danmark: SRH/Filmfabriken Danmarks historie og produktion* (Copenhagen: Multivers, 2003), 66.
16. E.g. Niels-Jørgen Dinnesen and Edvin Kau, *Filmen i Danmark* (Copenhagen: Akademisk Forlag, 1983), 29–20; Casper Tybjerg, *An Art of Silence and Light*, PhD thesis (University of Copenhagen), 73–74. Thomas C. Christensen, "Isbjørnens fald", in Helle Haastrup, Helle Kannik and Torben Kragh Grodal, *Sekvens 97. Filmæstetik og Billedhistorie. Filmvidenskabelig årbog 1997* (Copenhagen: Institut for Film og Medievidenskab, University of Copenhagen, 1997), 235. Tybjerg, "Teltholdernes verdensteater", 31.
17. Engberg, *Dansk Stumfilm*, 225.
18. Engberg, "Plagiarism", 79.
19. Engberg, *Dansk Stumfilm*, 229.
20. Cf. note 3.
21. NFS: II, 12. DFI. 304–305.
22. Corinna Müller, *Frühe deutsche Kinematographie. Formale, wirtschaftliche und kulturelle Entwicklungen 1907–1912* (Stuttgart and Weimar: Metzler, 1994), 126.
23. E-mail from assistant secretary in the Danish Ministry of Culture, Peter Schønning (15 February 2006).
24. The following material has been analysed in Landsarkivet for Sjælland (Provincial Archives of Zealand): Landover, – samt Hof og Stadsretten: Fogedkontoret-kendelsesprotokoller 1910–12. Navneregister 1892–1917. Forretningsregistre 1910–12.
25. Nielsen, *A/S Filmfabriken Danmark*, 66.
26. Richardt Gandrup, *Redaktør Louis Schmidt – en levnedsbeskrivelse* (Copenhagen: Gad, 1957), 38.
27. Stephan Michael Schröder, *Ideale Kommunikation, reale Filmproduktion. Zur Interaktion von Kino und dänischer Literatur in den Erfolgsjahren des dänischen Stummfilms 1909–1918*. 2 vols (Berlin: Nordeuropa-Institut, 2011), 426–427.
28. NFS: II, 14. DFI. 376-378. Sweden from January 1912. NFS: II, 18. DFI. 329.
29. NFS: II, 13. DFI. 475 and NFS: II, 14. DFI. 324.

30. Erhvervsarkivet (The Danish National Business Archives). Generalforsamlingsprotokol f. Hotel Royal 1908–23 (2 March 1911).
31. Tybjerg, "Spekulanter og Himmelstormere", 31.
32. Olaf Fønss, *Films-erindringer gennem 20 Aar* (Copenhagen: Nutidens Forlag, 1930), 66.
33. Arnold Hending, *Da Isbjørnen var lille* (Copenhagen: Urania, 1945), 82.
34. Ole Olsen, *Filmens Eventyr og mit eget* (Copenhagen: Jespersen og Pios Forlag, 1940), 91.
35. Ibid., 92.
36. NFS: I, 1:10. DFI.
37. Erhvervsarkivet (24 April 1911).
38. NFS: I, 23. DFI. 3.
39. NFS: II, 16. DFI. 25.
40. Janet Marie Wasko, "Relationships Between The American Motion Picture Industry and Banking Institutions", PhD thesis (Urbana, IL: University of Illinois at Urban-Champaign, 1980), 23.
41. NFS: II, 12. DFI. 172 and 897.
42. NFS: II, 30. DFI. 968. NFS: II, 13. DFI. 813. NFS: II, 11. DFI. 712.
43. Contract between Frede Skaarup and Asta Nielsen, 2 May 1911. Nordisk Film's Archive, Valby. The contract is apparently now stored in a warehouse. A digital copy of the contract is held at the Danish Film Institute.
44. Copy of contract between A/S København Kunstfilms Fabrik and Urban Gad dated 8 April 1908. In a note attached to the contract dated 29 February 1911 Gad denounced the contract effective 1 July 1912. Nordisk Film's Archive, Valby. The contract is apparently now stored in a warehouse. A digital copy of the contract is held at the DFI.
45. Christoph Mülleneisen Sr., "Wie ich Asta Nielsen engagierte", *Erste Internationale Film-Zeitung* (25 April 1914), repr. in Renate Seydel and Allan Hagedorff, *Asta Nielsen. Ihr Leben in Fotodokumenten, Selbstzeugnissen und zeitgenössischen Betrachtungen* (Berlin, GDR: Henschelverlag Kunst und Gesellschaft, 1984), 48–49. Asta Nielsen: *Den Tiende Muse*, bind II (Copenhagen: Gyldendal, 1946), 9–14.
46. NFS: II,15. DFI. 937.
47. Marguerite Engberg: *Filmstjernen Asta Nielsen* (Aarhus: Klim, 1999), 62. Nielsen, *Den Tiende Muse*, 14.
48. Mülleneisen, "Wie ich Asta Nielsen engagierte".
49. NFS: II, 16. DFI. 25.
50. Tybjerg, "Spekulanter og Himmelstormere", 31.
51. Olsen, *Filmens Eventyr og mit eget*, 92.
52. Ibid., 93.
53. NFS: I, 2: 3. DFI.
54. NFS: I, 2: 34. DFI.
55. NFS: I, 25. DFI.
56. Københavns Stadssarkiv (Copenhagen City Archive). Handelsregistret. Afdeling B. 2763.

Julie K. Allen

Ambivalent Admiration
Asta Nielsen's Conflicted Reception in Denmark, 1911–14

Asta Nielsen became a film actress as an attempt to boost her career prospects on the Danish stage, but ended up becoming the most famous Danish cinema actress in the world instead. The story of her rise to international fame not only illustrates the economic factors driving the rapid growth of the film industry and the movie star system, but also the role of nationalism and social class in early twentieth-century Danish bourgeois culture. Nielsen's debut film AFGRUNDEN (THE ABYSS) was tremendously popular with Danish audiences, but the low status of film as an art form thwarted Nielsen's hopes that it would lead to leading roles in the theater. Poul Reumert, an actor at the Danish Royal Theater and Nielsen's co-star in AFGRUNDEN, described the contemporary Danish opinion of film as "that miserable bastard, that despicable mix of photographic technique and penny-ante entertainment, the most outrageous antithesis to all spirit and art".[1] Even the reaction of the Danish film industry to Nielsen seemed lukewarm, however. AFGRUNDEN's success garnered Nielsen just a handful of film roles with the Danish studios Fotorama and Nordisk, on the short-term contracts that were typical for the time.

Fortunately for Asta Nielsen, AFGRUNDEN's staggering box-office revenues attracted the attention of German film companies on the lookout for potential stars whose popularity could facilitate their new monopoly film-distribution business model.[2] While Nielsen had been paid just 200 Danish crowns for starring in the film, Ludwig Gottschalk, who had purchased the German distribution rights for AFGRUNDEN, earned 800,000 marks on the film, enough to "pave Düsseldorf with them", as contemporary newspapers trumpeted.[3] In stark contrast to the indifference of the Danish studios, the German film industry recognized Nielsen's star potential and courted her with enthusiastic promises, made possible by the monopoly system's generous profit margins, of long-term contracts, creative autonomy, and astronomical earnings. Within just a few months of AFGRUNDEN's premiere, Deutsche Bioscop had engaged Nielsen and her director Urban Gad to make an entire series of films that would be pre-sold to distributors solely on the strength of their names. In the spring of 1911 Christoph Mülleneisen Sr., film distributor and cinema owner of Cologne, spent several frantic days persuading a group of businessmen, including Paul Davidson, the head of Projektions AG Union (PAGU), to co-found a new monopoly-distribution company, the Internationale Films-Vertrieb-GmbH (IFVG), for the express purpose of marketing and distributing Asta Nielsen's future films. The unprecedented terms of the contract, which included an annual salary of 80,000 marks and one third of the revenues of the films to Asta Nielsen, reflect the realization that star power was the key to conquering the burgeoning European cinema market.

Faced with such enticing prospects in Germany, Asta Nielsen opted to leave Denmark and its limited opportunities behind in order to make her professional home in Berlin, together with Gad, whom she married in 1912. IFVG had to pay a penalty of 10,000 crowns to Nordisk for causing Nielsen to breach her contract, but it was a necessary investment in the creation of a star whose name alone could sell films that had not yet even been conceptualized. As Nielsen explained to the Danish film journalist Viggo Schiørring in October 1911:

> The films we are going to make in 1912 have already been sold to the whole world, although the buyers have no idea what they will be about. All they know is that *I* am in them. ... You can see that a 'World-Monopoly-Patent' has been taken out on me![4]

The attention of the public was fickle, however, so market saturation with a steady supply of Nielsen films was an integral part of the creation of Asta Nielsen's stardom. New films appeared every four to six weeks during the peak season,[5] so that she would never be out of the public eye for long. Rather than be subject to the vagaries of the weather or limited by space constraints, Deutsche Bioscop built the first studios at Babelsberg to accommodate the production of Nielsen's films. During the 1911/12 season, eight films appeared in the first 'Asta Nielsen series', followed by eight more in 1912/13 and seven in 1913/14. These 23 films make up the entirety of Asta Nielsen's German series that premiered prior to the outbreak of World War I, though she made seven more films in 1914 that were not released until the 1915/16 season. This hectic production schedule, combined with frequent publicity events, kept Asta Nielsen very busy, with little time to spend back in Denmark, where she had left her adolescent daughter Jesta in the care of her family.

The international success of AFGRUNDEN, as well as Asta Nielsen's subsequent meteoric rise to global stardom, came as a tremendous surprise to her Danish contemporaries, most of whom knew her only from the minor roles she had played in Copenhagen theaters during the preceding decade. The Danish reception of Asta Nielsen's German-made films between 1911 and 1914 reflected both Nielsen's countrymen's delighted amazement that a Danish actress had attained such global renown and their defensive refusal to accord her the same level of celebrity in Denmark. While most Danish critics appre-

Ambivalent Admiration: Asta Nielsen's Conflicted Reception in Denmark, 1911–14

Urban Gad and Asta Nielsen-Gad, 1912. [Renate Seydel Collection, Berlin.]

ciated the prestige that Asta Nielsen's fame brought to her homeland, other Danes disparaged their countrywoman's international success and her cinematic work, for reasons ranging from aesthetic distaste to moral outrage. Close examination of the Danish print media's reception of Asta Nielsen's films from this pre-war period reveals a curious blend of approbation and disdain for

Denmark's most internationally famous star. In this paper, I examine the ways in which Nielsen and her films were alternately celebrated and censured in the Danish press in the years 1911 to 1914 in order to reveal the economic, social, and artistic tensions underlying her conflicted reception in her homeland.

During this first phase of Asta Nielsen's career, the Danish media generally basked in the reflected glory of her success. It was an era when Denmark viewed film as a means of extending Denmark's influence and enhancing its reputation abroad, a task that Nielsen managed most exceptionally. The announcement in the Danish newspaper *Politiken*, on 16 April 1911, of the Danish premiere of Asta Nielsen's first German film, DET HEDE BLOD (HEISSES BLUT, BURNING BLOOD), notes that the film should be of particular interest to Danes because "the film industry in Berlin has selected a Danish actress, Miss Asta Nielsen, to perform the female lead. This is the first time such a thing has happened".[6] Picking up the same theme, in the column "With the Film-Diva" in the same edition of *Politiken*, the columnist notes the significance of the fact that "Deutsche Bioscop, which is one of the world's largest film production companies, has become interested in Asta Nielsen, whose success in AFGRUNDEN, which has conquered the world from New Zealand to Hammerfest, has made her Denmark's first world-famous actress".[7] A year later, describing the opening of the new cinema Palads-Teatret (Palace Theater) in 1912, which Asta Nielsen attended for the Danish premiere of GENERALENS BØRN (DIE KINDER DES GENERALS, FALSELY ACCUSED), Niels Thomsen admitted: "There is something nationally pleasing in the fact that we here at home have not just been able to create one of Europe's largest theaters for moving pictures, but have also produced a true *prima donna* to adorn its inauguration".[8]

The fact that Nielsen was Danish generally trumped the fact that she worked in Germany in terms of the distribution and reception of her films in Denmark, a situation that would dramatically reverse itself after World War I.

In the immediate pre-war years, however, Asta Nielsen's German-made films received top billing in Danish newspapers and Copenhagen movie palaces. Danish newspapers in the early 1910s carried glowing reviews and sprawling advertisements for each new Asta Nielsen film, alongside detailed accounts of every visit that "our famous countrywoman",[9] "the most world-famous of all Danish actresses", paid to Denmark.[10] The tone of these reviews could be rather spiteful on occasion, for example in an article heralding the Danish premiere of PIGEN UDEN FÆDRELAND (DAS MÄDCHEN OHNE VATERLAND, A GIRL WITHOUT A COUNTRY) in *Politiken* on 21 December 1912, which begins with the statement that "the diva of film glides once more over the screen in the city of her birth, which now seems distant and small to her. Mrs. Asta Nielsen-Gad has conquered the world, her name is uttered with reverence in European metropolises and African villages, and on Monday evening Copenhagen must kneel before her art".[11] The global reach of Asta Nielsen's stardom suggested, to that particular reviewer at least, that the devotion of Copenhagen audiences would count for little by comparison.

Ambivalent Admiration: Asta Nielsen's Conflicted Reception in Denmark, 1911–14

Shooting of ENGELEIN (UP TO HER TRICKS) which required Asta Nielsen to wade out into the lake in her character's thwarted suicide attempt. [Det Danske Filminstitut.]

As was the custom at the time, the release of each of Asta Nielsen's films in Copenhagen was a major event, in which the screening of the feature film was preceded by orchestral music and various short films, which served as a type of psychological and emotional *amuse bouche*. A review of ILDEN (DAS FEUER, VENGEANCE IS MINE) in *Berlingske Tidende* on 10 May 1914 reports that Mrs. Asta Nielsen-Gad's performance was the high point of the evening, crowning "an excellent, varied program, consisting of an exciting action movie with a car chase, a series of lovely nature images from the coast of Bretagne, a current events survey from Canada's snowy plains to the race in Auteuil and a wonderful children's film: a baby playing with its beloved household pets". The mélange of genres and styles on what the reviewer in *Folkets Avis* on 12 May dubs "the Palace Theater's menu" [which offers] "something for every taste", recalls the variety show style of the cinema before the advent of the feature-length film, but the tone of the cinema experience was elevated in the new movie palace. Embossed programs printed on thick paper provided a summary of the film, in the style of program notes for an opera or theater performance.

The Palace Theater had the honor of hosting the Danish premiere of several of Nielsen's early films, which it did in grand style. The premiere of PIGEN UDEN FÆDRELAND in late December 1912 was a particularly high-profile affair, organized as a Christmas charity benefit. An energetic publicity campaign included a series of articles published in *Politiken* in the days leading up to the premiere and immediately afterward. On 21 December, the announcement of the premiere advises that "several well-known authors, actors, and actresses have been invited. It is much like when old Ibsen had a premiere."[12] The article published on 23 December, the day of the premiere, reads as if the author is reporting live from the red (or white, as they say in Danish) carpet and explicitly foregrounds both the luxurious surroundings of the Palace Theater and the high artistic niveau of the evening:

> At 8:15 this evening, as the new Asta Nielsen film PIGEN UDEN FÆDRELAND rolls across the screen in the Palace Theater, a very fine audience is present in both the box seats and the orchestra. The comfortable blue velvet chairs are filled with literature and art, which is naturally, in keeping with tradition, offered at a film premiere.[13]

The cinema's ascendant position relative to the preeminence of the stage is also defended with the assertion that "in modern cinemas one now receives just as much art in two-three hours as in half a year's diligent attendance at the talking theaters".[14] Just two years after Asta Nielsen's film debut, the cinema had established itself as a respectable and aggressive competitor to the stage.

Regardless of the merits of the particular film in which Asta Nielsen appeared, she earned acclaim for her talent from Danish critics. The rapid turnaround required to produce a new film every six weeks meant that the films were of widely disparate quality, but the practice of pre-selling the entire series safeguarded against the occasional flop,[15] since cinema owners had already committed to showing Asta Nielsen's upcoming films. ILDEN provides a good example of such a situation; Danish reviewers criticized the lack of exciting plot twists and the tragic ending, but they praised Nielsen's artistry – "she performs the role with all of her mimetic film talent as well as it can be played"[16] – and her beauty:

> One could have wished for a less theatrical conclusion. Mrs Asta Nielsen's acting was so beautiful that one would have rather admired the changeful brilliance of her eyes and the expressive curvature of her lips a little longer than watch the pavilion burn.[17]

By contrast, *Folkets Avis* raved about the originality of the content of STEMMERETSDAMEN (DIE SUFFRAGETTE, THE SUFFRAGETTE) a few months earlier, in November 1913, but still reserved its highest commendation for Nielsen, noting that it is "unfortunate that the rest of the cast is so inferior to her in the cinematic arts".

The fact that the evaluation of Nielsen's performance was positively colored by her Danish citizenship comes through in a review of PROLETARPIGEN (DIE ARME JENNY, POOR JENNY) that appeared in *Politiken* on 3 June 1912; the reviewer notes the usual excellence of Nielsen's performance, then remarks dismissively, "The rest of the cast is German".[18] Similarly, in a review of DEN STORE ELSKOV (DIE VERRÄTERIN, THE TRAITRESS) in *Politiken* on 22 March 1912, the reviewer notes that while the film will likely be a great success in Germany, it will not appeal to Danish tastes, aside from "Miss Asta Nielsen's passionate acting".[19]

Yet although Danes flocked to theaters to see the latest Asta Nielsen film, they

For her role in GENERALENS BØRN (DIE KINDER DES GENERALS, FALSELY ACCUSED) Nielsen donned long blond braids that made her look more like the stereotypical Nordic ideal of beauty than her usual dark hair. [Det Danske Filminstitut.]

remained somewhat perplexed by her popularity, in light of the fact that she had not been a major presence in Danish cultural life prior to her film debut. An article in the *Maanedsmagasin* in late 1912 noted: "It came as somewhat of a surprise for Danish audiences a few years ago to suddenly learn that Miss Asta Nielsen was an actress who mattered because she enjoyed worldwide fame."[20] In Denmark, Nielsen lacked the elaborate marketing apparatus that existed in Germany to plaster her name on a cornucopia of wares, from cinemas to perfumes, cigarettes, champagne, harmonicas, corsets, and feather boas. Fans could buy Asta Nielsen pastries in Berlin, cutlets in Budapest,[21] and in Cologne an "Asta Nielsen-Schnittchen", a slice of bread with salmon, caviar, and oysters for 1 Mark 75.[22] In Denmark, by contrast, the media made a point of reminding readers that Nielsen was no one special, "the same as when she lived on Bagerstræde in a rear building and had to fetch the cream and liqueur for her coffee herself".[23] For good or ill, Nielsen's films alone had to do all the work of building her reputation in Denmark, without assiduous branding to keep her in the public eye and demonstrate her exceptionality, an undertaking that would have been counterproductive in Denmark in any case, in light of the widespread resolutely egalitarian, often rigidly narrow mindset the Dano-Norwegian author Aksel Sandemose would dub "the Jante law" (*janteloven*) in his 1933 novel *En flygtning krysser sitt spor* (*A Refugee Crosses his Tracks*).

In keeping with this attitude, Danes tried very hard not to make a fuss over Asta Nielsen, particularly once she had become world-famous. In a profile of Asta Nielsen in *Verden og Vi* in 1915, the author reveals the deliberateness of the indifference with which Danes reacted to Nielsen's celebrity status:

> We Copenhageners, who are known for our tact and discretion, have perhaps glanced fleetingly over at the world famous star who glided past us like a dark, foreign mystery, but we did not allow ourselves to be more affected by the celebrated lady's presence. In Germany, people are very differently affected by being able to rub up against the Queen of Film. Ladies run after her on the street, touch her clothing, and people name cookies and sandwiches after her.[24]

This determination not to treat Asta Nielsen any differently because of her fame can be read both as a manifestation of Danish "tact and discretion", as the author suggests, and as evidence of Danish society's unwillingness to acknowledge Nielsen's newly-elevated social status. The contrast to Nielsen's imagined German audiences is clear – Danes are too level-headed to indulge in fan hysteria, even, or rather, especially toward a fellow Dane.

If anything about Asta Nielsen seemed particularly noteworthy and admirable to the Danish press, it was her connection, by marriage, to the highly respected Gad family, particularly her mother-in-law Emma Gad, who had earned a reputation for herself not only as a successful playwright and hostess, but also as an expert on polite society, Denmark's equivalent to Emily Post, the American author famous for writing on etiquette. Asta Nielsen's marriage to Urban Gad, undertaken after their move to Germany, not only satisfied bourgeois morality by regularizing their highly productive collaborative working relationship and cohabitation, but it also enabled Asta Nielsen to transcend

Ambivalent Admiration: Asta Nielsen's Conflicted Reception in Denmark, 1911–14

Asta Nielsen's character in DAS MÄDCHEN OHNE VATERLAND (A GIRL WITHOUT A COUNTRY) is caught in the act of stealing information from the man she has been trying to seduce. The title of the film is particularly appropriate in terms of the difficulties Asta Nielsen faced in obtaining recognition from the Danish film establishment. [Det Danske Filminstitut.]

her working-class origins in the eyes of the class-conscious early 20th century Danish society. After her 1912 wedding to Gad, the Danish press generally referred to Asta Nielsen as Mrs. Asta Nielsen-Gad, reminding readers of her membership in this rarefied social sphere. The announcement of the Danish release of her film SPANSK ELSKOV (TOD IN SEVILLA, SPANISH BLOOD), which appeared in *Politiken* on 9 June 1913, begins with mention of the fact that Mrs. Asta Nielsen-Gad is currently visiting her in-laws, Admiral and Mrs. Gad, in Humlebæk,[25] while the review of the premiere a few days later devotes several lines to the fact that Nielsen delegated responsibility for receiving her admirers to her mother-in-law. It also points out Urban Gad's considerable contributions to making the film a success, in particular his ability to capture the essence of the Spanish landscape on film. Corinna Müller explains that German film distributors had been initially uncertain whether to market Asta Nielsen or Urban Gad in developing the star system, but quickly opted to foreground the actress in favor of the director and stopped including Gad's name in ads for Nielsen's films after the first two.[26] In Denmark, however, the reviews of Asta Nielsen's early films nearly always included Urban Gad's name.

Despite her respectable family connections, however, many Asta Nielsen films were considered fairly scandalous and were frequently subject to censorship in Denmark and other parts of Scandinavia. Though the situation would become acute in the 1920s, with the result that many of Nielsen's later films were not released in Denmark at all, Danish censors in the 1910s were already quite strict about approving her films, on guard against transgressive behaviors either depicted in the films or inspired by them. In the case of DØDEDANSEN (TOTENTANZ, THE DANCE TO DEATH), the decision to label the film "forbidden for children" in Denmark seems to have been excessive, at least in the opinion of *Politiken*'s reviewer, who found the film "extremely decent".[27] For some viewers, however, enough of Nielsen's films pushed the limits of decency to justify condemning her, in an editorial in the *Aarhus Stiftstidende* on 23 October 1912, as "the priestess of sensuality", whose films are blamed for "awakening disturbing sensual joys in the viewer and making reprehensibility fashionable across Europe through her performance".[28] This puritanical view of Nielsen's films as a threat to bourgeois morality was not limited to Denmark, but also influenced the censors in the rest of Scandinavia, particularly Norway and Sweden, as demonstrated by Asta Nielsen's public dispute with the Swedish censorship board over her film IN DEM GROSSEN AUGENBLICK (THE GREAT MOMENT).[29]

Yet at the same time as some Danes were offended by the vulgarity of Nielsen's films, others were concerned that Asta Nielsen was being misrepresented as more culturally significant than she deserved to be. They took issue with the fact that German ads for Nielsen's films occasionally attributed to her a distinguished theatrical career at the Royal Theater in Copenhagen. For a variety of reasons including her dark coloring and her preference for drama in an era when operettas were in demand, Asta Nielsen's theater career in Copenhagen had not been terribly successful, hence her decision to try her luck in film. Sometimes maliciously, other times regretfully, Danish critics were quick to correct any misapprehension that Nielsen had been an integral or prominent part of the Danish theater community. In *Politiken*'s review of NATSVÆRMEREN (NACHTFALTER, RETRIBUTION), Asta Nielsen's second German film, the reviewer comments disparagingly of Nielsen's dancing that her "abilities as such are only just adequate for the cinema; a real music hall would hardly hire her in that capacity",[30] *Politiken*'s review of her previous film, DET HEDE BLOD (HEISSES BLUT, BURNING BLOOD), six weeks earlier, had included a similar observation about Asta Nielsen's unsuitability for Copenhagen theater, though with a more positive spin, noting that the film allowed Nielsen to demonstrate her talent, "which she has now dedicated to the service of international cinema, since the Copenhagen stages, with which she was affiliated, had no occasion to make use of it".[31] The implicit question that many of Asta Nielsen's Danish critics seem to struggle with is how she could have become so famous around the world without being famous in Denmark first.

Given her representative function for Denmark and Danish film, Asta Nielsen's dark hair and eyes compounded the problem, since she did not have a stereotypically Danish appearance. Writing about a cinema visit in Paris in an article in *Politiken* in 1911, Sophus Claussen objected to Nielsen's "southern complexion", which threatened to convey an inaccurate impression of Denmark to the world, and argued that Danish film ought to show "a certain degree of blondness, [which] suits us and awakens affection. ... Keep your films pure!"[32] Claussen's article reveals that Danes perceived Asta Nielsen as looking exotic and foreign, though this did not always evoke negative connotations. After interviewing her in Berlin in 1912, Viggo Schiörring emphasized this facet of Nielsen's looks, commenting admiringly on her "magnificent, red silk kimono with gold embroidery, which looks so exotic that it could easily have come from *The Mikado*! But this Yum-Yum costume suits her dark, bizarre physiognomy perfectly and reminds me of Polaire one moment, Mistinguett the next".[33] By comparing Nielsen to these two popular contemporary French dancers, Schiörring's goal seems to be to convey a sense of her aura of sensuality and exoticism, yet in so doing he too reaffirms her failure to embody the Danish norm.

It was not just her dark coloring that did not conform to Danish ideals of beauty, but also her body type. In a 1913 article in *Ekstrabladet* entitled "Heroes of our Time: Asta Nielsen-Gad", the future director Carl Theodor Dreyer, writing under the pseudonym Tommen, bluntly disparages Nielsen's physical appearance. He criticizes her for appearing in *Hosenrollen* (breeches parts) that reveal "how terribly she is built" and explains:

> Asta Nielsen-Gad truly has some terribly unfortunate features. She is lanky and overgrown, flat like an ironing board in back, flat-chested and with no calves to speak of. (…) But what does Asta Nielsen-Gad do? In half of her films, she wears a tight jersey, and when she is no longer interested in the jersey, she dons men's clothing. She is determined (…) to reveal her scrawniness.[34]

Dreyer's acerbic comments confirm that, at a time when the aesthetic ideal for a Danish woman was blond and buxom, Nielsen's slender figure was perceived as unattractive, though it corresponded very closely to the athletic, somewhat androgynous body type that was already becoming fashionable in France, through the work of Paul Poiret and Coco Chanel,[35] and would shape the image of the new woman across the world in the 1920s.

Yet even the most malicious criticisms of Asta Nielsen's appearance by Danish critics – and those were exceptions to the rule – never cast any doubt on Nielsen's credentials as an actress or as a Dane. There was little Asta Nielsen could do to change her body type or coloring to look more stereotypically Danish and even less cause to do so, given that most of her fans worldwide found her stunning just as she was. Her response to such petty Danish criticisms was to ignore them and concentrate on her work. During the years before the war, she continued to film in Germany, relying on the merits of her films to win fans in Denmark as anywhere else, while maintaining her personal connections back home. Even after her marriage to Urban Gad fell apart in 1915, she remained on good terms with her mother-in-law and emulated her by hosting her own artistic gatherings in her Copenhagen apartment during the war.

After World War I, however, when Asta Nielsen decided to return to Germany once more, both the economic basis of the Danish film industry and the political views of Danish cinema audiences had undergone a fundamental shift that complicated Nielsen's reception in her homeland and stripped her, in her countrymen's eyes, of her Danish identity. The nature of this paradigm shift in Asta Nielsen's Danish reception, which was demarcated by the increasing use of the moniker "die Asta" in the Danish press in the early 1920s to refer to Asta Nielsen,[36] is articulated very poignantly in a Danish review of Nielsen's film I.N.R.I. (CROWN OF THORNS) in December 1923. This review confirms Asta Nielsen's new status in Denmark as an outsider, in contrast to the emphasis that had been placed on her Danish origins before the war, with the announcement that one of the film's main attractions is that it stars "our own, or rather, the Germans' own Asta Nielsen".[37]

Notes

1. Poul Malmkjær, *Asta. Menneket, myten og filmstjernen* (Copenhagen: P. Haase & Søn, 2000), 63. All translations from Danish are my own.
2. Corinna Müller, *Frühe deutsche Kinematographie. Formale, wirtschaftliche und kulturelle Entwicklungen 1907–1912* (Stuttgart and Weimar: Metzler, 1994), 148.
3. Malmkjær, *Asta*, 78.
4. Viggo Schiörring, "Kino-Kunstens Duse", *Masken* (15 October 1911): 20.
5. Müller, *Frühe deutsche Kinematographie*, 149.
6. "Teater og Tribune", *Politiken* (16 April 1911).
7. Column "With the Film-Diva", *Politiken* (16 April 1911).
8. Niels Th. Thomsen, "Asta Nielsen-Gad", *Masken* (27 March 1912): 23.
9. "Teater og Tribune", *Politiken* (24 August 1912).
10. A characteristic example of such an article appeared in *Politiken* on 8 October 1912, under the byline Hektor and the title "The Visit of a Famous Artistic Couple. Asta Nielsen Gad and Peter Urban Gad. Brief Interview".
11. Helge, "En ny Asta Nielsen-Film. Paa Mandag Premiere i Paladsteatret. Hele Indtægter gaar til Juleindsamlingen", *Politiken* (21 December 1912).
12. Ibid.
13. Smut, "Filmen i Aften. Kl. 8¼ er der Premiere paa Paladsteatret", *Politiken* (23 December 1912).
14. Ibid.
15. Müller, *Frühe deutsche Kinematographie*, 150.
16. *Folkets Avis* (12 May 1914).
17. *Berlingske Tidende* (10 May 1914).
18. *Politiken* (3 June 1912).
19. "Kosmorama", *Politiken* (22 March 1912).
20. "Asta Nielsen", *Maanedsmagasin* (24 November 1912).
21. Malmkjær, *Asta*, 118.
22. Müller, *Frühe deutsche Kinematographie*, 152.
23. Thomsen, "Asta Nielsen-Gad", 24.
24. V.S., "Mellem Film-Slagene. Et Besøg hos Asta Nielsen", *Verden og Vi* 1 (1915): 20.
25. Anon., "En Tyrefægtnings-Film med Asta Nielsen i Hovedrollen", *Politiken* (9 June 1913).
26. Müller, *Frühe deutsche Kinematographie*, 150.
27. Hektor, "Films-Premiere. 'Dødedansen' af Urban Gad med Asta Nielsen i Hovedrollen", *Politiken* (10 July 1913).

28. Malmkjær, *Asta*, 130. *Aarhus Stiftstidence* (23 October 1912).
29. Cf. Anne Bachmann's essay in this volume.
30. "Levende Billeder", *Politiken* (30 May 1911).
31. "Panoptikon-Teatret", *Politiken* (18 April 1911).
32. Stephan Michael Schröder, "Fra Babel til Nørrebro, fra Berlin til Frederiksberg: Filmens Internationalisiering og Nationalisiering", in Henning Bech and Anne Scott Sørensen (eds), *Kultur på kryds og tværs* (Aarhus, Denmark: Klim, 2005), 114.
33. Schiörring, "Kino-Kunstens Duse", 20.
34. Carl Theodor Dreyer, "Vor Tids Helte. Asta Nielsen-Gad", *Ekstrabladet* (2 October 1913), in Peter Schepelern (ed.), *Tommen. Carl Th. Dreyers filmjournalistiske virksomhed* (Copenhagen: C.A. Reitzel, 1982), 36.
35. José Teunissen, "Mode und Modernität", in Heide Schlüpmann et al. (eds), *Unmögliche Liebe. Asta Nielsen, ihr Kino* (2nd edn) (Vienna: filmarchiv austria, 2010), 241–251.
36. Stephan Michael Schröder, "Die Duse des Kinos als 'Frau Nielsen': In Dänemark", in Schlüpmann, *Unmögliche Liebe*, 427–435, here 430.
37. Felix., "Hvad Verden Taler Om: I Julen skal Kæmpefilmen INRI gaa over hele Jorden med Asta Nielsen som Magdalena", unidentified Danish newspaper (1923), 10.

Agnes Schindler

"Aðalhlutverkið leikur: Frú Asta Nielsen Gad"
Asta Nielsen Films in Reykjavík, 1912–1915

Iceland belonged to the Kingdom of Denmark as a colony for centuries. In 1904, Denmark accorded its Icelandic colony the status of autonomy. The island's very close ties to the Danish mainland at the beginning of the 20th century permitted Danish merchants to operate businesses in Iceland. For example, a Danish merchant named Fr. Warburg sent Alfred Lind to Iceland to open a cinema (*bíó* in Icelandic). Lind later served as cameraman for Asta Nielsen's debut film AFGRUNDEN in 1910. The film screenings in the Reykjavíkur Biograftheater, which had 260 seats at that time, started on 2 November 1906.[1] Lind was accompanied to Iceland by the photographer Peter Petersen, who assisted Lind in setting up the cinema and who was to function as projectionist.[2] Soon after the beginning of screenings, Lind and Petersen produced the first local films for the cinema programme of the Reykjavíkur Biograftheater. One month after the cinema's opening, they screened SLÖKKVILIDSÆFING Í REYKJAVÍK, a fire drill in Reykjavík.[3] Alfred Lind returned to Denmark as early as the beginning of 1907. From this point on, Peter Petersen managed the Reykjavíkur Biograftheater. When owner Warburg died in 1913, Petersen bought the cinema and became the new owner on 1 April 1914. He operated the cinema until the end of 1939 and returned to his native city, Copenhagen, in 1940. Petersen was well-known in Iceland as 'Bíópetersen' (Cinema Petersen).

A second cinema in Reykjavík started its showings on 29 June 1912, the Nýja Bíó (new cinema).[4] From then on, the Reykjavíkur Biograftheater placed its cinema adverts under the name Gamla Bíó (old cinema) as well. Before the First World War, Reykjavík had not quite 14,000 inhabitants. Each of the cinemas offered one showing daily in the evening, amounting to about 300

Facing page:
Above: Reykjavíkur Biograftheater, after 1912 also named Gamla Bíó, in Aðalstræti 8, Reykjavík (c. 1925).
Below: The Nýja Bíó was operating in the former dining room of Hótel Ísland, Reykjavík, until 1920. [Both images Icelandic Film Archive.]

Peter Petersen, called 'Bíópetersen', who managed Gamla Bíó from 1907 until 1939. [Icelandic Film Archive.]

screenings a year.⁵ The Nýja Bíó was located in the former dining room of the Hótel Ísland. The opening was well received by the local public. The news magazine *Lögrétta* expected strong competition between the two cinemas.⁶ And, in fact, the managers attempted one-upmanship, not least with Asta Nielsen films.

With the aid of the digital archive *Tímarit*, cinema adverts as well as news texts can be found for some Asta Nielsen films in the news magazines *Ísafold* (named after the girl's name Ísafold) and *Reykjavík*, and in the daily newspapers *Vísir* and *Morgunblaðið*. The search at *Tímarit* was conducted using different spellings of Asta Nielsen's name (Asta Nielsen, Ásta Nielsen, Ásta Níelsen and Asta Níelsen). According to the cinema adverts by Gamla Bíó and Nýja Bíó, seventeen Asta Nielsen films were shown in Reykjavík from 1912 to 1915.

An advert in *Ísafold* announcing the opening of the Nýja Bíó on 29 June 1912 offers no information about the film programme. However, the column 'Reykjavíkur-annáll' (news from Reykjavík) points out that the Nýja Bíó was to open with an Asta Nielsen film: "The Nýja Bíó begins its screenings this evening in the old dining room of the Hótel Ísland. Among others, FIÐRILDIÐ [NACHTFALTER, RETRIBUTION] will be shown, featuring the film queen Asta Nielsen-Gad".⁷ A few days later, *Ísafold* covers the festive opening of the new cinema theatre in the presence of the mayor, the governor, journalists and many others.⁸ The opening of the Nýja Bíó was seen as proof how big Reykjavík had become, so that by now cinema entertainment was in such large

Advert for SPANISH BLOOD: "The leading role plays: Asta Nielsen Gad. Take this opportunity to view this gorgeous film." *Morgunblaðið* (4 April 1914).

demand in the city that two cinemas could co-exist.[9] *Ísafold* underlined the significance of the cinema for the city's social life. With the opening of the Nýja Bíó, the Danish actress, the film star Asta Nielsen, had arrived in Iceland which had, thus, drawn level with continental European countries.

Asta Nielsen Gad and Urban Gad

As in Denmark, also in Iceland Asta Nielsen often was referred to as Asta Nielsen Gad, to remind readers that she belonged, by marriage, to the highly respected Gad family.[10] We can find both name variants, Asta Nielsen and Asta Nielsen Gad, in the Icelandic adverts for Asta Nielsen films. The application of either one of the variations does not seem to follow any systematics. But between 1912 and 1914 the name Asta Nielsen Gad was apparently used more often. The exception from the rule is in the adverts for Á ÚRSLITA STUND (IN DEM GROSSEN AUGENBLICK, THE GREAT MOMENT). Starting on 9 June 1914 with FEIGÐARDRAUMUR (DEN SORTE DRØM, THE CIRCUS GIRL) the actress is solely referred to as Asta Nielsen – the only exception here is KVENRJETTIN-DAKONUR (DIE SUFFRAGETTE, THE SUFFRAGETTE). All in all, both variants were used in equal frequency. In a short note on the screening of SPÆNSK ÁST (DER TOD IN SEVILLA, SPANISH BLOOD) in *Morgunblaðið*, it is said that the leading role is played by Urban Gad's wife, Asta Nielsen Gad.[11]

> # NÝA BÍÓ.
> Í kveld—gamlárskveld—engin sýning
> Nýársdag kl. 6-10:
> ## Stundin mikla.
> Sorgarleikur í 3 þáttum eftir P. URBAN GAD
> Aðalhlutverkið leikur FRÚ ASTA NIELSEN.

Advert for THE GREAT MOMENT, emphasizing Urban Gad's authorship. *Vísir* (31 December 1913).

Stephan Michael Schröder maintains that the authorship of the early Asta Nielsen films was claimed over and over again by both, Urban Gad and Asta Nielsen.[12] Moreover, he says:

> "In the research literature [Gad] is still mentioned *en passant* only, although it were his narratives which appeared on the screen, and although, as the films' director, he was obviously also in charge of the editing, the framing of the images, the mise en scène, and although his name often appeared on the same level with Asta Nielsen in the marketing of the 'Asta-Nielsen-Urban-Gad series'".[13]

Urban Gad's authorship of the stories narrated in the Asta Nielsen films is highlighted in almost all of the adverts that I looked at, which corresponds with Schröder's observations. Only in the adverts for FIÐRILDIÐ, KVENRJETTINDAKONUR, and ÁSTAR-FÓRN (DIE VERRÄTERIN, THE TRAITRESS) Gad is not mentioned at all. Moreover, Urban Gad's as well as Asta Nielsen's name is printed in most cases in the same size and are likewise highlighted by boldface or spaced out print, or italics. The newspaper *Vísir* printed Urban Gad's name in an advert for Á ÚRSLITA STUND even in a larger font than Asta Nielsen's.[14] In the rare and short editorial notes on ÞEGAR GRÍMAN FELLUR (WENN DIE MASKE FÄLLT, WHEN THE MASK FALLS)[15] and SPÆNSK ÁST.[16] Urban Gad is even named first, before the authors go on to describe detailedly Asta Nielsen's acting skills in the films. Remarkably, in an advert of *Vísir* Urban Gad is referred to as "kvikmyndahöfundur" (film author); apart from that his authorship is usually described in the terminology of the legitimate stage: "leikrit eftir Urban Gad" (a play by Urban Gad). His contribution to the film is referred to in the adverts solely as that of a screen writer, while his role as director is not explicitly mentioned. This once again corresponds with Schröder's statement, according to which his task as director of the films was seen as being secondary.[17] The same goes for the names of film genres which are usually represented as compounds with terms like "leikinn" or "leikur" (play, rendition, presentation); as, for instance, *sjónleikur* (drama), *gamanleikur* (comedy), *nútíðar sjónleikur* (drama of the present day). These terms are taken from the realm of the legitimate stage and it seems as if at the time there had not yet been developed a specific Icelandic film terminology.

Asta Nielsen's Persistent Presence

After FIÐRILDIÐ, it evidently took almost a year before the next Asta Nielsen film was shown in Reykjavík. A Nýja Bíó advert on 19 April 1913 explicitly announced Asta Nielsen in the leading role to promote the film ÁSTAR-FÓRN.[18] Three weeks later the Nýja Bíó announced Asta Nielsen's next film UNG HJÖRTU (DER FREMDE VOGEL, THE COURSE OF TRUE LOVE): "In this film, Asta Nielsen demonstrates a new facet of her acting talent".[19]

In the 1913/14 season, the Gamla Bíó also screened Asta Nielsen films and started to place adverts nearly every day, as the daily newspaper *Morgunblaðið* began publishing on 2 November 1913. This new situation gave both cinemas the opportunity of advertising their current programme for the respective day. On the basis of the cinema adverts appearing daily at that time, it can be seen that both cinemas changed their programmes twice a week. A new film programme appeared each Tuesday and Saturday. On occasion, however, single adverts appeared announcing film screenings for only one to two days, deviating from the normal system of programme change. Significantly, Asta Nielsen films were not excluded from the twice-weekly programme change as it was the case in many other places, probably since the smallness of the city did not allow for longer runs of single films.

On 27 September 1913 both *Ísafold* and *Reykjavík* announced the screening of BÖRN HERSHÖFÐINGJANS (DIE KINDER DES GENERALS, FALSELY ACCUSED) at the Gamla Bíó from 26 to 29 September 1913, again advertising Asta Nielsen in the starring role.[20] The Gamla Bíó advertised ÞEGAR GRIMAN FELLUR daily in the *Morgunblaðið* and in *Vísir* from 29 November to 2 December 1913. The *Morgunblaðið* published a notice in its news section:

> The Gamla Bíó will screen the film ÞEGAR GRIMAN FELLUR this evening. The drama was written by Urban Gad and is outstanding in every respect. The leading role is played by Mrs. Asta Nielsen-Gad with her renowned skill. Whoever is not lying sick in bed should see her performance, as she is so well-known here that only a few do not know what a brilliant actress she is.[21]

On New Year's 1914, the Nýja Bíó again offered an Asta Nielsen film in its programme, THE GREAT MOMENT (IN DEM GROSSEN AUGENBLICK) which had already been released in Germany in September 1911. The adverts in *Ísafold*, in the *Morgunblaðið* and in *Vísir* advertised this film under four different titles: Á ÚRSLITA STUND, STUNDIN MIKLA, Á SÍÐUSTU STUNDU and ÚRSLITA-STUNDIN. Although there is no big difference of meaning in these variants, it may still be surprising that the adverts do not use consistently the same title, since readers might easily be confused. Still, similar examples of title variations can be found in yet the one or other film. A news item in the magazine *Ísafold* also announced the screening of this film:

> The Nýja Bíó will show a film on New Year's Day which attracted great attention where it has already been shown, a film which may be considered significant. The film is called Á ÚRSLITA STUND. Mrs. Ásta Nielsen, the renowned actress, plays the starring role, and it is said that such natural and touching acting as hers has seldom been seen in film.[22]

Agnes Schindler

Asta Nielsen films shown in Iceland, 1912 and 1915.

Icelandic title	Original title / English title	Reykjavík screenings	Berlin premiere
Fiðrildið	Der Nachtfalter Retribution	29 June 1912	13 May 1911
Ástar-fórn	Die Verräterin The Traitress	19 April 1913	9 December 1911
Ung hjörtu	Der fremde Vogel The Course of True Love	10 May 1913	11 November 1911
Börn hershöfðingjans	Die Kinder des Generals Falsely Accused	27–29 September 1913	5 October 1912
Þegar gríman fellur	Wenn die Maske Fällt When the Mask Falls	29 November–2 December 1913	1 November 1912
Á úrslita stund / Stundin mikla / Á síðustu stundu	In dem großen Augenblick The Great Moment	31 December 1913–3 January 1914	28 August 1911
Spænsk ást	Der Tod in Sevilla Spanish Blood	31 March–April 1914	4 April 1913
Synd feðranna / Syndir feðranna	Die Sünden der Väter Temptations of Drink	21–24 April 1914	28 February 1913
Æskubrek	Jugend und Tollheit In a Fix	16–18 May 1914	3 January 1913
Feigðardraumur	Den sorte drøm The Circus Girl	9–12 June 1914	19 August 1911
Komedianter	Komödianten The Heart of a Pierrot	4–7 August 1914	31 January 1913
Kvenrjettindakonur / Kvenrjettindakonan	Die Suffragette The Suffragette	10–14 August 1914	12 September 1913
Kvikmyndadrottningin	Die Filmprimadonna The Prima Donna	20–23 December 1914	5 December 1913
Litli Engillinn	Engelein Up to her Tricks	24–30 December 1914	3 January 1914
S.1.	S 1 A Girl's Sacrifice	23–25 May 1915	14 November 1913

In spring 1914, the Gamla Bíó advertised SPÆNSK ÁST daily in *Morgunblaðið* und *Vísir* from 31 March to 4 April. For the first time, the adverts for an Asta Nielsen film also contained the notice that children were not permitted to see the film.[23] In addition, the size and text of the adverts for this film varied more widely than was the case for previously shown Asta Nielsen films. On 2 April, *Vísir* printed a 42-line article on SPÆNSK ÁST with a plot description and a recommendation of the film:

> The Gamla Bíó has now shown a film on two evenings called SPÁNVERSK ÁST[24] by the well-known screenplay author Urban Gad. This film is one of the director's best, although all of his films are considered good. The starring role is played by the currently best-known actress, Mrs. Asta Nielsen Gad. (...) As we cannot give an exact description of the film here, we advise everyone to see the film, one surely

"Aðalhlutverkið leikur: Frú Asta Nielsen Gad" / Asta Nielsen Films in Reykjavík, 1912–1915

Advert for THE PRIMA DONNA, a long drama of the present day with Asta Nielsen in the leading role, that "all women and men should view".

worth seeing. It is clear-cut, yet shows new aspects; the coherence is good, the acting outstanding and the film, on the whole, thrilling.[25]

No other Asta Nielsen film had ever received such a comprehensive review. On the following day, the *Morgunblaðið* also printed a news item, however, only seven lines long. Again, it was emphasised that Asta Nielsen was the leading lady and that the film was the best one ever shown in Iceland.[26] Although the last showing of SPÆNSK ÁST was announced for 4 April, four days later the Gamla Bíó announced that SPÆNSK ÁST would be screened one more time on 8 April because of great demand.

As soon as two weeks later, SYNDIR FEÐRANNA (DIE SÜNDEN DER VÄTER, TEMPTATIONS OF DRINK) followed from 21 to 24 April 1914. The adverts were rather small and, except for the title, just mentioned that the film was by Urban Gad, and added: "Aðalhlutverkið leikur: Frú Asta Nielsen-Gad" (with Asta Nielsen-Gad in the leading role).[27] In mid-May the advert for the comedy ÆSKUBREK (JUGEND UND TOLLHEIT, IN A FIX) emphasised that adults as well as children would be amused by this film.[28] On 18 May adverts in both *Vísir* and the *Morgunblaðið* announced the last showings of ÆSKUBREK. A brief news item appeared in the *Morgunblaðið*, describing mainly the plot but also concluding that the film was very entertaining.[29]

After the Gamla Bíó had screened SPÆNSK ÁST, SYND FEÐRANNA and ÆSKUBREK, three films of the second 'Asta Nielsen series', shortly one after the other, the Nýja Bíó followed with the first film of this series, FEIGÐARDRAUMUR (DEN SORTE DRØM, THE CIRCUS GIRL), from 9 to 12 June 1914. The *Morgunblaðið* lauded the film and stressed Asta Nielsen's acting talent. It was said that she was an actress who always provided enjoyment for the viewers, and that the film was exceedingly popular.[30]

During the 1914/15 season, the Gamla Bíó again screened five Asta Nielsen films. A small advert in the *Morgunblaðið* announced KOMEDIANTER (KOMÖDIANTEN, THE HEART OF A PIERROT), always pointing out "Aðalhlutverkið leikur: Frú Asta Nielsen-Gad" (Asta Nielsen in the leading role), and printed a brief plot description with the remark that it was thanks to Asta Nielsen that the film received great public attention.[31] The author of the text, signing with 'X.', described Asta Nielsen's continuing popularity in Reykjavík: "Asta Nielsen is known for the artistry of her acting, and she has many admirers here in the town who never tire of watching her acting".[32] Adverts for KVENRJETTINDAKONUR were published daily in *Morgunblaðið* and *Vísir*, from 10 to 14 August 1914, and a short news item emphasised that this unusually long film of two hours was very entertaining, and praised Asta Nielsen's acting talent in the film.[33] After a long pause, the Gamla Bíó showed KVIKMYNDADROTTNINGIN (DIE FILMPRIMADONNA, THE PRIMA DONNA), from 20 to 23 December 1914, and then, as Christmas programme, it offered LITLI ENGILLINN (ENGELEIN, UP TO HER TRICKS). The advert in *Vísir* announced the showing in superlative terms and stated that it was the grandest and best comedy that had been seen in the town for some time.[34] Furthermore, the film would be screened twice a day instead of once as it was usual, from 7 to 9 pm and from 9 to 11 pm respectively.[35] Thus, the film is shown for an entire week with two screenings a day, instead of three, sometimes four days with only one screening. No other Asta Nielsen film was exhibited so generously in Reykjavík as this one. After five days of screenings, *Morgunblaðið* reported that LITLI ENGILLINN, after it had been shown at Palads-Haus in Copenhagen, was now to be seen at the Gamla Bíó.[36] The author additionally reported that the film had been screened twice daily and that the cinema had been full. He recommended everybody who had not yet seen it to do so before it had to be returned abroad. Moreover, the brief note maintains that the film had been shown especially for 350 children the previous day. An association of businessmen had provided for this opportunity at the Gamla Bíó.[37] A hitherto unheard-of event that is, to the best of our knowledge, not paralleled in continental Europe.

Advert for UP TO HER TRICKS: "The twelve year old Jesta is played by the world famous film actress Mrs. Asta Nielsen." *Vísir* (30 December 1914).

In the spring of 1915, the adverts finally document the presentation of the film S.I. (S 1, A GIRL'S SACRIFICE, 1913)[38] from 23 to 25 May 1915; again, Asta Nielsen's popularity was used to advertise the film. However, it ended the series of Asta Nielsen films in Iceland.

Conclusion

Altogether seventeen Asta Nielsen films were shown in Reykjavík between 1912 and 1915. There are significant temporal intervals between the premieres of these films in Germany and Iceland: the shortest is ten months, the longest even two years and four months. Where the two cinemas got the prints from is not clear and cannot be reconstructed from the information given in the adverts. Gamla Bíó appeared more frequently with its adverts for Asta Nielsen films in the newspapers than did the Nýja Bíó. Nevertheless, with altogether ten Asta Nielsen films shown at the Gamla Bíó, the number was only slightly higher than the number shown at the Nýja Bíó, altogether seven during that period. Whereas the Nýja Bíó presented more Asta Nielsen films at the beginning of the studied period, it was the Gamla Bíó which presented her films mainly towards the end of the period from 1912 to 1915. Both local cinemas competed intensively with each other, clearly using Asta Nielsen's popularity for their advertising strategies in the design of their programme adverts in the local media. It is remarkable, though, that in the adverts placed by both cinemas in the magazines and newspapers of Reykjavík usually no other film besides the Asta Nielsen film is mentioned. Urban Gad's reputation as author of the film narratives was also used in the promotion of the films.

Asta Nielsen's presence in Iceland is as persistent as in continental Europe. The Nýja Bíó shows an Asta Nielsen film on the occasion of its festive opening in June 1912 by referring to her as a great film "queen", thus introducing the star to Icelandic audiences. But in the 1914/15 season, when Asta Nielsen films had already vanished from continental European screens as a consequence of the outbreak of the First World War, Asta Nielsen is not only still to be seen in Reykjavík cinemas, but rather ENGILLINN is her greatest success on the island. It runs longer than any other Asta Nielsen film in Reykjavík and it is screened more often than any of the others. Moreover it is presented, in a special screening, to children, sponsored by local business people. While most other Asta Nielsen films were restricted for adult viewing only in most countries, ENGILLINN had become a family entertainment in Iceland.

Notes

1. Cf. on this Eggert Þór Bernharðsson, "Landnám lifandi mynda", in Guðni Elísson (ed.), *Heimur kvikmyndanna* (Reykjavík: Forlagið, 1999), 806.
2. Ibid.
3. Cf. Erlendur Sveinsson, "100 ára fæðingarafmæli Bíópetersens", in *Kvikmyndir á Íslandi 75 ára*, (Reykjavík: Prentrún, 1981), 17, and Bernharðsson, "Landnám", 806.
4. Cf. *Ísafold* (29 June 1912): 159.
5. Bernharðsson, "Landnám", 811. Here, the author refers to texts from *Morgunblaðið* (17 October

1915): 3. The Gamla Bíó moved to a new building on Ingólfsstræti in 1927 in which, according to Bernharðsson, there were almost 600 seats. According to Erlendur Sveinsson, in 1912 the Siglufjörd Bíógraftheater in Siglufjörður and in 1913 the Árna Bíó in Hafnarfjörður were opened.

6. Cf. *Lögrétta* (3 July 1912): 133.
7. *Ísafold* (29 June 1912): 158.
8. *Ísafold* (6 July 1912): 163.
9. Ibid.
10. Cf. Julie K. Allen's essay in this volume.
11. *Morgunblaðið* (3 April 1913): 706.
12. Cf. Stephan Michael Schröder: "Und Urban Gad? Zur Frage der Autorschaft in den Filmen bis 1914", in Heide Schlüpmann et al. (eds), *Unmögliche Liebe. Asta Nielsen, ihr Kino* (2nd edn) (Vienna: filmarchiv austria: 2010), 194.
13. Ibid., 197.
14. *Vísir* (31 December 1913): 24.
15. *Morgunblaðið* (30 November 1913): 132.
16. *Vísir* (2 April 1914): 1.
17. Schröder, "Und Urban Gad?", 204.
18. *Ísafold* (19 April 1913): 121.
19. *Ísafold* (10 May 1913): 148.
20. *Ísafold* (27 September 1913): 303; *Reykjavík* (27 September 1913): 155.
21. *Morgunblaðið* (30 November 1913): 132.
22. *Ísafold* (31 December 1913): 410.
23. *Morgunblaðið* (31 March 1914): 693.
24. This variant also means "spanish".
25. Author's translation, *Vísir* (4 April 1914): 1.
26. *Morgunblaðið* (3 April 1914): 706.
27. *Vísir* (21 April 1914): 1; (22 April 1914): 1; *Morgunblaðið* (22 April 1914): 789; *Morgunblaðið*, (23 April 1914): 791; *Vísir* (23 April 1914): 1; *Morgunblaðið* (24 April 1914): 795 and *Vísir* (24 April 1914): 1.
28. *Morgunblaðið* (16 May 1914): 897.
29. *Morgunblaðið* (18 May 1914): 910.
30. *Morgunblaðið* (11 June 1911): 1014.
31. *Morgunblaðið* (6 August 1914): 127.
32. *Morgunblaðið* (6 August 1914): 127.
33. *Morgunblaðið* (12 August 1914): 129.
34. *Vísir* (24 December 1914): 1.
35. Ibid.
36. *Morgunblaðið* (29 December 1914): 2. A similar hint – that a certain film had previously been shown at the Palads Teatret in Kopenhagen – was given in numerous adverts for Asta Nielsen films. On Christmas 1914, *Morgunblaðið* even maintains that LITLI ENGILLINN had been daily shown at the Palads Teatret for an entire month and had attracted 120,000 viewers (cf. *Morgunblaðið* (24 December 1914): cover).
37. *Morgunblaðið* (29 December 1914): 2.
38. *Morgunblaðið* (23 May 1915): 1; (24 May 1915): 1; (25 May 1915): 1.

PART II

AFGRUNDEN – DEBUT FILM OF AN UNKNOWN ACTRESS

Förevisas från och med den 23:dje januari å

SCALA
N. Esplanadgatan 21

Extra attraktionsbild
Med garanterad ensamuppföranderätt
i Finland för

Nordiska Biograf Komp.

Konstfilmen
Heltimmes skådespelet

Afgrunden

Kinematografiskt drama
i 2 akter och c:a 50 afdelningar

af

Urban Gad

Outi Hupaniittu

AFGRUNDEN aka KUILU in Finland
Nordiska Biograf, Exclusive Distribution and Newly Established Censorship

Asta Nielsen's debut film AFGRUNDEN premiered in Helsinki in January 1911, on the verge of the breakthrough of the Danish long-features in Finland. It was also the time when the official censorship took control over cinema exhibitions. In this paper, I will discuss two issues both focusing on AFGRUNDEN's unique status on the verge of a new era of the Finnish cinema culture. The first issue concerns the distribution of AFGRUNDEN in Finland. It was one of the first feature films purchased and distributed with exclusive rights by Nordiska Biograf Kompaniet, one of the biggest cinema companies in the country. A few surviving letters and advertisements describe the new business model to promote and advertise the film. The second issue concerns AFGRUNDEN and the newly established censorship system. The film went through censorship procedures three times in January and February 1911, but the censors found nothing to remark, although the film was full of such same 'indecent' material that had initially led to the establishment of the censorship.

Finland is a bilingual country. In the early 1900s most of the Finnish cinema companies were owned by speakers of Swedish just as most of the large enterprises in the capital city. The original sources used for this article are either in Swedish (e.g. censorship application, business correspondence) or in Finnish (e.g. adverts and interviews in newspapers). Asta Nielsen's debut film AFGRUNDEN was also known as KUILU among speakers of Finnish. In this article, I use the Swedish title AFGRUNDEN which is synonym with the original Danish title.

Long-features and the changes in the film distribution

The film trade in the Russian Grand Duchy of Finland was based upon a small number of companies operating in the capital city Helsinki. The film business

Facing page:
Cover of the programme leaflet for the premiere of AFGRUNDEN. Supplement to the application for censorship (23 January 1911). [National Archive of Finland.]

was independent from the rest of the Russian empire, but this was not extraordinary, as the autonomy gave wide independence to the business in Finland in general. However, 'Mother Russia' was an important trade partner to the Finnish entrepreneurs. The companies operating the Finnish film trade were quite modest in their structures, but they controlled the distribution, operated cinemas and produced films (mostly actualities, but also other sorts of non-fiction and some fictional films). These companies purchased films abroad, mostly from Western Europe, but some trade was made with companies operating from St Petersburg. The film programmes were first screened in the cinemas owned by the companies, then rented to others across the Grand Duchy.[1] In the end at least some of the films were sold onwards to St Petersburg with 30 to 40 per cent of the original price.[2] This system of trade proved to be effective, stable and profitable: it was established around the year 1906 and big structural changes occurred only in the late 1910s. In the turn of the 1910s, the expenses for film imports increased radically in consequence of the new multi-reel features. This was not just a Finnish phenomenon; just as elsewhere, the trade changed at least partially from bulk sales to one-off deals. It seems that the leading company in the transition period was Nordiska Biograf Kompaniet as it gained many of the best exclusive deals of the early months. Based in Helsinki since 1906, it was one of the biggest trading companies in Finland, and was owned by two entrepreneurs, the Norwegian Rasmus Hallseth and the Swede David Fernander.[3] Nordiska Biograf had strong business ties with the Danish film companies and imported some of the first Danish long-features in late 1910 and early 1911, before the rivals joined the competition.

The standard procedure of film distribution in Finland throughout the 1900s and 1910s was that the local cinema owner made annual deals with a trading company. By contract, he received a weekly programme, consisting of films compiled into a standard length set. The price depended upon the rank in the distribution chain – the cinemas first in line paid more than the later ones as they received the films at an earlier date, with fewer scratches and cuts. If the cinema owner preferred two premieres a week, he would have had to arrange a deal with two companies. While the twice-weekly change of programme seemingly was common to a certain degree in the rural towns, in Helsinki the programmes were usually exchanged once a week, the big companies had no need to supply more films than their own premiere cinemas in the capital city were able to screen. The rural cinema owners had no influence on the contents of the programmes but they were able to bargain when choosing a provider and the deals did not prevent them from stating their minds and demands if the programmes were considered inadequate. They also had the right to veto and get a replacement for a film previously screened in the town. Most of the time the films arrived as a bulk to the cinema and they were also promoted as a bulk by both, the distributor and the cinema owner with slogans as: "Our programmes are of the highest quality" or "Our programmes attract the biggest audiences".

The long-features altered these practices significantly in the turn of the 1910s. The costs were drastically higher than those of the bulk films, which resulted in the distributors not including them in the ordinary programmes: the cinemas had to pay extra to be supplied with them. The first recorded cases of exclusive film deals of this kind is from November 1910, when Nordiska Biograf Kompaniet advertised to its customers the Danish feature DEN HVIDE SLAVEHANDEL (THE WHITE SLAVE) for 100 FIM for a week whereas the normal fee was only 50 FIM (both prices for the fourth week in the distribution chain).[4] The company announced that the film had been a great success both abroad and in Finland, and that it had been screened for several weeks at the company's own cinemas.[5] It seems that the promotion paid off, as a few weeks later Nordiska Biograf did report that it was not yet able to schedule the screening, as there had been so many bookings.[6] In the beginning of February 1911, Nordiska Biograf received another Danish feature, which was considered

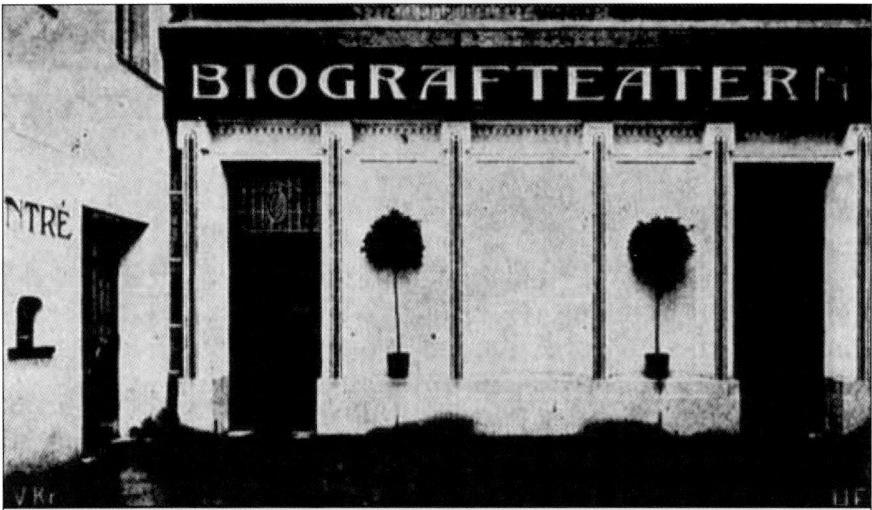

Cinema Scala in Helsinki, photos published on the occasion of the opening, *Veckans Krönika* (18 September 1909)

even more valuable, as it was offered at the price of 200 FIM (fourth week). Director Fernander signed the promotional letter stating:

> As we have succeeded with enormous expenses to obtain the picture AFGRUNDEN with exclusive rights to Finland, we take the privilege to ask, if You wish to rent it. The length of the picture is 850 metres and it is very exciting and magnificent, the most magnificent that has ever been produced in the cinema business. From the enclosed poster You can see what the foreign press has said about the picture. Most of them have wished to get it for two weeks, but no delays without mentioning are expected, as we have two copies of the picture. The rent (…) for a week is 200 FIM."[7]

It seems that the letter itself, similarly to the one promoting DEN HVIDE SLAVEHANDEL, was written by someone else and the price was added later: a clerk or secretary typewrote several similar letters and the director added the suitable price. As of both letters only one copy survives, we do not know how the prices varied, but as they were not added while they were being typed, they probably were consistent with the normal fees in a way that the first weeks were more expensive than the later ones.

The weekly rent asked for AFGRUNDEN was four times the standard price and double as much as it had been for DEN HVIDE SLAVEHANDEL which had gained a mound of bookings, so Nordiska Biograf saw an opportunity in AFGRUNDEN to make extra revenues and it pumped up the price. Also the company had bought two copies of the film, which must have been very exceptional at the time – possibly this film was the first to be distributed in Finland with more than one copy. Still, it was not yet the time when Asta Nielsen was the most adored actress and the Danish long features were the favorites, and there was not enough demand for two copies at the requested prices, as the promotional letter was followed by bargaining. A few weeks later Nordiska Biograf offered a deal: one could have AFGRUNDEN for 100 FIM if also FRA DET MØRKE KØBENHAVN was booked at the same price.[8] The company tried to make four times as much than normally from the renting of AFGRUNDEN, but had to settle for double at least in this case.

According to a newspaper advert, the company had paid 5600 FIM to obtain the film,[9] which was a high price even for two copies and exclusive rights. It is not known how much Nordiska Biograf had paid for other early exclusive films or how much the price of an ordinary film was, but at the beginning of 1914 the average fee for imported films were 1,25 FIM (non-colored), 1,40 FIM (toned) or 1,65 FIM (tinted) per metre.[10] As the inflation was very modest in the early 1910s, the rates can be considered somewhat equivalent to those common when AFGRUNDEN was bought in January 1911. With them, two tinted copies of 850 metres would have cost each only 1400 FIM, just half of the actual price paid for each of the AFGRUNDEN copies.

When comparing the purchasing price and the original offer made to rural cinema owners, it is evident that Nordiska Biograf Kompaniet saw a special opportunity to make extra revenue with exclusive rights to rent AFGRUNDEN in Finland, as it had paid double as much as normally but was trying to rent

Advert for the premiere of KUILU aka AFGRUNDEN, *Helsingin Sanomat* (22 January 1911).

out with four times as high a price. Simultaneously it is evident that the distribution to rural towns was not the key to compensate the expenses, as 200 FIM per week was not that much when compared with the price of the film, 5600 FIM. Gerben Bakker has outlined, that the biggest revenues in film business were in the distribution,[11] but the case of AFGRUNDEN suggests that the distribution to local cinemas was not that important. For the big Finnish film companies most of the income came from their own cinemas, and the distribution to others was a welcomed surplus to it. Nordiska Biograf ran four cinemas around Finland (Scala at Helsinki, Olympia at Turku, Kulmahalli at Viipuri and Biografiteatteri at Kuopio) of which the most important one was the flagship cinema Scala in Helsinki. It was not large, as it had only 283 seats, but it was at the very center of the city, at the Northern Esplanade Street, where all the most luxurious cinemas of the 1910s were situated. AFGRUNDEN premiered at it for one week at the end of January 1911, but, given all screenings were sold out, and everyone paid the full 1 FIM ticket, the box office income would have been almost 18,000 FIM for just that one week. According to the advert the screenings were held once in an hour between 2 pm and 11 pm, and the prices were not higher than normally and no half price children's tickets were sold.[12] This means nine screenings a day, in total 63 screenings and up to 17,829 visitors in a week. It is highly unlikely that the prices for all the tickets were neither that high nor that all the screenings were full, but even with half of the income and even when considering the other costs, including rent, taxes and wages for the personnel and the orchestra, the film could have been profitable already in the first week.

The acquisition price was amortized by the screenings in the company's own cinemas, but it was not the only way to make profits. Renting the films to the rural cinemas was a good way to make some additional income - and even after that there were possibilities for business, as part of the used prints were sold over to St. Petersburg. Still, the figures highlight that AFGRUNDEN had to attract much more audiences than an average film programme. The long feature started a new era in the film exhibition and distribution, as the scale of business multiplied instantly. There were large audiences, and the revenues in both box office and rental were high, but the risks grew as well.

AFGRUNDEN and the newly established censorship

The film censorship was a hot topic in the public discussion in the late 1900s. The rapid emergence of fixed-site cinemas begun in 1906, and by the end of the decade there were more than a dozen of them in the capital city and at least a few in every major rural town. As cinema became a common form of entertainment, the concerns about its disadvantages were raised as well. Responding to persistent lobbying by those concerned about the chastity and morality in the society and likewise persistent objections by the cinema owners, the Finnish senate imposed censorship on films in the turn of 1911. The local police departments were to inspect all films to be shown within their jurisdiction, and pay special attention to aspects of indecency, immorality, violence, and mocking of official authorities within the films.[13]

The censorship was not based upon legislation but only on regulation, which is not surprising when considering the political situation in the Grand Duchy of Finland. In the early 1910s the second wave of Russification had been in force for a few years with vast amounts of policies aimed to narrow down the

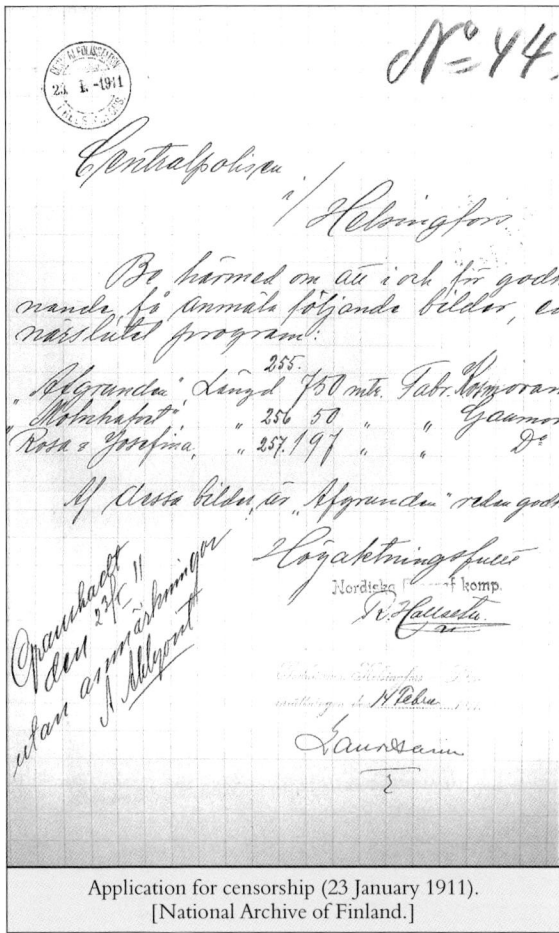

Application for censorship (23 January 1911).
[National Archive of Finland.]

Finnish autonomy or to 'equalize the legislation' with Russia. In this scope it was evident that the Finnish senate was not ready to impose a law about preventive censorship even if it considered films. Also the senate avoided using the word censorship in the regulation, instead was used the word "inspection". The same biased vocabulary can be found in the discussion preceding the regulation: the lobbyists were promoting inspections, as the cinema owners were resisting censorship.[14]

In Helsinki, the inspection board started to operate from the beginning of February 1911. Only one week before, on 23 January, AFGRUNDEN had its premiere at Nordiska Biograf Kompaniet's flagship cinema Scala. This could suggest that the company intended to screen the film before the inspections would start in order to avoid the censorship, but this was not entirely the case. Instead Nordiska Biograf sent a censor application to the police department on the very day of the premiere, which indicates that there actually was an unofficial film censorship in place in Helsinki before the senate's regulation was passed.[15] The police had all the time been bound to monitor the cinemas and to prevent or stop any screening considered indecent or otherwise discriminating. The censorship records indicate that Nordiska Biograf sought official approval for AFGRUNDEN before it became obligatory. There are a few other hints at such cooperation,[16] but this document shows how elaborate it was at least in this case.

In comparison with censorship applications for other films the one for AFGRUNDEN does not look any different. It is handwritten on a grid paper and it includes one cinema programme, consisting of AFGRUNDEN and two films by Gaumont.[17] The film titles and manufacturers of the films and their lengths are stated on the paper. At this point AFGRUNDEN was stated as 750-metres long.[18] Maybe the company cut the 'gaucho dance' scene or some other part of the film to prevent problems, but the length is not necessarily a proof of a cut, since the company marketed the film only two weeks later as 850-metres long.[19] In addition, the film measures given on the applications in general are notoriously inaccurate; and the difference can be explained by other reasons. Maybe already at this time the fee for the inspection was based upon the length of the film and the company wanted to cut the costs. Maybe the company did not include the inter-titles in the length, or made a plain mistake.

The application was accompanied by a programme, an eight page long leaflet consisting of the plot of AFGRUNDEN. The leaflet was made for the grand premiere in Helsinki, as on its cover the venue, cinema Scala, and the premiere day, the 23 January, are stated; and moreover a declaration that Nordiska Biograf had the exclusive right to screen the film in Finland. Both the leaflet and the application were stamped on arrival at the Helsinki Police Department, on the day of the premiere. There is also a note "Granskadt den 23 / I 11 utan anmärkingar. A. Ahlqvist" testifying that the police inspected the programme on the very day and found nothing to remark.[20]

On the application there is a short notice by Rasmus Hallseth, the owner of Nordiska Biograf Kompaniet, to the police stating that "Af dessa bilder är AFGRUNDEN redan godkänt" ("Of these pictures AFGRUNDEN is already approved").[21] The film had been reviewed even before the unofficial inspection on the premiere day, still, there is no information on the public body which had examined the film – nor whether Nordiska Biograf had sent similar documents to the police department earlier or whether there had been discussions between Rasmus Hallseth and the police officers. At any rate, Rasmus Hallseth wanted to remind the police of a procedure already done before the day of the premiere – most probably that the police would not pay such a close attention to the film.

Both of these inspections occurred before the official censorship board commenced work, but there was yet another inspection, which took place some three weeks after the premiere, on 14th February. In the official records it was stated that AFGRUNDEN was approved for public screenings within the area of the capital city Helsinki.[22] The initial screenings had lasted only for one week, so there was no need for censorship, but the approval of the capital city police was extremely important, as the rural police departments depended heavily upon the decisions made in Helsinki from the very beginning of regular censorship – or even before, during the time of the unofficial inspections. If a film was approved in Helsinki, the other departments usually gave the permit for screenings in their own area as well, sometimes even without inspection. This helped the distribution of films and eliminated the risks: if a local police would have prohibited screenings, the system of distributions would have faltered by interrupting the steady flow of film programmes from town to town. The unofficial inspections testify that the relationship between the owners of the major cinemas, who also run the trading companies, and the Helsinki police department was desirable and they had a good understanding upon what kind of film programmes were suitable for the audience. During the debate about the necessity of film censorship, the owners of large cinemas had endorsed the Helsinki police departments as inspection officials, which helps to interpret the fact that the number of prohibited films in Helsinki was very small during the 1910s. Nevertheless, there were problems between the same companies and the local police departments outside Helsinki which highlight the importance of the inspection in the capital city.

Consequently, AFGRUNDEN was inspected by the Helsinki police department in total three times in January and February 1911. Nothing alarmed the censors, as each time the film on its entirety was classified as suitable for screenings. The officials did not even impose a restriction for underage audiences, although the film was full of the very issues the censorship was intended to prevent: indecency, immorality, violence. Nordiska Biograf Kompaniet played it safe and restricted the screenings only for adults, as the story was so daring and racy, that it could have raised objections would children had been allowed to see it. The restriction was not just a preventive measure, but part of the profit making and advertising strategy. In the newspaper adverts was stated with large letters that no tickets for children were sold for these screenings. The exclusion of children suggested that there was something unique and exciting to be screened. Nordiska Biograf created interest in the film and made sure that the box office income was as large as possible.

The surprising outcome of the censorship decisions on AFGRUNDEN was favoured by the inspection practices of the Helsinki police department. Before regular film censorship commenced at the beginning of February 1911, it seems only a few cinema owners had sought approval, and only for part of their films. But now there was a huge flood of censorship applications, which brought an enormous work load to the police, According to the senate's regulation cinemas had to send to the police department the basic information about each film: the title and length of the film, the name of the manufacturer, and "a sufficiently complete account of the content of the film".[23] If the police considered the film to be suspicious, they had the right to call for a screening or to ban the film without any further inspection. In practice the police leafed and glanced through the hundreds of applications, and viewed practically none of the films. The Helsinki police department had no film projector at hand and neither time nor interest in screenings, especially if there was nothing particularly suspicious in the application. Markku Nenonen, who studied the beginnings of film censorship in Finland, estimated that it could have taken up to December 1911 before the Helsinki police actually started systematic screenings.[24]

When the application of AFGRUNDEN was submitted to the Helsinki police department on 23 January 1911, the premiere day, seemingly there was nothing suspicious in it. The programme leaflet accompanying the application explained the plot of the film in depth, but left out the 'gaucho dance' scene: it told that Magda and Rudolf worked at a variety theatre, and that there was a scene in which Magda and another woman on the stage were jealous of one another, but the notorious dance was not mentioned. Maybe it was left out with the intention not to draw attention on it, maybe because it did not develop the plot any further. The available information depicted the film to be a melodramatic story of a woman falling from the right path and ending up in the custody of the police. As the censorship guidelines emphasized that the wrong-doers and those behaving unsuitably had to be held responsible for their actions, which meant that despite the bold topic, AFGRUNDEN treated its story according to these standards. Furthermore, as Rasmus Hallseth had written on the application, the police had already approved the film, so there was nothing conspicuous or suspicious to be expected.

Somehow the film did not provoke discussions or create objections even after the premiere and the screenings in and outside the capital city. Maybe the premiere one week before the enforcement of the censorship was the redeemer of the film: the moralists had no grounds for complaints at that point, as the inspections were starting just the following week. Maybe the premiere and screenings in the best neighborhoods of the city were not considered that hazardous, especially as they were not allowed for children. Maybe the moralists saw it more necessary to monitor the indecencies at the outskirts of the city, at the second class cinemas. Maybe the film company eventually decided to cut the film, or intentionally showed different lengths of the film without any alterations to it. Regardless of the reason, the film made a successful tour around the cinemas of the Grand Duchy of Finland, and it seems that in every town it was screened without problems or difficulties.

On the verge of a new era

AFGRUNDEN was a groundbreaking film in many ways. It must have been quite an experience, watching the story of Magda on the verge of AFGRUNDEN, especially when the 'gaucho dance' was not cut out, with Asta Nielsen's body in a skinny leather dress without the harnesses of petticoats, corset or even a camisole squirming and wriggling against the body of Poul Reumert. One could almost say that the practices of cinema were never the same again: the concept of film performance changed, as well as the notion of the long-feature film, and the practices of film advertising.

There are no sources on the success of the film in Finland, except some words of self-praise and boasting in the marketing letters, but it must have been great. In the fall of 1911, when Nordiska Biograf Kompaniet opened a new cinema in Turku, the first programme was highlighted with the story of Magda, and in the upcoming years the Danish long features and Asta Nielsen were extremely popular in Finland.[25] And just like anywhere else, in Finland AFGRUNDEN was also one of the first films to be advertised with the name of the leading actress, Asta Nielsen, and the director, Urban Gad.[26] Nevertheless the changes were at least as big off the screen as on the screen.

AFGRUNDEN was a groundbreaking film in the practices of Finnish cinema, and it was screened on the verge of a new era. It was one of the very first Danish long features that brought the system of exclusive rights to Finland. It was also possibly the first film to be distributed with two copies. It even could have been the cause for the first large censorship battle or a scandal, but somehow it escaped it all in the turmoil of the implementation of the censorship – most probably due the good tactics and relations of the trading company Nordiska Biograf Kompaniet with the capital police department.

Acknowledgements: I have previously written about AFGRUNDEN in Finland; cf. Outi Hupaniittu, "Näihin näytäntöihin ei myydä lasten pilettejä. Asta Nielsen in Kuilu-elokuva Helsingissä vuonna 1911", in Leila Koivunen and Taina Syrjämaa (eds), *Samanaikaisuuksia: Kansainvälisiä näköaloja vuoden 1911 maailmaan, Histories 2* (Turku: Yleinen historia, Turun yliopisto, 2010), 49–65.

Notes

1. The information about the distribution practices is based upon the research conducted for my upcoming doctoral thesis (2013) which will examine the Finnish cinema business of the 1900s and 1910s. The most important source on the distribution is the correspondence between cinema Opiksi ja Huviksi, situated in the rural town of Jyväskylä in Central Finland, and major cinema companies and trading houses (Nordiska Biograf Kompaniet, Olympia, Apollo, Maxim etc) in 1907–1914. F:1, Correspondence 1907–1914. Archive of Opiksi ja Huviksi, Jyväskylä Provincial Archive.
2. Pseudonym Haastattelija, "Eläväin kuvain sensuroiminen. Biografiteatterien omistajia haastattelemassa" (Censoring the Motion Pictures. Interview with the Cinema Owners), *Helsingin Sanomat* (13 February 1912).
3. Fernander and Hallseth had joined in business already around the year 1900. The first years of the new century they travelled around Scandinavia and Finland with their film tour, but in the year 1906 they settled in Helsinki. There is little evidence of their tours outside Finland and Iceland, where they were the first ones to exhibit films in 1904.
4. Finland was part of the gold exchange standard, and the value of the Finnish mark (FIM) was exactly the same as the French, Swiss and Belgian francs and the Italian lira.
5. Nordiska Biograf Kompaniet to Opiksi ja Huviksi, 12 November 1910. F:1, Correspondence 1907–1914. Archive of Opiksi ja Huviksi, Jyväskylä Provincial Archive.
6. Nordiska Biograf Kompaniet to Opiksi ja Huviksi, 25 November 1910. F:1, Correspondence 1907–1914. Archive of Opiksi ja Huviksi, Jyväskylä Provincial Archive.
7. Nordiska Biograf Kompaniet to Opiksi ja Huviksi, 8 February 1911. F:1, Correspondence 1907–1914. Archive of Opiksi ja Huviksi, Jyväskylä Provincial Archive. Original in Swedish, translation by the author.
8. Nordiska Biograf Kompaniet to Opiksi ja Huviksi, 27 February 1911. F:1, Correspondence

1907–1914. Archive of Opiksi ja Huviksi, Jyväskylä Provincial Archive. Original in Swedish, translation by the author.

9. Advertisement of cinema Scala, *Helsingin Sanomat* (22 January 1911).
10. Erik Estlander, Finlandia Film, to John Uggla, 1 February 1914. Act KD 20/306, 1912. Archive of the Senates Finance department, National Archive of Finland.
11. Cf. Gerben Bakker, *Entertainment Industrialized: The Emergence of the International Film Industry 1890–1940*, (London: London School of Economics and Political Science, 2008), 179–181.
12. Advertisement of cinema Scala, *Helsingin Sanomat* (22 January 1911).
13. Guidelines to the Governors, 15 December 1910. Da:47, Transcripts. Archive of the Senates Office of the Civilian Operations (Interior Ministry), National Archives of Finland. See also Markku Nenonen, *Elokuvatarkastuksen synty Suomessa (1907–1922)* (Helsinki: Suomalaisen Kirjallisuuden Seura SKS, 1999), 25–56, 70–72.
14. Cf. for example The Kolmisointu Association to the Senate, 17 May 1910. Act KD 65/94, 26.6.1910. Archive of the Senates Finance department, National Archive of Finland; Haastattelija, "Eläväin kuvain sensuroiminen".
15. Inspection 44, 2 February 1911, including films 255–257, Fc:1, Censorship records 1911, Archive of the State Board of Film Classification, National Archive of Finland.
16. The Governor of Uusimaa to the Senate, 15 June 1910. Act KD 65/94, 26.6.1910. Archive of the Senates Finance department, National Archive of Finland; Haastattelija, "Eläväin kuvain sensuroiminen".
17. MOLNHAFVET / PILVIMERI (THE SEA OF CLOUDS), 50 metres, and ROSA OCH JOSEFINA / RUUSA JA JOSEFIINA (A L'INSTAR DE ROSA-JOSEPHA, LIKE ROSE AND JOSEPHINE), 197 metres.
18. Film 255, 14 February 1911, Ba:1, List of censored film 1911, Archive of the State Board of Film Classification, National Archive of Finland.
19. Nordiska Biograf Kompaniet to Opiksi ja Huviksi, 8 February 1911. F:1, Correspondence 1907–1914. Archive of Opiksi ja Huviksi, Jyväskylä Provincial Archive.
20. Programme leaflet and application, Inspection 44, 14 February 1911, including films 255–257, Fc:1, Censorship records 1911, Archive of the State Board of Film Classification, National Archive of Finland.
21. Ibid.
22. Film 255, 14 February 1911, Ba:1, List of censored film 1911, Archive of the State Board of Film Classification, National Archive of Finland.
23. Guidelines to the Governors, 15 December 1910. Da:47, Transcripts. Archive of the Senates Office of the Civilian Operations (Interior Ministry), National Archives of Finland.
24. Markku Nenonen, *Elokuvatarkastuksen synty Suomessa*, 65–66.
25. More about the popularity of Danish films and Asta Nielsen in Finland in Outi Hupaniittu, "Nuori Apollo, vanhan mamsellin ystävä: Helsinkiläisten suosikkinäyttelijä Valdemar Psilander ja 1910-luvun elokuvakulttuuri", in Heta Mulari and Lauri Piispa (eds), *Elokuva historiassa, historia elokuvassa* (Turku: K&h, 2009), 49–82.
26. Advertisement of cinema Scala, *Helsingin Sanomat* (22 January 1911).

Andrzej Dębski

AFGRUNDEN in Warsaw and Asta Nielsen's Popularity in Polish territories

In the years before the First World War, Poland did not exist as a sovereign state on the map of Europe. Polish territories lay within the borders of the Russian Empire, the German Empire and Austro-Hungary. Warsaw was the largest Polish cultural centre within the borders of the Russian Empire. Karl Baedeker's city guide from 1914 noted on Warsaw: "It resembles the cities of Western Europe much more than it resembles Russia".[1] The number of cinemas reflects the enormous popularity of cinema-going among over 870,000 inhabitants: "After 1910, 63 cinemas in Warsaw commenced showings every evening".[2] But only around fifteen of them placed their advertisements in the local press, especially in the most popular newspapers such as *Kurier Warszawski* and *Kurier Poranny*. Half of them were located in close proximity to each other at Marszałkowska Street: Olimpja (No. 114), Sfinks (No. 116), Illusion (No. 118), Kultura (No. 125), Czary (No. 129), Alabastra (No. 138). This demonstrates the high competitiveness of these cinemas in the shopping centre of Warsaw. Fierce competition for the audience took place especially between the neighbouring cinemas Sfinks and Illusion. The latter was opened in 1908 and belonged to the Siła company established by Mordechaj Towbin, whereas Sfinks was opened in 1909 and belonged to the company Towarzystwo Udziałowe Sfinks established by Aleksander Hertz, Józef Koerner, Alfred Silberlast and Mojżesz (Marek) Zuker. The atmosphere of this competition has been described by Edward Zajiček:

> It was a challenge which gave rise to a long-standing and fierce rivalry between the two protagonists of the industry. The rivalry was abound in controversial incidents of unfair competition, provoked by Mordka Towbin who used to say about his rival: Hertz is the same thief as I am – except that he wears white gloves.[3]

DEN HVIDE SLAVEHANDEL precedes AFGRUNDEN

On 28 September 1910, the Warsaw newspaper *Kurier Poranny* announced an "excellent programme" of short films as something usual in cinema Sfinks, while from 8 pm onward the repertoire contained "a propaganda picture by the Society for the Protection of Women in London entitled BIAŁA NIEWOLNICA [DEN HVIDE SLAVEHANDEL, THE WHITE SLAVE] – from the history of

Kurier Poranny (29 September 1910).

slave trade".[4] Readers were informed that this film was intended for adult audiences only; tickets for children and adolescents were not sold after 7 pm. Although the advertisement announced the usual short film programme by naming some of the films to be shown, and, whereas those which were particularly interesting were highlighted with the heading "beyond the programme", presumably THE WHITE SLAVE was one of the first films in Warsaw which came across as an element of the repertoire in its own right. The programme presented after 8 pm most probably included this one film alone. The question regarding the number of screenings per evening remains open, but there is no doubt as to the special status of the film, as reflected by the advertisements. On 29 September the announcement said: "Today from 7 pm BIAŁA NIEWOLNICA, the regular programme until 7 pm".[5]

The motif of the 'white slave' – a woman seduced or kidnapped and forced into prostitution – was extremely popular in the mass culture around 1900. The combination of sexuality and the big city demonstrated the discomfort associated with the transformations brought about by industrialisation and urbanisation, but also with the emancipation of women in terms of professional occupation and sexual behaviour. Sociologist Emilie Altenloh, author of the first dissertation on cinema audiences, articulated her observation: "The arrival of the first modern sensation drama THE WHITE SLAVE meant a fundamental change in cinema programmes, and a boom for the entire film industry".[6]

In 1910, two feature-length films were produced in Denmark with the title DEN HVIDE SLAVEHANDEL: The first version was directed by Alfred Cohn in the spring of 1910 for the Danish cinema company Fotorama. This film was 706 metres long and ran 35 minutes, three times longer than standard films screened in short film programmes. However, in the summer of 1910, the competing Nordisk Film Compagni plagiarised Fotorama's version, scene by scene, and produced a film of 603 metres under the same title, DEN HVIDE SLAVEHANDEL, directed by August Blom. Because of the technical quality, but perhaps more because of the contacts of Ole Olsen who had founded Nordisk Film, it was Blom's version which achieved international renown. In Great Britain, Nordisk's version was released under the title THE WHITE SLAVE,[7] whereas Fotorama's original version was distributed as THE WHITE SLAVE TRADE. Nordisk Film sold prints of its plagiarism through its international representatives, while the purchasers resold them or leased them. In October 1910, there were several prints in circulation under the title DIE WEISSE SKLAVIN, in Germany.[8] A print of this film was at the disposal of the owners of cinema Sfinks. However, this was not the only print of THE WHITE SLAVE in Warsaw: in cinema Sfinks, THE WHITE SLAVE was shown from 28 September to 21 October; but, on 11 October, it was also found in the programme of cinema Moulin Rouge. This would have hardly been possible had the movie been distributed in the exclusive system.

Local Rivalry for AFGRUNDEN

The rivalry between the cinemas Sfinks and Illusion is splendidly reflected by their exhibition practices in the case of AFGRUNDEN which was shown in Warsaw under the title OTCHŁAŃ (THE ABYSS). The exclusive system meant higher profits for the exhibitors who had purchased a licence. It seems that the success of AFGRUNDEN in Copenhagen was a strong stimulus for the owners of Sfinks and Illusion (as for other exhibitors in Warsaw) to try to get hold of this long-feature film. As reported by Lauri Piispa, the Warsaw based cinema Sfinks, together with the Moscow based company Globus, purchased from the producer the exclusive rights to the exhibition for the territory of Russia. AFGRUNDEN was shown in Warsaw before it was shown in Moscow.[9]

AFGRUNDEN was in Sfinks' repertoire on 30 November 1910. The advertisement announced the film as follows: "The story of the collapse of a woman, a picture of international renown from the 'white slaves' series".[10] The reference testifies to the success of THE WHITE SLAVE in Warsaw, though AFGRUNDEN was not about a young woman forced into prostitution. The associations which were supposed to be formed by the audience upon reading the announcement seem to have a twofold dimension: thematic and feature-related. The last dimension is demonstrated by additional information: the screenings began at: "7, 8, 9 pm etc."[11] which suggests that 9 pm was not the last hour of the film screenings. There is no doubt that the screenings of AFGRUNDEN enjoyed a special status. The adverts announcing AFGRUNDEN under the Polish title OTCHŁAŃ in cinema Sfinks were published daily from 30 November until 19 December and on 21 December 1910, in *Kurier Poranny*.

AFGRUNDEN was 850 metres long. The full hours given as starting times of the screenings in the adverts correspond to the running time of 47 minutes at 16 frames per second. AFGRUNDEN was presumably the longest film shown in

Warsaw up to that time. The screenings of AFGRUNDEN in cinema Sfinks had various starting times. On the assumption that cinemas in Warsaw were open until 11 pm, as in most large cities of Europe, AFGRUNDEN was shown in cinema Sfinks 85 times in total.

Table 1. Screenings of AFGRUNDEN in cinema Sfinks, 30 November to 20 December 1910[12]

Date	Show times from	Showings	Date	Show times from	Showings
30 November	7 pm	4	11 December	6 pm	5
1 December	7 pm	4	12 December	7 pm	4
2 December	7 pm	4	13 December	7 pm	4
3 December	6 pm	5	14 December	7 pm	4
4 December	5 pm	6	15 December	8 pm	3
5 December	6 pm	5	16 December	8 pm	3
6 December	7 pm	4	17 December	8 pm	3
7 December	7 pm	4	18 December	6 pm	5
8 December	6 pm	5	19 December	8.30 pm	2
9 December	7 pm	4	20 December	9 pm	2
10 December	6 pm	5	**TOTAL**		**85**

However, the owners of Sfinks in Warsaw had a second outlet, since Towarzystwo Sfinks also owned the Uranja hall in the Philharmonic. There the film was announced on 12 December 1910:

> On account of an unprecedented success of a renowned cinematographic drama, AFGRUNDEN, in order to make it available to larger audiences we will soon commence to screen it in the cinema Uranja in the Grand Hall of the Warsaw Philharmonic, simultaneously with the cinema Sfinks.[13]

As Uranja's advertisements were not published every day (whereas those of Sfinks were published daily), it remains open whether these were occasional screenings. The adverts were published on 13 December (showing time from 8 pm), 18 and 19 December (showing times from 9 pm). From the additional three screenings, we conclude that Towarzystwo Sfinks organised all in all 88 screenings of AFGRUNDEN in Warsaw. This demonstrates the considerable popularity of this film, especially when we take into consideration the prestige associated with screenings in the grand hall of the Philharmonic.

The Danish producer sold AFGRUNDEN as an exclusive. In Warsaw, no cinema apart from those which belonged to Towarzystwo Sfinks was allowed to rent a print from elsewhere or to show AFGRUNDEN during the period when cinema Sfinks was screening it. However, competing cinemas did not give up fighting for audiences. Strikingly, the day after the first screening of AFGRUNDEN in cinema Sfinks, on 1 December, the following information was published in *Kurier Poranny*:

> Illusion, Marszałkowska 118, would like to inform the Distinguished Audience that beginning on Saturday the 3rd day of this month, not only in special hours and not only for special Audiences, but for everyone, we will be showing between programmes, with a change on Tuesdays and Saturdays, the pictures by the author of THE WHITE SLAVE, from the series of DZIEJE UPADKU KOBIETY [THE STORY OF

Afgrunden in Warsaw and Asta Nielsen's Popularity in Polish territories

Kurier Poranny (13 December 1910).

THE COLLAPSE OF A WOMAN], OTCHŁAŃ [AFGRUNDEN, THE ABYSS], ROMANS PANICZA Z SUBRETKĄ [The Romance of the Young Master with a Soubrette], DWIE SŁUŻĄCE [Two Slaves] etc.[14]

The competition not only underlined the broader availability of the film (which can also indicate a large number of those willing to attend the screenings in Sfinks), but it also made a reference to the main title THE ABYSS as well as to the subtitle "The Story of the Collapse of a Woman", simultaneously suggesting that in fact it held the licence for the film featuring Asta Nielsen. In view of such a turn of events, the response of the owners of Sfinks becomes understandable. The following day they notified the readers of *Kurier Poranny*:

> On account of the announcements of the unreliable competition we would like to emphasize that the renowned cinematographic drama AFGRUNDEN: "The Story of the Collapse of a Woman" from the 'white slaves' series has been purchased by us as our exclusive property and until it stops being screened in the cinemas Sfinks and Uranja, it will not be shown anywhere else in Warsaw. We warn against the imitation of titles.[15]

The next day the competition retorted:

> The cinema Illusion, Marszałkowska 118, would like to inform the Distinguished Audience that despite the denial by the extremely unreliable competition, beginning as of Saturday, the theatre will be showing the whole series of pictures from the Copenhagen factory for everyone and not only during special hours

Kurier Poranny (21 December 1910).

between the regular programmes, with a change on Tuesdays and Saturdays. Today a change of programme, among others: ROMANS PANICZA Z SUBRETKĄ [THE ROMANCE OF THE YOUNG MASTER WITH A SOUBRETTE]. The 'human trafficking' series by the author of THE WHITE SLAVE.[16]

The owners of Sfinks explained once again, even more forcibly, on the following day:

> We would like to draw the attention of the Distinguished Audience to the fact that the renowned drama by Urban Good [sic], entitled AFGRUNDEN: "The Story of the Collapse of a Woman", the second from the 'white slaves' series, proffered with such a tremendous success exclusively in cinema Sfinks, Marszałkowska 116, has nothing to do with the pictures shown under that title in other cinemas, apart from the title 'borrowed' from us. Until now there have been no more pictures from the 'white slaves' series. As far as the reliability of the competing advertisements, meant to mislead the Audience, is concerned, the judgement thereof should be made at the discretion of the Audience itself.[17]

What attracts attention is that the owners of cinema Sfinks warned readers not only against the showings in the cinema owned by Mordka Towbin, but also against those "in other cinemas". The advertisements indicate that, on 3 December 1910, Kinema-Corso had "UPADEK KOBIETY [THE COLLAPSE OF THE WOMAN] by the author of THE WHITE SLAVE, THE ABYSS etc."[18] in its repertoire, whereas several days later cinema Piękna 15 advertised "DWIE SUBRETKI [TWO SOUBRETTES] the picture by the author of THE WHITE SLAVE".[19] Presumably, these were short feature films, thematically alluding to 'dramas' which were trendy at that time but which were not distributed through the exclusive system. AFGRUNDEN was found in the repertoires of Sfinks and Uranja only, which – bearing in mind the number of screenings and the reactions of the competition and the owners of Towarzystwo themselves – must have been extremely lucrative. Until 20 December AFGRUNDEN was shown in cinema Sfinks, and later it found its way to the cinema Moulin Rouge where it was screened "from 7 pm in the evening",[20] presumably until the end of the year.[21]

In Warsaw, the enormous success of BIAŁA NIEWOLNICA (THE WHITE SLAVE), and subsequently also of OTCHŁAŃ (AFGRUNDEN, THE ABYSS), marked the beginning of a change in shaping cinema programmes – an 'exclusive' single film was supposed to attract audiences magnetically to the cinema. Cinema owners became aware of the advantages of exclusive exhibition. They designed their advertisements in the newspapers in such a way that readers could deduce that no other cinema in Warsaw would screen the same film at the same time. On 18 December 1910, that is, during the period when cinema Sfinks screened AFGRUNDEN, cinema Illusion introduced into its repertoire "from 7 pm ZE SZPONÓW HAŃBY [From the Talons of Dishonour], a drama from the human trafficking series, the only film print in Warsaw".[22] On 15 January 1911, cinema Sfinks announced another film which was supposed to be a hit: "From 6 pm OFIARA PÓŁŚWIATKA [Victim of the Underworld]. The story of a man, according to Urban Good [sic]. The only film print purchased as the exclusive property of Towarzystwo Udziałowe 'Sfinks'. We warn against the imitation of titles."[23]

Moreover, the length of the films themselves began to constitute an attraction emphasised in the announcements. Towards the end of January 1911, cinema Illusion Kultura advertised NOWY OGRÓD ZOOLOGICZNY W RZYMIE (The New Zoological Garden in Rome), highlighting the favourable features of the film: "This picture, 600 metres long, has the most brilliant camerawork".[24] On 16 February, cinema Olimpja recommended its own film in the following manner: "Today from 7 pm W MATNI ŻYCIA [In the Dire Straits of Life], a tragedy against the background of human trafficking. A picture with a length of 1200 metres".[25] It is worth adding that this film was probably DEN HVIDE SLAVEHANDELS SIDSTE OFFER (IN THE HANDS OF IMPOSTORS), the most frequently advertised as the second part of THE WHITE SLAVE. It was 930 metres long, but it was not an exclusive: in the cinemas Sfinks, Illusion, Oaza and Kultura, this film was screened under the title W WIRZE ŻYCIA (In the Whirl of Life), and presented with the remark that it was a continuation of the popular title BIAŁA NIEWOLNICA, 2 (THE WHITE SLAVE, part 2).[26] This also indicates that exhibitors were looking around for long-feature films which were still rare on the market.

At the turn of the year 1911, a fundamental change in film programming was initiated in Warsaw, shifting from short film programmes to those based on a long-feature film. The success of AFGRUNDEN became a prelude to the emergence of Asta Nielsen as the first film star who attracted audiences to long dramas. Even though her name did not appear in the local adverts of AFGRUNDEN, the popularity of this film does not raise any doubts about her success because the actress became a renowned celebrity in Warsaw. This is further reinforced by her popularity in other cities inhabited by Polish-speaking people.

Asta Nielsen's Popularity in Galicia

That Asta Nielsen attained the status of a major celebrity also in Galicia is confirmed by Włodzimierz Łada who wrote an article in Cracow on 25 January 1913:

> The 'elite' audiences prefer Asta Nielsen's troupe exclusively. A blessed actress! (...) Therefore, we admire Asta Nielsen. Not because of her good figure, because she has got meaningful eyes, an expressive gesture, because she plays roles created exclusively for her – that is why she does not need to shy away from playing Shakespeare, as the virtuosos do. Here Cracow audiences reach out to – please do not laugh – their traditions. Perhaps, they are not even aware of the fact that, in the Danish actress, they like the moderation of the gesture, the self-restraint in affect, the entire treatment of the role, once referred to as the 'Koźmian school'. (...) This is an important matter. Since Asta Nielsen is good and it is great that we spontaneously admire her style which is similar to our tastes. However, when the theatre starts to struggle financially, then the only thing left after the 'Koźmian school' might turn out to be Asta Nielsen.[27]

While appreciating the virtues of Asta Nielsen, the author also expressed his fears about the future of the theatre: Thus he confirmed the superior status of the actress from the point of view of the inhabitants of Cracow. – Asta Nielsen's live theatre performance in May of the same year in Lvov demonstrates that she enjoyed a considerable renown also in this city. Barbara Gierszewska writes:

> In May of 1913 the Lvov-based cinema Colosseum hosted the Danish actress Asta Nielsen who is popular in all of Europe. Her visit ought to be regarded as a cinema event not only in Lvov, but in pre-war Eastern Galicia. All the newspapers reported that the star was coming to Lvov on Thursday [2 May] at 11 at night, and that she would be staying at the George Hotel, and the following day her 'first performance' would take place. The arrival of the favourite lead character of cinema dramas was almost like a holiday for the inhabitants of Lvov, all the more proud because the actress came to Lvov 'straight from Vienna', passing over Cracow. [...] Nielsen appeared 'live' in the 'Colosseum' in a 20-minute long 'mimodrama' *Cyganka* [The Gipsy Woman] which had attracted crowds of local and nearby audiences who were watching the actress's 'remarkable skill with respect to mimetic acting'. (...) The other cinemas prepared a retrospective of the films which featured the celebrity. Cinema Bajka screened ZDEMASKOWANI [WENN DIE MASKE FÄLLT, WHEN THE MASK FALLS] and KOMEDIANCI [KOMÖDIANTEN, THE HEART OF A PIERROT]; cinema Vaudeville showed 'the most beautiful Asta Nielsen exclusive dramas' GRZECHY OJCÓW [DIE SÜNDEN DER VÄTER, TEMPTATIONS OF DRINK] and DZIEWCZYNA Z LUDU [DIE VERRÄTERIN, A WOMAN OF THE PEOPLE]. On those days no dramas were screened other than the ones featuring 'the divine Asta'.[28]

These examples demonstrate that among Polish audiences Asta Nielsen enjoyed a renown similar to the one she enjoyed among German audiences.[29] For the local history of cinema-going it would be interesting to examine the change in film programming in Cracow and Lvov and how significant those early long-feature films starring Asta Nielsen were in the said locations.

Translated from Polish by Agnieszka Dziołak

Notes

1. Quoted in Norman Davies, *Boże Igrzysko. Historia Polski* (Kraków: Wydawnictwo Znak 2001), 599.
2. Małgorzata Hendrykowska, "Początki kinematografii polskiej. Pierwsze dwie dekady", in Grażyna Grabowska (ed.): *Sto lat polskiego filmu. Kino okresu wielkiego niemowy. Część pierwsza: początki* (Warsaw: Filmoteka Narodowa 2008), 26.
3. Edward Zajiček, "Towarzystwo Udziałowe Sfinks – Domena Aleksandra Hertza", in Grabowska, *Sto lat polskiego filmu*, 50.
4. *Kurier Poranny* (28 September 1910).
5. *Kurier Poranny* (29 September 1910).
6. Emilie Altenloh, *Zur Soziologie des Kino. Die Kino-Unternehmung und die sozialen Schichten ihrer Besucher* [1914], ed. by Andrea Haller, Martin Loiperdinger and Heide Schlüpmann (Frankfurt and Basel: Stroemfeld, 2012), 9.
7. Cf. Marguerite Engberg, "Plagiarism, and the Birth of the Danish Multi-Reel Film", in Lisbeth Richter Larsen, Dan Nissen (eds): *100 Years of Nordisk Film* (Copenhagen: Danish Film Institute, 2006), 75.
8. Cf. Corinna Müller, *Frühe deutsche Kinematographie. Formale, wirtschaftliche und kulturelle Entwicklungen 1907–1912* (Stuttgart and Weimar: Metzler, 1994), 110–115.
9. Cf. Lauri Piispa's essay in this book.
10. *Kurier Poranny* (30 November 1910).
11. Ibid.
12. The Sfinks advertisement was not published on 20 December 1910, but on 21 December. However, on the same day AFGRUNDEN was screened for the first time in the cinema Moulin Rouge, and therefore it is feasible that the Sfinks advertisement on 21 December had been mistakenly published one day late.
13. *Kurier Poranny* (12 December 1910).
14. *Kurier Poranny* (1 December 1910).
15. *Kurier Poranny* (2 December 1910).
16. *Kurier Warszawski* (3 December 1910).
17. *Kurier Poranny* (4 December 1910).
18. *Kurier Warszawski* (3 December 1910).
19. *Kurier Warszawski* (13 December 1910).
20. *Kurier Poranny* (21 December 1910).
21. On Christmas Eve, 24 December 1910, the advertisement in *Kurier Poranny* informed that AFGRUNDEN would be screened in cinema Moulin Rouge "for several days only". I have not found any subsequent advert for it.
22. *Kurier Poranny* (18 December 1910).
23. *Kurier Poranny* (15 January 1911).
24. *Kurier Warszawski* (28 January 1911).
25. *Kurier Poranny* (16 February 1911).
26. Cf. *Kurier Poranny* (16 and 17 February 1911); *Kurier Warszawski* (16 February 1911).
27. Włodzimierz Łada, "Plakaty i oczy. – Dobroczynne 'kino'. – Zawsze z artystami. –'Nasza szkoła'. – Panna Asta Nielsen. – Czy taki koniec?" *Kurier Warszawski* (26 January 1913). Stanisław Koźmian, a theatre reformer, was director of the Cracow theatre from 1871 to 1885.
28. Cf. Barbara Gierszewska, *Kino i film we Lwowie do 1939 roku* (Kielce: Wydawnictwo Akademii Świętokrzyskiej, 2006), 98–99.
29. For information about the tour of Asta Nielsen in the year 1914 in Breslau please see Andrzej Dębski, *Historia kina we Wrocławiu w latach 1896–1918* (Wrocław: Wydawnictwo Uniwersytetu Wrocławskiego, 2009), 211–214.

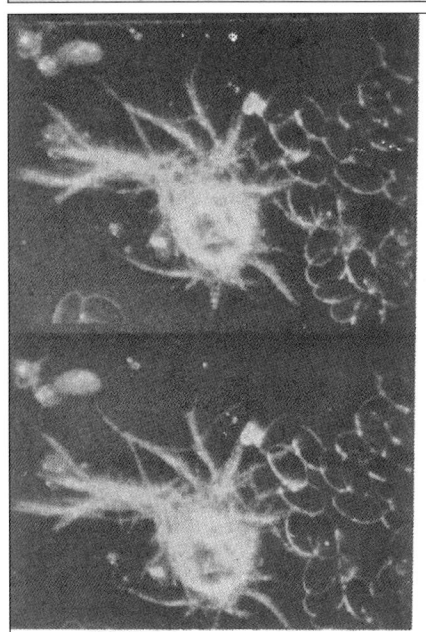
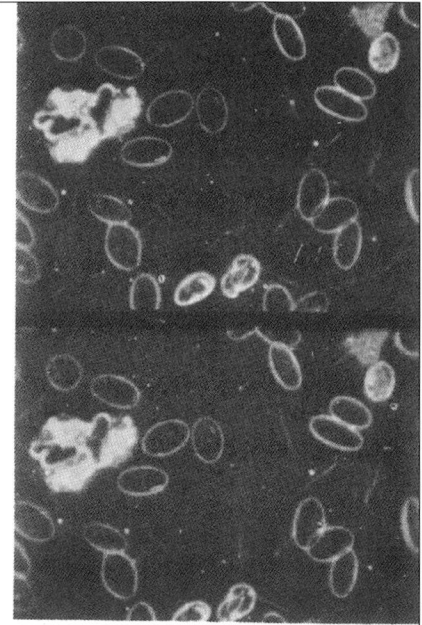

[Copyright, Pathé Frères

1.   2.
CINEMATOGRAPH FILMS OF MICROBES.

Ouissal Mejri

AFGRUNDEN and Professor Ehrlich's Magic Bullet in Alexandria

Film historiography in the Arabic countries treats the silent film era rather superficially. Only rarely are a few aspects treated in more detail. Bibliographical information is often unclear, or it is missing altogether. Institutional structures to preserve the film heritage such as film museums or archives are hardly developed or suffer from an insufficiency of material. In the historical archives, access to paper documents is impeded by the poor quality of preservation. Researching into a magazine or a newspaper over a longer period of time requires months of on-site work. I decided to take on this task for my research on the foreign influence on the development of cinema in the Maghreb countries from 1896 to 1930.[1] In European countries as well, it is often very difficult to find information on the important questions concerning the history of cinema in sources of the time. As Egypt was a protectorate under British rule, the situation is even more complicated with respect to very specific questions. Finding information on the distribution and exhibition of Asta Nielsen films in Egypt turned out to be extremely difficult. My research in the National Film Archive in Cairo, in the library of the Cairo Film School, in the National Library of Cairo and in the Library of Alexandria turned up only one periodical giving one bit of information on an Asta Nielsen film: *La Réforme*, a daily paper in French that was issued in Alexandria beginning in 1896. The studies of the Egyptian film historian Ahmed Al Hadari have shown that initially only the foreign-language Egyptian magazines reported on films and the cinema.[2] My research in Arabic-language newspapers and magazines such as the weekly journals *Al Ahram* (founded in Alexandria in 1875) and *Misr* (founded in Cairo in 1875) and the daily newspapers *Al Muayed* (founded in Cairo in 1817), *Al Mokatam* (founded in Cairo in 1882), and *Al Akhbar* (founded in Cairo in 1881) have produced no information on Asta Nielsen films in Egypt.

Facing page:

Above: AFGRUNDEN, the 'gaucho dance'. [Filmarchiv Austria.]
Below: Illustration from Frederick A. Talbot, *Moving Pictures. How they are made and worked* (1912).

In general, it can be determined that information on film showings was placed in the press in advance. They functioned as advertisements for the respective event. As *La Réforme* appeared in French, the newspaper was addressed primarily to the foreign public in Alexandria. Being the most open and liberal city in Egypt, Alexandria was the much diversified cultural and intellectual centre, with its golden age at the turn of the century when the first stage plays and film screenings were launched and the first Egyptian news organisations were founded. In the early 1910s, audiences of film projections in cinemas as well as in coffee shops were essentially connected to the foreign communities who arranged elegant evenings around the cinematograph. Cinema was considered a foreigners' institution. As in many European countries, the film programmes combined a long-feature film with several short films. In Alexandria, those programmes were shown in a projection hall called Cinema and Theatre Chantecler which opened on 6 March 1911. According to *La Réforme*, the French national anthem was heard in the presence of the French Consul, and Monsieur Du Lagarine, the manager, was preparing another evening to accommodate inspectors and French sailors who were to arrive in Alexandria Harbour on 20 March.[3] It seems that this cinema programmed Pathé films exclusively, combined with long features from Nordisk Film. In 1914, short comedies with Max Linder were shown, and a prominent long feature was ATLANTIS which tells the story of the sinking of a luxury liner with its passengers.

Two months after the grand opening of the Cinema and Theatre Chantecler, *La Réforme* announced that Pathé's projection hall "in old Boursa street", which had not been in use for some time, would be revived, starting with a "Scientific Art Film Festival" on Monday, 1 May 1911: "Two films will be shown which are already successful with the public in Cairo. The titles of these films were 606, about the discovery by Doctor Ehrlich, and AL HAWIYÀ, a drama in two parts."[4] A week later, the same information concerning the projection of these two films was repeated: this time the opening was announced for Sunday, 7 May.[5] The following day, *La Réforme* reported:

> The reopening of the Cinema Pathé, located in the old Boursa street, took place under the supervision of Signor Fernando, the owner of Cinema Pathé in Cairo. The French Consul in Alexandria and his wife attended the opening ceremonies. The films 606 and AL HAWIYÀ, plus a comedy film were projected. The music was performed by the orchestra conducted by Grasso.[6]

The French Consul was present again – as he had been at the grand opening of the Cinema and Theatre Chantecler, two months earlier. It seems that Monsieur Du Lagarine, the sole owner of the Cinema and Theatre Chantecler, was upset and complained that it was illegal to show Pathé films in Alexandria outside of his cinema. In addition, he expressed his stupefaction at the reopening of this small projection hall, previously abandoned and situated in a populous neighbourhood. Monsieur Du Lagarine planned to take Signor Fernando to court because the only cinema which, in his point of view, was allowed to show new Pathé films was to be the Cinema and Theatre Chantecler.

Nonetheless, the projection of the two films 606 and AL HAWIYÀ took place,[7] and in order to avoid the law suit the name of the old Cinema Pathé was changed to Cinema Palace.[8]

But what about the two 'scientific art films' which comprised the re-opening programme of Alexandria's old Pathé Cinema? AL HAWIYÀ is simply the translation of the Danish title AFGRUNDEN (THE ABYSS). Though neither Asta Nielsen nor Urban Gad is mentioned in this context, "a drama in two parts" called AL HAWIYÀ, without any doubt, is identical with AFGRUNDEN. In the last article *La Réforme* dedicated to the film on 19 May 1911, it was specified that the film AL HAWIYÀ was produced in Denmark. But Asta Nielsen's debut film certainly is not a 'scientific art film'. Science comes into play with the second film of the programme: The film's title, the abbreviation '606' refers to 606 CONTRE SPIROCHÈTE PÂLE, then a brand new Pathé film released in April 1911. Pathé's catalogue description reads:

> The pale spirochete is the agent of the terrible sickness which Professor Erlich [sic] of Frankfurt has tried hard to combat using the serum 606 or hydrochloride of dioxydiaminoarsenobenzene. The spirochete has a thickness of 0.5 thousandths of a millimetre; it is shaped in a helix like a drill; it is the smallest of known microbes.[9]

This description does not reveal that spirochaeta pallida is the agent of syphilis. As early as July 1910, Pathé had released a whole series of fifteen scientific films on human blood and microbes called 'La Cinématographie ultramicroscopique' which were meant for instruction at colleges and universities. These films were produced under the scientific direction of Dr. Jean Comandon and caused a great sensation, not only with medical experts.[10] 606 CONTRE SPIROCHÈTE PÂLE, which Pathé released as 'Scène de vulgarisation scientifique' in April 1911, took as its theme the scientific defeat of the sexually transmitted disease syphilis, presenting it to the general public. This popular science film treated a controversial subject in which medical questions were thrown together with problems of sexual morality. At the time it was highly topical: In 1909, Professor Paul Ehrlich in Frankfurt, with the help of his assistant Sahachiro Hata, had discovered that compound 606, Arsphenamine, effectively combatted *spirochaetes* bacteria. In late 1910, after extensive clinical testing, the Hoechst company began to market the compound as 'Salvarsan', which proved to be most effective, particularly when compared with the conventional therapy of mercury salts. Salvarsan became the most widely prescribed drug worldwide and was known as Professor Ehrlich's 'magic bullet' – a term that Ehrlich had coined himself for a compound that targeted a disease selectively.

606 CONTRE SPIROCHÈTE PÂLE is a one-reeler of 14 minutes, whereas AFGRUNDEN is one of the first Danish long-feature films and takes about 45 minutes projection time. In *La Reforme*, there is no information on the succession of the two films which formed Monsieur Fernando's "Scientific Art Film Festival",

and there is no report on how Ehrlich's 'magic bullet' worked when combined with the famous 'gaucho dance' – and vice versa. It seems that AL HAWIYÀ did not suffer any censorship in Alexandria. This can be explained by the changes in the judicial system in Egypt at the end of the 19th century which were a result of the multitude of specific laws which each newly arrived community brought into the country. These foreign communities, which were predominantly located in Alexandria and Cairo, were protected and the lives of the community members were never threatened; in fact, their presence was part of the British policy of imposing their protectorate on Egypt. The liberal cultural conditions which resulted from this unique situation allowed the public in Alexandria to watch Asta Nielsen's eroticism and her 'gaucho dance', unrestricted by any censorship, und in the assurance that finally an effective medication had been found to treat syphilis.

Notes

1. My doctoral thesis *Il cinema in Egitto e in Tunisia dal 1896 all'avvento del sonoro: l'influenza straniera* (Theatre and Cinema Studies, Bologna University, 2011).
2. Ahmed (el) Hadari, *El Tarikh essinima fi Misr: al-Juz' al-awwal min bidayat 1896 li-akhir 1930* [The History of Cinema in Egypt, Part 1: From Its Beginnings in 1896 to 1930] (Cairo: Nadi al-Sinima, 1989).
3. *La Réforme* (9 March 1911).
4. *La Réforme* (8 May 1911).
5. *La Réforme* (4 May 1911).
6. *La Réforme* (8 May 1911).
7. *La Réforme* (13 May 1911).
8. *La Réforme* (19 May 1911).
9. See http://filmographie.fondation-jeromeseydoux-pathe.com/
10. See Béatrice de Pastre (ed.), *Filmer la science, comprendre la vie: le cinéma de Jean Comandon* (Paris: CNC, 2012); as a contemporary source the chapter "Moving Pictures on Microbes" in Frederick A. Talbot, *Moving Pictures. How they are made and worked* (Philadelphia 1912, Reprint Arno Press: New York, 1970), 161–167.

PART 3

THE MAKING OF THE FILM STAR IN GERMANY

Internationale Film=Vertriebs=Gesellschaft
m. b. H.

BERLIN SW 68 Zimmerstr. 16=18

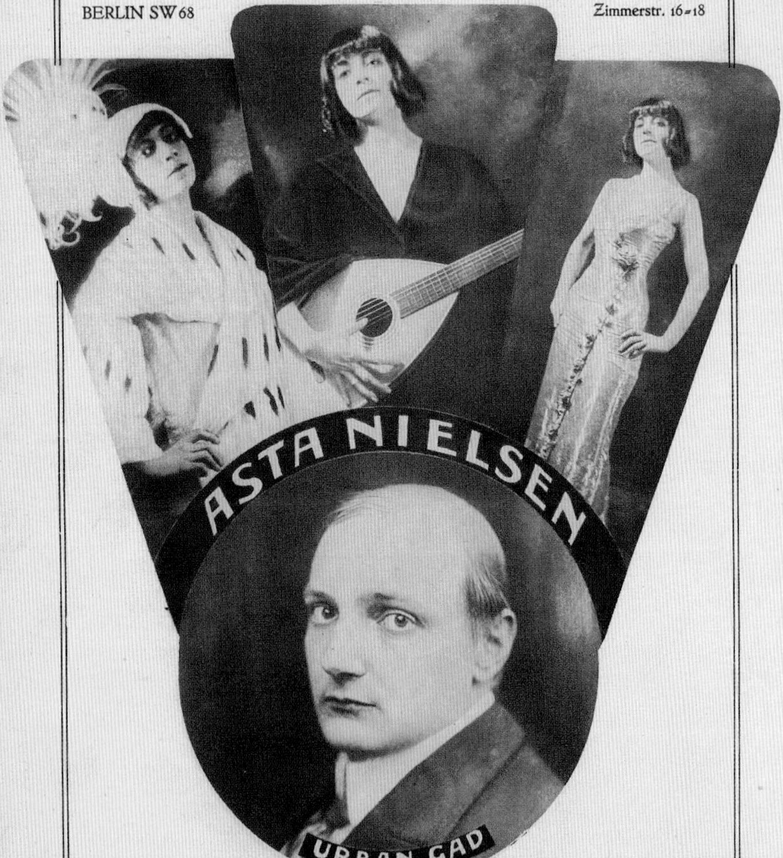

J·F·V·G J·F·V·G

Tiefdruck=Radio=Gravure Richard Falk, Berlin

Martin Loiperdinger

"Die Duse der Kino-Kunst"
Asta Nielsen's Berlin Made Brand

The film market in Germany ranked third in size only to that of the US and the UK and was first to see a systematic combination of the long-feature format with exclusive renting called *Monopolfilm* and branding the new product by using the name of the leading actress or actor. Introducing this innovation into film production, distribution and exhibition was an economic venture undertaken by film businessmen from Cologne, Frankfurt, Berlin and Vienna who engaged Asta Nielsen and Urban Gad exclusively for a period of three years to make 30 long-feature films. The contract was signed by the end of May 1911 in the office of Projektions-AG Union, Kaiserstrasse 64, Frankfurt. The film trade in Germany had already been suffering for three years from the overproduction of short films, inside and outside of the country. The Frankfurt contract with the artist couple from Denmark proved to be a decisive action to overcome the crisis by introducing a new film product which, in economic terms, worked very differently from selling short films. As always in the film business, the investments of film producers, distributors and exhibitors had to be amortised with considerable interest by box-office proceeds. It was the public that played the final and decisive role. Producers and distributors relied on exhibitors who booked their films with Asta Nielsen in the leading role, and exhibitors relied on audiences that flocked into the cinema theatres to watch Asta Nielsen on screen.

AFGRUNDEN, HEISSES BLUT, NACHTFALTER:
long-feature films with Asta Nielsen, 1910/11

The fundamental transformation of film as a commodity began in the Danish cinema industry in 1910. The transition from short films of a maximum length of one-reel to multiple-reel films started with Fotorama's DEN HVIDE SLAVE-HANDEL (THE WHITE SLAVE TRADE), which was 706 metres long and ran 35 minutes (when projected at 16 fps). Urban Gad, the artistic advisor and stage

---

Facing page:
Erste Internationale Film-Zeitung, no 23 (7 June 1913).

designer of Copenhagen's New Theatre, directed for the Copenhagen cinema theatre Kinografen an even longer film of 970 metres on the Danish-Prussian war, EN REKRUT FRA 64 (A RECRUIT OF 1864). And Gad wrote the script of the third Danish long-feature film, the erotic melodrama AFGRUNDEN (THE ABYSS), for his ensemble colleague Asta Nielsen. Gad's friend Hjalmar Davidsen, who owned the cinema theatre Kosmorama in Copenhagen, invested 8,000 crowns for a week's shooting in June of 1910. Asta Nielsen played Magda Vang who runs off with the 'cowboy' of a travelling variety theatre. On stage, she performs the highly erotic 'gaucho dance' with her lover. She ropes the 'cowboy' with her lasso and ties him up to make him suffer tantalising tortures while she dances around him, dressed in a long, tight leather skirt, sways with her hips, rubs her body against his – yet he must remain still and must not touch her. The couple is fired after an argument. Magda then earns money by playing the piano in cafés while the former 'cowboy' drinks away her money. During an argument she stabs him in self-defence.

Anticipating 'better audiences' by featuring actors from reputable Danish theatres, AFGRUNDEN was a 'sex and crime' drama intended only for adults. Asta Nielsen's debut film achieved a long run of seven weeks at the Kosmorama.[1] Davidsen sold exclusive rights to foreign countries.[2] He awarded the film distributor Ludwig Gottschalk, who owned the Düsseldorf Film-Manufaktur, the exclusive rights to distribute and exhibit AFGRUNDEN in Germany.[3]

Beginning on 16 November 1910, Gottschalk promoted AFGRUNDEN under the title ABGRÜNDE on the German market with an advertising campaign the likes of which had never before been seen for a single film.[4] Almost every week, up to January 1911, he ran numerous full-page text adverts in trade papers such as *Der Kinematograph*. Gottschalk offered German cinema owners the opportunity to secure the unrivalled premiere rights to this hit in their town for up to ten weeks.[5] Gottschalk demanded graduated prices for this offer, a tactic thus far unknown. Exhibitors who booked ABGRÜNDE could be certain that no other cinema in town could show this film at the same time. This exclusive mode of distribution was called *Monopolfilm*.[6] ABGRÜNDE was the first *Monopolfilm* to be distributed in Germany.

On 26 November 1910 the German premiere of ABGRÜNDE took place at the Palast-Theater in Düsseldorf. Gottschalk promised enormous box-office revenues if cinema owners decided to programme long-feature *Monopolfilms* for long periods of time. ABGRÜNDE ran for three weeks in Düsseldorf,[7] a unique occurrence at the end of 1910 for an extremely long single film with a running time of 45 minutes. It seems that ABGRÜNDE was an attraction for middle-class audiences influenced by the taste of Düsseldorf's community of artists:

> Up to now, it was assumed that all film dramas were 'kitsch'. But ABGRÜNDE, showing at the Palast-Theater, has all of a sudden made artists enthusiastic fans of cinema pantomime. [...] I have met almost no artist or actor there who had not seen ABGRÜNDE for the third, fourth, fifth or even the eighth time. [...] At any rate, ABGRÜNDE has contributed a great deal, if not the most, to turning the

conversation in society more than usual to film theatre and to leading people whom you would never expect to go to the cinema.[8]

To drum up business, the daily press printed large-format adverts, and local exhibitors highlighted the number of their screenings of ABGRÜNDE in their promotion of the film:

> The talk of the town in Cologne still remains the showing of the theatre drama ABGRÜNDE DES LEBENS, for everyone is full of enthusiasm about the fabulous true-to-life drama never before seen. By now, this fantastic drama has been shown 42 times in our Cologne cinema, and the crowds are still coming. So don't miss coming to our theatre named above.[9]

According to an advert two days later, ABGRÜNDE had already been screened 66 times (within only five days), in the two venues of the Cinéma-Palais, in Cologne.[10] In Breslau (today Wrocław, Poland), then the German centre of the Silesian border region, ABGRÜNDE was shown altogether 86 times in the 450-seat Palast-Theater, and in the Monopol-Theater, both owned by Franz Thiemer, who appparently 'bicycled' one print between his two theatres.[11] Introducing one-film showings with ABGRÜNDE was only another promising way to increase proceeds at the box-office. As entrance fees for these one-hour shows were equal to those for the usual two hours of short film programmes, exhibitors could double their income, at least for evening shows. After a while, Thiemer in Breslau programmed ABGRÜNDE this way in response to the great demand. To combine one-film showings and the 'bicycling' of reels between two venues was most promising – and was practiced not only in Breslau but also in Cologne and other cities.

The most convincing evidence for fundamental changes emerging in programming practices is the case of ABGRÜNDE in Hamburg. In 1910, Hamburg was an industrial agglomeration with a population of 1.2 million inhabitants. According to cinema adverts in the *Hamburger Fremden-Blatt*, there was obviously no print of ABGRÜNDE available for the Christmas 1910 programmes. Screenings of ABGRÜNDE in the Hamburg area started in the middle of January 1911, and by mid-March, the number of screenings had added up to altogether 223. No cinema programme or single film by far had previously been offered so many times to patrons in Hamburg over such a long period. The capacity of seats reserved by Hamburg cinema owners for possible audiences to watch ABGRÜNDE amounted to 184,182 seats.[12] What does that mean in respect to the potential audience in the Hamburg area? According to the 1910 census, about 35% of the German population was under fifteen years of age (and was banned from screenings of ABGRÜNDE); in addition, five per cent was over 65 and probably did not attend cinema showings at all. Taking this into account and applying it to the Hamburg area, we see a potential audience of up to 700,000; that is, one seat was available for every 3.8 potential patrons.[13] The major portion of this capacity was located in five cinemas owned by James Henschel who was called the 'cinema king' of Hamburg.

The Danish film industry made no further offers to Urban Gad and Asta Nielsen. Their next two films, HEISSES BLUT (BURNING BLOOD) and NACHT-

FALTER (RETRIBUTION), were produced by the Deutsche Bioscop in Berlin. HEISSES BLUT was distributed as a so-called *Terminfilm*, so that every cinema owner was free to order the film and was guaranteed to receive it on the announced release date. Deutsche Bioscop placed full-page adverts in trade papers, sometimes even on the cover pages, from 11 March 1911 onward, announcing 22 April as the day on which this "Weltschlager" (world hit) would be released.[14] For interested parties, Deutsche Bioscop offered daily showings of the film at its premises in Berlin at 10 am and 5 pm.[15] Distributors avidly took up this offer. From the end of March to the end of May 1911, altogether 19 companies advertised in the trade journal *Erste Internationale Filmzeitung* prints of HEISSES BLUT which they had bought from Deutsche Bioscop to rent them out to cinemas. Martin Dentler, distributor and cinema owner from Brunswick, offered ten prints, and the Deutsche Film-Gesellschaft, Cologne, offered five prints for rent.[16] Two weeks later Martin Dentler had already made contracts for eight first-run weeks. It took him three more weeks to place the two remaining first-run weeks with his customers.[17] At this time, that is five weeks after the first advert, Martin Dentler still had three second-run weeks on offer. HEISSES BLUT was in demand by the cinema owners, but the second long-feature film with Asta Nielsen was not exactly snatched from the distributors. As it was, her name was not yet to play a role. The Deutsche Bioscop focussed on the title of the film. In its first advert the company asked the rhetorical question: "Do you like the title?", and maintained: "You will like the film even better!"[18] In their adverts, the 19 distributors advertised in most cases the length of 860 metres along with the film title. Only Martin Dentler mentions Asta Nielsen and Urban Gad in some adverts, both in respect to ABGRÜNDE.

On 13 May 1911, only three weeks after HEISSES BLUT, Asta Nielsen's third film, NACHTFALTER, was released by the Aktien-Gesellschaft für Kinematographie und Filmverleih [Stock Company for Cinematography and Film Distribution] in Strasbourg. The largest German film company had bought the exclusive rights for Germany and the world from the producer, the Deutsche Bioscop. Rental prices were fixed from 40 pfennigs per metre for the first-run week to 10 pfennigs per metre for the 11th-run week.[19] The adverts focused again on the title, but also stated that Asta Nielsen would play the leading role:

> Asta Nielsen, the famous Danish actress, plays the leading role in this pictorial drama. There's no need to explain to film consumers who Asta Nielsen is. The connoisseur knows and understands the significance of this dramatic artist who has already earned everlasting laurels with her creation of true-to-life figures in THE ABYSS and in BURNING BLOOD.[20]

This advert sheds some light on the emerging film star Asta Nielsen. In his advertising campaign, Ludwig Gottschalk had underlined the author's part by announcing ABGRÜNDE as "theatre drama in 2 acts by Urban Gad".[21] Only in his last advert did he mention for the first time six 'main personae', featuring "famous members from Copenhagen theatres". First on the list was Asta

Nielsen in the role of Magda Vang.[22] After the debut film ABGRÜNDE had become a box-office success, promotion for her third film placed Asta Nielsen in the foreground without saying one word about her writer-director yet. A later advert even calls Asta Nielsen the "Schöpferin der ABGRÜNDE "(creator of ABGRÜNDE).[23] With these words, author's credit was given to the leading actress. After the breathtaking box-office success of ABGRÜNDE in Germany, this clearly indicates a shift in importance from the writer-director (Urban Gad) to the actress who played the main character (Asta Nielsen).[24] This shift grows from the positive audience response to ABGRÜNDE. The entire film industry – producers, distributors and exhibitors – immediately reacted by creating an innovative business model to incite and exploit the public's enthusiasm for the Danish actress. The idea of making Asta Nielsen a film star was just around the corner.

Mülleneisen's coup: the exclusive engagement, May 1911

On 22 June 1911, in the column "Continental Notes", the British trade journal *The Bioscope* informed readers on upcoming film productions in Germany:

> The Internationale Film Vertrieb Gesselschaft [sic], whose headquarters are in Vienna, has opened a branch at Frankfurt a/M. The well-known writer Urban Gad and the Asta Nielson [sic] Company of artists have undertaken to produce fresh subjects for the above-named firm in the immediate future.[25]

What was behind this news? The above-mentioned advert for NACHTFALTER informed readers that the exclusive rights for ABGRÜNDE for Austria-Hungary were held by the Lichtspiel-Gesellschaft in Cologne.[26] The owner of this company was Christoph Mülleneisen Sr. He ran several cinemas in the Western parts of Germany, and he was the film distributor who gave Asta Nielsen's career the decisive turn. Her autobiography calls him "Mr. X". Mülleneisen devised for the exploitation of future Asta Nielsen films a business model to introduce the star system to the German film industry and, with his successful coup, provided "an example still impressive today in its professionalism, visionary elegance and audacity".[27]

With his two *Monopolfilms*, HEISSES BLUT and NACHTFALTER, Mülleneisen encountered diverging reactions in Vienna and Budapest. Regardless of the success of ABGRÜNDE, the distributors wanted nothing to do with Asta Nielsen. The cinema owners, however, were prepared to pay almost the complete copy sales price as rental fee just for the first week. Mülleneisen had, as he himself said, "the satisfaction of seeing what Asta Nielsen was worth to the public".[28] He effected Asta Nielsen's prolonged engagement with the Deutsche Bioscop, with which he concluded at the same time a "contingency contract" for exclusive distribution of future films in Europe outside Austria. Mülleneisen evidently pursued the idea of exclusive film distribution, that is, trade with exclusive screening rights linked to expanding the production monopoly to the work of the sought-after film actress. However, Asta Nielsen was initially engaged by Deutsche Bioscop for further filming as it was customary at the time, only by the month, June and August. For the free months of July and

After signing the ground-breaking contract. Sitting left: Asta Nielsen; to her right Christoph Mülleneisen Sr., cinema owner and film trader from Cologne. Standing from left to right: Erich Zeiske, head of Deutsche Bioscop; Dr jur Kühnelt, manager of Österreichisch-Ungarische Kino-Industrie Gesellschaft; Urban Gad; Paul Davidson, head of PAGU. [Deutsche Kinemathek.]

September, she had already signed a contract with the Danish Nordisk Film. Mülleneisen recognised the risk for his lofty plans. To retrieve the intended monopoly on the acting achievements of Asta Nielsen, he travelled immediately to Copenhagen. He attempted to effect a dissolution of the engagement with Nordisk, failed, however, because of the hard-line position of the Danish competition. But he did succeed in concluding an eleven-day temporary contract with Urban Gad and Asta Nielsen to engage them exclusively for several years.

To acquire an associate and partner for his ambitious plans, Mülleneisen immediately conducted personal negotiations with Erich Zeiske, the manager of Deutsche Bioscop, with the Strasbourg Stock Company for Cinematography and Film Distribution as well as with the Austro-Hungarian film industry. As he himself vividly described three years later, Mülleneisen was underway without interruption eleven days and nights between Copenhagen and Lugano, Vienna, Strasbourg, Frankfurt am Main and Berlin.[29] Three days before the expiration of the temporary contract, he received confirmation from Vienna and from Deutsche Bioscop in Berlin, pledges which were in no way sufficient financially. By telephone, Paul Davidson, manager of the PAGU, agreed to participate in negotiations. Mülleneisen called Urban Gad and Asta Nielsen to Frankfurt am Main to the offices of PAGU. In her autobiography Asta Nielsen offers a graphic description of the course of the negotiations.[30] They threatened to fail because the actress insisted on receiving a third of the films' box-office take. Asta Nielsen remained adamant – the consortium of film businessmen agreed only after a long tug of war. The Danish artist couple committed themselves to collaborating exclusively on ten long-feature films each year over a period of three years. Asta Nielsen was to play the leading role in each film, and Urban Gad was to write the script and direct. On 27 May 1911, in Frankfurt am Main, Mülleneisen Sr., PAGU and Österreichisch- Ungarische Kino-Industrie founded the Internationale Films-Vertrieb- Gesellschaft (IFVG), with headquarters in Vienna. They named Paul Davidson as managing director. Before the First World War, Asta Nielsen and Urban Gad made altogether 29 films with Deutsche Bioscop and PAGU respectively – they almost completely fulfilled the three-year contract. Unfortunately, this important contract must be considered lost.

Three exclusive 'Asta Nielsen series', 1911–1914

By "proclamation" on 7 June 1911 in the trade journal *Der Kinematograph*, the German exhibitors received immediate news of the founding of the company and the commitment of the artistic couple.[31] Six weeks later, on 19 July 1911, came the announcement of the first two *Monopolfilms* for the season 1911/12 – with a bang. The new company intended to make a turnover of 1,400,000 marks by distributing *Monopolfilms* with Asta Nielsen up to 3 February 1912. "That's gutsy!" chimed the advertisement.[32] Banking on the appeal of Asta Nielsen and Urban Gad, IVFG, however, had "no fear of placing this bet".[33] The film businessmen concluded from the resounding success of ABGRÜNDE, HEISSES BLUT and NACHTFALTER that Asta Nielsen guaranteed the value of their future films for the entertainment needs of the public. Asta Nielsen and Urban Gad, "both of these names have gone into the flesh and blood of cinema-goers and guarantee full houses!!" claimed the advert.[34] At Deutsche Bioscop "700,000 running metres of Nielsen films were ordered at 1 mark per running metre for 1911 and 1912".[35]

The distribution of the films produced with Urban Gad and Asta Nielsen was organised in exclusive 'Asta Nielsen series'. The first 'Asta Nielsen series' in the 1911/12 season comprised eight films, followed by eight films in the second series in 1912/13 and by seven films in the third series in 1913/14. There were seven more films made in 1914, which were released in Germany only in the 1915/16 season because of the First World War. The first film of the first series was DEN SORTE DRØM (DER SCHWARZE TRAUM, THE CIRCUS GIRL) which was bought from the Danish producer Fotorama to avoid harmful local competition against the exclusivity of the first 'Asta Nielsen series'. Apart from ABGRÜNDE, HEISSES BLUT and NACHTFALTER, which had already been circulating for some time, exclusivity was still threatened by another fresh Danish long-feature film with Asta Nielsen available on the free market: BALLETDANSERINDEN (BRENNENDE TRIEBE, THE BALLET DANCER), which Nordisk Film was not willing to give away for exclusive distribution by the IFVG.

Branding a series of exclusive long-feature films with the name of the actress who played the leading role was a ground-breaking innovation in the film trade. Films which belonged to an 'Asta Nielsen series' were 'Asta Nielsen films' – and thus a new film commodity was introduced to the market requiring a new habit of cinema going: films which were made attractive for mass consumption not by subject, genre, plot or action but by the actress whose appearances on screen characterised them as being *her* films, 'Asta Nielsen films'. Thus Asta Nielsen was made the star of this undertaking and, as such, had to ensure that exhibitors booked the exclusive 'Asta Nielsen series' in advance, even before the films were produced – the only way to get their hands on fresh 'Asta Nielsen films'. The star needed to be promoted. First of all, the brand 'Asta Nielsen' was equipped with a resounding epithet: In the above-mentioned advert of 19 July 1911, Asta Nielsen is called "die Duse der Kinokunst" (the Duse of cinema art) for the first time, equating her with Eleonora Duse, the world-famous Italian theatre diva. This epithet was invented by Arthur Mellini, chief editor of the German trade journal *Lichtbild-Bühne*, a man who had been hired for the promotion of the first 'Asta Nielsen series'.

The sale of the 'Asta Nielsen series' was conducted by travelling salesmen who transacted contracts with exhibitors concerning the respective series. As early as the first "proclamation" of 7 June 1911, it says: "Do you want to have your theatre sold out daily in the 1910/11 season? Then don't sign a contract for *Monopolfilms* before the representative of Internationale Films-Vertrieb-Gesellschaft has paid you a visit in the very near future".[36] Following the announcement of the release dates of the first two *Monopolfilms*, the second advert promised "Our general representatives are underway!"[37] Large-scale advertisement campaigns in the trade press, as was otherwise customary for *Monopolfilms* and *Terminfilms*, were not run for the first 'Asta Nielsen series'. The customers who had booked the entire series sight unseen for one of ten weeks learned of the dates for their films according to the contract. In the trade journal *Der Kinematograph*, only four adverts were published for the first 'Asta Nielsen series'. On 11 October 1911, an unadorned portrait photo of Asta Nielsen and enthusiastic news about the initial success of the 'Asta Nielsen series' attempted to encourage exhibitors to book the whole series of "10 Monopol-Films" in advance.[38] In contrast, the third advert on 28 February 1912 was full of confidence: A pyramid-like graphic showed the exhibitors the foundation of their business success and announced in the form of a question the last building block, the eighth film of the 'Asta Nielsen series'.[39] The last advert flirts with self-satisfaction with only one sentence: "Nobody can explain the unequalled monumental success of the Asta Nielsen series".[40]

Along with the customary advertising material such as posters, stills, programme booklets, the exhibitors' promotional adverts in the local press played an important role. An article by Mellini in the *Lichtbild-Bühne* offers the cinema owners tips with good and bad examples for designing an effective newspaper advert.[41] The cinema adverts on the newspaper pages which published the

"Die Duse der Kino-Kunst". Asta Nielsen's Berlin Made Brand

Advert for the first 'Asta Nielsen series'. *Der Kinematograph*, no. 270 (28 February 1912).

Advert announcing a slide promoting the 'Asta Nielsen series', addressed to cinema owners. *Der Kinematograph*, no. 313 (25 December 1912).

> A few remarks about Asta Nielsen:
>
> The name awakens great enthusiasm in the hearts of those who were able to marvel at this incomparable artist in ABGRÜNDE, in HEISSES BLUT or even NACHTFALTER. This woman seems to possess a sheer supernatural power; she can do anything in any situation, "as if written for her and her alone". Whether the artist is playing a loving wife, a hapless mother or the fallen lover of a degenerate fellow, she always knows how to enthral the viewer with her vital acting. She portrays a lady of high society with the same mastery as that of a dancer or a circus rider who storms through the ring on her white horse. For everyone who has seen it, the boundless expression of her eyes remains unforgettable; those eyes can tell more than the loveliest words; their portrayal artistry removes all hindrances, eyes capable of replacing the most artistic speech with only a few movements. She has reached the zenith of her own artistry because she never gives more than she should, never too little, never too much and, at the height of emotion, she can always add a crowning touch. Never to exaggerate, that is the greatest of arts, and she possesses that art to the utmost degree.
>
> During the season 1911/12, the public will be offered ten new films in which Asta Nielsen plays the starring role, directed by her ideally matched author, Urban Gad. Asta Nielsen, who knows how to bring her fellow actors to unheard-of masterly achievement through her inspiring acting, and the circumspect yet relaxed directing by Urban Gad, who does not overlook even the smallest detail – all this offers the best guarantee for dramatic and acting quality in the film. Technically as well, this film is on a level which has never before been achieved. Brilliant photogrammes, mostly hand in hand with well-shaded tinting which always sets the right mood, turn hours into minutes for the delighted viewers, who never tire from the tension-filled images undisturbed by flickering or dancing about. The eyes of the viewers follow the continually mounting dramatic situations.
>
> Asta Nielsen received a fee of 85,000 marks for playing in these ten *Monopolfilm* dramas, the so-called "Asta Nielsen Series" (filmed over about 5 months).
>
> I have secured for Trier the rights to the first showings *of all Asta Nielsen* dramas rom the Internationale Film-Gesellschaft, [recte: Internationale Films-Vertrieb-Gesellschaft, IFVG], and, with these works of cinematographic art obtained only at colossal cost and licence fees, I promise my guests artistic pleasure as they might be offered only in the *pre-eminent theatres of the world*.
>
> A picture will appear every month. (…)
>
> Increased prices: Preferred seating: 100 p., 2nd rank seating: 70 p., 3rd rank seating: 50 p.
>
> School children under age 14 are not admitted to the showings.
>
> ---
> From the cinema advert of Peter Marzen's Central-Theater, Trier, for DER SCHWARZE TRAUM, first film of the first 'Asta Nielsen series'.

announcements for local entertainment offers such as theatre, variety shows, concerts, lectures and cinema programmes were, in fact, clearly larger and more elaborate, as can be demonstrated, for example, in the case of Mannheim.[42] Some cinema owners took over texts passages from the information material the distributors provided to familiarise their local audience with the special features of the innovative film commodity of the 'Asta Nielsen series'. For example, the cinema owner Peter Marzen in Trier placed an advert of almost an entire newspaper page for DER SCHWARZE TRAUM to announce the new programme format of the 'Asta Nielsen series' and to introduce Asta Nielsen as the new type of an enormously versatile actress.

In contrast to short film series with cowboys, detectives or comics, who remained in a single genre with always recognisable roles, the 'Asta Nielsen series' followed the principle of variety. With each new film, the audience saw the star of the series in a new role. Apart from one historical drama, the first 'Asta Nielsen series' admittedly consisted of social dramas which, with one exception, ended tragically and founded Asta Nielsen's reputation as a 'great tragedienne'. To demonstrate to the audience on an emotional level the depths to which the leading lady falls, the dramatics of these films inserted humorous accents as well. Furthermore, Asta Nielsen played a diversity of social characters: In the first 'Asta Nielsen series' she played in turn a circus rider, a serving maid, an home worker, a Gypsy girl, the daughter of an English nobleman, the daughter of a French count, a country girl, a proletarian girl in Berlin as well as an office clerk in a Berlin architect's office. Her roles were similarly diversified in the second and in the third 'Asta Nielsen series', which expanded the genre canon of social dramas and morality films by a 'comedy of errors' (JUGEND UND TOLLHEIT, IN A FIX), a topical drama set in the Balkans (DAS MÄDCHEN OHNE VATERLAND, A GIRL WITHOUT A COUNTRY), a political social drama set in England (DIE SUFFRAGETTE, THE SUFFRAGETTE), a teenage comedy (ENGELEIN, UP TO HER TRICKS) and an adventure comedy set in the mountains of Italy (ZAPATAS BANDE, ZAPATA'S GANG).[43] Thus, IFVG and PAGU presented the newly branded commodity in widely varied fashion for a week's run every four to six weeks to the buyers of the 'Asta Nielsen series' and their audiences.

Local case studies of cities in south-west Germany demonstrate that this system worked very well in large cities with more than 100,000 inhabitants such as Mannheim and Saarbrücken. All three 'Asta Nielsen series' were also shown in Metz, a garrison city of 68,000 inhabitants, but only the first series was booked in Trier, a garrison city of 50,000 inhabitants.[44] Further research into local distribution may outline the limits of the 'Asta Nielsen series' business model in environments where exhibitors were not able to rely on audiences large enough to return the investments required to screen an exclusive 'Asta Nielsen series'. Anyway, in many large cities of the German Empire, the Asta Nielsen series had no trouble with sales because the films could be shown in the first week in the Union-Theaters of the PAGU. The PAGU commissioned Deutsche Bioscop, which manufactured the first and second 'Asta Nielsen series'; the third one was manufactured by PAGU itself. The distribution was handled by the IFVG, which had been founded by PAGU and its partners. PAGU's head, Paul Davidson, was also head of IFVG. PAGU's Union-Theater chain was the first buyer of the three 'Asta Nielsen series', which means that PAGU actually anticipated what was later called 'vertical integration', in the Hollywood studio system.

Asta Nielsen – a Berlin Actress in Berlin's Union-Theater Chain

In the early 1910s, Berlin, capital of the German Empire, was a city of nearly four million people, third in the world to London and New York.[45] The PAGU Union-Theater, U.T. for short, was the largest cinema chain in Germany. As in other large cities, the well-equipped Union-Theater cinemas were centrally located in Berlin as well and appealed to all levels of the public. Every new Asta

Asta Nielsen in her home. Picture post card.

Nielsen film was placed on the programme in all Union-Theater cinemas in Berlin for one week at the same time. In the 1911/12 season, while the first 'Asta Nielsen series' was running, the five Union-Theater cinemas in Berlin had, according to their own adverts, up to 14,000 viewers daily.[46] In 1913 four additional Union-Theater houses were founded in Berlin. From 1912 to 1914, the weekly *Union-Theater-Zeitung* was published every Saturday, the day of programme change. Chief editor Paul Ehren addressed the patrons of Berlin's five Union-Theater houses as "a large community".[47] An examination of the available years of the *Union-Theater-Zeitung*, 1912 and 1913, indicates that Asta Nielsen was presented as the definitive star persona of Berlin's Union-Theater chain. No one else appears in the programme overviews or film descriptions of the *Union-Theater-Zeitung* so often or so regularly. Each Asta Nielsen Film

> ### All Round the Cinema
>
> Chief Superintendent of Police von Jagow has been kind enough to issue a permit for an extremely dangerous cinema shooting taking place on Monday, 1 April. From 1:00 to 1:30 p.m., he will personally carry out a strict blockade of Friedrichstrasse at the corner of Leipzigerstrasse with the assistance of 60 policemen. Following prolonged negotiations, the Traffic Commissioner's office at police headquarters has just now given the long-sought written approval. In the sensational film 'Opfermut einer Mutter' (a mother's willingness to make sacrifices), now in preparation, wild lions play an important role. Sitting on one of the circus wagons coming into the city is the lion tamer, who has an unrequited passionate for the married daughter (Asta Nielsen) of the circus director. Unsuspectingly, she goes with her small child behind the wagon, and suddenly the lion tamer opens the cage doors in his insane jealousy, and two wild beasts jump onto the street, empty of people because of the blockade. The two lions start to attack the child, but mother love lends the courageous Asta Nielsen superhuman strength. A mighty struggle ensues; the attacked mother succeeds in driving the beasts back into the cage, and mother and child are saved. The dehumanised lion tamer sees that his horrible plan has failed and flees into Kronenstrasse. – Incidentally, Ms. Nielsen will be in no danger, for the scene has been carefully rehearsed in the Sarransani Circus for several weeks. The lions have become so sweet-natured by the ingratiating personage of the great artist that their bestial nature will not assert itself against her. – The business owners on Friedrichstrasse, corner of Leipzigerstrasse have already received instructions from the police to leave their shutters closed during the critical half hour. Electric trams and omnibuses are to be diverted. The government will have
>
> April Fool's Joke. *Union-Theater-Zeitung* 1:3 (29 March – 5 April 1912): 15.

received an announcement, some an additional advert as well as a detailed description in the column "The story in the film". Remarkably, neither Asta Nielsen films nor other long-feature films are prominent in the programme lists published in the *Union-Theater-Zeitung*; rather they are listed as just a number in the film programmes, which contained up to nine "numbers". Only at the end of March 1913 was the title of an Asta Nielsen film printed in boldface and emphasised in capital letters for the first time with DER TOD IN SEVILLA (SPANISH BLOOD), something which became the rule from then on. Each film programme of the Berlin Union-Theater chain featured from then on, emphasised in conspicuous letters, a main film or a so-called hit. In addition, stills from Asta Nielsen films displaying the actress were placed in the newspaper remarkably often – with or without the addition of a text.

Marketing and public relations clearly focussed on the visible Asta Nielsen – Urban Gad was kept in the background. He wrote and directed the 29 Asta Nielsen films made under the exclusive contract signed by both Nielsen and Gad.[48] In the *Union-Theater-Zeitung* credits, the programmes of the Berlin Union-Theater chain listed Asta Nielsen "in the starring role", and it was only from 20 February 1913 onward that Gad's authorship was given credit with the phrase "by Urban Gad" added to the title and genre of the Asta Nielsen films.[49] The film descriptions either do not mention Urban Gad at all or just mention him as a helping hand, who, for example, wrote for Asta Nielsen "the very roles for this sensuous actress".[50] True, the chief editor Paul Ehren wrote a double-page cover essay on "Regiekunst" (the art of directing) dedicated to Urban Gad as the writer-director who, "modestly remains in the shadows".

Ehren claims: "Urban Gad, the Danish writer, is the master of the modern art of film directing." The essay underlines Gad's "art of lighting effects" (which may also be attributed to the cameraman, Guido Seeber), and his mastery in arranging location shootings (which may once again be attributed to Guido Seeber).[51] Urban Gad remains invisible in the background. An unusual exception to this marketing practice is an IFVG advert in the trade journal *Erste Internationale Filmzeitung* which shows Asta Nielsen in three figures somehow emerging from Urban Gad's head: the leading actress as the brainchild of the writer-director![52] It goes without saying that Urban Gad's backstage status in the marketing of the 'Asta Nielsen series' also seduced film historians into focussing quite exclusively on Asta Nielsen and leaving her partner behind the scenes.[53]

The editors of the *Union-Theater-Zeitung* cover and promote Asta Nielsen as a star persona even without referring to any of her films in distribution. At the end of March 1912, the *Union-Theater-Zeitung* announced sensational filming out on the Berlin streets: With her bare hands Asta Nielsen has to drive two released lions back into their cage – a successful April Fool's joke![54] In April, the newspaper featured a full-page photograph titled "Die Duse der Kino-Kunst" showing "Asta Nielsen in her home" (as the caption states) standing before a mirror as if she were checking her dress before going out for an evening's entertainment. A chandelier visible in the mirror symbolises prosperity. A further caption adds to a number of attributes which indicate her status:

> The famous Danish actress, whom audiences will see today in a new film drama, enjoys unchallenged popularity. Her acting, the vivid expression of her gestures, have earned her the honorary title of a 'Duse of cinematic art', and the films in which the 'Asta' plays have become her own popular brand for the literary connoisseur of the cinema. The celebrated tragedienne, whose achievements are honoured with enormous fees, has now returned from a study trip in Spain and sends the readers of the U.T.Z. this portrait and best regards from her Copenhagen home.[55]

One month after this remarkable exhibition of Asta Nielsen's ostensible privacy in Copenhagen, promising news followed that "Asta Nielsen, our famous Copenhagen actress and film tragedienne, has taken such a liking to Berlin that she is considering exchanging her residence in her northern home country for Berlin".[56] And after two months, she finally fully arrived in Berlin:

> The 'Duse of cinematic art' has now furnished a cosy as well as tasteful home, and the colourful, diversified life of the young cosmopolitan metropolis of Berlin is just the right place to chase away not only the last remains of home sickness but also to learn to love the new home more and more.[57]

If that was not enough, Asta Nielsen "has also become a citizen of busy, industrious Berlin […] to add to the glamour of the city herself", for example, to make new Asta Nielsen films. "Thus Asta Nielsen is very industrious, is making surprising progress in learning German, which she earlier considered 'wery hart' and, as a soon completely acclimated Berliner, has asked us to send

Compassion. "Oh Gosh – how deep down this Asta Nielsen must wash herself".
Union-Theater-Zeitung 1:30 (12–18 October 1912).

her kindest regards to her new countrymen".[58] The Danish émigré 'now belongs' and has been taken into the community of Berlin because she has moved to Berlin to work. With the expression "new countrymen" the public relations office of the Berlin Union-Theater had raised the residence change from Copenhagen to Berlin to an internal metamorphosis of citizenship: as if Asta Nielsen, through her move, had changed her Danish nationality to a kind of Berlin nationality, distinguished by her special diligence. Thus Asta Nielsen then became predestined to play Berlin characters in Berlin. At the end of September 1912, DIE KINDER DES GENERALS (FALSELY ACCUSED) was introduced to Berlin audiences as a "heimatlicher Film" (home-based film): "Asta Nielsen plays a Berlin child in this film, a brave, clever and proud girl." But not only that:

> For the first time Asta Nielsen is playing *in* Berlin. We have, however, already seen her in dramas where the Berlin streets served as the milieu; but now she is here for the first time in the Berlin marches; Berlin's surroundings appear before our eyes and with those realistic details that only film can express; we can take in the whole atmosphere emanating from this, in a sense, home-based film.[59]

Between the spring of 1912 and the autumn of 1913, in the public relations

> **To the Editor,**
>
> In the paper what I like, the *Berliner Morgenpost*, I just read the bosses at the U.T. Kintop have a newspaper of theirs own. I were glad to hear that, cause I go to the pictures in Wedding evry week with my other half and our littluns and it's a bit embarrassin when me people ask me fings I don't know about them films wot we watched. I mean, wot do I know about them foreign lands shown in them pictures? I didn't learn nofing about all that at my rubbish ol school! So I want to kindly ask the honourable editors that they might please explain them pictures properly in their paper. See, how it is with my boy, he's learnin more at school now than I ever learnt them 30 years ago! But still, he don't learn nofing about them foreign lands neither. And then there's that Asta Nielsen. They really got somefing going there, right! My girl, she's doin her apprenticeship in some department store, but she wants to play Asta Nielsen, of all people! On Sundys, all the day, she stands front the mirror and plays wot she seen in the films. O course, I gave her wot for. I mean, wot's a department store apprentice sposed to do with all that? She'd be better off usin her time to help her ol mum doin the dinner. Still, tis nice when she pretends to be Asta Nielsen, so touchin, that girl! And we can always hardly wait for Saturday night, when the newest film with Asta comes. Anyway, back to the grindstone for me, now, but I have a look forward to your paper!
>
> *August Bäcker, locksmith*
>
> **Answer from the Editor**
>
> Our column "The story in the film" will show you that we have followed your suggestion. Where your daughter is concerned, we do not in the least doubt her talent, which we do not know about. Let the young lady play "film". One can't start too early to become an Asta Nielsen!
>
> Letter to the editor, written in Berlin dialect. *Union-Theater-Zeitung* 1:1 (16–22 March 1912): 5

statements of the *Union-Theater-Zeitung*, Asta Nielsen mutated from a foreign Danish actress to a "fully acclimated Berliner" among her Berlin compatriots. Why this advertising campaign was conducted remains open to speculation and might be answered by further historical research. Did chief editor Paul Ehren think it was disadvantageous to her popularity with the Berlin audience to promote an actress from a foreign country as a foreigner? In any case, it is a fact that the public relations department of the Union-Theater used the occasion of Asta Nielsen's move from Copenhagen to Berlin to make the star of the 'Asta Nielsen series' produced in the Berlin area more accessible to Berlin audiences.

Not only the content but also the persistence of the Asta Nielsen brand was cultivated very carefully by the editors of the *Union-Theater-Zeitung*. For the readers of this newspaper who attended the Union-Theater, it was just a matter of course to encounter Asta Nielsen again and again. The difference between the in-the-flesh presence on the stage and the technical reproduction of the cinematographic image on the screen was thus obliterated. She was announced as if she were a theatre diva: "The highly celebrated artist will appear before audiences today in her role in the Balkans film drama DAS MÄDCHEN OHNE VATERLAND (A GIRL WITHOUT A COUNTRY)" reads the caption of a full-page photographic portrait.[60] The *Union-Theater-Zeitung* stylised Asta Nielsen as a greatly honoured resident of the Union-Theater houses who regularly appeared to her cult following – not on the balcony of a palace but on the screens of the cinema chain.

Ambivalent audience response

Pointers to the audience's attitude toward Asta Nielsen hardly appear in the *Union-Theater-Zeitung*. A letter from a locksmith invented by the editors, written in Berlin dialect refers to Asta Nielsen and her audience right in the first issue: The daughter, apprentice in a department store, allegedly stands in front of the mirror all day Sunday and imitates Asta Nielsen.[61] This fictional story corresponds to the report of a cinema reformer who attended the second examination of Asta Nielsen's debut film ABGRÜNDE at Berlin police headquarters:

> This film was released by the censors only after a fairly lewd scene – a gaucho dance representing a disgustingly sensual belly dance – was cut. Where the film (it comes from Denmark) has been permitted to be shown unrestrictedly, it can happen (as in Hamburg) that young girls can be seen to practice these snake-like belly movements in the street.[62]

A prize competition by the Union-Theater asking cinema goers to write literary film descriptions brought in "hundreds of submissions", but only three of them were fit to print. As an "interesting aside", the editors stated, "that the greater number of writers by far had turned their interest to the Asta Nielsen films".[63] At the end of 1913, the audience magazine *Illustrierte Kino-Woche* conducted a survey among the presumably mostly women readers about their favourite film actor. The winner far and away was the Danish male actor Valdemar Psilander with 382 votes, followed by Asta Nielsen with 271 votes and by Henny Porten with 258 votes.[64] Six months before this survey, Emilie Altenloh, a Heidelberg student of economics under the supervision of Alfred Weber, concluded her dissertation *Zur Soziologie des Kino. Die Kino-Unternehmung und die sozialen Schichten ihrer Besucher* [On the sociology of the cinema. Cinema companies and the social classes of their viewers]. She conducted her audience survey in Mannheim during the 1911/12 season as an outsider and may thus be considered an unprejudiced observer of cinema theatres in the early 1910s. Altenloh called the "Asta Nielsen dramas" "Kassen-Stücke" (box-office hits).[65] The interest of the inner city audience in the cinema theatres centred around these hits, whereas the number of viewers for the Asta Nielsen film ZU TODE GEHETZT (DRIVEN OUT) in a Mannheim suburban cinema declined:

> If we consider those programmes which proved to be especially popular, the success can be traced for the most part to certain dramas. For example, without exception, the Asta Nielsen dramas were the preferred ones in the inner city cinemas. (In contrast, the effect was the reverse in the suburbs. The number of viewers sank even below the average for the film ZU TODE GEHETZT, with Asta Nielsen in the leading role).[66]

In her categorisation of individual classes, Altenloh underscores twice 16- and 17-year-old "Gehilfen im Kaufmannsstand" (shop assistants), who go to the cinema "extremely often", that they named "most frequently" Asta Nielsen films when asked about their favourite films.[67] The shop assistants have "a quite pronounced class consciousness" and "are looking for any ways to differentiate themselves from workers: [...] For example, they never go to the small cinemas in the suburbs".[68] They are among the patrons of the cinema theatres in the city centre of Mannheim.

A series of clues points to the fact that Asta Nielsen polarised the cinema-going audiences in Germany.[69] This may have limited her box-office records in some sectors of the cinema business in Germany as well as her popularity among some classes of the cinema-going public. Audience response to Asta Nielsen films and to Asta Nielsen as star persona in Germany is a difficult task belonging to further research. The texts of numerous contemporary publications of essays in magazines and film reviews in the daily and trade press should be critically examined to explore the profile of German public discourse about Asta Nielsen. However, texts inspired by distributor and cinema advertising must be strictly distinguished from statements by independent authors. Conversely, the varied distribution and exhibition in different regions, localities and social milieus can be *indirectly* established by the popularity of Asta Nielsen films with audiences in Germany.[70] Apart from the statements by the large number of professional writers und teachers, comments by the cinema audiences referring directly to Asta Nielsen and her films were seldom printed.[71] It is therefore all the more important to investigate answers to prize contests and surveys as well as letters to the editor, likewise unpublished reports by cinema viewers written for local authorities or clubs involved with supervision of the cinemas. Asta Nielsen polarised. She had fans – and detractors ... .

Notes

1. In the Kosmorama, AFGRUNDEN was screened from 12 September to 30 October 1910, with 10 to 13 showings daily, according to local newspaper adverts (information kindly provided by Stephan Michael Schröder, e-mail to the author, 17 March 2009).
2. See Andrzej Debski's, Outi Hupaniittu's and Lauri Piispa's essays in this volume for the example of Russia, including the Grand Duchy of Finland and the Polish territories.
3. See Marguerite Engberg. *Filmstjernen Asta Nielsen* (Aarhus, Klim 1999), 53–54.
4. See in detail Martin Loiperdinger, "*Afgrunden* in Germany: *monopolfilm*, cinema-going and the emergence of the film star Asta Nielsen", in Daniel Biltereyst, Richard Maltby and Philippe Meers (eds), *Cinema, Audiences and Modernity. New perspectives on European cinema history* (London: Routledge, 2012), 142–153.
5. *Der Kinematograph*, no. 204 (23 November 1910).
6. The German word 'Monopolfilm' has no English equivalent. Rachael Low uses the term 'exclusive film' in her ground-breaking *The History of the British Film, 1906–1914* (London, George Allen & Unwin, 1949), 42–49. According to Low, the first film handled in Britain as an exclusive was Nordisk Film's IN THE HANDS OF IMPOSTORS (DEN HVIDE SLAVEHANDELS SIDSTE OFFER), in March 1911.
7. According to the adverts from the Düsseldorf Palast-Theater, ABGRÜNDE had a run of three weeks. See the adverts in *Düsseldorfer Neueste Nachrichten*, no. 276 (26 November 1910) and no. 288 (10 December 1911).
8. Niko, "Düsseldorf im Januar 1911", *Kinematograph*, no. 213 (25 January 1911).
9. Advert from the Cinéma-Palais and Theater Hohe Pforte 10, *Stadt-Anzeiger* (Cologne), no. 555 (6 December 1910).
10. Advert from the Cinéma-Palais and Theater Hohe Pforte 10, *Stadt-Anzeiger* (Cologne), no. 559 (8 December 1910).
11. Advert from the Breslau Palast-Theater, *Breslauer General-Anzeiger*, no. 31 (1 February 1911); see

also Martin Loiperdinger, "ABGRÜNDE - poczatek dlugometrazowych filmów fabularnych we Wrocławiu", in Andrzej Debski and Marek Zybura (eds), *Wrocław bedzie miastem filmowym. Z dziejów kina we Wrocławiu* (Wrocław: Wydawnictwo GAJT 1991, 2008): 55–63.

12. See for details Loiperdinger, *"Afgrunden* in Germany", 150.
13. For seating capacities in Hamburg cinemas see Film- und Fernsehmuseum Hamburg: www.film-museum-hamburg.de, and Michael Töteberg. "Neben dem Operetten-Theater und vis-à-vis Schauspielhaus. Eine Kino-Topographie von Hamburg 1896–1912," in Corinna Müller and Harro Segeberg (eds), *Kinoöffentlichkeit (1895–1920) – Entstehung, Etablierung, Differenzierung / Cinema's Public Sphere – Emergence, Settlement, Differentiation (1895–1920)* (Marburg: Schüren Verlag, 2008), 105–125.
14. Cover advert, *Der Kinematograph*, no. 221 (22 March 1911).
15. See *Der Kinematograph*, no. 220 (15 March 1911) to no. 223 (5 April 1911).
16. *Erste Internationale Filmzeitung*, no. 14 (8 April 1911): 40; and no. 17 (29 April 1911): 44.
17. *Erste Internationale Filmzeitung*, no. 12 (25 March 1911).
18. *Der Kinematograph*, no. 220 (15 March 1911).
19. Advert from the Aktien-Gesellschaft für Kinematographie und Filmverleih, Strasbourg, *Der Kinematograph*, no. 224 (12 April 1911).
20. Ibid.
21. *Der Kinematograph* , no. 206 (7 December 1910); 209 (28 December 1910); 211 (11 January 1911).
22. *Der Kinematograph*, no. 212 (18 January 1911).
23. *Der Kinematograph*, no. 228 (10 May 1911).
24. *Der Kinematograph*, no. 228 (10 May 1911).
25. *The Bioscope*, no. 245 (22 June 1911): 625.
26. Ibid.
27. Corinna Müller, *Frühe deutsche Kinematographie. Formale, wirtschaftliche und kulturelle Entwicklungen* (Stuttgart and Weimar: Metzler, 1994), 144.
28. Christoph Mülleneisen Sr., "Wie ich Asta Nielsen engagierte", *Erste Internationale Film-Zeitung* (25 April 1914); repr. in: Renate Seydel and Allan Hagedorff (eds), *Asta Nielsen. Ihr Leben in Fotodokumenten, Selbstzeugnissen und zeitgenössischen Betrachtungen* (Berlin, GDR: Henschelverlag Kunst und Gesellschaft, 1984), 48–49.
29. Ibid.
30. Asta Nielsen, *Die schweigende Muse* (Berlin, GDR: Henschelverlag Kunst und Gesellschaft, 1977), 139–140.
31. Advert "Bekanntmachung!", *Der Kinematograph*, no. 232 (7 June 1911).
32. Advert "Ein Unikum in der Kino-Branche!", *Der Kinematograph*, no. 238 (19 July 1911).
33. Ibid.
34. Ibid.
35. Mülleneisen Sr., "Wie ich Asta Nielsen engagierte".
36. Advert "Bekanntmachung!", *Der Kinematograph*, no. 232 (7 June 1911).
37. Advert "Ein Unikum in der Kino-Branche!", *Der Kinematograph*, no. 238 (19 July 1911).
38. PAGU advert "Asta Nielsen-Serie", *Der Kinematograph*, no. 250 (11 October 1911); the next PAGU advert was placed in no. 256 (22 November 1911).
39. PAGU advert announcing the eighth film of the first 'Asta Nielsen series', *Der Kinematograph*, no. 270 (28 February 1911).
40. PAGU advert, *Der Kinematograph*, no. 277 (17 April 1912).
41. Arthur Mellini, "Reklame-Kunst im Zeitungsinserat", *Lichtbild-Bühne*, no. 33 (19 August 1911); see Corinna Müller, *Frühe deutsche Kinematogaphie*, 151.
42. See Andrea Haller's essay in this volume.

43. See the lavishly illustrated documentation of all Asta Nielsen films: Karola Gramann and Heide Schlüpmann (eds), *Nachtfalter. Asta Nielsen, ihre Filme* (2nd edn) (Vienna: filmarchiv austria, 2010).
44. See Andrea Haller's essay on Mannheim and Pierre Stotzky's essay on Metz in this volume. For Saarbrücken. Saarbruck and Trier, see Christina Rönz, "'Asta Nielsen kommt' – Der Filmstar und die Kinobetreiber im Deutschen Reich", in Heide Schlüpmann et al. (eds), *Unmögliche Liebe. Asta Nielsen, ihr Kino* (2nd edn) (Vienna: filmarchiv austria, 2010), 187–193.
45. In 1910, Berlin had around two million inhabitants, and the cities which formed Greater Berlin in 1920 had nearly another two million inhabitants.
46. See Union-Theater adverts in the *Berliner Tageblatt*, no. 342 (8 July 1911) and no. 448 (3 September 1911). Thanks to Jeanpaul Goergen for this clue.
47. Paul Ehren, "Unsere Zeitung", *Union-Theater-Zeitung* 1:1 (16–22 March 1912): 2.
48. Only the script of ZIGEUNERBLUT (GIPSY BLOOD) was not written by Urban Gad, and it is not quite clear who wrote and directed DIE FALSCHE ASTA NIELSEN (THE FALSE ASTA NIELSEN); see Gramann and Schlüpmann, *Nachtfalter*, 33 and 173.
49. The phrase "by Urban Gad" was added for the first time when DER FREMDE VOGEL (THE COURSE OF TRUE LOVE) appeared in the programme lists; see *Union-Theater-Zeitung* 2:8 (20–27 February 1913).
50. Announcement of JUGEND UND TOLLHEIT (IN A FIX), *Union-Theater-Zeitung* 1:42 (27 December 1912 – 2 January 1913): 7.
51. Paul Ehren, "Regiekunst", *Union-Theater-Zeitung* 1:35 (8–14 November 1912): 1–2.
52. IFVG advert, *Erste Internationale Filmzeitung*, no. 23 (7 June 1913).
53. See Stephan Michael Schröder, "Und Urban Gad? Zur Frage der Autorschaft in den Filmen bis 1914", in Schlüpmann, *Unmögliche Liebe*, 194–210.
54. *Union-Theater-Zeitung* 1:3 (30 March – 4 April): 15.
55. *Union-Theater-Zeitung* 1:5 (13–19 April 1912): 3. Unfortunately, *Union-Theater-Zeitung* is accessible only on microfilm. Due to the poor quality of microfilm reproduction, this photograph of Asta Nielsen cannot be printed here.
56. "Asta Nielsen bleibt dauernd in Berlin", *Union-Theater-Zeitung* 1:11 (25–31 May 1912): 12.
57. "Asta Nielsen als Berliner Bürgerin", *Union-Theater-Zeitung* 1:19 (20–26 July 1912): 15.
58. Ibid.
59. "DIE KINDER DES GENERALS", *Union-Theater-Zeitung* 1:30 (5–11 October 1912): 8.
60. *Union-Theater-Zeitung* 1:38 (29 November – 5 December 1912): 3.
61. *Union-Theater-Zeitung* 1:1 (16–22 March 1912): 5.
62. Ernst Schultze, *Der Kinematograph als Bildungsmittel. Eine kulturpolitische Untersuchung* (Halle Verlag der Buchhandlung des Waisenhauses, 1911), 86–87.
63. "Unser Preisausschreiben", *Union-Theater-Zeitung* 1:33 (25–31 October 1912): 12.
64. "Das Resultat unserer Rundfrage", *Illustrierte Kino-Woche*, 2:1 (1914): 7. For details see Annemone Ligensa's essay in this volume.
65. Emilie Altenloh, *Zur Soziologie des Kino. Die Kino-Unternehmung und die sozialen Schichten ihrer Besucher* [1914], edited by Andrea Haller, Martin Loiperdinger and Heide Schlüpmann (Frankfurt and Basel: Stroemfeld, 2012), 57.
66. Ibid.
67. Ibid., 84 and 86.
68. Ibid., 82.
69. See Annemone Ligensa's essay in this volume.
70. See Andrea Haller's and Pierre Stotzky's local case studies in this volume.
71. Quotations from the "prize survey" of *Illustrierte Filmwoche* on the "most popular film artist" from the spring of 1918 are located in Andrea Haller, "'Nur meine Asta! Und damit basta!' Ein Blick in die Frauen- und Fanzeitschriften der 1910er Jahre", in Schlüpmann, *Unmögliche Liebe*, 325–336.

Pierre Stotzky

Screening Asta Nielsen Films in Metz before the First World War

Metz is located in the North Eastern French department of Moselle, which borders on Germany and Luxembourg. Between 1870 and 1918, Metz was a German city integrated to the German Reich along with the department of Moselle and the Alsace region. The city counted 68,000 inhabitants in 1914, half of them native French speakers, the other native German speakers. German was the teaching and administrative language, yet in 1914 one could still live in Metz without speaking a word of German. One fourth of the population in this garrison city were soldiers.

The first cinema opened in Metz in December 1907 and by Summer 1914, seven cinemas (close to 2500 seats) were showing films daily, renewing programmes twice a week (on Saturdays and Wednesdays). Each programme was made up of about ten short films, split between comic and dramatic shorts, newsreels and documentaries, as well as one feature-length film or several medium-length films taking the top billing. In spite of a timed schedule indicating the beginning of the programme, one could enter the showings at any time. During these years, cinema became the foremost leisure activity of the inhabitants of Metz. It went from being a mere attraction to becoming a regular night out, prepared for by reading detailed programmes in the local press or booklets accessible in the cinemas, and motivated by spectators' budding tastes.

Between 1910 and 1914, at least 28 Asta Nielsen films were shown in Metz. Apart from the two first films, her name was always mentioned in advertisements published in the local press, in some cases in larger font than the film title. Twenty-seven of these films got top billing in their accompanying programmes. They even outshone the rest of the programme, as the titles of accompanying films were very rarely mentioned. Furthermore, Asta Nielsen's name was featured early and durably in the press: she was by far the actress most often mentioned in Metz newspapers between 1911 and 1914.

Most of the films starring Asta Nielsen which were distributed before the First World War were shown also in Metz. Her films were shown in Metz on dates close to their national release dates, which suggests that the star became quickly popular in Metz.

| Advert for AFGRUNDEN, *Lothringer Zeitung* (4 January 1911). [Médiathèque de Metz, P REV 20.] | First sketch of Asta Nielsen published in the daily press of Metz. *Metzer Zeitung* (20 September 1913). [Archives Départementales de la Moselle, 1 AL 53–77.] |

Nielsen's films were offered to cinema owners through a peculiar system of distribution: the 'Asta Nielsen series' which forced owners to buy exclusive screening rights for an entire series which involved an important cost. Owners showing Asta Nielsen films therefore had actively made that choice.

Asta Nielsen's single films in Metz

AFGRUNDEN was screened in Metz, from Saturday, 31 December 1910, to Saturday, 6 January 1911, in two downtown film theaters, Cinématographe Hirdt, also known as "the old Hirdt theater" (274 seats)[1] and the Nouveau Cinématographe Hirdt (170 seats).[2] They belonged to two different owners, Alois Hirdt and Hans Lang, who worked together and were to jointly found together the Société Luxembourgo-allemande de Cinéma (SLAC) on 30 November 1911. Their cinemas stood about a hundred yards apart, and the film was not screened at the same time in both theaters, hence the ability of 'bicycling' to share the same reel.[3]

Screening Asta Nielsen Films in Metz before the First World War

Table 1. Asta Nielsen films screened in Metz from 1910 to 1914.

Season	Film title	Film theatre	Screening dates *Saturday
1910/11 3 films	*Afgrunden (Abgründe, The Abyss)*	Cinématographe Hirdt	31★December 1910 – 6 January 1911
	Heisses Blut (Burning Blood)	Nouveau cinéma Hirdt	6★–12 May 1911
		Landstuhl cinéma	6–7 June 1911
	Der Nachtfalter (Retribution)	Nouveau cinéma Hirdt	22★–28 July 1911
1911/12 8 films 1 reissue	*Der Nachtfalter (Retribution)* reissue	Landstuhl cinéma	30 August 1911
	Den sorte Drøm (Der Schwarze Traum, The Circus Girl) 1st Asta Nielsen series, no 1	Cinématographe Hirdt	30★September–13 October 1911
	In dem großen Augenblick (The Great Moment) 1st Asta Nielsen series, no 2	Excelsior	7★–13 October 1911
	Zigeunerblut (Gipsy Blood) 1st Asta Nielsen series, no 3	Excelsior	4★–10 November 1911
	Balletdanseriden (Brennende Triebe, The Ballet Dancer)	Cinématographe Hirdt	4★–10 November 1911
	Die Verräterin (The Traitress) 1st Asta Nielsen series, no 5	Excelsior	30★December 1911–5 January 1912
	Die Macht des Goldes (The Better Way) 1st Asta Nielsen series, no 6	Excelsior	21★January–2 February 1912
	Zu Tode gehetzt (Driven Out) 1st Asta Nielsen series, no 8	Excelsior	23★–29 March 1912
	Der Fremde Vogel (The Course of True Love) 1st Asta Nielsen series, no 4		29 May
1912/13 8 films	*Der Totentanz (The Dance to Death)* 2nd Asta Nielsen series, no 1	Palais-Cinéma	19★–22 October 1912
	Die Kinder des Generals (Falsely Accused) 2nd Asta Nielsen series, no 2	Palais-Cinéma	13★–15 November 1912
	Wenn die Maske fällt (When the Mask Falls) 2nd Asta Nielsen series, no 3	Palais-Cinéma	7★–10 December 1912
	Das Mädchen ohne Vaterland (A Girl without a Country) 2nd Asta Nielsen series, no 4	Palais-Cinéma	4★–7 January 1913
	Jugend und Tolheit (In a Fix) 2nd Asta Nielsen series, no 5	Palais-Cinéma	1★–4 February 1913
	Komödianten (The Heart of a Pierrot) 2nd Asta Nielsen series, no 6	Cinématographe Hirdt	12–14 March 1913
	Die Sünden unserer Väter (The Temptations of Drink) 2nd Asta Nielsen series, no 7	Palais-Cinéma	12★–15 April 1913
	Tod in Sevilla (Spanish Blood) 2nd Asta Nielsen series, no 8	Palais-Cinéma	10★–13 May 1913
1913/14 7 films 2 reissues	*Die Suffragette (The Suffragette)* 3rd Asta Nielsen series, no 1	Palais-Cinéma	20★–23 September 1913
	S 1 (A Girl's Sacrifice) 3rd Asta Nielsen series, no 2	Palais-Cinéma	22★–25 November 1913
	Engelein (Up to Her Tricks) 3rd Asta Nielsen series, no 4	Palais-Cinéma	14–16 January 1914
	Im großen Augenblick (The Great Moment) reissue 1st Asta Nielsen series, no 2	Krystall-Lichtspiele	24★–27 January 1914
	Das Kind ruft (The Cry of a Child) 3rd Asta Nielsen series, no 5	Palais-Cinéma	31★January–3 February 1914
	Zapatas Bande (Zapata's Gang) 3rd Asta Nielsen series, no 6	Cinéma de l'Esplanade	7★–10 March 1914
	Tod in Sevilla (Spanish Blood) reissue 2nd Asta Nielsen series, no 8	Eldorado	10–11 March 1914
	Das Feuer (Vengeance is Mine) 3rd Asta Nielsen series, no 7	Palais-Cinéma	4★–8 April 1914

The advertisement for AFGRUNDEN is interesting on several accounts: in 1910, adverts for single films in the local press were still rare. They listed the titles of the showings together with some information about the genre of the films (comic, dramatic, news,...). The most important titles in the programme (generally a selection of one to three titles) are signaled typographically. Here AFGRUNDEN alone is advertised, even though as most films of the time, it is part of the weekly programme.[4] Most importantly, information about the film is very precise: its length of two acts for a total running time of 50 minutes is emphasised; its Danish provenance is mentioned as a guarantee of quality ("artists of the Copenhagen Royal Theatre;" the film "shown 700 times to enormously large audiences in Copenhagen movie houses"). One particular scene is singled out: the memorable "dance of the Gaucho",[5] and the advertisement calls upon the spectator's memory: it claims that this film surpasses THE WHITE SLAVE (DEN HVIDE SLAVEHANDEL, 1910), a film previously screened in Metz.[6] The screening of AFGRUNDEN and its advertisement in the local press illustrate the evolution of cinema as spectacle in Metz in the beginning of the 1910s, with the advent of the feature film in cinema programming, and the birth of the star system. Indeed, although her name is not mentioned on the advert, this is the first Asta Nielsen film screened in Metz.

Between May and August 1911, HEISSES BLUT (BURNING BLOOD) and NACHTFALTER (RETRIBUTION), the first German films featuring Asta Nielsen were shown in the Nouveau Cinématographe Hirdt and in a beer-hall where films were screened while customers drank and ate. The first advert for NACHTFALTER, of 22 July 1911, mentions the actress's name. From now on, Asta Nielsen's name was always included in advertisements and soon became an argument for the quality of the spectacle. The advert for NACHTFALTER at the Landstuhl cinema[7] notes that the film was authorised by the censors: the indirect mention of Asta Nielsen's sultriness marks a first period of the exploitation of her films in Metz.[8]

'Asta Nielsen series' at the Excelsior and the Palais-Cinéma

An exhibitor who bought the exclusive exhibition rights for the first 'Asta Nielsen series' essentially catered to an informed, adult audience. The Excelsior cinema (135 seats) opened in July 1911 at the heart of a vast leisure center, the Crystal Palace, located in the German neighbourhood around the new train station favoured by soldiers.[9] Among the favourite film genres were dramas of manners, 'big city pictures', and war dramas. In May and June 1912, the Excelsior was the only theatre in the city to have adults-only screenings.[10] According to adverts in the local press, the Excelsior screened five of eight of the films in the first 'Asta Nielsen' series of 1911/12: IN DEM GROSSEN AUGENBLICK (THE GREAT MOMENT), ZIGEUNERBLUT (GIPSY BLOOD), DIE VERRÄTERIN (THE TRAITRESS), THE BETTER WAY (DIE MACHT DES GOLDES), and ZU TODE GEHETZT (DRIVEN OUT).[11] These films were all screened from Saturday to Wednesday, along with an extra programme. The advert for the screening of IN DEM GROSSEN AUGENBLICK (from 7 to 11 October 1911) stipulated that children under the age of 16 be not admitted to the cinema. This certainly followed the Berlin Censorship Bureau's decision to ban this and most of the subsequent Asta Nielsen films for the youth. The themes developed in these films fitted perfectly the Excelsior's programming aimed at an informed audience.

The exclusive second and third 'Asta Nielsen series' were shown at the Palais-Cinéma (twelve titles), at the Esplanade theatre (one title) and at the old Hirdt cinema (one title), three venues owned by the aforementioned Société Luxembourgo-allemande de Cinéma (SLAC), founded by Hans Lang and Alois Hirdt. The Palais Cinéma was the first 'cinema palace' in Metz: opened with much fanfare on 10 November 1911, it was the first purpose-built cinema in Metz. A building in the main business street in Metz was razed in order to make room for this 'modern cinema theatre' with a capacity of 400 spectators. This company managed also two cinemas in Esch-sur-Alzette (Luxembourg), and one in Ludwigshafen (Germany). The company had a capital of 225,000 Marks.[12] On 31 January 1914, the Esplanade opened in the Cigogne building, where the Nouveau Cinématographe Hirdt was previously housed. This modern 600-seat cinema, the biggest in town, was also born of the collaboration between Lang and Hirdt. With its two new cinemas in the heart of the city, by 1914 the SLAC could offer 1,000 theater seats in a city boasting 68,000 inhabitants. With two modern cinemas and a consequent financial capital, SLAC had the means to pay exclusive rights for the 'Asta Nielsen series' of 1912/13 and 1913/14, which were shown in their totality between 19 October 1912 when DER TOTENTANZ (THE DANCE TO DEATH), the first film in the second series, was launched in Metz, and 4 April 1914 when DAS FEUER (VENGEANCE IS MINE), the seventh and last film in the third series, was screened for the last time.[13] In the season 1912/13, cinemas in Metz began renewing programmes twice a week, on Saturdays and Wednesdays. Most Asta Nielsen films were shown on Saturdays, arguably the best attended day of the week along with Sunday.

Feature-length standardisation and the leading actress as quality proof

Between 1910 and 1914, increasing film length was a major trend. Multiple-reel films were an exception before 1911; they became common that year, and as early as 1912 each programme included one or two films longer than half an hour. It was not uncommon for top billing films to boast an average length of 45 minutes. This trend towards lengthening reached its apex in 1913, when several 'monster length' films, sometimes up to three hours long, were screened in Metz. It deserves to be noted that the gradual assertion of the feature film did not come with radical changes in the organisation of cinema as spectacle: long-length films were still part of a programme, and customers could still enter screenings at any time, except for a few rare cases. However, advertising increasingly focused on feature length films, and it soon became more difficult to find full programmes in the local press. The case of Asta

Nielsen is interesting in that regard, because all of her films have the characteristics of the long-feature film: their length,[14] the way they were promoted, and of course the emphasis on the main actress make them all dominate the rest of the programme. Thus, as early as the screening of her first film in December 1910, it is impossible to know the full content of the programmes in which her films are were featured.

Table 2. Actresses whose name is mentioned at least twice in the Metz press between 1911 and 1914 (number of films by the actress whose press advert includes at least one occurrence of the actress's name).

Name	1911	1912	1913	1914	Total
Asta Nielsen	7	7	7	5	26
Henny Porten		1	4	7	12
Suzanne Grandais			5	3	8
Gabrielle Robinne			7	1	7
Lissi Nebuschka			1	5	6
Rita Sachetto			1	3	4
Wanda Treumann		3	1	1	5
Erna Morena			3		3
Magde Lessing				3	3
Ellen Aggerholm				3	3
Sarah Bernhardt		1	1	1	3
Clara Wieth	1		3		4
Betty Nansen				2	2
Hedda Vernon			1	1	2

The introduction of the feature-length film format was paralleled by the development of the star system: the names of headline actors from Germany, Denmark, Italy, France or the United States began appearing more regularly in adverts. Among them, Asta Nielsen was the earliest to be cited this way, and second only to French comedian Max Linder in number of mentions. The actress's name gradually became even more important than the film title. Her films soon came to be advertised as "Asta Nielsen-Schlager" (Asta Nielsen hits; the same way westerns were known as "Wild West-Schlager" and detective films as "Detektiv-Schlager"). Advertising, sometimes masqueraded as news items appeared in the 'local entertainment' columns: thus film programmes were often announced in articles titled after the cinemas in question. Yet in the *Metzer Zeitung* (the main German-language newspaper in Metz, belonging to Hans Lang, owner of the Palais-Cinéma and member of SLAC), adverts for Asta Nielsen films only bear the actress's name as titles. Her name is usually accompanied by words of praise underlining Asta Nielsen's acting talent and her popularity. Her acting is constantly celebrated, and she is often presented as the "famous tragedienne". Here is an excerpt from such a piece praising her performance in DIE SUFFRAGETTE:

> The contribution of a first-rate artist being indispensable to a production of this

For the first time, another film (HIAVATHA, Colonia Film, 1913) gets top billing above an Asta Nielsen film. *Metzer Zeitung* (7 March 1914). [Archives Départementales de la Moselle, 1 AL 53-78.]

nature on the cinema stage, the author gave the main role to the famous tragedienne Asta Nielsen. Those used to seeing shows at the Palais-Cinéma have long known Asta Nielsen's merits who interprets the most complex roles with extraordinary gusto. In Urban Gad's new opus, THE SUFFRAGETTE, the artist is without compare and admirably personifies a high born woman who goes down the wrong path until repentance leads her to her true destiny as woman and spouse.[15]

Asta Nielsen films were not the only ones to benefit from this kind of coverage in the local press of Metz. None of her films were promoted on the scale of the very long feature films of 1913 and of some German *Autorenfilms* such as DER ANDERE (THE OTHER). Furthermore, in 1914 she finds serious competition in the German star Henny Porten, who headlines several feature films whose adverts sometimes spread half a page in the Metz press. Asta Nielsen stands apart for being recognised already in 1911 by Metz audiences as a star, and for the length of time she remained a star. Her films screened during this period illustrate the gradual standardisation of cinema entertainment around 90-minute long films which featured a familiar star in the lead.

The emergence of cinephilic memory in Metz

In 1914 two older Asta Nielsen films were shown in Metz: IM LETZTEN AUGENBLICK at the Krystall-Lichtspiele and TOD IN SEVILLA (SPANISH BLOOD) at the Eldorado, both of them getting top billing. IM LETZTEN AUGENBLICK had been shown two years and two months earlier, and TOD IN SEVILLA about ten months prior. Reprises were then very rare in Metz: of more than 3,600 recorded film titles from 1908 to 1914, only about fifty appear in two different programmes, and only a handful were re-released months or years later. Beyond the fact that such reprises constitute an obvious sign of these films' qualities, they may also show the increasing differences between the city's film theatres. The Krystall-Lichtspiele was the cinema at the Crystal Palace, taken over on October 1913 by an independent owner. The Eldorado (234 seats), owned by the eponymous Strasbourg company, was located on the outskirts of town in a working-class, mostly French-speaking neighbourhood. These two cinemas were not as fancy as the downtown palaces and did not have the means necessary to acquire exclusive rights on Nielsen's films, and therefore had to settle for old titles.

Asta Nielsen and her films played a central role in the formation of the cinematic culture of Metz audiences. Cinephilia developed through seeing films, accumulating knowledge about them, and comparing their respective qualities, a comparison made possible by calling upon memories of the experience they left in each spectator. The screening and promotion of Asta Nielsen films in Metz form these three constitutive elements of cinephilia.

To begin with, the number of her films screened and the fact that they were all directed by the same person undoubtedly contributed to shape the tastes of spectators. Serial screening necessarily invited spectators to compare films which were part of the series. Being able to watch films several times is also obviously constitutive of cinephilia: the screenings in 1914 of two of Nielsen's old hits (IN DEM LETZEN AUGENBLICK[16] and TOD IN SEVILLA) let the star's fans discover or rediscover these titles. As already mentioned, this was a very rare occurrence in Metz: only a few films – such as QUO VADIS? for example – were granted the privilege of a second screening. It is worth noting that IN DEM GROSSEN AUGENBLICK, the first Asta Nielsen film shown at the Excelsior in October 1911, was announced in the French-language press under its German title. The French advertisement for her following title included the original German title, ZIGEUNERBLUT, along with the French translation. These are the only examples of titles advertised in German in the French-language press of the time. Either the audience already knew these films by their German titles and the owner meant to profit from this notoriety, or the mention of the original title can be analysed as another piece of information helping spectators to build their cinema culture. Furthermore, the promotions of Asta Nielsen films were progressively accompanied with more and more information: length of the films in metres, number of acts and scenes, secondary actors' names, scene descriptions, references to other cities where these films had been successful, plot summaries. All these elements could contribute to the constitution of a nascent cinema culture. The fact that Urban Gad's name was almost always mentioned in the adverts is also worthy of note: he was the first film director to see his name and work thus recognised in the Metz press. Finally, spectators of Asta Nielsen's films were very early asked to reminisce older films. The advert for ZIGEUNERBLUT published in the French-language newspaper *Le Messin* notes the actress's previous films.[17] The advert for DIE SUFFRAGETTE also calls upon the memory of Nielsen's previous roles, without citing them. Though it was not common, this way of calling upon spectators' memories was not exclusive to adverts for Asta Nielsen films. Other examples compare new films with others screened previously in Metz. Nevertheless, regularly as Asta Nielsen films were screened, they appear to have played a singular role in the constitution of the cinephilic memory of the Metz public.

Translated from French by Grégory Pierrot, Pennsylvania State University

Acknowledgement: This article is based on Pierre Stotzky, *Le spectacle cinématographique à Metz, naissance d'un nouveau loisir (1908–1914)* B.A. thesis (Metz: Université Paul Verlaine, 2004), 138 pp. Based on research in local archives, this work offers analysis of related news and recovers the original programmes of the city's film theatres (a total of 709 programmes announcing 3593 films).

Notes

1. Cinématographe Hirdt was the first film theatre in the city, located on the main business street. It was opened by the Kaiserslautern fairground showman Heinrich Hirdt in December 1907, managed by Emile Nutz from Summer 1909 to May 1910 and by Hans Lang (a printer from Metz, editor for the German-language newspaper *Metzer Zeitung*) until 15 November 1913.
2. This screening room was active between 23 October 1909 and 1 October 1911. It was located in *La Cigogne*, a big building of several stores comprising a beerhall, a dance hall, a concert hall. It was managed by Henri Hirdt's son, Alois Hirdt, hence the name: Nouveau Cinéma Hirdt.
3. This print-sharing practice also attests to the proximity and collaboration between the two cinemas' managers from May 1910 to November 1911: during this time period, nine films were announced on the same week in both cinemas. This proximity led to the creation of the SLAC on 30 November 1911.
4. There were exceptions to this rule: in 1913, nine films were screened alone, at fixed times, because of their singular topic or their exceptional length: MORT VIVANT (2150 metres), GERMINAL (3020 metres) and LES MISÉRABLES (3010 metres), DER ANDERE (2000 metres), RICHARD WAGNER (2055 metres), MARCANTONIO E CLEOPATRA (2000 metres) and QUO VADIS? (2400 metres). The advertisement for the screening of LES MISÉRABLES announces that the nine acts will be shown in a row, for a total running time of three hours. In 1914, at least two films were screened on their own, at fixed times: BISMARCK (1853 metres) and ATLANTIS (2280 metres – some adverts announce up to 4000-metre long versions).
5. A hundred years later, this scene still mesmerizes spectators online: "Erotic Dance by Asta Nielsen in AFGRUNDEN (1910)": http://www.youtube.com/watch?v=criEcLXgUQ0
6. Nevertheless, a film with this title was screened as part of the Cinéma Hirdt programe for 22 to 28 October 1910, and that for 19 to 25 November 1910 ("by general demand"). Considering the number of films about white slavery produced at the time, it is difficult to assert with certitude if indeed this was DEN HVIDE SLAVEHANDEL.
7. Daily, free screenings were organised in the Landstuhl cinema which was located in the imperial neighbourhood around the new train station between 2 June 1909 and Fall 1911. It is likely that mostly German-speaking spectators patroned this venue.
8. The Berlin censorship bureau barred youth from screenings of NACHTFALTER, while in Munich it was banned altogether. Most Asta Nielsen films were censored by both of these bureaus. Cf.

http://www.earlycinema.uni-koeln.de. In Metz, following the police decree of 12 April 1912, film theatres had to submit detailed lists of programmed films to the police three days before the first screening, or one day if first approved in Berlin. The police could visit cinemas without notice or demand to see any suspicious film. In reality, as police was short on material and human means, it is likely that these rules were not rigorously applied.

9. The Strasbourg based company Excelsior Cinema-Gesellschaft managed the Excelsior cinema until it closed on 30 July 1913. The company owned at least two other cinemas, the Weltkinematograph in Saarbrücken and the Excelsior-Cinema in Dudweiler.

10. On 22 May 1912 began the screening of FUNKE UNTER DER ASCHE, presented as a "picture of the big modern city", and on 12 June 1912 WENN FRAUEN LIEBEN. These films were announced as adult-only, yet a police decree dated 12 April 1912 forbids entry in the city's film theatres to people under the age of 16, except during screenings expressly reserved for children. The announcement might appear superfluous (unless the decree was not respected): it nevertheless gives adult spectators an idea of the programme's content.

11. DER SCHWARZE TRAUM (DEN SORTE DRØM, THE CIRCUS GIRL) and DER FREMDE VOGEL (THE COURSE OF TRUE LOVE), films number 1 and 4 in the first 'Asta Nielsen series', were shown in the Hirdt cinemas and at the Palais-Cinéma which contradicts the *Monopolfilm* rules by which only the Excelsior should have screened the films in Metz. They may have been first screened at the Excelsior: advertisements for the Excelsior were rare in the local press which makes reconstructing the Excelsior film programmes a difficult task.

12. Cf. *Der Kinematograph* no. 264 (17 January 1912).

13. Only DIE FILMPRIMADONNA, third film in the third series of 1913/14, was not mentioned in Metz programmes: taking into account gaps of documentation, this does not necessarily mean that the film was not shown.

14. All Asta Nielsen films screened in Metz comprise several reels: the shortest is 731 meters long (DAS KIND RUFT, 1914), the longest 1878 meters (DIE SUFFRAGETTE), 1913). The average reel length for the 28 Asta Nielsen films screened in Metz is around 1000 metres.

15. *Le Messin* (19 September 1913).

16. IN DEM LETZTEN AUGENBLICK was shown in the same venue (now renamed and with a different owner) where it had been screened two years earlier.

17. "Luscha: Asta Nielsen the famous tragédienne who gained universal admiration in ABÎMES, AMOUR BRÛLANT, SANG GÉNÉREUX, PAPILLON DE NUIT, LE SONGE NOIR, DANS LE GRAND MOMENt." Advert for DAS MÄDCHEN OHNE VATERLAND, *Le Messin* (4 November 1911).

Andrea Haller

Advertising Asta Nielsen and the Long-Feature Film – the Case of Mannheim

Asta Nielsen was a key figure in the increase of film length, the introduction of the exclusive rental system, and the implementation of film stars: three changes the German film industry underwent in 1911–12. She was not only the first star in feature-length films: her appearance on screen helped to introduce a new 'genre', the *Kinodrama* or social drama, and to establish the 'one-hour film' as the norm of cinema programming in Germany after 1912. This will be shown in my article by a closer analysis of Mannheim cinema programmes and of the way Asta Nielsen films were advertised in the local press, in 1911 and 1912.

Why should Mannheim serve for a local analysis to answer these questions? Mannheim might be the city about which we know most in regards to early cinema history. Mannheim is where Emilie Altenloh conducted her empirical research on cinema audiences for her dissertation *Zur Soziologie des Kino* which was published in 1914.[1] Altenloh had studied *Nationalökonomie* (political economy) and attended law courses in Munich, Kiel, Vienna, and in Heidelberg. She was among the first women to receive a doctoral degree at a German university by writing her dissertation under the supervision of sociologist Alfred Weber in Heidelberg. She collected empirical data on the cinema audiences in Mannheim between mid-1911 and mid-1912 with a female colleague, Else Biram, who was researching art education and urban reception of art. During that time Altenloh often visited the cinemas in Mannheim, and one might assume that she had seen Asta Nielsen films there. These visits to the cinema formed the basis of her theory on the cinema audience. Thus, comparing her findings with what the local press and the programme adverts tell us seems to be an appropriate means of finding out more about Asta Nielsen and her reception in Mannheim. Although the data Altenloh collected are merely based on a local case study, she presents her findings as typical of general tendencies in audience taste and the cinema in industrial towns in Germany.[2] Her findings on the audience and their 'taste' can add to the analysis of the programming and advertising of the Asta Nielsen films in the trade press in Mannheim. Furthermore, it can underpin the idea that Asta Nielsen was an outstanding figure in the cinema programmes of Mannheim. Her name stands for her products, i.e. her films, and it was able to draw people into the cinema.

Mannheim and its cinema topography in 1911

Mannheim is located in south-west Germany where the rivers Rhine and Neckar meet. At the beginning of the 19th century the city underwent a massive upswing in the ongoing process of industrialisation; it became a real boomtown. Many workers from the countryside moved to the city seeking employment in the new industries. Mannheim was connected to the railway and boasted of a large industrial harbour; many new factories, especially steelworks and chemical plants, were erected. The 'industrial reserve army' that fed the new factories mainly lived near the factories in the suburbs, where residential areas exclusively for workers and their families were built around 1900. Many of these new workers were confronted with conflicts caused by overcrowding and housing shortage. Within fifteen years, between 1885 and 1900, Mannheim's population increased by about 82 per cent. Thus Mannheim had around 217,000 inhabitants by 1910. However, Mannheim also had a substantial higher social class: a long-established middle class because it was also a residence of the Grand Duke of Baden. Compared to the working classes the members of this social segment lived in a totally different world: They resided in the noble part of the city centre near the Grand Duke's palace, which was clearly separated from the workers' areas. Here, every second household kept servants and maids.[3] The middle class neighbourhood was located between the two areas where the lower middle class, the tradesmen and the craftsmen lived and worked.

In 1911 Mannheim had twelve cinemas, seven of which were located in suburban areas where the industrial workers lived with their families. These cinemas were small, mostly between 50 and 200 seats, and not very comfortably furnished and in some cases located side by side, predominantly on the major thoroughfares. The inner city, i.e. the more middle-class neighbourhoods with their shopping areas, had five cinemas. Two of them, the Union-Theater and the Saalbau cinema, were quite large and elegantly furnished, accommodating from 700 up to 2000 people. They had a proper orchestra, always tried to show the latest and most successful films and gave themselves an air of nobility. According to Altenloh, people from all classes, and especially women, liked to go to those two more elegant inner city cinemas. During the day they were mainly frequented by a walk-in patronage who went to the city centre to go shopping or to run errands and the likes. The smaller suburban cinemas were frequented mainly by workers, primarily male workers, and school children, i.e. people from the neighbourhood.

Only the Union-Theater and the Saalbau cinema regularly advertised their programmes in the daily press. The Saalbau cinema, a former variety theatre, boasted that it was the "largest and most elegant cinema in Germany". The Union-Theater was not only the oldest cinema in Mannheim; it was also the

Union-Theater in 1907. [Stadtarchiv Mannheim, Bslg. KF0101343.]

first cinema of the Frankfurt-based Allgemeine Kinematographen-Theater-Gesellschaft, which was the most important cinema chain in Germany in the beginning of the 1910s. In 1910 it was renamed Projektions-Aktiengesellschaft Union, in short PAGU, one of the companies that formed the consortium which later contracted Asta Nielsen and Urban Gad.[4] Two businessmen from Mannheim were members of the supervisory board, the lawyer Dr. Max Jeselsen, and the factory owner Heinrich Hellwig.[5] In an advert from 1911 the Union-Theater boasted its "luxurious but dignified interiors" and also soon claimed to be the "most elegant cinema in Germany".[6] Both cinemas advertised their programmes in the local newspaper *Mannheimer Generalanzeiger* twice a week, whenever the programmes changed, whereas the smaller workers' cinemas hardly every announced their programmes in the newspapers.

Asta Nielsen in Mannheim

The Union-Theater started the new year of 1911 with a real smash hit: It was the film about the fight between the two heavyweight boxing champions Jack Johnson and Jim Jeffries to which PAGU had bought the exclusive rights. THE JACK JOHNSON AND JIM JEFFRIES FIGHT, 1800 metres long and running approximately two hours, was a non-fiction film. It was heavily advertised and screened on 28 January.[7] On the same day, the Saalbau cinema less prominently advertised Asta Nielsen's debut film AFGRUNDEN, the first film that was rented out as a *Monopolfilm* in Germany. The so-called *Monopolfilm* rental system granted exhibitors the exclusive right to show a film regionally without the competition of a neighbouring cinema.⁸ Exhibitors could then select a single film, rather than an entire short film programme from the distributors. Hence, the Saalbau cinema claimed in its first advert from 28 January 1911 to own the "exclusive rights to show the film for Mannheim".⁹ With 850 metres and about 47 minutes running time (at 16 fps), AFGRUNDEN was longer than most of the other fictional films of that time. Consequently, the adverts for AFGRUNDEN emphasised the length of the film. Asta Nielsen was not yet mentioned. This advert mentions only one single film whereas usually cinema adverts specified all eight to twelve (or even more) short films of which a programme commonly consisted at that time.

On 7 February, the Saalbau cinema published a second advert for AFGRUNDEN which said in large letters: "Confiscated!" In the meantime the local censorship board had seized the film, supposedly on the grounds of the eroticism of the 'gaucho dance'. But then the Saalbau was allowed to put it back into the programme. Suggesting risky content as the reason for the ban was likely to make the film appear even more interesting for the local audience. All in all, AFGRUNDEN was shown in an extremely long run of two weeks, apparently never paralleled before in Mannheim. Usually the programme was changed twice a week. Looking at the screenings of AFGRUNDEN in Hamburg, Martin Loiperdinger has stated that this film was the "starting point for the media upheaval that marks the transition from the short film programme to the long feature film format" and "a new era in film exhibition".¹⁰ One might suppose that the extraordinarily long run of AFGRUNDEN in Mannheim was the first signal of that change in Mannheim.

AFGRUNDEN was also pioneering in regards to its content. It marked the beginning of the *Kinodrama* (cine-drama) or the social drama, as Altenloh calls it, a new genre which was to dominate the programmes in Mannheim in the next years: "What is symptomatic of this new genre is the social momentum. Indeed, the fondness for this term is so deep that the word "social" became the most common word in the adverts".¹¹ According to Altenloh, the social drama deals with social problems of the day through real examples and in the most powerful possible form.¹² The basic conflict developed mostly around the contradiction between the women's feelings and the opposing social conditions. In AFGRUNDEN Asta Nielsen embodies the piano teacher Magda who falls in love with a travelling variety actor, leaves her fiancé and elopes with the actor. After they leave the troupe she must earn their living by playing the piano in shady cafés while he is drinking too much. After a quarrel, she kills him in self-defence.

After AFGRUNDEN had served as a kind of initial spark for other *Kinodramen*, about 1000 metres long and dealing with the fate and fortune of women, more of them were shown in Mannheim in early 1911, e.g. DIE WEISSE SKLAVIN II (DEN HVIDE SLAVEHANDELS SIDSTE OFFER, IN THE HANDS OF IMPOSTORS), at the Union-Theater from 16 to 25 February; or on 22 April, DAS GEFÄHRLICHE ALTER (THE DANGEROUS AGE), a drama about an elderly woman still looking for love, based on a popular book by the Danish author Karen Michaelis. In June, the Danish films DIE MORPHINISTEN (MORFINISTEN, THE MORPHINE TAKERS), "a psycho-pathological drama from modern life",[13] and AUF ABWEGEN (GONE ASTRAY), "a modern *Sittendrama* [drama of manners]",[14] were heavily advertised. Asta Nielsen and the popularity of her films had probably already paved the way this early for the popularity and effectiveness of other long-feature films in which the fate of a female protagonist struggling with social circumstances is at the centre of the story.

Asta Nielsen's second film, HEISSES BLUT (BURNING BLOOD), was shown at the Union-Theater from 29 April onward. In this drama, Nielsen plays a woman who betrays her husband but the love of her child reunites the family in the end. The only advert, which is quite large but not overly so, mentions the name Asta Nielsen and the length of the film. After that, HEISSES BLUT was shown from 3 May in the Eldorado cinema, a smaller inner city cinema. The Eldorado seldom advertised its programme, but HEISSES BLUT seemed to be a film worth advertising. As HEISSES BLUT was not a *Monopolfilm*, a small cinema such as the Eldorado had the opportunity to show an Asta Nielsen film shortly after its release. From 20 May on, NACHTFALTER (RETRIBUTION), Asta Nielsen's third film, was shown in the Saalbau cinema which held the exclusive exhibition right for Mannheim, as was distinctly indicated in the advert. Furthermore, the running time of one hour is emphasised. And, the advert mentions Asta Nielsen playing the leading role in this "boulevard drama from Paris",[15] where she portrays the seamstress Olga, who, after stealing her sister's money, becomes a variety star and unknowingly starts an affair with her sister's husband. Her suicide reunites the couple.

In August, the Union-Theater showed DER SCHWARZE TRAUM (DEN SORTE DRØM, THE CIRCUS GIRL), the first film of the first 'Asta Nielsen series' Asta Nielsen plays Stella, a circus rider. Torn between two men who fight for her, she sacrifices herself for the one she really loves. The promotion for this film took a new level: Some days before the film started the cinema placed mysterious little adverts in the local newspaper to draw attention to the film. The first advert was only a black box in a corner of the newspaper page saying "DER SCHWARZE TRAUM".[16] On the next day the black box announced "DER SCHWARZE TRAUM. A sensation in the field of film art".[17] The following day an advert solved the mystery and invited readers to the premiere of the film at the Union-Theater the next evening. On the day of the premiere, one day later, on 26 August, a huge advert praised DER SCHWARZE TRAUM as "a first-rate attraction" and promoted Asta Nielsen as the "Eleonore Duse of film art", while Urban Gad as the author of the script was mentioned in letters of the same size.[18] While the film was shown at the Union-Theater some other adverts were placed in the local newspaper telling of sold-out screenings and of people storming the theatre. After two weeks, a last advert announced the "irrevocably last large farewell screening".[19] All in all, the Union-Theater posted seven adverts for this film. This was in fact the first publicity campaign

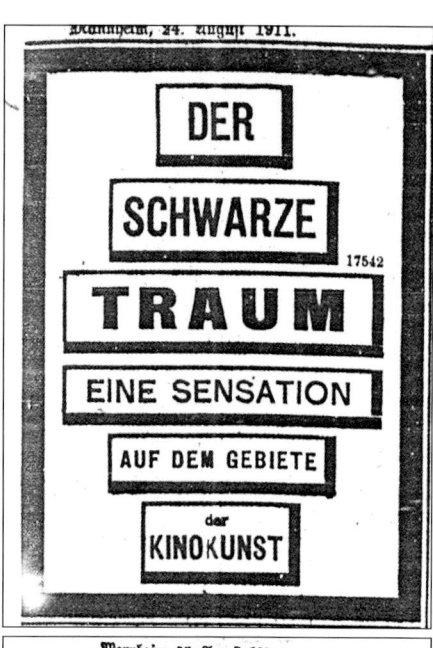

Advertising Asta Nielsen and the Long-Feature Film – the Case of Mannheim

Publicity campaign for DER SCHWARZE TRAUM, *Mannheimer Generalanzeiger* (23 August – 1 September 1911).

for a single film in Mannheim. Whereas DER SCHWARZE TRAUM had been bought from the Danish producer Fotorama, the next Asta Nielsen films shown in Mannheim were made under the exclusive contract with Asta Nielsen and Urban Gad. They were produced by Deutsche Bioscop for PAGU. In Mannheim, they were shown at the Union-Theater, which belonged to PAGU. Asta Nielsen films were now shown in Mannheim on a regular basis. On 22 September, a huge advert that puts "Asta Nielsen" literally at the centre of attraction announced the "Gala-Premiere" of IN DEM GROSSEN AUGENBLICK (THE GREAT MOMENT), the second film of the first 'Asta Nielsen series'. Urban Gad's name appears far smaller. Besides, the advert refers to a larger orchestra and fixed screening times. The resemblance to a 'proper' theatre premiere was to give this film premiere the air of a great event. The advertising strategy of DER SCHWARZE TRAUM was repeated: Another advert from 23 September reported traffic jams because huge crowds were rushing to the cinema. Hence the next screening was sold out, as the adverts from 25 September remarked.[20] A last advert from 29 September announced the last day of the "Asta Nielsen *Gastspiel* [guest performance]", again, a term from theatre jargon. All in all, the Union-Theater advertised this film five times.

IN DEM GROSSEN AUGENBLICK demonstrated Asta Nielsen's acting abilities in portraying a house maid in a rural manor who is seduced by the landlord's nephew and becomes pregnant. She therefore has to move to the big city where she tries to earn a living as a seamstress for herself and her child. As it happens she meets her former landlady in the tramway, who offers to adopt the child. Annie finally gives in with a heavy heart since her financial situation has become unbearable. Years later, she kidnaps her child and is sent to prison for a year. When she returns to the manor and recognises the house is on fire she rushes in and saves her child, sacrificing her own life. For many women in the Mannheim audience, the fate of Annie might have come close to their own experiences, because many of the female workers and servants originally came from rural areas to the big city and knew well the problems of earning one's living and finding the 'right' man. Mannheim had an extremely high percentage of unmarried women with illegitimate children at that time.[21]

ZIGEUNERBLUT (GIPSY'S BLOOD) was screened in October and promoted with five adverts.[22] The name Asta Nielsen clearly stands out in the adverts and is printed as large, or even larger, than the title of the film. Urban Gad is mentioned in far smaller type or not mentioned at all. In the advert on 21 October, the day of the premiere, the Union-Theater asked its patrons to visit the screenings in the afternoon because masses of cinema-goers were expected for the evening shows. This strategy of anticipating huge crowds storming the cinema might have created even larger crowds. The advert from 23 October actually reports that the box-office had been stormed two days earlier and that "every single one of the thousands of visitors was very satisfied with the captivating virtuoso dramatics of the great tragedienne Asta Nielsen".[23]

From 3 to 8 November, the residents of Mannheim viewed BRENNENDE

Adverts for BALLETTDANSERINDEN by both inner city cinemas in Mannheim on the same day, *Mannheimer Generalanzeiger* (4 November 1911).

TRIEBE (BALLETTDANSERINDEN, THE BALLET DANCER) which was shown at the Union-Theater as well as in the Saalbau cinema. This Asta Nielsen film was not an exclusive: the prints were sold by Nordisk Film, the Danish producer, on the free market. Both cinemas rented prints from distributors at the same time. This clearly indicates how much they already trusted in the appeal of Asta Nielsen, who was held capable of filling two major cinemas in one town. Both cinemas advertised the film in the local press. The Union-Theater paid for three adverts while the Saalbau cinema advertised twice. Both cinemas extended the screening for some more days, so that they both showed it for a whole week. As BALLETTDANSERINDEN was not rented as a *Monopolfilm*, it would normally have vanished from the programme after half a week like the other films. Therefore both cinemas felt the need to proclaim that they would keep it for another half week. In none of the adverts was Urban Gad mentioned. Although PAGU had made the contract with both, Nielsen and Gad, Asta Nielsen was the focus of attraction in public. The cinema owners anticipated that their audience would pay to watch the actress Asta Nielsen who was visible on screen. Urban Gad virtually vanished from the public consciousness as the author of the films.[24]

On 17 November 1911, EIN FREMDER VOGEL (THE COURSE OF TRUE LOVE) was advertised with two pre-announcements, one of which covered a press screening in Berlin for over 400 journalists and writers.[25] The daily press seldom reported on films or cinema showings at all. Press screenings of films were quite unusual at that time. But they became part of the effort to increase the cultural reputation of cinema and to establish film as art. Mentioning the press screening in the adverts was meant to attract the 'better audiences', i.e. the middle classes. Therefore the advert also mentions Nielsen's co-star, Carl Clewig, an actor from the Royal Theatre in Berlin. However, the advert left no doubt about the fact that it was Asta Nielsen who drew the masses into the cinema. In December the Union-Theater programmed DIE VERRÄTERIN (THE TRAITRESS). Similar to the campaign for DEN SORTE DRØM this film was also advertised by small mysterious pre-announcements days before the first screening. The large advert on the day of the premiere labels DIE VERRÄTERIN as the "best film" of the first 'Asta Nielsen series' and the "biggest and most thrilling sensational drama" and claimed that the story about a woman willing to sacrifice herself to another man for the release of her lover aroused "Amazement, Admiration, Delight".[26]

In comparison to the adverts for the Asta Nielsen films, no other films were advertised that prominently in Mannheim in 1911 in regards to the number, size and design of the respective adverts. But it seems as if the Asta Nielsen films and the way they were advertised were a forerunner of a more general trend in advertising: other long *Kinodramen* were promoted likewise in large and elaborate advertising. In August 1911, the audience viewed the German film DAS MODELL (THE MODEL), a film that drew a "shocking yet true picture of many metropolitan existences".[27] This film was very popular: The local newspaper indicated that 8736 patrons saw this picture in the Saalbau cinema on the first day of its exhibition. Furthermore, DIE BALLHAUS-ANNA (BALLROOM ANNA) was intensely advertised, "a demimonde drama from Berlin",[28] in which a girl has become the slave of money and ruins her lover. In general, 'demimonde' films became a real fad in Mannheim. VERIRRTE SEELEN (STRAY SOULS), "a realistic demimonde drama",[29] shown in October, was so popular that the Saalbau cinema had to extend it by another week. At the end of August, ROMAN EINES BLUMENMÄDCHENS (THE NOVEL OF A FLOWER GIRL) by Berlin-based Vitascope was shown. The trend of the social drama continued in September 1911 with DER AVIATIKER UND DIE FRAU DES JOURNALISTEN (FLYVEREN OG JOURNALISTEN HUSTRU, THE PILOT AND THE JOURNALIST'S WIFE), a drama of jealousy, and SÜNDIGE LIEBE (FOOLS OF SOCIETY), "a modern tableau of manners from the elegant world",[30] about a woman who

Advert for DER TOTENTANZ, *Mannheimer Generalanzeiger* (13 September 1912).

Advert for DER TOTENTANZ, *Mannheimer Generalanzeiger* (14 September 1912).

loves two men and in the end is forced to commit suicide. That film was extremely popular in Mannheim and was shown in both inner city cinemas which promoted it with great fanfare.[31] All these *Kinodramen* so prominently advertised had a running time of around one hour, most of them dealing with women's stories. Thus it is even more probable that Asta Nielsen and her female film characters laid the foundation on which this new kind of films could prosper and gain popularity, films which especially the female audiences could easily connect with.

In 1912 Asta Nielsen's films remained popular in Mannheim and were still aggressively advertised. What differentiated the first adverts from 1912 from other adverts for social and sensational dramas was the emphasis put on the fact that Asta Nielsen was playing the leading role, a fact that was as important, if not more so, than the title and content of the film. On 13 January, DIE MACHT DES GOLDES (THE BETTER WAY) was shown at the Union-Theater, followed by DIE ARME JENNY (POOR JENNY) on 10 February. On 6 April, the Union-Theater programmed ZU TODE GEHETZT (DRIVEN OUT). In general, the adverts were somewhat smaller than in 1911 and more standardised. It seems as if Asta Nielsen had already been well established as a brand, so there was no need for very large, conspicuous adverts anymore.

However, Asta Nielsen's remaining appeal is evidenced by the fact that the Saalbau cinema was programming older Asta Nielsen films as re-runs: In March and April 1912, NACHTFALTER and AFGRUNDEN which had been shown in 1911 were screened again for three days respectively.[32]

The second 'Asta Nielsen series' started in September 1912, prominently advertised as "The return of Asta Nielsen", with DER TOTENTANZ (THE DANCE TO DEATH). Furthermore, the advert mentions that the film was the first of a whole series of Asta Nielsen films ("Asta Nielsen Serie II"), all of which would be shown exclusively in the Union-Theater.[33] The next advert included even a picture of Asta Nielsen. Her face had become an icon, a symbol for her films.[34] From then on, one Asta Nielsen film per month was programmed: KINDER DES GENERALS (FALSLY ACCUSED) on 12 October, WENN DIE MASKE FÄLLT (WHEN THE MASK FALLS) on 9 November, and DAS MÄDCHEN OHNE VATERLAND (A GIRL WITHOUT A COUNTRY) on 7 December. All these films were advertised with one medium-size advert each and three other small adverts.

In comparison, the name of Asta Nielsen's rival Henny Porten is not mentioned once in cinema adverts until MASKIERTE LIEBE (MASKED LOVE), screened at the Union-Theater on 2 April 1912, is first promoted in the press. DES LEBENS WÜRFELSPIEL (THROWING THE DICE OF LIFE) was announced by both the Union-Theater and the Saalbau cinema on 27 April, but in this advert the name of Saharet, a then world-famous Australian cancan dancer, was written in even larger letters than Henny Porten's name. Many Henny Porten films were programmed in Mannheim during late 1912 and advertised as such, but the adverts were smaller and less elaborate than the adverts for Asta Nielsen films. Besides these two actresses, there was only a handful of other names that were mentioned – if only occasionally – in the adverts, among others Wanda Treumann and Viggo Larsen, Max Linder or Lissy Nebuschka.[35]

Audience response to Asta Nielsen in Mannheim

Extent and content of the abovementioned advertising campaigns for Asta Nielsen films in the local press suggest some popularity of Asta Nielsen in the city of Mannheim. Altenloh notes in her study that women, no matter from which social class, were among her fans.[36] But still this was even more true for women of the upper class: "Asta Nielsen dramas and historical productions in particular motivated them to attend a screening".[37] Her name is the only one that is particularly mentioned in Altenloh's book, standing *pars pro toto* for a whole new genre of films which especially catered to the interests of women in the audience: "If one looks at those programmes that have proven especially popular, this success can usually be traced to particular dramas. For example, the Asta Nielsen dramas were without exception the most popular ones shown in the better theatres".[38] Here she refers to the two inner city cinemas, Union-Theater and Saalbau cinema, which were by and large visited by women. In the suburban cinemas in the worker's neighbourhoods, Asta Nielsen was not that popular: "In contrast, the situation in the suburbs was exactly the opposite. For the film ZU TODE GEHETZT [DRIVEN OUT], with Asta Nielsen in the lead role, audience numbers fell below average."[39] Altenloh believes she knew the reason why Asta Nielsen dramas were so popular: Writing about the cinematic preferences of female clerical assistants, she traces their enthusiasm for Asta Nielsen's films back to the fact that her passionate character and the images of guilt and ultimate destiny shown in her films correspond to an outlook on life these women and girls already had: "It goes therefore without saying that Asta Nielsen enjoys huge popularity and arouses great admiration".[40] Her screen personality helped to increase the popularity of this new type of film, the long-feature *Kinodrama*, that was often telling stories never told on screen before, i.e. stories about women. Altenloh offers another reason why these films mainly catered to the interests of women: "Films that allow members of an audience to make a connection with their own social environment, whether depicting life as it is or as they wish it could be, are most popular and allow for greater emotional identification".[41] This was especially true of Asta Nielsen, who seemed to be exceptionally capable of affecting the audience on an emotional level by giving her film characters a special truthfulness and authenticity,[42] be they a single mother fighting for her child (as in IN DEM GROSSEN AUGENBLICK), a lower-class girl longing for social advancement (as in ARME JENNY) or just a loving woman or caring mother, as in most of her films. Thus, one might assume that it was mainly the women in the audience who helped Asta Nielsen become the first German film star and thus establish the *Kinodrama*, and with it the long feature film as a standard film form. The way the Asta Nielsen films were advertised in the local press indicates that they prepared the foundation for other long-feature films, especially the *Kinodramen*. Asta Nielsen can thus be seen as a catalyst of the transition from short film programmes to the long-feature film.

Notes

1. Emilie Altenloh, *Zur Soziologie des Kino. Die Kino-Unternehmung und die sozialen Schichten ihrer Besucher* [1914], edited by Andrea Haller, Martin Loiperdinger and Heide Schlüpmann (Frankfurt and Basel: Stroemfeld, 2012). A part of her dissertation appeared in an English translation: Emilie Altenloh, "A sociology of the cinema and the audience" [Kathleen Cross, trans.], *Screen* 42:3 (2001): 249–293.

2. Cf. Martin Loiperdinger, "Emilie Altenloh als historische Quelle lesen", in Altenloh, *Zur Soziologie des Kino*, ★103–★115.

3. Michael Caroli, "Fin de siècle oder Aufbruch zu neuen Ufern? Mannheim an der Schwelle zum

20. Jahrhundert", in Michael Caroli and Friedrich Teutsch (eds), *Mannheim im Aufbruch: die Stadt an der Wende vom 19. zum 20. Jahrhundert* (Mannheim: Verlagsbüro von Brandt, 1999), 25.

4. Cf. Martin Loiperdinger's essay in this volume; cf. also his "Der erste Filmstar im Monopolfilmverleih", in Heide Schlüpmann et al. (eds), *Unmögliche Liebe. Asta Nielsen, ihr Kino* (2nd edn) (Vienna: filmarchiv austria, 2010), 177–186, here 182–185.

5. Peter Lähn, "Die PAGU. Ein Filmunternehmen aus Frankfurt", in Rudolf Worschech et al. (eds), *Lebende Bilder einer Stadt. Kino und Film in Frankfurt am Main* (Frankfurt: Deutsches Filmmuseum, 1995), 52–59, here 56.

6. *Mannheimer Generalanzeiger* (11 August 1911; 29 September 1911).

7. THE JACK JOHNSON AND JIM JEFFRIES FIGHT marked the beginning of the practice to treat the mere length of a film as quality criterion and an argument in advertising. Cf. Corinna Müller, *Frühe deutsche Kinematographie. Formale, wirtschaftliche und kulturelle Entwicklungen 1907–1912* (Stuttgart and Weimar: Metzler, 1994), 119.

8. Cf. Müller, *Frühe deutsche Kinematographie*, 126–157.

9. *Mannheimer Generalanzeiger* (28 January 1911).

10. Martin Loiperdinger, "*Afgrunden* in Germany. Monopolfilm, cinemagoing and the emergence of the film star Asta Nielsen in Germany", in Daniel Biltereyst, Richard Maltby and Philippe Meers (eds), *Cinema, Audiences and Modernity. New perspectives on European cinema history* (London: Routledge, 2012), 149.

11. Altenloh, *Zur Soziologie des Kino*, 9.

12. Altenloh, "A sociology of the cinema", 258.

13. *Mannheimer Generalanzeiger* (24 June 1911).

14. Ibid.

15. *Mannheimer Generalanzeiger* (20 May 1911).

16. *Mannheimer Generalanzeiger* (23 August 1911).

17. *Mannheimer Generalanzeiger* (24 August 1911).

18. *Mannheimer Generalanzeiger* (26 August 1911).

19. *Mannheimer Generalanzeiger* (1 September 1911).

20. *Mannheimer Generalanzeiger* (23 and 25 September 1911).

21. Cf. Sabine Heißler, "'Stets habe ich mir ein nahes Ziel gewählt, doch hat ein fernes mich dazu beseelt.' Sexualreform, der Bund für Mutterschutz und der Kampf gegen den §218 in Mannheim von 1907–1933", in Frauenbeauftragte der Stadt Mannheim und die Autorinnen (eds): *Stadt ohne Frauen? Frauen in der Geschichte Mannheims* (Mannheim: Edition Quadrat, 1993), 185–200, here 187–189.

22. *Mannheimer Generalanzeiger* (10–23 October 1911).

23. *Mannheimer Generalanzeiger* (23 October 1911).

24. For a detailed study on the importance of Urban Gad and for his influence on the first Asta Nielsen films, cf. Stephan Michael Schröder, "Und Urban Gad? Zur Frage der Autorschaft in den Filmen bis 1914", in Schlüpmann, *Unmögliche Liebe*, 194–210. Schröder, furthermore, finds that Urban Gad re-emerges into the public as the film author during the wave of the *Autorenfilme* around 1913.

25. *Mannheimer Generalanzeiger* (17 November 1911).

26. *Mannheimer Generalanzeiger* (16 December 1911).

27. *Mannheimer Generalanzeiger* (5 August 1911).

28. *Mannheimer Generalanzeiger* (12 August 1911).

29. *Mannheimer Generalanzeiger* (28 October 1911).

30. *Mannheimer Generalanzeiger* (23 September 1911).

31. Cf. Jon Burrows' essay in this volume on FOOLS OF SOCIETY in Great Britain. For a detailed analysis of the *Kinodramen* and social dramas shown in Mannheim, cf. my dissertation: Andrea Haller, *Weibliches Publikum, Programmgestaltung und Rezeptionshaltung im frühen deutschen Kino (1906–1918)* (doctoral thesis, Trier: University of Trier, 2009), 209–259.

32. NACHTFALTER: 20–23 March 1912, AFGRUNDEN: 17–19 April 1912.
33. *Mannheimer Generalanzeiger* (13 September 1912).
34. *Mannheimer Generalanzeiger* (14 September 1912).
35. Cf. Haller, *Weibliches Publikum*, 209–259.
36. Altenloh, "A sociology of the cinema", 259 and 283.
37. Ibid., 285.
38. Ibid., 259.
39. Ibid.
40. Ibid., 283.
41. Ibid., 259.
42. Cf. for example the results and answers of a survey about the favourite film star in the fan magazine *Illustrierte Filmwoche*: "Unsere Preisrundfrage: Wer ist die beliebteste Filmkünstlerin?" *Illustrierte Filmwoche*, no 17 (1918): 141, where the authenticity of Nielsen's acting is emphasised several times, a kind of authenticity that triumphs over personal vanity.

PART IV

ASTA NIELSEN FILMS IN LOCAL EXHIBITION

Café Lehners Kinotheater Karlstrasse 11

Nur für Erwachsene — **Ab heute:** — **Nur für Erwachsene**

Höchst spannend! — Polizeilich genehmigt! — Höchst spannend!

Die Abgründe

Grossartiges Theaterdrama!
in 2 Akten von Anton Gad
in 100.000 Einzelaufnahmen.
Vorführungsdauer ¾ Stunden.

J943

Bitte überzeugen, dann urteilen sie selbst!

Wir besitzen das **alleinige** Vorführungsrecht dieses **nie wiederkehrenden Attraktionsstückes!**

Staunend! — Durchschlagender Erfolg! — Staunend!

Ermässigungskarten haben keine Giltigkeit

Tausend Kronen

derjenigen Konkurrenzfirma, welche im Stande ist, das Bild gleichzeitig mit uns aufzuführen.

Zentral-Kinematograph.

Ein Rekord. — **Nie wiederkehrend.**

Alles bisher Dagewesene in Schatten stellend.

Nur bei uns zu sehen. — **Ab Ostermontag** — Nur bei uns zu sehen.

Kinder haben keinen Zutritt.

Konkurrenzlos!

Heißes Blut

Das alleinige Aufführungsrecht für Innsbruck erworben.

2000 Kronen zahlen wir demjenigen Konkurrenz-Unternehmen, welches im Stande ist, das Bild mit uns heute aufzuführen.

Theater-Drama in 2 Abteilungen von Urban Gad.
In 100.000 Einzelaufnahmen.

Vorführungsdauer dieses Bildes zirka 1 Stunde.
Filmlänge 900 Meter.
Außerdem 2 weitere erstklassige Prachtnummern.

Dieses Bild übertrifft alle bis jetzt gezeigten Schlagerfilms, die spannendsten Handlungen von Urban Gad, dem Verfasser von **Abgründe** mit Asta Nielsen, Kopenhagen, in der Hauptrolle.

J2282

Verantwortlicher Schriftleiter: Hermann Prechtl.
Herausgegeben von der Wagner'schen Universitäts-Buchhandlung. — Druck der Wagner'schen Universitäts-Buchdruckerei. — Papier von Othmar Tschurr.
Die heutige Nummer besteht aus 48 Seiten.

Patric Blaser

Asta Nielsen Films in Innsbruck before the First World War

The first star of the German film industry as well as audience response to the exhibition of long feature films in Austria-Hungary – these are topics which have been rarely treated by Austrian film scholars so far. This is all the more astonishing as the distributor of Asta Nielsen films, the Internationale Films-Vertrieb-Gesellschaft (IFVG), was based in Vienna. IFVG was founded by Christoph Mülleneisen Sr., owner of several cinemas in Cologne and the Rhineland, by Paul Davidson, head of the Frankfurt based Projektions AG Union (PAGU), and by Dr. Kühnelt of the Österreichisch-Ungarische Kino-Industrie Gesellschaft (ÖUKI). The business of the IFVG was the marketing of the 'Asta Nielsen series' all over the world.

Mülleneisen's interest was attracted by Ludwig Gottschalk's enormous success in distributing AFGRUNDEN which was the introduction of the exclusive system into Germany's film business. In the beginning of 1911, from the Strasbourg based Aktien-Gesellschaft für Kinematographie und Filmverleih, Mülleneisen bought the exclusive distribution licence for the territory of Austria-Hungary of two other films with Asta Nielsen in the lead role, HEISSES BLUT (BURNING BLOOD) and NACHTFALTER (RETRIBUTION), produced by Deutsche Bioscop in Berlin, and written and directed by Urban Gad. Since, as he claimed later in the trade press, that no distributor was really interested in any of these two films,[1] he offered HEISSES BLUT and NACHTFALTER directly to the cinema owners. Thus, already in April and May 1911, interested parties could read the names Urban Gad and Asta Nielsen several times in Mülleneisen's advertisements for these two exclusive films.[2] This obviously turned out to be a fortunate decision that inspired him to arrange the groundbreaking deal with Asta Nielsen and Urban Gad.

In 1912 the IFVG was for the first time listed in Vienna's company register *Lehmann's Allgemeiner Wohnungsanzeiger für Wien*. The company's original capital was 90,000 crowns. Paul Davidson and a partner named Felix Franz Forster

---

Facing page:
Above: *Innsbrucker Nachrichten*, no. 40 (18 February 1911).
Below: *Innsbrucker Nachrichten*, no. 87 (15 April 1911).

were named as executive directors. The adress of the IFVG was Neubaugasse 33 in the 7th district in Vienna which was also the address of the ÖUKI. At the end of May 1911, in PAGU's office in Frankfurt, Asta Nielsen and Urban Gad signed the contract stipulating that in the following three years ten films be made per year, exclusively for the IVFG.[3] Unfortunately we did not succeed yet in finding any business documents, in Vienna, neither of the IFVG nor of the ÖUKI.

In the first week of June 1911, the IFVG informed German cinema owners in the trade press that Asta Nielsen and Urban Gad had signed a contract with them. In Austria-Hungary, advertising and booking of the first 'Asta Nielsen series' was handled by the ÖUKI. On 10 June 1911, cinema owners in Austria were informed via the trade journal *Österreichischer Komet*: "We brought off a special deal for years with Urban Gad and Asta Nielsen. More information is coming soon".[4] This advertisement was again published on 24 June and on 10 July with the notice: "Advanced bookings requested immediately, because only a few weeks available".[5] This was the beginning of a considerable promotion campaign for Asta Nielsen films in the Austrian trade press. This paper will focus on the question, how the campaign affected the exhibition and programming of films in Austrian cinemas, or, in other words, how cinema owners reacted to this campaign and brought Asta Nielsen to Austrian cinema-goers.

Besides posters in the streets, local newspapers were the most important media used by exhibitors to advertise their weekly or twice-a-week changes of film programmes. There is still not much known on programming and exhibition in Austria-Hungary's capital, Vienna. Strikingly, we know little to nothing about Asta Nielsen's appearances on screen in European film trading centres as London, Paris, and Berlin. There were simply too many newspapers published in these cities as to place advertisements in an effective, yet reasonable way. On the contrary, in a middle-sized provincial town as Innsbruck, for instance, the situation was much different: Here, the leading newspaper on local affairs of that time is still extant, thus exhibition practices of local cinemas and the film programmes they advertised to their patrons can be studied.

Around 1910 Innsbruck was a provincial boom town with a very vital and growing civic cultural life. From 1900 to 1910, due to demographic factors, to migration and incorporation, Innsbruck's population almost doubled from 29,000 to more than 53,000 inhabitants. Migration alone had a share of 30 per cent of the population's growth.[6] Innsbruck was a 'young' city: More than 57 per cent of the population were 30 years of age and younger.[7] Maybe for that reason cinema-going was a growing leisure time activity. In 1911 there were four cinemas running in Innsbruck: Zentral-Kinematograph, Café Lehners Kinematograph, Theater-Kinematograph, and Bierwastl-Kinematograph. All of them were located in the historic city centre, and they announced their film programmes regularly in the leading local newspaper *Innsbrucker Nachrichten*. Studying their many advertisements allows detailed insights into Asta Nielsen's appearances on local screens, and in addition it enables researchers to study the implementation of the exclusive system in the business of film distribution, on a more general level.

In Innsbruck, screenings of Asta Nielsen's first film AFGRUNDEN started on 18 February 1911, with the title DIE ABGRÜNDE, according to an unusually large half-page advertisement of Café Lehner's Kinematograph in *Innsbrucker Nachrichten*. Lehner promoted DIE ABGRÜNDE as a "great theatre drama in two acts by Anton [sic] Gad", consisting of "100,000 single photographs [i.e. single frames] which implied "three quarters of an hour" of projection time.[8] Asta Nielsen was not mentioned yet. This first advertisement focused on the exclusivity of this unusually long feature film. In Germany, Ludwig Gottschalk had started distribution of ABGRÜNDE as an exclusive *Monopolfilm* already at the end of November 1910.[9] Café Lehner claimed the exclusive screening licence for DIE ABGRÜNDE in Innsbruck and promised "one thousand crowns to any rivaling company who would be able to show this picture, at the same time".[10] Readers were also informed about censorship restrictions: DIE ABGRÜNDE had been passed by the police, but access to screenings had been limited "for adults only". Three days later, the next advertisement promoted ABGRÜNDE! as "the gossip of the whole city of Innsbruck".[11] After six days at Café Lehner's Kinematograph, the film print shifted to the rivaling Zentral-Kinematograph and was shown there as DIE ABGRÜNDE! on Friday, 24 February, for only one single day.[12] This must have been accomplished on very short notice, as the day before readers of *Innsbrucker Nachrichten* were still notified about a short film programme that was to be screened on Friday.[13] Zentral-Kinematograph had programmed DIE WEISSE SKLAVIN – ZWEITES BILD (DEN HVIDE SLAVEHANDELS SIDSTE OFFER, IN THE HANDS OF IMPOSTORS) one day before, consisting of "100,000 single photographs" [i.e. single frames]", before Café Lehner launched DIE ABGRÜNDE. It is not known to us, from whom the owners of Zentral-Kinematograph purchased the licence to screen Asta Nielsen's first film, but seemingly the cinema was very keen to get ahold of DIE ABGRÜNDE! if only for one day.

Seven weeks later, Zentral-Kinematograph announced Asta Nielsen's second film HEISSES BLUT (BURNING BLOOD) with a half page advertisement trumpeting "This will be dwarfing everything you could have seen in the past!"[14] Editorial publicity in the column 'Schaustellungen' (shows) of *Innsbrucker Nachrichten* confirmed this: "According to the unisonous judgement of experts, artists and dramatists, this photoplay is the most fabulous, beautiful picture which will amaze customers to the highest degree".[15] Both the advertisement and the editorial text referred to Urban Gad as the author of ABGRÜNDE, and mentioned Asta Nielsen as playing the lead character. Zentral-Kinematograph underlined the exclusivity of these showings by promising to pay 2,000 crowns to any competing company that would be able to screen HEISSES BLUT at the same time. HEISSES BLUT was screened, with two additional first class programme numbers, on Easter Sunday and Monday, from 10 am to 10 pm, without a break.

Innsbrucker Nachrichten, no. 268 (22 November 1911).

Less than two months later, the week-end after Pentecost, the third film directed by Urban Gad with Asta Nielsen playing the lead character was shown in Innsbruck. The Zentral-Kinematograph announced DER NACHTFALTER (RETRIBUTION) as a tragedy of a woman, adapted from a boulevard theatre play of Paris. Meanwhile, Asta Nielsen seemingly was a well-known screen personality as the advertisement invited readers: "Do not hesitate a minute!", because "how Asta Nielsen plays the part must be seen".[16] But patrons had only a three days chance to see, from Saturday until Monday, 10 to 12 June.[17] During the summer weeks of 1911, there was growing competition between Lehner's Kinematograph and Zentral-Kinematograph, according to their newspaper advertisements. Innsbruck's two leading cinemas tried to cry up each other by promoting so-called 'Schlager' (hits), e.g. single films which they screened only for two or three days, sometimes only for one day, underlining the uniqueness of sensation that those films offered the audience to be experienced. In the middle of June, both cinemas praised their own local films which they had taken of the Corpus Christi procession at Innsbruck,[19] and during the last week-end of June, both cinemas screened DIE WEISSE SKLAVIN III (THE WHITE SLAVE III), produced by Vitascope in Berlin.[19]

In the beginning of the 1911/12 season, Café Lehner's Kinematograph annonced "Monopol-Films" which were "in preparation", and challenged to pay

Innsbrucker Nachrichten, no. 73 (30 March 1912).

2,000 crowns to any person who would be able to screen one of these "Monopolbilder" ('monopol' pictures) in the month of September.[20] A few days later, on 11 September, Zentral-Kinematograph responded by promoting DER SCHWARZE TRAUM (DEN SORTE DRØM, THE CIRCUS GIRL) "with the famous Nilsen" [sic], and offered, for his part, 2,000 crowns to any competitor who would be able to screen this "world hit" during the same two days when Zentral-Kinematograph showed it.[21] DER SCHWARZE TRAUM had been produced in Denmark by Fotorama, but was sold to Germany, including exhibition rights for all countries but Denmark, and became the first of eight films that made up the first 'Asta Nielsen series' marketed by the Internationale Films-Vertrieb-Gesellschaft in Vienna. Exactly one month later, on 11 October, ABGRÜNDE II. TEIL (THE ABYSS, 2nd series) with the subtitle "Das Schicksal einer Verlorenen" (The Fate of a Lost Woman) was announced, in bold type, as "Monopol-Kunstfilm" ('monopol' art film) by Café Lehner's Kinematograph.[22] This "Sittendrama" (drama of manners)[23] was produced by Vitascope in Berlin and distributed by Ludwig Gottschalk as some kind of 'remake' to repeat the tremendous success he had made with ABGRÜNDE. Not surprisingly, Gottschalk's advertisements in the German trade press do not reveal the name of the actress who played the lead character (thus, so to speak, suggesting that it was Asta Nielsen).

Innsbrucker Nachrichten, no. 243 (21 October 1912).

On 31 October, in a half-page advertisement, Café Lehner's Kinematograph admitted to a certain extent to a deception; while claiming that there had been "No deception!", it promised screenings of the "Asta Nilsen [sic] Kunstfilm" (art film) BRENNENDE TRIEBE (BALLETDANSERINDEN, THE BALLET DANCER), the "Greatest Nordic hit of the season".[24] Produced in Denmark with Urban Gad and Asta Nielsen by Nordisk Film, this film was available without any marketing restrictions. Café Lehner's Kinematograph claimed triumphantly: "Even if my enemies turn upside down, I will still present the best of the best!"[25] But such rhetoric of self-praise could not help Lehner's falling behind his most important competitor: Zentral-Kinematograph showed five films of the first 'Asta Nielsen series' in Innsbruck: After DER SCHWARZE TRAUM, Zentral-Kinematograph announced ZIGEUNERBLUT (GIPSY'S BLOOD) on 22 November, with both Urban Gad and Asta Nielsen named in the advert.[26] On 5 January 1912, a "Dienstmann" (barker) advertised DIE VERRÄTERIN (THE TRAITRESS) as an "Asta Nilsen [sic] Schlager" (Asta Nilsen [sic] hit).[27] On 30 March, the barker design announced DIE ARME JENNY (POOR JENNY) as an "Asta Nielsen Gastspiel" (guest performance).[28] On 4 May, the "Asta Nielsen Schlager" ZU TODE GEHETZT was promoted as the "last film of this series 1912", shown between a Gaumont newsreel and Gaumont's KATASTROPHE DER TITANIC (THE TITANIC DISASTER) of which a detailed description was added.[29]

On Easter Sunday, 7 April 1912, not far from the Zentral-Kinematograph, the Triumph-Kino "newly built and equipped with all comfort of modern age" opened with a benefit show at Maria Theresienstraße 17, in one of Innsbruck's noblest shopping streets.[30] For a short period there were five cinemas in Innsbruck. But already at the end of May, the Bierwastl-Kinematograph stopped screening films and reduced its shows to concerts and cabaret. On 11 May, the *Innsbrucker Nachrichten* started the daily column 'Innsbrucker Allgemeiner Kino-Anzeiger' (Innsbruck General Cinema Advertiser) where all cinema announcements were published side by side. This innovation was an advantage for customers and readers, because information on the film programmes of Innsbruck's cinemas was now available in every issue of the local newspaper and easy to locate for their patrons. For a while the 'Kino-Anzeiger' abandoned printing single cinema advertisements of different sizes and designs.

Triumph-Kino, the new player on Innsbruck's film market, obviously had purchased the exclusive rights for Innsbruck to the Asta Nielsen films of the season. On 23 September 1912, Triumph-Kino advertised DER TOTENTANZ (THE DANCE TO DEATH), "the first drama of the new Asta Nielsen series 1912/13 – definitely for only 4 days", from Saturday to Tuesday, 21 to 24 September.[31] For exactly the same period, Zentral-Kinematograph launched GLÜHENDE LIEBE – LODERNDER HASS (DOCKAN ELLER GLÖDANDE KÄRLEK, TURNED ADRIFT) – with an actress called Ida Nielsen! A coincidence – made up consciously or just a chance circumstance? Two days before, the Zentral-Kinematograph had placed an article on Ida Nielsen in the local newspaper *Innsbrucker Nachrichten* saying:

> From today on the Zentral-Kinematograph will present the first picture of the excclusive Ida Nielsen series. Contrary to all other allegations, Ida Nielsen were not an actress and called herself Ida Nielsen as a preudonym, it is hereby intimated that Ida Nielsen is the first opera- primadonna at the biggest stages of her Nordic home and bound herself to the Swedish Art Film Company for one year. The first Tyrolian film distributor A. Marx purchased the exclusive distribution rights for Tyrol, Salzbourg, Upper Austria, Styria and Carinthia, and the first of these pictures GLÜHENDE LIEBE – LODERNDER HASS is presented at the Zentral-Kinematograph.[32]

Adolf Marx, cinema owner, managed the Zentral-Kinematograph. The Danish actress Ida Nielsen (1887–1918), born Ida Kier, played in operettas in Copenhagen and Aarhus. In 1910, she married Holger Nielsen, a bandmaster. In 1911 and 1912, she played the lead characters in a series of several long feature films produced by Frans Lundberg of Malmö which were promoted in the German trade press. She was certainly not a double or look-alike of Asta Nielsen, but cinema owners used her name somehow pretending to show 'Nielsen' films. A film distributor even advertised GLÜHENDE LIEBE – LODERNDER HASS as an Asta Nielsen film.[33]

On Tuesday, 8 October 1912, readers of *Innsbrucker Nachrichten* were informed about four long feature films with an actress called Nielsen playing the lead character: Zentral-Kinematograph announced "today for the last time" BRENNENDE TRIEBE (THE BALLET DANCER) which had already been shown in Innsbruck one year before by Café Lehner's Kinematograph.[34] But the days before, BRENNENDE TRIEBE does not show up at all in Zentral-Kinematograph advertisements. As it seems, Adolf Marx got ahold of a print of this Danish Asta Nielsen film on short notice and screened it for only one or two days. Then, from 19 to 22 October 1912, parallel screenings of films with Asta Nielsen and Ida Nielsen respectively occurred again: When Triumph-Kino screened DIE KINDER DES GENERALS (FALSELY ACCUSED) as "Asta Nielsen guest performance" and "second film of the series 1912/13", Zentral-Kinematograph screened ZIRKUSLUFT (CIRKUSLUFT, CIRCUS QUEEN), "second picture of the

Ida Nielsen Series 1912".[35] With good reason we can assume that, at the end of 1912, (Asta) Nielsen was a celebrated name which cinema managers attempted to benefit from. This assumption is supported by another strange case: On 14 October, Theater-Kino announced the "Asta Nielsen drama" SCHWARZES BLUT (BLACK BLOOD). In Asta Nielsen's filmography this title does not exist. But in 1912, Harry Piel produced and directed a film called SCHWARZES BLUT – with Curt Goetz, Ernst A. Becker and Erna Nitter, but not with Asta Nielsen! A consciously concocted coincidence or just another chapter of the confusing comedy of errors?

From 16 November to 10 December, according to the announcements in *Innsbrucker Nachrichten*, the programmes of four week-ends (which were screened, as usual, from Saturday to Tuesday) consisted of the four episodes of MENSCHEN UNTER MENSCHEN, adapted from Victor Hugo's famous novel *Les Misérables* – they were shown in three of the four cinemas of Innsbruck: Triumph-Kino, Zentral-Kinematograph, and Café Lehner's Kinematograph.[36] Asta Nielsen was placed in the interval between the second and the third episode of MENSCHEN UNTER MENSCHEN, from Wednesday to Friday, 27–29 November: Triumph-Kino announced WENN DIE MASKE FÄLLT (WHEN THE MASK FALLS) as "third drama of the series 1912/13", with "the artist Asta Nielsen in the lead role". In the column called 'Schaustellungen' (shows) of *Innsbrucker Nachrichten*, a few lines of editorial publicity portrayed the programmes and the popularity of the Triumph-Kino in highest praise:

> One thing is sure that the audience is highly satisfied by the programme of the Triumph-Kino. This is proven by the scores of visitors which the shows of this company can boast of. Accordingly the owner of this theatre will from today on present the newest drama of the Asta Nielsen series WENN DIE MASKE FÄLLT, truly a masterpiece of film art. Since this outstanding piece will only be shown for three days (Wednesday to Friday), therefore it should be all the more so drawn to everybody's attention that nobody should miss to get to know this grandiose drama.[37]

At Christmas 1912, Zentral-Kinemotograph moved from Maria Theresienstrasse no. 10 to a huge new theatre at no. 37. A full-page advertisement praised the new venue as a "first class showplace", with a capacity for audiences of 500 patrons and with an orchestra of nine musicians.[38] "Beautiful interior, splendid pictures and good music are the main reasons for a bulk of visitors every day", it was emphasised.[39] From August onward, Zentral-Kino even showed vaudeville acts at the evening performances.[40] Simultaneously with its new house and the numerous restructurings, Zentral-Kino started running individual advertisements again which were placed outside the 'Innsbrucker Allgemeiner Kino-Anzeiger' column. As a consequence, all cinema owners in Innsbruck restarted their agressive advertising activities.

On 11 January, Triumph-Kino announced a "New appearance of Asta Nielsen" with JUGEND UND TOLLHEIT (IN A FIX),[41] which was followed, in the last days of March, by her "guest performance" in DER TOD IN SEVILLA (SPANISH

BLOOD).⁴² Editorial publicity describes the latter as the "most important hit by Asta Nielsen, because significant difficulties were faced during the shooting".⁴³

Triumph-Kino's extra advertisement trumpeted: "The newest hit DER TOD IN SEVILLA. Asta Nielsen causes a sensation. A bullfight shot on location."⁴⁴ From 17 to 20 May, Triumph-Kino finished the series with DIE SÜNDEN DER VÄTER (TEMPTATIONS OF DRINK), "the last Asta Nielsen drama of the season".⁴⁵

For the opening of the new season 1913/14, Triumph-Kino started a campaign with a half-page advertisement claiming on 6 August: "Asta Nielsen plays only at Triumph-Kino! Henny Porten plays only at Triumph-Kino! Wanda Treumann und Viggo Larsen play only at Triumph-Kino!"⁴⁶ Three days later, Triumph-Kino declared: "Attention! Triumph-Kino programmes can not be surpassed! We have always been the leader in the market concerning the compilation of our programmes. But due to our manifold contracts of purchase we now are standing out uniquely!"⁴⁷ A large sized advertisement published on 27 August assured readers: "We do not need to advertise separately, because everybody knows the exquisite quality of our programs. And one tells the next one!"⁴⁸

Asta Nielsen's "first guest performance" of the season was DAS MÄDCHEN OHNE VATERLAND (A GIRL WITHOUT A COUNTRY), "a drama from the Balkan war", from 18 to 21 October.⁴⁹ Asta Nielsen's "second guest performance" followed with DIE SUFFRAGETTE (THE SUFFRAGETTE), from 15 to 18 November. Then, from 3 to 6 January 1914, Triumph-Kino screened MILITÄRLUFT-SCHIFF "S1" (A GIRL'S SACRIFICE),⁵⁰ and, from 21 to 23 February, DIE FILM-PRIMADONNA (THE FILM PRIMADONNA) was shown.⁵¹

In the beginning of march 1914, the advertisement activities outside the 'Innsbrucker Allgemeiner Kino-Anzeiger' column decreased noticeably. Competition between the cinemas in Innsbruck shifted to the question of admission fees. On 20 March, Triumph-Kino published an exhausting and large sized advertisement designed as an "open letter" to justify the reduction of admission fees by underlining "that the point is not to attract patrons, but to give all the world the opportunity to see for oneself that our programmes are unrivaled".⁵² One day later, a large extra advertisement announced ENGELEIN (UP TO HER TRICKS).⁵³ Asta Nielsen's "last guest performance for this season" – and, due to the First World War, for a long period of time – was ZAPATAS BANDE (ZAPATA'S GANG). Triumph-Kino promised: "This magnificent comedy moves the audience into the most cheerful mood".⁵⁴

The appearance of Asta Nielsen can be considered as a key moment in film promotion by cinema owners in Innsbruck. AFGRUNDEN was the first film which was purchased and distributed with exclusive rights and Café Lehner's numerous adverts in the *Innsbrucker Nachrichten* in February 1911 were part of one of the first campaigns for a single film in Innsbruck, which became standard soon. In connection with this, it becomes obvious, how fast the introduction of the exclusive rental system took place and how important it must have been for local cinemas to secure the unrivalled screening-right for a long feature in a city like Innsbruck.

Last but not at least, cinema adverts indicate how Asta Nielsen affected the campaigns. She was not only one of the very first actors whose names appeared regularly in adverts, her name functioned like a label which could be used in advertisements. And this can be read as something we nearly know nothing about: the effect Asta Nielsen must have had on contemporary patrons, how she must have been admired and honoured by cinema goers at that time, so we can speak about her as the first female film star.

Notes

1. Cf. Christoph Mülleneisen, "Wie ich Asta Nielsen engagierte", *Erste Internationale Film-Zeitung*, (25 April 1914), repr. in Renate Seydel and Allan Hagedorff (eds), *Asta Nielsen. Ihr Leben in Fotodokumenten, Selbstzeugnissen und zeitgenössischen Betrachtungen* (Berlin, GDR: Henschelverlag Kunst und Gesellschaft, 1984), 48–51.
2. *Österreichischer Komet*, no. 67 (10 May 1911), 4.
3. Cf. Martin Loiperdinger's essay in this volume.
4. *Österreichischer Komet*, no. 69 (10 June 1911), 4.
5. *Österreichischer Komet* , no. 71 (10 July 1911), 4.
6. *Statistische Monatsschrift*, vol. 39 (Vienna: 1913), 212–213.
7. "Ergebnisse der Volkszählung vom 31. Dezember 1910", *Österreichische Statistik*, Neue Folge 1:3 (Vienna: 1917).
8. *Innsbrucker Nachrichten*, no. 40 (18 February 1911).
9. *Der Kinematograph*, no. 204 (23 November 1910).
10. *Innsbrucker Nachrichten*, no. 40 (18 February 1911).
11. *Innsbrucker Nachrichten*, no. 42 (21 February 1911), 10.
12. *Innsbrucker Nachrichten*, no. 45 (24 February 1911), 16.
13. *Innsbrucker Nachrichten*, no. 44 (23 February 1911), 6.
14. *Innsbrucker Nachrichten*, no. 87 (15 April 1911), 16.
15. Ibid., 6.
16. *Innsbrucker Nachrichten*, no. 132 (10 June 1911), 10.
17. *Innsbrucker Nachrichten*, no. 133 (12 June 1911), 11.
18. *Innsbrucker Nachrichten*, no. 136 (16 June 1911), 12 and 15.
19. Cf. *Innsbrucker Nachrichten*, no. 142 (23 June 1911); 16; no. 143 (24 June 1911), 9 and 36.
20. Cf. *Innsbrucker Nachrichten*, no. 204 (6 September 1911), 15.
21. *Innsbrucker Nachrichten*, no. 207 (11 September 1911), 16.
22. *Innsbrucker Nachrichten*, no. 233 (11 October 1911), 16.
23. *Innsbrucker Nachrichten*, no. 236 (11 October 1911), 15.
24. *Innsbrucker Nachrichten*, no. 250 (31 October 1911), 15.
25. Ibid.
26. *Innsbrucker Nachrichten*, no. 268 (22 November 1911), 16.
27. *Innsbrucker Nachrichten*, no. 4 (5 January 1912), 10.
28. *Innsbrucker Nachrichten*, no. 73 (30 March 1912), 37.
29. *Innsbrucker Nachrichten*, no.102 (4 May 1912), 28.
30. *Innsbrucker Nachrichten*, no.79 (6 April 1912), 42.
31. *Innsbrucker Nachrichten*, no. 218 (23 September 1912), 16.

32. *Innsbrucker Nachrichten*, no. 217 (21 September 1912), 5.
33. Cf. Jan Olsson, *Sensationer från en bakgård. Frans Lundberg som biografägare och filmproducent i Malmö? och Köpenhamm* (Stockholm: Symposion, 1988).
34. *Innsbrucker Nachrichten*, no. 231 (8 October 1912), 16.
35. *Innsbrucker Nachrichten*, no. 243 (21 October 1912), 15.
36. The day before the series started Triumph-Kino placed a leaflet in the *Innsbrucker Nachrichten*, no. 263 (15 November 1912), referring explicitly to the new series produced by Pathé (which premiered in Paris only on 3 January 1913). Already in 1909, Vitagraph had produced an American version of Hugo's novel, directed by Stuart Blackton. The question of which cinema in Innsbruck screened which particular version of Hugo's *Les Misérables* parts remains open to further research.
37. *Innsbrucker Nachrichten*, no. 273 (27 November 1912), 9.
38. *Innsbrucker Nachrichten*, no. 3 (4 January 1913), 16.
39. *Innsbrucker Nachrichten*, no. 20 (25 January 1913), 6.
40. *Innsbrucker Nachrichten*, no. 176 (2 August 1913), 6.
41. *Innsbrucker Nachrichten*, no. 8 (11 January 1913), 15.
42. *Innsbrucker Nachrichten*, no. 72 (31 March 1913), 10.
43. *Innsbrucker Nachrichten*, no. 71 (29 March 1913), 23.
44. *Innsbrucker Nachrichten*, no. 72 (31 March 1913), 10.
45. *Innsbrucker Nachrichten*, no. 112 (19 May 1913), 15.
46. *Innsbrucker Nachrichten*, no. 179 (6 Augsut 1913), 16.
47. *Innsbrucker Nachrichten*, no. 182 (9 August 1913), 16.
48. *Innsbrucker Nachrichten*, no. 196 (27 August 1913), 16.
49. *Innsbrucker Nachrichten*, no. 263 (15 November 1913), 11.
50. *Innsbrucker Nachrichten*, no. 2 (3 January 1914), 9.
51. *Innsbrucker Nachrichten*, no. 42 (21 February 1914), 36.
52. *Innsbrucker Nachrichten*, no. 64 (20 March 1914), 11.
53. *Innsbrucker Nachrichten*, no. 65 (21 March 1914), 38.
54. *Innsbrucker Nachrichten*, no. 105 (9 May 1914), 9.

Mattia Lento

Asta Nielsen in Zurich
Film Exhibition and Reviews

Doing research on the exhibition of Asta Nielsen films before the First World War means always more than a case study on an early film star. Asta Nielsen and her films were crucial for the transformation of film exhibition in the beginning 1910s. Corinna Müller and Martin Loiperdinger have demonstrated how the emergence of the Danish film star was intertwined with substantial changes in German film trade and film exhibition.[1] Between 1908 and 1910, the prospects for German film producers and distributors were not promising, because the film supply exceeded by far the demand. Films were still sold per metre and only something like twice the price of Eastman's raw film stock could be asked for them.[2] In late 1910, distributor Ludwig Gottschalk from Düsseldorf started a massive advertising campaign in the trade press to promote Asta Nielsen's first film AFGRUNDEN (THE ABYSS) as a *Monopolfilm* with exclusive local exhibition rights. This mode of film renting enabled individual films to be intensively exploited for a considerable profit. AFGRUNDEN, released as ABGRÜNDE, was screened in the entire country with enormous success.[3] In May 1911, Asta Nielsen and Urban Gad were exclusively contracted to produce three exclusive film series consisting of ten long feature films each which were to be distributed by the newly founded Internationale Films-Vertrieb-Gesellschaft (IFVG). For the release of the first series in August 1911, Asta Nielsen was advertised 'the Eleonora Duse of Film Art', and she became the most popular film actress among German film audiences in the early 1910s.

Asta Nielsen's popularity was not limited to Germany. The exclusive rights of her films were sold to distributors in many countries, not only in Europe. In Switzerland, there was no considerable film production at that time, as compared with other European countries as France, Italy, Great Britain, or Germany. Thus, Switzerland as a small country gives us an opportunity to study more easily the impact of international film production companies on the distribution and exhibition of their films. The film trade in Switzerland allows

Facing page: *Tagblatt der Stadt Zürich*, no. 63 (15 March 1913).

Tagblatt der Stadt Zürich, no. 88 (13 April 1911).

to test the reception of a film or the popularity of a film actor in a 'neutral' market that is not engaged in the defence of a national film production. Recent research in film distribution, exhibition and reception in Switzerland before the First World War has underlined the vitality and the originality of this cinematic context.[4] This paper traces the exhibition of Asta Nielsen films during the seasons 1910/11, 1911/12 and 1912/13 in Zurich and presents some early reviews of Asta Nielsen and her films from Switzerland.

Zurich, a city of circa 230,000 inhabitants in 1910,[5] was the economic centre of Switzerland. Here, 18 cinemas opened between 1907 and 1913.[6] The most important cinemas in the city centre at the beginning of the 1910s were Löwenkino, Elektrische Lichtbühne (Centraltheater), Olympia-Kino, Kinematograph Radium, and Speck's Kinematograph. The daily paper *Tagblatt der Stadt Zürich*, a tabloid of advertisings and an official gazette, reveals detailed information about film programming in Zurich. Short slapsticks, foreign and local non-fiction films, comedies and short dramas, for example, comprised the programmes of Speck's Kinematograph and Löwenkino still at the beginning of 1911.[7] The 'flow' of these short film programmes was suddenly interrupted on 23 February 1911 when the long Danish feature film DEN HVINDE SLAVEHANDELS SIDSTE OFFER (IN THE HANDS OF IMPOSTORS) was announced as DIE WEISSE SKLAVIN II by Löwenkino, Speck's Kinematograph, Kinematograph Radium and Centraltheater for the same week, from 24 February to 2 March.[8] The advertisements praised the film as "ein belehrendes Sittenbild" (an instructive picture of manner) which was intended for adolescents and their parents, due to its supposed pedagogical values, but forbidden for children. The advent of long feature films brought about a change in marketing strategies: the word 'sensation' became prominent in cinema advertisements which often underlined a foreign film's success in big cities of leading European countries.

Just five weeks after DIE WEISSE SKLAVIN II, on 7 April 1911, Asta Nielsen's first film AFGRUNDEN (THE ABYSS) was announced with the German title ABGRÜNDE by the Löwenkino.[9] The next advertisements by Löwenkino and by Speck's Kinematograph drew the attention to ABGRÜNDE on 12 April, just one day before the first screenings took place.[10] Asta Nielsen's and Urban Gad's names were not given in these advertisements. The Danish screenwriter and director appeared one day later in an advertisement of the Central-Theater, a cinema managed by the Elektrische Lichtbühne A.G., an important company which owned a number of cinemas in Switzerland and was engaged in film distribution.[11] ABGRÜNDE was promoted as "Eine lebenswahre Tragödie, dramatisiert von Urban Gad! Das sensationellste und spannendste Theater-Drama, das bis jetzt erschienen! " (A realistic tragedy written by Urban Gad! The most sensational and exciting theatrical drama ever released so far!)[12] The advertisement reported triumphant screenings of six to eight weeks in Berlin, Düsseldorf, Copenhagen, and, last but not least, in Paris, and it claimed that "all the artists" had taken sides with AFGRUNDEN. The advertisement announced an unusual permanence on screen of fifteen days as well as an original score that had been composed for the musical accompaniment. Slightly increased admission prices were justified by saying that the costs of the rights to the film were exorbitant for the company. It was also stated that the same company, Elektrische Lichtbühne A.G., had purchased the exclusive rights for all of Switzerland only with big sacrifices.[13]

This cinema advertisement may be the first proof of the introduction of the exclusive rental system to the film trade in Switzerland. Though Asta Nielsen's name is not mentioned yet, it may also testify to the importance of Asta Nielsen in this process. At any rate, the Elektrische Lichtbühne A.G. apparently was not able to maintain the exclusivity of her commercial exploitation of Asta Nielsen's first film in Zurich, more than four months after the premiere of ABGRÜNDE in Germany. In Zurich, ABGRÜNDE screenings actually started in four cinemas at the same day, on 13 April 2011: The Centraltheater showed

Table 1. Asta Nielsen films in Zurich in the seasons 1910/11 to 1912/13, according to cinema advertisements in *Tagblatt der Stadt Zürich*.

Original title / English title	Elektrische Lichtbühne	Löwenkino	Olympia-Kino	Kinematograph Radium	Speck's Kinematograph
Afgrunden / The Abyss	13–27 Apr 1911	13–21 Apr 1911★	8 Mar 1912★★	13 Apr 1911★★	13–15 Apr 1911★
Heisses Blut / Burning Blood				8 May 1911★★	
Nachtfalter / Retribution		19–27 May 1911★		20–27 May 1911★	
In dem grossen Augenblick / The Great Moment		13–20 May 1911			13–14 Oct 1911★★
Den sorte drøm / Vengeance is Mine		17–23 Nov 1911			
Zigeunerblut / Gipsy's Blood				25–31 Jan 1912	
Die arme Jenny / Poor Jenny			10–16 Oct 1912	10–16 Oct 1912	
Die Verräterin / The Traitress				24–30 Oct 1912	
Der fremde Vogel / The Course of True Love				11–17 Apr 1912	
Wenn die Maske fällt / When the Mask Falls	14–16 Nov 1912★★				
Der Totentanz / The Dance to Death			14–20 Nov 1912	14–20 Nov 1912	
Die Kinder des Generals / Falsely Accused			12–18 Dec 1912		
Jugend und Tollheit / In a Fix	13–15 Mar 1913★★				
Komödianten / The Heart of a Pierrot	22–24 May 1913★★				
Das Mädchen ohne Vaterland / A Girl Without a Country	17–20 Jul 1913★★				

(★) The permanence of the film in the movie theatre programme is probably longer as indicated.
(★★) This date indicates only the day when the film advert appeared.

ABGRÜNDE for the very unusual duration of fifteen days, Löwenkino for nine days, Speck's Kinematograph for three days – while the period of time when audiences could see Asta Nielsen on Kinematograph Radium's screen is not known to us.

Many advertisements which promoted Asta Nielsen films in the *Tagblatt der Stadt Zürich* referred to the great success of ABGRÜNDE in retrospect, but it is not possible to calculate the exact number of screenings and seats which were available to audiences in Zurich. Asta Nielsen's name was not mentioned at all in the adverts for ABGRÜNDE in Zurich. Her name appeared for the first time only one month later in an advertisement for HEISSES BLUT (BURNING BLOOD) which reminded readers of her role in AFGRUNDEN and underlined the international success of this film.[14] A fortnight later, in the middle of May, an advertisement for NACHTFALTER (RETRIBUTION) promoted Asta Nielsen as well as the length of the film and a wonderful colourisation. HEISSES BLUT and NACHTFALTER had been produced in Berlin by Deutsche Bioscop. Exclusive rights outside of Germany were sold by the Allgemeine Kinematographen- und Filmverleih-Gesellschaft based in Strasbourg, at that time the biggest film company in Germany. Both films were programmed by Kino Radium.[15] The size of Asta Nielsen's name was bigger in the next advertising which appeared in the middle of October for IN DEM GROSSEN AUGENBLICK (THE GREAT MOMENT), the second film of the 'Asta Nielsen series' 1911/12.[16] Five weeks later, her name was placed even bigger in the advertisement for DEN SORTE DRØM (VENGEANCE IS MINE), the Danish production which became the first film of the series. For the first time, in the *Tagblatt der Stadt Zürich*, this advertisement characterised Asta Nielsen as "Duse der Kinokunst" (Duse of the art of cinema).[17] This demonstrates once more the international public relations effort made by the German distributor of the 'Asta Nielsen series' to promote her as a genius of the screen, comparable only with Eleonora Duse, the unchallenged diva of the stage.

Information about film screenings are not complete because newspapers printed advertisements for films only irregularly and because the adverts do not give always information about the days of programming and the number of screenings per day. However, there is no doubt about the success of Asta Nielsen's films in Zurich during the seasons 1910/1911 to 1912/1913.

Asta Nielsen's success with her films which were distributed in many countries provoked major changes in the film trade and in film programming: within a short time, film exhibition began to be shaped around long feature films, film actors acquired much more visibility, and cinemas gained even more space in the public sphere of the city or town where they were located. Film stars, in particular Asta Nielsen, became arguments for the respectability of cinemas. In contrast to most Kinoreform activists who stuck by their condemnation of cinema as poison for young souls, more commentators demonstrated enthusiastic respect for the new medium as they began to consider it as art. In Switzerland, the trade journal *Kinema* was established in 1911 and worked out of the canton of Zurich. Together with *Die Ähre*, the journal of the association of Swiss writers, which started to publish film reviews in 1913, *Kinema* started a campaign in defence of cinema.

Karl Bleibtreu, a German writer who had been living in Zurich since 1908 was among the first and most important film reviewers at that time in German speaking countries. In April and May 1913, *Kinema* published his "Theater und Kino" (theatre and cinema), a series of five articles on his principles of film reviewing. After that he wrote numerous columns on his visits to cinemas in Zurich, first for *Kinema*, and from July 1913 to January 1915 for *Die Ähre*.[18] He intended to defend the cinema against those accusing it of immorality and triviality. For Bleibtreu, cinema was a matter of art. His texts on Asta Nielsen reveal a great passion for the actress. For him, she was the most convincing argument to sustain his cinephile point of view. In one of his columns he wrote: "In every moment, the Nielsen is the life, the nature, in every of her aspects she is real truth".[19] He declared also her superiority over Elenora Duse:

> The light came from the North to us, facing Asta every criticism is silenced, here boundless admiration is the primary obligation [...] The great Asta is quite simply a genius, a patent of nobility which I, contrary to the misuse of this esteemed word, would not have wasted on actors, not even on Duse or Wolter. Both of them always remain reproducers only, while Asta Nielsen, this muse of poetic mimic art, is a creator, herself a woman poet, her own poet. Those stupids and ignorants who speak about cinema as an attraction of the fairground stage should be seized by their ears and dragged here to watch the highest art.[20]

In Bleibtreu's eyes, nature and culture seemed to merge in Asta Nielsen's screen personality. His columns make the Danish star a sort of yardstick for evaluating other film actors. Moreover, her art was adduced as an argument to support the idea of cinematic specificities in comparison with theatre, as Bleibtreu shows at length by using JUGEND UND TOLLHEIT (IN A FIX) as paradigm.[21]

Karl Bleibtreu was not the only film reviewer interested in Asta Nielsen. In his *Kinema* article in defense of cinema an anonymous writer quotes a panegyric of the conservative newspaper *Berner Tagblatt* which was in favour of the seventh art. The leading newspaper of the Swiss capital reclaims reforms and sustains the idea that cinema cannot survive by programming non-fiction films only. It says that the cinema has the right to offer the same "human experience" as theatre does, and that the new medium has made some progress, since it had left 'childhood' years behind. The mimetic art of Asta Nielsen would have been the confirmation of this progress for the anonymous author.[22]

In the columns of *Kinema*, Asta Nielsen is not only the sublime artist used as an argument in defense of cinema, but also a film star to be valorized with opportune communicative strategies. In a series of short international chronicles made by the editorial staff, for example, we can find the description of a theatrical tournée made by Asta Nielsen in Budapest with all the corollary of anecdotes typical of a big star: the immense crowd of fans waiting for her at the train station, her automobile blocked by the multitude of people, the

Die Aehre 2:11 (1914): special issue Karl Bleibtreu.

flowers, the applause and so on.²³ Another *Kinema* article is focused on Asta Nielsen's toilettes as an important aspect of her art. The text describes her passion for *art nouveau*, brocade, soft furs, and underlines her attention to fashion in her private life, too. The author analyses her choices of toilettes in DIE SUFFRAGETTE (THE SUFFRAGETTE). According to him, Asta Nielsen was conscious of the communicative power of film costumes on female audiences and so she had chosen fashionable as well as popular clothes which could enforce the identification of female audiences of all social strata with the struggling heroine. *Kinema* tried to shape the image of an intelligent star who incorporated female modernity.[24] In a *Kinema* article entitled "Von Ibsen zum Kino", the anonymous writer reported an interview with Asta Nielsen made by a Viennese newspaper.[25] Asta Nielsen welcomed the interviewer in a hotel of the city centre dressed with an eccentric Japanese kimono. She told the story of her first theatrical audition in Copenhagen with a scene taken by Ibsen's *Brand* and her first encounter with a film projection in the same city, which took place with the same scene by Ibsen on the screen. She also told the story of AFGRUNDEN and she explained how much the interpretation of film roles were difficult for her, because her extreme metamorphic and emotionalist acting exhausted her.[26] The film star was very conscious of her incredible impact on cinema audiences due to the ubiquity of her films. She maintained to the interviewer that "she was being screened in around six hundred movie theatres" and "facing half a million of viewers over the world at the exact moment of the interview".[27] This sublime film artist and incredible screen personality was well aware of her innovations and her most prominent status within the international film business and cinema culture. She was a clever, sensitive and struggling diva who contributed to the revaluation of cinema not only in a small country as Switzerland but over the world.

Notes

1. Cf. Corinna Müller, *Frühe deutsche Kinematographie. Formale, wirtschaftliche und kulturelle Entwicklungen 1907–1912* (Stuttgart and Weimar: Metzler, 1994) ; Martin Loiperdinger, "*Afgrunden* in Germany. *monopolfilm*, cinemagoing and the emergence of the film star Asta Nielsen, 1910–11", in Daniel Biltereyst, Richard Maltby and Philippe Meers (eds), *Cinema, Audiences and Modernity. New perspectives on European cinema history* (London, New York: Routledge, 2011), 142–153.

2. Corinna Müller, "Emergence of the feature film in Germany between 1910 and 1911 / Le origini del lungometraggio nel cinema tedesco, 1910–1911", in Paolo Cherchi Usai and Lorenzo Codelli (eds), *Before Caligari. German cinema, 1895–1920 / Prima di Caligari. Cinema tedesco, 1895–1920* (Pordenone: Le Giornate del Cinema Muto, 1990), 96.

3. Cf. Loiperdinger, "*Afgrunden* in Germany".

4. Cf. Ernest Prodolliet, *Die Filmpresse in der Schweiz: Bibliographie und Texte* (Freiburg: Universität Freiburg, 1975); Paul Meier-Kern, *Verbrecherschule oder Kulturfaktor? Kino und Film in Basel 1896–1916* (Basel: Helbing & Lichtenhahn, 1993), 38; Mariann Lewinsky: "Schweizer National Cinema Leuzinger, Rapperswil (SG): Aktualitätenfilmproduktion und regionale Kinogeschichte der Zentral- und Ostschweiz, 1896–1945", *KINtop* 9 (2000); Stefano Mordasini, „La naissance et le développment de l'exploitation cinématogrpahique dans le Tessin 1896–1946", in Vinzenz Hediger et al. (eds): *Home Stories: neue Studien zu Film und Kino in der Schweiz / nouvelles approches du cinéma et du film en Suisse* (Marburg: Schüren, 2001), 71–79; Rémy Pithon (ed.), *Cinéma suisse muet: lumières et ombres* (Lausanne: Antipodes, 2002); Gianni Haver and Pierre-Emmanuel Jaques, *Le spectacle cinématographique en Suisse 1895–1945* (Lausanne: Antipodes, 2003).

5. Cf. Martin Illi, *Von der Kameralistik zum New Public Management. Geschichte der Zürcher Kantonsverwaltung von 1803 bis 1998* (Zurich: Chronos, 2008), 224.

6. Cf. Christoph Bignens, *Kinos: Architektur als Marketing* (Zurich: Hans Rohr, 1988), 99–137.

7. *Tagblatt der Stadt Zürich*, no. 16 (19 January 1911): 4–5.

8. *Tagblatt der Stadt Zürich*, no. 46 (23 February 1911): 5.

9. *Tagblatt der Stadt Zürich*, no. 83 (7 April 1911): 7.

10. *Tagblatt der Stadt Zürich*, no. 87 (12 April 1911): 5–7.
11. *Tagblatt der Stadt Zürich*, no. 88 (13 April 1911): 3.
12. Ibid.
13. The advertising announced admission prices: from 2 CHF (balcony) to 0,60 CHF (gallery).
14. *Tagblatt der Stadt Zürich*, no. 107 (8 May 1911): 6.
15. *Tagblatt der Stadt Zürich*, no. 119 (19 May 1911): 6; no. 117 (19 May 1911): 6; no. 122 (26 May 1911): 6.
16. *Tagblatt der Stadt Zürich*, no. 241 (14 October 1911): 7.
17. *Tagblatt der Stadt Zürich*, no. 271 (17 November 1911): 7.
18. On Karl Bleibtreu, his biography and his writings on cinema cf. Fritz Güttinger (ed.), *Kein Tag ohne Kino. Schriftsteller über den Stummfilm* (Frankfurt am Main: Deutsches Filmmuseum, 1984), 207–208.
19. "Die Nielsen aber ist in jeder Faser das Leben selbst, die Natur, jeder Zug ist unverfälschte Wahrheit." Karl Bleibtreu, "Zürcher Kino", *Die Ähre*, (27 July 1913): 9; reprinted in Güttinger, *Kein Tag ohne Kino*, 256.
20. Karl Bleibtreu, "Zürcher Kino", *Die Ähre* (27 July 1913): 8–9, reprinted in Güttinger, *Kein Tag ohne Kino*, 255–256.
21. Karl Bleibtreu, "Theater und Kino", *Kinema* 3:16 (1913): 1.
22. Cf. Anonymous, "Den Kino-Gegnern ins Stammbuch", *Kinema* 3:10 (1913): 5–6.
23. Anonymous, "Asta Nielsen in Budapest", *Kinema* 3:17 (1913): 11. The stardom strategy for the coeval film actors seems to be that of stressing their theatrical commitment alongside the cinematic activity but, at the same time, describing this latter as an original and specific form of expression. Cf. Cristina Jandelli: *Le dive italiane del cinema muto* (Palermo: L'Epos, 2006).
24. Anonymous, "Verschiedenes", *Kinema* 3:43 (1913): 13.
25. Anonymous, "Von Ibsen zum Kino", *Kinema* 3:11 (1913): 4.
26. On emotionalism and silent film acting cf. Mattia Lento, "Basta la mossa! or Not? Theatre, Silent Film and Pedagogy of Actors in Italy", in Katharina Klung, Susie Trenka and Geesa Tuch (eds), Dokumentation des 24. Film- und Fernsehwissenschaftliches Kolloquiums (Marburg: Schüren, forthcoming).
27. Anonymous, "Von Ibsen zum Kino", *Kinema* 3:11 (1913): 4.

Adrian Gerber

Advertising Asta Nielsen
Traces of Local Trade Rivalry in Zurich and Transnational Circulation

Johannes Kamps pointed to an incomplete preservation of posters for Asta Nielsen films of the 1910s. According to him, only unusual movie posters, the sophisticated ones that were considered of artistic value even at that time, survived in contemporary poster collections.[1] Two new chance finds in Zurich, Switzerland, have helped to narrow this gap in the legacy of cinematographic commercial art.

The first discovery is a photograph of the junction Weinbergstrasse / Leonhardstrasse in Zurich, dating back to 1913. The advertising column in the centre of the photograph, owned by the Allgemeine Plakatgesellschaft, shows a text-only poster from the Löwen-Kino that was situated close to the Bahnhofstrasse in Zurich.[2] The column was placed about a kilometre's distance from the Löwen-Kino. The placard advertised an "Asta Nielsen Cyklus" comprising six films starting on Wednesday, 3 September. From Karl Bleibtreu's reviews of the city's cinema programmes, we know that this 'cycle' dedicated to the film star included at least the 'older films' DIE KINDER DES GENERALS (FALSELY ACCUSED, second film of the second 'Asta Nielsen series' of 1912/13), and JUGEND UND TOLLHEIT (IN A FIX, fifth film of that series).[3] The 'cycle' played for approximately one week and even included films that did not feature Asta Nielsen. Otherwise little is known about these reruns. The Zurich *Tagblatt* newspaper, in which local cinemas advertised most regularly, contains only a small advance notice.[4] Those responsible for marketing the Löwen-Kino's film programmes most probably resorted to posters and handbills to advertise this special programme. Furthermore, the timing was not coincidental but tactically motivated from an advertising point of view. Only a few days later, the

---

Facing page:
Above: Photo of Weinbergstrasse / Leonhardstrasse in Zurich, September 1913.
[Archiv Tram-Museum Zürich.]
Below: Löwen-Kino's advert for the "Asta Nielsen Cyklus", *Tagblatt der Stadt Zürich* (1 September 1913).

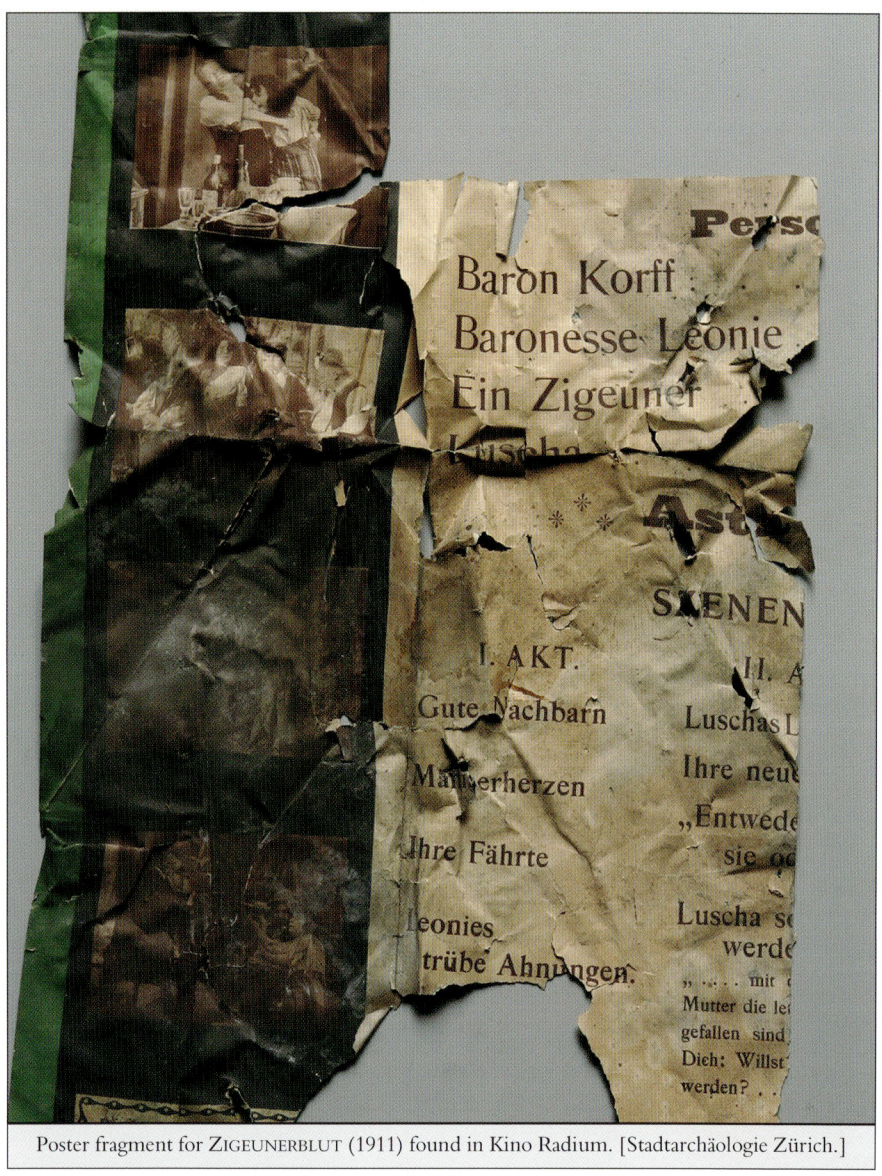

Poster fragment for ZIGEUNERBLUT (1911) found in Kino Radium. [Stadtarchäologie Zürich.]

new 'Asta Nielsen series' of 1913/14 started at the Kino Radium in Zurich with DIE SUFFRAGETTE (THE SUFFRAGETTE)!

The manager of the Kino Radium, Carl Simon-Sommer, who had bought the exclusive rights to the latest Asta Nielsen films at great expense, must have been bewildered to see his local competitor's posters. Simon-Sommer launched a marketing counterattack on this very same 3 September that Löwen-Kino launched its "Asta Nielsen Cyklus" and placed an unusually large preview advertisement in the *Tagblatt*. He used the advertisement as well to draw the

Poster for DIE VERRÄTERIN (1911) found in Kino Radium. [Stadtarchäologie Zürich.]

public's attention to the disreputable programme strategy of the Löwen-Kino: "All other Asta Nielsen films being shown in Zurich from today onwards are older films that have already been shown here".[5]

The Kino Radium not only showed films from the 'Asta Nielsen series' of 1912/13 and 1913/14. As early as January and October 1912 ZIGEUNERBLUT (GYPSY BLOOD, third film of the first series of 1911/12) and DIE VERRÄTERIN (THE TRAITRESS, fifth film of that series) had also been playing. This is indicated not only by the relevant newspaper advertisements[6] but also by two recently discovered posters of the Kino Radium. Shortly after the closure of Kino Radium in the summer of 2008, archaeologists stumbled upon a pile of film posters hidden behind a timber wall. These posters dating from the years before the First World War comprise both simple text posters commissioned by the cinema, similar in style to the poster for the Löwen-Kino shown in the photograph, and posters of international origin that were of a more complex design.[7] The international placards include a poster and a fragment of a poster for the two aforementioned films of the 1911/12 series. These so-called *Clichéplakate* (i. e. text posters with several inserted photographic reproductions) were designed in the same style. Moreover, they are comparable to the German-language poster for the Asta Nielsen film DEN SORTE DRØM (DER SCHWARZE TRAUM, VENGEANCE IS MINE) held in the Amsterdam-based EYE Film Instituut Nederland.[8] Although this latter film was produced independently in Denmark, it was marketed on distribution by the Projektions-AG Union (PAGU) as the first film of the first 'Asta Nielsen series' in the 1911/12 season. It is thereby apparent that there was a kind of corporate design in place for the series' posters, which circulated transnationally in Central and Western Europe. It is certain that these posters were used in Germany, Austria[9] and Switzerland. They probably found their way into the Netherlands as well in the 1910s: the Amsterdam poster originates from the exceptional legacy of the Dutch distributor Jean Desmet.

Though some time prior to the rise of Asta Nielsen, the names of well-known stage actors in sophisticated *films d'art* or the comic Max Linder were occasionally mentioned on French film posters;[10] the prominent naming of the main actor on film posters was an innovation of 1911/12, closely linked to the introduction of the star system. As a newspaper article on the occasion of Asta Nielsen's visit to Vienna illustrates, Nielsen posters attracted considerable attention, thereby fulfilling their advertising purpose. The journalist wrote:

> Some time ago I spotted an unusual crowd in front of a shabby cinema close to the Augarten. What is going on, I asked? A young schoolboy silently pointed to a poster on which the name of Asta Nielsen was emblazoned in large bold lettering. Asta Nielsen is a magnet with an extraordinary attraction. She draws people into cinemas. She is the only female film actor whose name is engraved on the minds of the masses and who has achieved astonishing popularity in a short time.[11]

The photograph of Weinbergstrasse / Leonhardstrasse, which unintentionally immortalises a perishable film poster, along with the rather unassuming posters from an archaeological poster find, are not the usual kind of material that film historians generally have the opportunity to work with. The two accidental discoveries in Zurich provide an insight into the everyday advertising practices of cinemas in the beginning 1910s – an insight into marketing activities that cannot be fully covered by the analysis of the advertising sections of newspapers or by the traditional holdings of poster collections.

Notes

1. Johannes Kamps, "Pionierin des frühen deutschen Starplakats", in Heide Schlüpmann et al. (eds), *Unmögliche Liebe: Asta Nielsen, ihr Kino* (2nd edn) (Vienna: filmarchiv austria, 2010), 287–288.
2. The photograph is kept in the photographic archive of Zurich's tramway museum which was previously not considered in film studies. It was taken on the occasion of the impending rebuilding of the tramway tracks: H. Wolf-Bender, glass plate and print 1913, in Archiv Tram-Museum Zürich.
3. Karl Bleibtreu, "Filmkritik", *Die Ähre* 1:34 (14 September 1913): 9.
4. *Tagblatt der Stadt Zürich* (1 September 1913): 6.
5. *Tagblatt der Stadt Zürich* (3 September 1913): 5.
6. *Tagblatt der Stadt Zürich* (24 January 1912): 5; (24 October 1912): 7.
7. Adrian Gerber and Andreas Motschi, *Der Plakatfund aus dem Kino Radium in Zürich: Filmplakate der Jahre 1907 bis 1914 und weitere Materialien: Inventar*, edited by Stadt Zürich, Amt für Städtebau (Zurich: Online-Publikation Archäologie & Denkmalpflege, 2011). My article on the posters found in the Kino Radium, "Sensation im Schundkino! Archäologie der Kinowerbung in der Schweiz um 1910", will be published in a yearbook by Memoriav, expected 2013. The original posters are currently held by Stadtarchäologie Zürich.
8. Ivo Blom, *Jean Desmet and the early Dutch film trade* (Amsterdam: Amsterdam University Press, 2003), 219–220, 405. The poster, which is not mentioned by Kamps, is displayed in Karola Gramann and Heide Schlüpmann (eds), *Nachtfalter. Asta Nielsen, ihre Filme* (2nd edn) (Vienna: filmarchiv austria, 2010), 26.
9. The addresses of the German and Austrian distribution companies are stated on the posters.
10. See the French posters for Le Luthier de Crémone (1909) and Petite Rosse (1909) in Fondation Jérôme Seydoux–Pathé, Paris (online: http://www.fondation-jeromeseydoux-pathe.com). A historical photograph from the French-speaking town of Lausanne indicates that the Pathé poster for Petite Rosse was used in Switzerland before April 1910, cf. Roland Cosandey and François Langer, "Le Théâtre Lumen de Roth-de-Markus: défense et illustration du cinématographe (Lausanne, 1908–1912)", in *Equinoxe* 7 (Spring 1992): 49.
11. "Von Ibsen zum Kino", *Neues Wiener Abendblatt*, reprinted in *Kinema* 3:11 (15 March 1913): 4. It is, of course, uncertain whether the abovementioned advertising poster is one of the official posters for the 1911/12 Nielsen series, but this seems very likely because of the coincidence in style and timing.

Pierre-Emmanuel Jaques

Asta Nielsen in the Cinema Theatres of Lausanne, 1911–1913

Before the First World War, ten feature-length films starring Asta Nielsen were screened in Lausanne, a rapidly growing city in the French-speaking part of Switzerland. I will examine how these films found their place in a rather restricted market while focusing on the adverts in the local press, the only traces now available.

Historical sources and the state of research

Before the First World War, most of the films shown in Switzerland were imported from the major producing countries. It is difficult to identify many of them, as the files of the film distributors have disappeared and as no national censorship had been established in Switzerland. Before the 1930s, local cinemas were controlled by single police officers whose files were generally not preserved.[1] The programme leaflets distributed by the cinemas are almost entirely lost, and, in most cases, cinema adverts in local newspapers give only incomplete information on the composition of film programmes. Thus an important portion of the films which were shown in Switzerland will remain unknown.

An important source for the years before the First World War is the trade journal *Kinema*, which was founded in 1911. But this periodical is available only from March 1913 onward. In the second surviving issue an interview with Asta Nielsen was published that had previously appeared in the *Neue Wiener Abendblatt*,[2] thus highlighting the star's importance for Switzerland.

> Facing page:
> Above: On the right, cinema Royal Biograph in 1923 (no major transformation was made since inauguration in 1911). On the left the 'new Lumen' (opened in 1912). The poster announces LA VÉRITÉ (by Henri Roussel, screened between 2 and 5 March 1923 at the Lumen). Postcard (author unknown), publisher: Edition Art. Perrochet-Matile. [Musée historique de Lausanne: P.2.M.A.1.G.23.087 (fonds carte postale) © MHL.]
> Below: On the right, behind the trees, the cinema Royal Biograph in 1933. At the background, left, the Lumen. Photograph: Charles Gerber. [Musée historique de Lausanne: P.2.F.14.01.01.03.2219 (fonds urbanisme) © MHL, Phot. Charles Gerber.]

Only scarce data are available on the local film programmes before the emergence of regular film criticism in local newspapers at the beginning of the 1920s.[3] In the 1910s, with the exception of Karl Bleibtreu's reviews in the periodical *Die Ähre*[4] and some scarce and scattered articles, only the adverts inserted by the cinemas themselves named the titles of the programmed films, usually without any other information. In the early 1960s Freddy Buache and Jacques Rial had already used the local newspapers for their pioneering study *Les Débuts du cinématographe à Genève et à Lausanne 1895–1914*.[5] Buache and Rial attribute a substantial delay in cinematic developments in Lausanne to the lack of recognition of the new entertainment. Often Buache and Rial mock what they see as a form of provincial conservatism, notably the demand for better programmes and the ban on admitting children. On the other hand, Buache and Rial look closely at the significance given to some films, actors or actresses. About the advert for the Asta Nielsen film PUISSANCE MATERNELLE (IN DEM GROSSEN AUGENBLICK, THE GREAT MOMENT) they note: "For the first time a cinema advert presents the name of a performer in large print: the first sign of the 'star system'".[6]

Asta Nielsen on the screens of Lausanne

As already mentioned, between 1911 and 1913, ten films starring Asta Nielsen were shown in Lausanne, a striving town situated in the French part of Switzerland; the number of inhabitants increased from 53,000 in 1905 to 70,500 in 1912. The years before the First World War were a time of growth of cinematographic exhibition. Altogether, there were four cinemas in Lausanne: The first fixed-site cinema of the town, called Modern Cinéma, opened in December 1907. It became the Théâtre Lux in April 1908, and, after a major modification, Cinéma-Théâtre Palace in July 1913. A second cinema, the Lumen, opened in March 1908. It closed two years later and re-opened at the end of April 1912, now a large theatre with a gallery, able to welcome one thousand viewers who could see films but also theatre plays, operettas and other forms of live performance.[7] On 1 December 1911, the Royal Biograph, a travelling cinema which had permanently run film shows in town since the spring of 1911, was converted into Lausanne's third fixed-site cinema, with an Asta Nielsen film in its opening programme. The last cinema to open in Lausanne before the war was the Apollo in October 1913.

The openings of these cinemas coincided with the promulgation of a stricter control over the cinemas. Since 1909, children under twelve were not admitted to cinemas in town, unless a special authorisation was produced. In 1912, the municipality tried to stop the building of a new cinema, a motion prevented by a precedent ruling of the Federal Court. These measures reflect widespread official suspicion towards cinema in those years.

All in all, the Royal Biograph presented seven Asta Nielsen films, thus making it the main venue for the actress in Lausanne. Before it opened as Lausanne's third fixed-site cinema on 1 December 1911, the Royal Biograph had been

Cinema Lumen about 1910 with posters of films from 1909 (Film d'art: L'Epi; Une chasse à l'éléphant au Cambodge). Photograph: Charles Recordon / Company: Brandt & Cie, Lausanne. [Musée historique de Lausanne: P.1.A.1.G.23.058 (fonds topographie lausannoise) © MHL, Phot. Charles Recordon.]

situated for some months at the Grande Salle de Tivoli and, during the summer of 1911, in the Kursaal. Its manager, Georg Korb, was a travelling showman.[8] He was the first to screen a long feature with Asta Nielsen in Lausanne: her debut film VERS L'ABÎME (AFGRUNDEN, THE ABYSS), for only three days, from Friday, 7 to Sunday, 9 April. The advert indicates that the projection of this "moving drama" lasted one hour; children were not admitted, not even to the Sunday matinee.[9] Among the long features programmed by the Royal Biograph, we find more Danish "films of manners" such as L'ESCLAVE BLANCHE 2e série (DEN HVIDE SLAVEHANDELS SIDSTE OFFER, IN THE HANDS OF IMPOSTORS).[10] From 10 to 17 November 1911, always in the Grande Salle de Tivoli, Georg Korb screened PUISSANCE MATERNELLE, starring Asta Nielsen in the role of the mother who sacrifices herself for the life of her child. When Georg Korb opened his fixed-site cinema Royal Biograph, the main attraction screened at the opening night on 1 December 1911 was RÊVE NOIR (DEN SORTE DRØM, VENGEANCE IS MINE), again with Asta Nielsen playing the lead role. Georg Korb's Royal Biograph may be considered the cinema enterprise which introduced Asta Nielsen to Lausanne audiences, as it showed five films of the first 'Asta Nielsen series' 1911/12, plus her debut film AFGRUNDEN. Two more films of the second series and one film of the third series were programmed by Lux cinema (renamed the Cinéma-Théâtre Palace in July 1913). Both cinemas programmed the long features starring Asta Nielsen with considerable time lags of two-and-a-half to five-and-a-half and three-and-a-half to 5 months respectively compared to the Berlin premieres of those films. These times exceeded by far the window during which it would have been commercially viable to secure the exclusive distribution rights to Asta Nielsen films in Lausanne.

Table 1. List of Asta Nielsen films shown in Lausanne, 1911–1913.[26]

Title in Lausanne	Original title English title	Cinema	Lausanne screenings (Berlin premiere)
Vers l'abîme	Afgrunden The Abyss	Royal Biograph (Salle Tivoli)	7–9 Apr 1911 [Copenhagen: 12 Sep 1910]
Puissance maternelle	In dem grossen Augenblick The Great Moment	Royal Biograph (Salle Tivoli)	10–17 Nov 1911 (28 Aug 1911)
Rêve noir	Den sorte Drøm The Circus Girl	Royal Biograph	1–7 Dec 1911 (19 Aug 1911)
Amour tzigane	Zigeunerblut Gipsy's Blood	Royal Biograph	1–7 Mar 1912 (8 Oct 1911)
L'oiseau étranger	Der fremde Vogel The Course of True Love	Royal Biograph	26 Apr–2 May 1912 (11 Nov 1911)
La puissance de l'or	Die Macht des Goldes The Better Way	Royal Biograph	21–27 Jun 1912 (3 Feb 1912)
Danse macabre	Der Totentanz The Dance to Death	Lux	27–29 Dec 1912 (7 Sep 1912)
Les enfants du général	Die Kinder des Generals Falsely Accused	Royal Biograph	3–9 Jan 1913 (5 Oct 1912)
Les enfants du général	Die Kinder des Generals Falsely Accused	Lux	[7–13 Feb ?] (30 Aug 1912)
Les fautes des pères	Die Sünden der Väter Temptations of Drink	Cinéma-Théâtre Palace	7–13 Nov 1913 (28 Feb 1913)
La suffragette	Die Sufragette Sufragette	Cinéma-Théâtre Palace	21–27 Nov 1913* (12 Sep 1913)

*Adverts with wrong indications of 14–20 November
Sources: Lausanne-Plaisirs, La Semaine à Lausanne, Gazette de Lausanne

Asta Nielsen and the opening of the cinema Royal Biograph

According to a press report on the Royal Biograph's opening night, the first projection was rather problematic: The screening began with a half-hour delay and not all the guests could be seated although the cinema could accommodate 450 patrons. More embarrassingly even, some invited politicians were obliged to stand, as all the seats were taken. But the most shocking for the reporter of the *Gazette de Lausanne*, a conservative and high-brow daily newspaper, was the poor composition of the programme: "Some films were positively outrageous and will certainly bring comments to the Royal Biograph from the authorities in charge of monitoring the showings".[11] RÊVE NOIR was shown alongside Éclair's recent temperance drama LE POISON DE L'HUMANITÉ (ALCOHOL: THE POISON OF HUMANITY), a "great drama in two acts and approved for all

Cinema Lumen from another viewpoint before 1910. Photograph: Adolphe Dulex. [Musée historique de Lausanne: P.2.D.10.A.1.G.24.005 (fonds Bridel) © MHL, Phot. Adolphe Dulex.]

audiences".[12] In order to clear his reputation, Korb wrote to all local newspapers to explain the reasons for the delay. There had been a power failure because of water damage to the electrical panel. He sent a particular response to the *Gazette de Lausanne* to defend himself against the complaint about the low morality of his programme. The insistence of his response reflects the necessity for the cinema owners to clear their programmes of any moral charge:

> Regarding the morality of the screened scenes, I must vehemently protest against the judgements of your reporter. I always take scrupulous care to present only pieces that can be seen by everyone. And that is the first time that criticism of this nature has been addressed to me. I certainly do not deserve it.[13]

On the opening night of the Royal Biograph, only these two films were shown, but then more titles were added. A reporter returned to the Royal Biograph during this first week of screenings.[14] He gives a valuable hint about the composition of the programme: The journalist is astonished to see films with German titles (without giving details). As the programmes of the other two fixed-site cinemas in Lausanne were composed mostly of French films, we can interpret this manner of programming as a way of breaking into a rather closed market. To differentiate the Royal Biograph from the competing cinemas, Georg Korb selected films of Danish and German origin. In the local newspapers, numerous films were advertised stating that the actors were members of the Royal Theatre of Copenhagen. This leaning towards Denmark and Germany was reinforced, for instance, when MENSONGE FATAL (LIVETS LØGN), produced by Nordisk Film in 1911, was said to have had a tremendous success in Berlin just eight days earlier.[15] The long features starring Asta Nielsen seemingly played an important role in Korb's business venture. In addition to naming the origin, Royal Biograph adverts also stated the length of the Asta Nielsen films: For most of the titles from VERS L'ABÎME to L'OISEAU ÉTRANGER (DER FREMDE VOGEL, THE COURSE OF TRUE LOVE), the adverts specified the running times of these long features. Thus they appeared as a novelty on the film programmes of the cinemas in Lausanne. Finally, the Royal Biograph adverts also recognised the type of genre as significant by mentioning that the film was a drama, social drama, great drama of real life, etc. Origin, length and genres of Nordic films were publicised as a means of raising the quality of the exhibition and a means of differentiation from the competing cinemas of the town.

Asta Nielsen in local adverts

Buache and Rial had already noted that Asta Nielsen was the first actress whose name was mentioned in the cinema adverts of Lausanne newspapers. But she was not introduced as a film actress; rather she was first said to be a singer from the Opera of Copenhagen,[16] and later she was referred to as a 'tragedienne',[17] a term that refers clearly to the legitimate stage. This strategy of promoting actors recurred many times over in the adverts for films of Nordic origins. The reference to the stage is important not only for the Danish films but more generally for the star system of the period before the First World War. In adverts both in daily newspapers and local periodicals as *La Semaine à Lausanne* or *Lausanne-Plaisirs*, the film actors who were the earliest to be mentioned were always said to have already acquired a significant status on the theatrical stage. Asta Nielsen appears as a figure of transition: First called a 'tragedienne', she soon became an actress whose name is mentioned over and over again, defining at the same time her cinematic acting style as the key to successful screenings:

> The management of the Royal Biograph has not hesitated to make a great sacrifice in order to offer its well-regarded viewers and the public of Lausanne the exclusivity of a cinematographic film of a simple genre, moving and of a perfect moral correctness. AMOUR TZIGANE [ZIGEUNERBLUT, GYPSY BLOOD], a great true-to-life drama in three acts, is a wonderful piece regarding both the scenery the action is set against and the portrayal by the artists. It is true that each film which headlines the name of the celebrated Danish tragedienne Asta Nielsen could be nothing but a success. This woman has such an expressive face and interprets her roles so naturally that she provokes a shiver among the public. AMOUR TZIGANE reveals to us the strength of bohemian love and the generous sacrifice of a gypsy. Asta Nielsen interprets this role in a sublime fashion, and it is without a doubt that this film will attain great success in our town.[18]

But once her talent had been praised and audiences had already experienced her appearance on screen, other aspects of her films were also underlined:

> Asta Nielsen returns, the great star, the unique and incomparable artist who will once more affirm her talent with a triumph. Indeed, the Cinéma-Palace, which has acquired exclusive rights to this film, offers us LES FAUTES DES PÈRES [DIE

SÜNDEN DER VÄTER, TEMPTATIONS OF DRINK], with Asta in the role of Hanna. Who does not know this masterpiece by Urban Gad; who has not been shaken when reading this eminently social work where the human heart is cleft by the hand of a master, where the passions are depicted with almost brutal truth? This moving drama where alcohol, this terrible hereditary defect, makes of the most delicate young girl, Hanna, the most tarnished creature.[19]

In fact, this publicity article begins with the mention of Asta Nielsen, but the main accent is placed on the dramatic development of the film, characterised as the adaptation of a novel by Urban Gad. The detour via another cultural medium still seemed a useful way to attract a vast audience.

Regarding the implementation of a star system, Asta Nielsen stands unquestionably among the first names to appear regularly as a means of promoting films. At first she is presented in the adverts as a figure of the stage; then she becomes an attraction in her own right, even being called "la reine de l'écran" (the queen of the screen), in an advert for LA SUFFRAGETTE (DIE SUFFRAGETTE, THE SUFFRAGETTE).[20] The adverts for her last three films shown in Lausanne before the First World War do not contain any other information. She has become a film star in her own right and does not need any confirmation from another cultural field.

Genre and Asta Nielsen films

In the weekly *Lausanne-Plaisirs,* dedicated to the leisure and artistic programmes of Lausanne, and in the local columns as "Lausanne. Spectacles, conférences, concerts" of *La Tribune de Lausanne,* the weekly programme announcements of the Royal Biograph were usually accompanied by short comments. They mention the genres first and then always the names of the participating Danish (or Nordic) actors. This emphasis on the genre is also confirmed by an opinion poll from the spring of 1912, conducted by the weekly *Lausanne-Plaisirs,* which asks its readers "What is your preferred film genre?"[21] The results are difficult to interpret. They indicate that Asta Nielsen films were among the controversial genres as compared to news or comical films, which were the ones preferred by the respondents of the poll.[22] Many Asta Nielsen films are classified as "grands drames vécus" (great dramas of real life): 61 respondents prefer this genre against 45 negatives.

In the summer of 1913, a further inquiry into the 'taste of the audience' indicated that dramas are becoming the favourite genre, especially among the lower and middle classes.[23] The persistence with which Asta Nielsen's quality as 'great tragedienne' is placed in the forefront in newspaper adverts is not surprising, as most of her characters correspond to a genre that was becoming more and more praised by the public.

The films of Asta Nielsen play an important role in the emergence of the long feature as the main attraction of the film programme. In his aforementioned letter to the editor, Georg Korb maintains that the bad feelings one reporter had while watching one of the programmes were because of the lack of short comical or entertaining films that would have coloured up the show. He argues the feature-length films appear at the Royal Biograph as a specialty of the house: "As a speciality, our house presents a greatly interesting show each week, very captivating, at least one thousand metres long."[24] By comparison with the adverts of the cinema Lux, the Royal Biograph always tended to lay stress on the long features. Undoubtedly, exhibiting seven Asta Nielsen films helped Georg Korb break into a rather closed market where his strategy of programming a long feature each night guaranteed his success. In this regard, the films with Asta Nielsen and the films of Danish production companies at large played an important role in the acknowledgment of cinema as an art form in its own right. In terms of business, they were part of Georg Korb's effort to establish his Royal Biograph as a leading force in the exhibition and distribution of films in Switzerland.[25]

Notes

1. The situation differed from one canton to another, as no national censorship law had been passed. In the Canton de Vaud, until 1916, it was the respective municipal authorities who authorised or banned films.
2. "Von Ibsen zum Kino. Asta Nielsen", *Kinema* 3:11 (15 March 1913): 4.
3. Laurent Guido and Pierre-Emmanuel Jaques, "Les débuts de la critique cinématographique à Genève et à Lausanne", in Vinzenz Hediger et al. (eds), *Home Stories. Neue Studien zu Film und Kino in der Schweiz / Nouvelles approches du cinéma et du film en Suisse* (Marburg: Schüren, 2001), 221–235.
4. Cf. Mattia Lento's essay in this volume.
5. Freddy Buache and Jacques Rial, *Les débuts du cinématographe à Genève et à Lausanne 1895–1914* (Lausanne: Cinémathèque suisse, 1964). This book has just been republished, without any correction or bibliography (Gollion: Infolio, 2011).
6. Buache and Rial, *Les débuts du cinématographe*, 108.
7. For more details cf. François Langer, *"Per artem probam ad Lumen". Les débuts de l'exploitation cinématographique à Lausanne 1896–1930* (unpublished Master's thesis: Université de Lausanne, 1989); Roland Cosandey and François Langer, "Le Théâtre Lumen de Roth-de Markus: défense et illustration du cinématographe (Lausanne, 1908–1912)", *Equinoxe* 7 (1992), 45–61. Gianni Haver, *Les lueurs de la guerre. Écrans vaudois 1939–1945* (Lausanne: Payot, 2003), 74–94.
8. Georg Korb was a German citizen from Lausigk, a little village near Dessau, in Saxony-Anhalt. Korb eventually died in 1918 at the age of 37.
9. *Feuille d'avis de Lausanne* (8 April 1911): 27.
10. *Tribune de Lausanne* (18 March 1911).
11. *Gazette de Lausanne* (2 December 1911): 3.
12. *Feuille d'avis de Lausanne* (5 December 1911); given as LE POISON HUMAIN, "drame social en 2 actes" in *Gazette de Lausanne* (4 December 1911): 3.
13. *Gazette de Lausanne* (4 December 1911): 3.
14. TAC, "The Royal Biograph", *Lausanne-Plaisirs*, no. 12 (9 December 1911).
15. *Lausanne-Plaisirs*, no.23 (24 February 1912).
16. *Lausanne-Plaisirs*, no. 8 (11 November 1911).
17. *Lausanne-Plaisirs,* no. 32 (27 April 1912); *Lausanne-Plaisirs*, no. 33 (4 May 1912).
18. *Lausanne-Plaisirs*, no. 24 (2 March 1912).
19. *Lausanne-Plaisirs*, no. 112 (8 November 1913).
20. *Lausanne-Plaisirs*, no. 114 (22 November 1913). The name of Henny Porten in LA FOI QUI SAUVE (DER WANKENDE GLAUBE, WAVERING FAITH) appeared for the first time the same week .
21. *Lausanne-Plaisirs*, no. 36 (25 May 1912). The submitted genres were: actualité mondiale (journal

animé) / fines comédies / drames américains / reconstitutions historiques / films d'art / paysages en couleurs / scène d'après nature / féeries / voyages d'explorations / vulgarisation scientifique / scènes truquées / pièces policières / drames d'aventures / pièces pathétiques / grands drames vécus / drames sensationnels / scènes comiques. The results must be viewed with great caution as they rely on only some dozens of answers.

22. *Lausanne-Plaisirs*, no. 36 (25 May 1912).
23. "Le goût du public", *Le Nouvelliste vaudois* (8 July 1913). According to the unsigned article, this poll was undertaken by a cinema in Bern, the capital city of Switzerland, situated in the German speaking part of the country.
24. *Lausanne-Plaisirs*, no. 20 (3 February 1912).
25. On a local level, besides the Nordic long features, Swiss news and a Wilhelm Tell from Germany were also crucial for Royal Biograph's ranking in its competition with rival cinemas in Lausanne. Cf. my essay "Une diffusion 'nationale'? De la circulation d'images locales ou nationales à Lausanne 1896–1914", in Frank Kessler and Nanna Verhoeff (eds), *Networks of Entertainment: Early Film Distribution 1895–1915* (Eastleigh: John Libbey, 2007), 47–56.
26. I could not find any evidence that any Asta Nielsen film was screened in Lausanne from December 1913 to the outbreak of the First World War.

Cinéma Parisiana

Sans concurrence! — Pour les adultes seulement!

La fréquentation toujours croissante de notre établissement est la meilleure preuve que non pas seulement les notabilités, mais encore toute la bourgeoisie ont formulé leur jugement, déclarant que le cinéma Marzen est absolument sans concurrence et qu'il est

la perle de la cinématographie.

Nous abandonnons ce jugement au public même, puisque la clientèle constitue la meilleure réclame.

Venez, voyez, admirez et jugez vous-mêmes

Du samedi 17 février au mardi 20 février inclusivement.

PROGRAMME:

1) Mines de granit dans les Vosges; vue superbe d'après nature.
2) L'amour à bord; tragi-com'que.
3) Les eaux arrivent, les eaux croissent; drame ém t'onnant.
4) Un père de famille d'occasion; très exhilarant.
5) La rivale indienne; une petite perle.
6. Little Hans est soldat colonial; très humoristique.
7) Film sensationnel dont tout le monde parle et qui ne date que du 10 févr'er 1912; nous n'avons pas regardé aux frais pour nous procurer ce numéro exceptionnellement brillant comme intercalé spécial;

Sauvé des profondeurs de la mer

Drame sensationnel de premier ordre.

8) Maurice en domestique; à mourir de rire
9) **La perle des perles!**   **Sans concurrence!**

ASTA NIELSEN

Plus d'une heure de projection. Sujet extrêmement émouvant où la belle Française montre son aversion, dictée par le patriotisme, aux officiers allemands.

PRIX DES PLACES:

1re place 1.50 fr. — 2e place 1 fr. — 3e place 50 centimes.
Abonnements (10 représentations) 1re place 11.25 fr. — 2e place 7.50 fr.

Les premières sont numérotées et peuvent être prises d'avance. Les secondes peuvent également être retenues, mais ne sont pas numérotées. — Les enfants ne sont pas admis aux représentations Asta Nielsen et les militaires paient place entière. — Billets de faveur 25 centimes de supplément.

Les 3 jours de carnaval, on commencera à 3 h. précises.

2454   **La Direction.**

Paul Lesch

"Earning the audience's unbridled applause"
Asta Nielsen films in Luxembourg

Historians researching the history of film in Luxembourg in the first quarter of the 20th century are faced with a severe problem when trying to track down source material, which is why I will not be able to answer some of the core questions of this conference.

For instance, I do not have any information on the distribution of Asta Nielsen films in Luxembourg. The same is true for the censorship of her films in the Grand Duchy. The study of the distribution of Asta Nielsen's films and their reception by the Luxembourg audience is complicated by the fact that hardly any official documentation about cinemas and film screenings has survived. The same is true for private archives of film theatres. Since the government legislation concerning film screenings was passed only in 1922, there are no national censorship decisions (usually a historical source of great value) preceding this year. Moreover, no national trade or corporatist periodicals of either travelling showmen or cinema owners existed at the time. Furthermore, the first popular film journal, *Le Film Luxembourgeois*, was founded only in 1927. Then there is no collection of film posters, flyers or lobby cards published or distributed by cinemas. Unfortunately no sociological studies have been made about the composition of cinema audiences in Luxembourg. In addition, very few writers and intellectuals have voiced their thoughts publicly on the beginnings of cinema in the Grand Duchy.

So in conclusion, the reconstruction of the cinema programmes of the 1910s as well as the analysis of the reception of the films has to be performed solely with the help of the newspapers of the time. Unfortunately, not all newspapers commented on film programmes. And those which did normally discussed only the films of those cinemas that had placed advertisements in their columns. The commentaries were thus often reduced to a chorus of biased praise regarding the individual films and the programme as a whole. Film reviews in

Facing page: Programme advert emphasising Asta Nielsen, without mentioning the title of the film (which is THE TRAITRESS, DIE VERRÄTERIN). *Luxemburger Bürger-Zeitung* (4 January 1913).

the modern sense were almost totally absent in the Luxembourg daily press back then.

Nevertheless, a systematic examination of the country's main daily newspapers allows us to draw a number of conclusions concerning the success of certain films as well as the popularity of certain actors and actresses. Furthermore, the newspapers give us an idea of how advertisement for films worked at that time and how graphics and lettering as well as drawings were used to draw attention to certain films and actors. In the case of Asta Nielsen, the analysis of articles and advertisements that appeared in various Luxembourg daily newspapers from 1911 to 1932 have proved to be rather fruitful.

Asta Nielsen: a strong presence before 1918

By reconstructing the programming of the cinemas in Luxembourg City during the 1910s, we found that almost all of the Asta Nielsen films produced up to 1916 were shown before 1918. The first one to be shown was HEISSES BLUT (BURNING BLOOD), in June 1911, then shortly afterwards in July 1911, ABGRÜNDE (AFGRUNDEN, THE ABYSS). Between June 1911 and the beginning of the First World War, as many as twenty films featuring the Danish star were shown in the two main cinemas of Luxembourg City, 'Marzen's Cinéma Parisiana' and 'Medinger's Kinematograph', both located in the city centre. Between 1914 and 1918, seventeen more Asta Nielsen films found their way to Luxembourg. They were always part of a longer programme consisting of at least ten films, but they were almost always presented as the main attraction. With the exception of ABGRÜNDE, which was shown in Luxembourg only in June 1911, more than half a year after it was screened in Germany, the films with Asta Nielsen were generally shown two or three months after the German premiere.

In discussing and presenting the first films with Asta Nielsen in the years 1911/1912, the Luxembourg press always pointed out their international success, stressing that they had attracted crowds in the major European cities such as Paris, Brussels, London, Berlin or Cologne. Another important issue in advertising her films in those years was the Danish origin of Asta Nielsen and director Urban Gad. From 1911 onwards, Danish films and especially the "famous Copenhagen actors"[1] seem to have enjoyed a special reputation in Luxembourg. According to the adverts and the articles published in the Luxembourg press, Danish actresses and actors were the only ones able to compete with the French ones in terms of quality.

The star Asta Nielsen in newspaper adverts

Until the First World War, no other actress was as systematically emphasised in the adverts as Asta Nielsen. In the newspaper adverts her presence in a film was highlighted through a variety of graphic techniques (the name appeared in bold, oversized letters; the name was repeated several times in the same advert; and, sometimes, the adverts were illustrated with a portrait drawing of the

"Earning the audience's unbridled applause" – Asta Nielsen films in Luxembourg

Programme advert emphasising Asta Nielsen Festival with THE DANCE TO DEATH, *L'Indépendance Luxembourgeoise* (17 February 1912).

actress's head). In several adverts, her name appeared in even larger letters than the title of the film.

Asta Nielsen was, of course, not the only actress who was specifically mentioned by name in adverts and articles. In the period between 1911 and 1913, other renowned actresses referred to were, in particular, the French Gabrielle Robinne (an actress the Luxembourg public knew well, because she acted in French plays performed in Luxembourg City during this period), Stacia Napierkowska, Mistinguett and, of course, Sarah Bernhardt, but also the Germans Lissi Nebuschka, Erna Morena and Henny Porten.

The actors and actresses who enjoyed the greatest prestige at the time were either French (especially if they were members of the Comédie Française, the Théâtre Sarah Bernhardt or the Théâtre de l'Odéon), Danish or, to a lesser extent, Italian. Despite the popularity of the Asta Nielsen films (which were produced mostly in Germany), the prestige of the German film industry was not great enough to be used as a sales argument. The adverts therefore focused mainly on the Danish nationality of the director and leading actress.

From 1914/1915 on, other female stars started to challenge the rank of Asta Nielsen, particularly Henny Porten, whose name and portrait drawings were presented in the same way in the cinema adverts as Asta Nielsen's. Other actresses who were regularly quoted and highlighted in the adverts at that time were Fern Andra, Hella Moja, Mia May and Maria Carmi.

Urban Gad

It is also noteworthy that a number of newspaper articles on films starring Asta Nielsen not only focused on the actress, but also highlighted the creative and artistic contribution of director Urban Gad. At that time, mentioning a film director in an article or in an advert was much more the exception than the rule in the Luxembourg press. In fact, for years, Gad was one of the very few directors to be mentioned by name in newspapers. The articles praised his talent as a playwright,[2] his work as a "poet",[3] meaning 'screenwriter', but also his skills as a director.[4] When DIE SÜNDEN DER VÄTER (TEMPTATIONS OF DRINK), a film which touched on art and painting, was shown in Luxembourg in May 1913, a local newspaper pointed out that Urban Gad was himself a talented and prestigious painter and that he was very familiar with the topic.[5]

A crowd puller ...

According to the Luxembourg press of the time, films with Asta Nielsen were very popular with the public. The cinemas were regularly sold out and the newspapers recommended their readers to buy the tickets in advance in order to guarantee admission. The newspapers reported that, at the end of the screenings of Asta Nielsen films, the audience applauded on a regular basis.[6] In a small poem dedicated to the cinema Parisiana, run by the German Hubert Marzen, who had secured himself the exclusive exhibition rights to Asta Nielsen films in the years between 1912 and 1914, one can read not only that the cinema was sold out every night but also that Asta Nielsen "earned the audience's unbridled applause".[7] Even if such phrases were part of a promotional strategy aiming at attracting even more spectators, Asta Nielsen films are likely to have been huge commercial hits. If the two largest film theatres in Luxembourg city, the aforementioned Marzen's Cinéma Parisiana and Medinger's Kinematograph, regularly fought to obtain the exclusive rights to show Asta Nielsen films in the years 1911 to 1918, this most certainly was because the actress was considered to be a crowd puller in Luxembourg.

Even if no sociological study has been done on cinema audiences at the time, we can assume that a significant part of the cinema-goers in the City of

"Earning the audience's unbridled applause" – Asta Nielsen films in Luxembourg

Advert for Asta Nielsen Festival, *Luxemburger Zeitung* (9 December 1916).

Luxembourg consisted of middle-class citizens. This is evidenced by the fact that the three newspapers that published the largest number of cinema adverts and the longest articles devoted to film programmes in general, and the Nielsen films in particular (*Luxemburger Zeitung, Luxemburger Bürger-Zeitung, L'Indépendance Luxembourgeoise*), were publications aimed at a liberal middle class readership. All three newspapers regularly insisted on the cinemas being art venues. The word they normally used in these years was "temple of the arts".[8] They wrote their commentaries on film for what they called "an audience sensitive to the arts".[9] To our knowledge, as opposed to other countries, in Luxembourg no Asta Nielsen film provoked any controversy – at least not in the newspapers. All we know is that some adverts noted that children were not allowed to attend the screening of certain Asta Nielsen films.

... and a recognized artist

The few Luxembourg newspapers that showed an interest in the art of film showered Asta Nielsen (in the adverts as well as in the reviews of her films)

with extremely flattering attributes. The most frequently cited were "divinely gifted, unparalleled artist",[10] "the Pearl of Pearls",[11] "the queen of the cinemas",[12] "greatest tragedienne of cinema",[13] "unique artist"[14] or "queen of the art of cinema",[15] etc. etc. After 1913 she was, in an allusion to the Italian actress Eleonora Duse, praised over and over again as "(divinely gifted) *Kinoduse*".[16] The press regularly celebrated the talent of the Danish artist ("unsurpassable acting skills")[17] who was able to portray a vast variety of characters. In an article on DER TOD IN SEVILLA (SPANISH BLOOD), in which Nielsen played a Spaniard, a Luxembourg newspaper wrote:

> Asta Nielsen, the great actress, has once again delivered a masterpiece of *mimische Darstellungskunst* [mimic acting]. She, a child of the north, has succeeded completely in internalising the thinking and feeling(s) of the sister of the south. She has thus succeeded in creating a magnificent figure of the strongest effect.[18]

The fact that a spectator fainted during the screening of IN DEM GROSSEN AUGENBLICK / AU MOMENT DÉCISIF (THE GREAT MOMENT) was seen as testimony to the quality of both the film and Asta Nielsen's performance.[19] The critics particularly emphasised her talent for tragic parts ("the actress characterising all the passions that move the hearts and minds of people")[20] and her ability to create "soul portraits of poignant tragedy",[21] but they also insisted on the versatility of the actress, praising her performance in comic roles ("master of humour"),[22] as in JUGEND UND TOLLHEIT (IN A FIX) or DIE SUFFRAGETTE (THE SUFFRAGETTE). According to the critics, she could compete with the most popular comic actors of the time such as Max Linder or Charles Seigneur (better known under the name 'Prince').[23]

The films of Urban Gad and Asta Nielsen appeared at a time when the burgeoning cinema medium strove to prove its respectability and openly harboured the ambition to reach "audiences sensitive to art".[24] In order to prove the artistic value of films in general and those of Asta Nielsen in particular, both the cinema owners and the press repeatedly made reference to the world of theatre, which in their view was a guarantee for high artistic standards. In the case of the Asta Nielsen films, they often insisted on the actress's past successes on the best "Scandinavian stages".[25] When an Asta Nielsen film was shown, the programme was normally advertised as "Asta-Nielsen-Festspiele" (Asta Nielsen Festival), in reference to the world of theatre. In January 1912, when ZIGEUNERBLUT / SANG DE BOHÉMIEN OU LA VAGABONDE (GIPSY'S BLOOD) was shown in Luxembourg City, a Luxembourg newspaper wrote: "Asta Nielsen's great and genuine art is not only recognized by the cinema audiences, but also – and this is indicative of the importance of Asta Nielsen – by the colleagues of the theatre stages who came in droves to the cinemas in order to admire her and – learn from her".[26] The recognition by stage actors was regarded as the highest possible honour for a film actor.

These are the findings concerning Asta Nielsen and her films I could infer from the limited source material I was able to find in the Luxembourg papers. But even if the Luxembourg reception history of Asta Nielsen films is somewhat limited, due to the smallness of the country and the scarcity of documents, it may still serve as an interesting case study for researchers dealing with the phenomenon of film stars on an international level in the early years of cinema.

Notes

1. Advert for ABGRÜNDE in *Luxemburger Zeitung* (8 July 1911).
2. Review of DER TOTENTANZ, *Luxemburger Bürger-Zeitung* (9 November 1912) .
3. Review of DIE SÜNDEN DER VÄTER, *Luxemburger Bürger-Zeitung* (3 May 1913).
4. Review of DIE SUFFRAGETTE, *Luxemburger Bürger-Zeitung* (15 November 1913).
5. *Luxemburger Bürger-Zeitung* (3 Mai 1913)
6. *Luxemburger Bürger-Zeitung* (19 December 1913).
7. "Doch Marzen's Kino empfiehlt sich getreulich von selbst durch all'abends ausverkauftes Haus und Asta Nielsen – erntet erfreulich des Publikums unbändigen Applaus." *Luxemburger Bürger-Zeitung* (9 January 1912).
8. *Luxemburger Bürger-Zeitung* (1 February 1913).
9. *Luxemburger Bürger-Zeitung* (16 March 1912).
10. *Luxemburger Bürger-Zeitung* (19 December 1911); (6 January 1912).
11. *L'Indépendance Luxembourgeoise* (17 February 1912).
12. *L'Indépendance Luxembourgeoise* (6 April 1912).
13. *Luxemburger Bürger-Zeitung* (3 Mai 1913).
14. *Luxemburger Bürger-Zeitung* (3 Mai 1915).
15. *Luxemburger Zeitung* (16 June 1916).
16. *Luxemburger Bürger-Zeitung* (4 January 1913).
17. *Luxemburger Bürger-Zeitung* (20 January 1912).
18. *Luxemburger Bürger-Zeitung* (31 May 1913).
19. *Luxemburger Bürger-Zeitung* (19 December 1911).
20. *Luxemburger Bürger-Zeitung* (17 February 1912).
21. *Luxemburger Bürger-Zeitung* (5 April 1913).
22. *Luxemburger Bürger-Zeitung* (1 March 1913).
23. Ibid.
24. *Luxemburger Bürger-Zeitung* (16 March 1912).
25. Ibid.
26. *Luxemburger Bürger-Zeitung* (6 January 1912).

La sensacional película

Cuando se levanta la máscara

confirma una vez más el insuperable talento
de la gran trágica

Asta Nielsen

que arrebata a todos los públicos

Serie especial ASTA NIELSEN, presentada por

PATHÉ FRÈRES

Concesionario exclusivo para España y Portugal
LOUIS GARNIER
Paseo de Gracia, 43   □   BARCELONA

María Antonia Paz and Julio Montero

"Celebrada artista de fama mundial"
Asta Nielsen in Barcelona, 1911–1915

Between 1910 and 1920 Spanish film business had one fundamental weakness: its atomisation. This affected film production, distribution and exhibition in equal measure, and reflected the general situation of the Spanish economy. Around 1910, very few films were being made and production companies, except for some isolated cases, were small in size and short-lived. The distributors and exhibitors exploited the market, which was strong and consolidated in Catalonia (particularly in Barcelona) and in the towns along the Mediterranean coast. Barcelona was the heart of cinematography in Spain, in terms of film showings as well as of production and distribution. Madrid would not be able to offer a realistic alternative until the 1930s. The chronic need for foreign productions to show in the cinemas placed the Spanish market in full contact with innovations in the European film trade. These included the production and promotion of feature films, the exclusive system of film distribution, and the development of the star system.

The Spanish film market between 1910 and 1918

According to the trade journal *Arte y Cinematografía*, Barcelona had at least 100 cinemas in 1911. However, the city had little capacity to produce films, and the majority of those shown were foreign. An analysis of the advertisements and listings in the press indicates that the proportion of Spanish films being screened at any one time hovered around ten per cent at best. A small group of the most important distribution companies served the growing demand for films by imports. This gave rise to a relatively high degree of modernisation, since the companies were in contact with the most advanced production houses in Europe and the United States. From 1910, distribution across Spain was carried out via a network of regional representatives with agencies in Barcelona, Madrid, Seville, Malaga, Valencia, Bilbao and La Coruña. During the First World War there were around 50 distribution companies in Barcelona. Film distribution was based on diversified and efficient structures. It was the most

Facing page:
El Cine (8 March 1913).

robust part of the film business in the city, organised on two levels. At the top were the wholesalers or representatives: their activities focused on the import of films from the most important producers in the world.[1] They released their films to the retailers or hire companies who then made up their catalogues and offered them to the exhibitors. A few businessmen ran cinema chains of up to six theatres in the city – which tended to be the most centrally located and the most luxurious. The chains had an advantage in their negotiations with the hire companies. From around 1914 onwards, competition led them to offer longer and longer programmes of, allegedly, between 4,000 and 6,000 metres. From then on, feature films can be considered to have triumphed over shorts, though there were still plenty of short films available to complement the programmes.

Initially, the spread of feature-length films had a negative impact on the smaller cinemas which were the most common type in Spain, Barcelona included. The exhibitors protested about the hike in rental prices. Long-feature films were only profitable for those venues with large auditoriums. The small cinemas were obliged to reduce costs, since limited capacity meant they could not recoup the increased outlay, and raising admission prices would have put them at a disadvantage in a very competitive market. Pressure from distributors and audiences made long-feature films almost compulsory, although the smaller cinemas tried to resist at first. In fact, they saw that no feature films at all were shown in Barcelona during the summer of 1913. At the same time they resorted to illegal practices that the distributors were obliged to accept. The most common of these was 'bicycling' prints: "that is, transporting a single print around a number of theatres, thus getting several shows for the price of a single rental".[2]

This involved the screening of a long-feature film in several cinemas on the same day. Usually, the participating cinemas belonged to the same owner, although agreements between independent companies were also made. Showings of the film were scheduled at different times in each cinema and the reels were transported by bicycle from one to the next as soon as they had been screened.[3] Another dishonest practice, which was also tolerated for some time, was that of breaking exclusivity arrangements, which made it difficult for the exclusive system to take root.

Bicycling prints did not increase revenues for small cinemas but it did reduce the relative costs. The distributors and rental companies protested constantly, but the cinemas threatened to close if the practice was not tolerated. The smaller rental companies also proved eager to face up to competition from the larger ones. The conflict was resolved with a provisional agreement which allowed bicycling of the same film between two cinemas at a marginally higher price. The use of this system increased between 1915 and 1918, due to the scarcity of films as well as increased rental prices. It was prohibited in 1918 and almost died out. It is striking that an illegal practice was tolerated because of pressure from a market which was reluctant to restructure.[4] From then on, thepractice of breaking exclusivity arrangements can also be considered to have been overcome.[5]

There were no administrative barriers of any kind to importing films from abroad. It was a completely free trade and this put Spanish production companies up against insurmountable competition. There is no information available as to the existence of branches of German production and distribution companies in Spain between 1911 and 1918.[6] Statistics on film imports in 1912 provide the only insight into the matter. They show that 42 per cent of the imported metres of film came from Germany.[7] Imports from France and the United States accounted for 23.6 per cent and 23 per cent respectively. However, the number of films advertised in the trade press and daily newspapers in Barcelona does not bear any testimony to these figures, and instead shows the clear dominance of French films. This is corroborated by the early, deep-rooted presence of French production and distribution houses in Barcelona. The figures probably include both the printed reels as well as the raw film material from Germany which would be used to make additional copies of films from other countries.

German films arrived on the Spanish market in a variety of ways. For example, a Catalan businessman, J. Cánovas, represented Messter Film of Berlin, until 1915 when J. Pich i Pon took on that role. C. Carandini did the same for Hahn & Guerz of Germany. Another, Volart y Arenas, appears to have represented Levantische Films. In addition, an advert placed by the representative of Pathé in Barcelona in September 1912 states that Pathé was the distributor of the Asta Nielsen film EL BAÍLE TRÁGICO (DER TOTENTANZ, THE DANCE TO DEATH). Through its representative in Spain, Pathé would promote the exclusive presence of the actress. Two more names of German origin appear in the advertisements, Otto Mülhauser and a certain Eichenauer. All we know about these individuals is that they were dedicated to the business of film distribution in Barcelona, and it is possible they were involved in the import of German and Austrian films.[8]

In any case, the German producers and distributors were not able to centralise their exports to Spain via a representative or exclusive Spanish dealer. We do not know if the German companies attempted to do this, but it appears that it would have been difficult for them to find a partner in Barcelona who could provide sufficient guarantees in terms of volume of trade and robust management. In fact, the Asta Nielsen films which were shown in Barcelona were distributed by the Pathé representative in the city.

In terms of the timeline, the fundamental cut-off point is 1914. From this year on, German products almost disappeared from the usual suppliers, including even the raw film stock used to print copies.[9] French and Italian films would follow a similar path. First in 1917 and then definitively in 1918, the film trade with Spain was cut off as a reprisal for the country's economic relations with Germany during the First World War. The American film companies, however, did not let this opportunity pass them by.

Asta Nielsen films in Barcelona

Data on the films of Asta Nielsen in Barcelona refer exclusively to those advertisements which mention the actress's name. It is unlikely that there are any mentions of her films which do not include her name; but this has only been confirmed within a particular sample. The daily newspaper analysed is Barcelona's La Vanguardia.[10] There was only one magazine aimed at the professional cinematography trade at that stage, *Arte y Cinematografía*, which we consulted in the Filmoteca Española library (the collection is incomplete for 1912, but is complete from 1913 up to 1918). We also consulted a consumer cinema magazine entitled *El Cine. Semanario popular de espectáculos* at the library.

In 1912, most adverts mentioning the Danish star's films appeared in *La Vanguardia*. The film titles, with her name linked to them, appear on 70 occasions. The cycle closes in 1915, with just one reference. In 1913, there were a total of 28 references, and there is a slight decline to 20 references in 1914. This evidence should be considered in conjunction with other information. In 1912 six Asta Nielsen films premiered in Barcelona; in 1913, five were shown, and the highest number of releases was in 1914 when eight Asta Nielsen films premiered. It seems that the intensity of the advertising was focused on launching an actress who had been unknown in Spain until then. In 1912, there are 70 entries for six films. The following year there were just 28 entries for five films and in 1914, twenty advertising references were made to the actress for eight of her films.

One additional factor has a bearing on how we assess these figures. In 1912, the films were advertised more widely because they were given more screenings. For example, EL BAILE TRÁGICO could be seen in five cinemas at the same time, over three days. This is remarkable. In four of them it remained on the programme for one more day; and in two of them the screenings continued for two more days. Films were usually replaced after three days, because the public demanded such variety that programme changes were required twice a week. Those many screenings of EL BAILE TRÁGICO at the same time in Barcelona suggest two things: first, the powerful impact of the combination of feature films and the actress's popularity, which had been intensified by her presence in the *espectáculos* pages of *La Vanguardia*; second, the use of more than one print for exhibition in Barcelona, which was – by a considerable margin – the city with the most important cinema business in the country, as we have seen. Alternatively, this may also be an indication that bicycling was being used to reduce rental costs in a conservative and prudent market.

If a film having a longer than usual run in each cinema is taken as a sign of success, we must recognise that Asta Nielsen's success was unprecedented in the early period of cinema in Spain. Along with EL BAILE TRÁGICO, MOMENTO CRÍTICO also had an extended run in the same year. It was shown in five cinemas and remained on the programme at the cinema Walkyria for eight consecutive days. LOS HIJOS DEL GENERAL was shown over five days in the Cataluña and five more days in the Cinematógrafo Belliograff.

"Celebrada artista de fama mundial" Asta Nielsen in Barcelona, 1911–1915

Table 1. Asta Nielsen films premiered and programmed in Barcelona 1912–1915.

Spanish title	Original title English title	Berlin premiere	Barcelona premiere*	Barcelona numbers of programmes in cinemas
El momento crítico	In dem großen Augenblick The Great Moment	28 Aug 1911	24 Jan 1912	51 Iris, Walkyria, Bohemia, Triunfo, Príncipe
Sangre gitana	Zigeunerblut Gipsy Blood	8 Oct 1911	11 May 1912	15 Excelsior, Cataluña
La espía francesa	Die Verräterin The Traitress	9 Dec 1911	1 Oct 1912	3 Excelsior
La danza de la muerte o Baile trágico	Der Totentanz The Dance to Death	7 Sep 1912	3 Oct 1912	69 Iris, Belliograff, Excelsior, Kursaal, Royal
Los hijos del general	Die Kinder des Generals Falsely Accused	5 Oct 1912	7 Nov 1912	57 Belliograff, Cataluña, Excelsior, Iris, Royal
El hipócrita o Cuando se cae la máscara	Wenn die Maske fällt When the Mask Falls	1 Nov 1912	10 Dec 1912	27 Belliograff, Argentina, Fregoli
Las batallas del amor	Jugend und Tollheit In a Fix	3 Jan 1913	10 Feb 1913	15 Diana
La muerte de Pierrot	Komödianten The Heart of a Pierrot	31 Jan 1913	22 May 1913	24 Príncipe Alfonso, Ideal, Diana, Royal
Sangre Andaluza	Der Tod in Sevilla Spanish Blood	4 April 1913	7 June 1913	2 Cataluña, Gran Cine Eldorado
Hacia el abismo	Abgründe The Abyss	[Copenhagen] 12 Sep 1910	16 Jul 1913	15 Diana, Royal, Príncipe Alfonso
La sufragista	Die Suffragette The Suffragette	12 Sep 1913	11 Dec 1913	33 Ideal, Argentina, Cataluña, Bohemia
El aeroplano no. 1	S 1 A Girl's Sacrifice	14 Nov 1913	16 Jan 1914	9 Cataluña, Argentina
El sueño negro	Der schwarze Traum The Circus Girl	19 Aug 1911	19 Feb 1914	3 Kursaal
Subterfugio	Das Mädchen ohne Vaterland A Girl Without a Country	29 Nov 1912	14 Apr 1914	12 Príncipe Alfonso, Cataluña
Mater Dolorosa	Das Kind ruft The Cry of a Child	6 Feb 1914	7 May 1914	15 Príncipe Alfonso, Cataluña, Diana
La Reina del Cine	Die Filmprimadonna The Prima Donna	5 Dec 1913	12 May 1914	6 Príncipe Alfonso
Bandoleros de los Apeninos	Zapatas Bande Zapata's Gang	27 Feb 1914	22 May 1914	3 Príncipe Alfonso
La novela de la amazona	Zapatas Bande Zapata's Gang	27 Feb 1914	8 Jun 1914	9 Cataluña, Bohemia, Kursaal
El sentir del primer amor	Engelein Up to Her Tricks	3 Jan 1914	18 Aug 1915	3 Príncipe Alfonso

In 1913 in Barcelona, Asta Nielsen's most watched film was LA SUFRAGISTA: it was on at four cinemas and remained on the programme for four days at the Ideal cinema. In 1914, MATER DOLOROSA and SUBTERFUGIO were the most widely seen. MATER DOLOROSA was on in four cinemas, for an average of two days, and SUBTERFUGIO in two cinemas for two days. As we can see, the rhythm of showings was decreasing, which may indicate a normalisation of the market, including reduced use of bicycling these films, and the decreasing importance of the Asta Nielsen phenomenon.

The cinema advertisements did not usually provide information about the number of showings for each day. In Barcelona, from 1915 onwards and in the most important and central cinemas, they announced – at times – two screenings on weekdays and three on Sundays.[11] There were 367 adverts for Asta Nielsen films in Barcelona's daily newspaper *La Vanguardia*. Not all of the films had the same success: once the initial wave of expectation had passed, Asta Nielsen's capacity to draw audiences declined. Four films were subject to a total of 210 adverts (57.8%). The three films with the highest number of adverts premiered in 1912. The next highest incidence of adverts was in 1913. Figures from then on are less spectacular, as if demand for Nielsen had lost momentum in Barcelona.

Films advertised as exclusives in the press to lure audiences in were very rare. This occurred only for LA ESPÍA FRANCESA which was shown exclusively in the Excelsior Cinema in 1912, and SANGRE ANDALUZA in 1913, shown at the Teatro Cataluña and Gran Cine Eldorado respectively. LAS BATALLAS DEL AMOR was advertised as an exclusive in two cinemas belonging to the same company: the Diana and the Royal, in 1913. This is probably an example of a tolerated bicycling of prints. Exclusives are referred to on other occasions, but on further investigation the claims to exclusivity are found to be false. For example, the exclusive showing of LA SUFRAGISTA at the Argentina cinema on 9 December 1913 is disproved by its screening in the Ideal cinema. (It would not appear that exclusivity agreements were broken in this case.) Bicycling prints and the lack of demand for exclusivity from exhibitors paints a picture of a market which is still traditional and remains more focused on reducing costs than on investing in innovation.

Film star Asta Nielsen

Film advertisements placed in *La Vanguardia* refer to Asta Nielsen in 23 different ways. Twelve of them use the expression "célebre" (celebrated) or "famosa" (famous) to highlight her importance. In Spanish, these two terms are synonymous and mean that "she was famous", or was known for a particular characteristic which allows us to distinguish her from others who were otherwise apparently similar. This unique element which sets a famous person apart can be something they have done or something they have said which becomes widely known. Therefore the descriptions of an actress as "famosa" and "célebre" have a positive meaning which goes beyond her pure popularity, which is the primary meaning of these words and the most obvious to anyone who reads or hears them.

Asta Nielsen is "célebre" (celebrated), "célebre y famosa" (celebrated and famosa), "célebre artista" (a celebrated artist), "famosa y célebre artista" (a famous and celebrated artist), "famosa" (famous), "celebrada artista de fama mundial" (world-famous celebrated artist), "célebre y popular" (celebrated and popular), "celebridad mundial" (a worldwide celebrity), "renombrada artista" (a renowned artist)... Potential cinema-goers are left in no doubt: Asta Nielsen is an extraordinarily famous actress. Therefore going to see her film will give them an advantage over those who are not able to see it. In a film exhibition system which showed films for three days and then replaced them by the next film programme, intensive advertising was essential. There was no time to consider whether or not to buy a ticket: audiences had to be decisive and the extraordinary nature of the viewing seems to have played a key role in this decision.

The second set of phrases that the advertisements used for Asta Nielsen in her films refers to the quality of her work. The references come in seven different forms. The term "artist", the noun that defines Nielsen by her professional activity, is intensified with descriptions such as: "eminent" (elevated, outstanding; which sets one apart); "great"; "notable"; "matchless" (there is no-one else like her in this concept of an artist); "unrivalled" (no one could compete with her and hope to win); etc. In these cases, the actress's importance is attributed directly to her qualities rather than to what others think of her or what makes her popular and well known. An unusually long publicity phrase in January 1912 defined her as "Famous, great, extraordinary and recognised throughout the world as the cinema's best artist".[12]

A third set of references in the adverts contains a number of themes. One advert for LA REINA DEL CINE is particularly interesting because the film's title is used to promote the actress herself, and consequently the film. The film's title seems to apply to Asta Nielsen and thus crown her as the greatest cinema actress of the time. It seems paradoxical then, that the last reference to Nielsen in *La Vanguardia*'s film advertisements as a "great artist, a favourite among Barcelona audiences" took advantage of the actress's popularity in the city. It aimed to create a closeness and proximity that had previously been attempted in 1912 through a news story about Nielsen's trip to Spain (though no more was ever published about that event).[13]

Another interesting aspect of the promotion of Asta Nielsen and her films in Spain is the evolution of her public image, which was built around the advertising. The absence of detail about her personal life in comparison to the way the American stars later operated is striking. Throughout 1912, regular readers of the entertainment pages in *La Vanguardia* would only have discovered that she was a famous and celebrated actress. They would have to wait until September 1912 (the beginning of the second season of her films in Barcelona) for the promotion to begin to assess her artistic talent. The publicity

El Cine (7 December 1912).

did not mention her nationality until the following year,[14] while previously they had mentioned her status as a 'señorita' and, therefore, that she was single.[15] Neither the trade journal *Arte y Cinematografía* nor the consumer magazine *El Cine. Semanario popular de espectáculos* gave more information about her private life. The remainder of the phrases are aimed at Spanish cinema owners. For example: "The sensational film CUANDO SE CAE LA MÁSCARA confirms once again the unbeatable talent of the great tragedian Asta Nielsen, which captivates every audience".[16]

The actress herself is the most important feature in the advertising for these films. The film companies which the prints came from are mentioned in just two cases: LA SUFRAGISTA from Pathé, and LA ESPÍA FRANCESA from Nordisk. This is quite significant in a market where the name of the company had previously been used as an indication of the quality of its films (in the case of shorts). A film's genre does not appear to have been important to viewers either. They seem to have been more interested in *whom* and less in *what* they would see. Only dramas were frequently specified as such. Possibly the most specific praise given to Asta Nielsen's performance is for LA MUERTE DE PIERROT: "This is the most admirably interpreted film by this artist since its plot is ideal for this. The scenes in which the mother, pained by the death of her son, makes herself up to go out onto the stage are fantastic, as is the scene of her own death."[17]

Adverts for Asta Nielsen films do not contain any references that might suggest indecency or scandal, and therefore were not likely to appeal to audiences looking for shocking scenes. This strategy must be understood in context – film censorship had been established by Royal Decree on 29 November 1912. Those who had called for moral propriety in the cinema achieved their goal in the end. In reality, and particularly in the early stages of censorship, the practice merely involved the exhibitors sending the provincial authorities a summary of the plot of each film they intended to show. The summaries were sometimes published in the trade press and consumer magazines as well. The texts do not give any indication of scenes of impropriety, at least to a modern reader, which might have made the films more attractive to audiences. Distributors and exhibitors, mindful of attracting the attention of the censors, avoided making these aspects public, if indeed they cropped up in the films at all.

From all of the material analysed, just two details might lead us to think that potentially 'scandalous' aspects were promoted, albeit indirectly. The first is in the publicity for EL BAILE TRÁGICO, where audiences were reminded that the film shared its leading lady with TRATA DE BLANCAS (DEN HVIDE SLAVEHANDELS SIDSTE OFFER, IN THE HANDS OF IMPOSTORS),[18] which was not the case, but positioned this Asta Nielsen film in the fashionable tradition of the 'white slave' genre. The second detail is in the advert for HACIA EL ABISMO where no mention is made that the images had proved to be provocative in other countries. It is simply described as "extraordinary".[19] The references relied on audiences having seen, or heard about, the earlier films and drawing their own conclusions about the kind of scenes on offer.

The advertisements frequently point out the films' length, and in particular the fact that the advertised films are feature-length. The number of metres attributed to an individual film did not always match, but the important thing was that they exceeded 1,000 metres. LOS HIJOS DEL GENERAL is 1,000 metres long according to one advert, 1,110 metres in another and 1,040 metres in a third advert. The length of most Asta Nielsen films shown in Barcelona varied between 1,000 and 1,200 metres. The longest film is LA SUFRAGISTA, for which the German release version counted 1878 metres. The shortest film is MATER

DOLOROSA at 650 metres. Only adverts for LA MUERTE DE PIERROT and EL HIPÓCRITA specified that they comprised of three acts.

Offering information on a film's length was used as a means of promoting feature films. Features would have great importance in Barcelona as the city's population had significant proportions of both educated and regular viewers, who therefore preferred to have information about the films on offer. Furthermore, these data refer to concrete pieces of information (such as the length of the films), and providing objective details was particularly valuable to audiences at a time when cinema programmes were awash with adjectives. It also suggests that incorporating feature films into cinema programmes was considered to offer audiences added value. In fact, the trade press states emphatically that viewers preferred feature-length films.[20]

The system of advance information about forthcoming titles was used to create a certain sense of anticipation among the public. It was common to give details of upcoming premieres two days in advance, but in the case of EL MOMENTO CRÍTICO, details were given one week before it opened at the Iris Park cinema. The final showing of a film was also advertised, at least in the cases of six Asta Nielsen films. If a film was receiving a one-off showing this was also mentioned as in the case of EL SUEÑO NEGRO, at the Kursaal. On two occasions, 25 September 1912 and 7 February 1913, the listings advertise the forthcoming return of Asta Nielsen, without mentioning any particular film. This is a clear indication of her popularity and the fame she enjoyed among Spanish audiences.

Descriptions of the films are full of praise. The most often repeated element is success: "a success every day", "a great success", "sensational success". "Fantastic" is used in reference to EL BAILE TRÁGICO, LA SUFRAGISTA is described as "magnificent" and HACIA EL ABISMO "extraordinary". LOS HIJOS DEL GENERAL and EL HIPÓCRITA are praised as "artistic jewels". Another indication of Asta Nielsen's success in Spain is the re-release of EL SUEÑO NEGRO, a film from 1911, shown in Barcelona in 1914 "by popular request", according to the listings.[21]

Asta Nielsen among other stars

Films featuring foreign actors and actresses appeared freely on Spanish screens. The mentions of the star system's leading players made in the daily newspapers were not free of charge. They were a form of advertising which the cinemas paid for in order to differentiate their products from those offered by their competitors. The respective advertising was targeted at potential viewers of the film who read that particular newspaper. The price was established according to the number of words used. For this reason, advertising slogans were usually brief and very often just the name of the leading actress was used to draw patrons in. In fact, the most common reference states simply that this is an 'Asta Nielsen film'. The phrase occurs on 37 occasions in *La Vanguardia*.

When the star of a film was advertised in a trade journal, the distributor had to pay for it, as it enabled him to offer his catalogue of great productions to cinema owners. The advertising took various forms: from a full-page advert to feature articles, and outlines of the plots. All of this provided a set of materials to help potential customers decide between certain products. Of course, exclusive showings for exhibitors were also offered.

The table below looks at four prominent stars of different nationalities: Asta Nielsen (who in Spain was presented as being linked to German cinema); Francesca Bertini (Italian); Suzanne Grandais (French) and Mary Pickford (American). An analysis of references made to them in advertising published in the Barcelona daily newspaper *La Vanguardia*, provides the following results:

Table 2. Number of mentions★ of actresses in cinema adverts in *La Vanguardia*.

Year	Asta Nielsen	Francesca Bertini	Suzanne Grandais	Mary Pickford	Total for the year
1910	0	0	0	0	0
1911	9	0	0	0	6
1912	38	0	0	0	38
1913	19	0	1	0	20
1914	16	4	0	0	20
1915	1	41	0	0	42
1916	0	36	0	0	36
1917	0	16	0	0	16
1918	0	12	0	3	15
1919	0	14	0	4	18
1920	0	2	0	4	6
Total for the actress	80	125	1	11	217

★Days on which each star is mentioned in *La Vanguardia*. There may have been several mentions on a single day.

In Spain, the use of the star system as a means of intensifying film publicity among audiences began in the 1911/12 season in Barcelona. The figures for 1911 in the table above are relatively low because the system only came into use in October of that year. The implementation of the star system is directly linked to the promotion of Asta Nielsen films. This is an important point as the French star Suzanne Grandais enjoyed enormous popularity in the same period, but her celebrity was not used as a key factor in adverts for her films in the daily press. In contrast, it was heavily used to advertise films starring Asta Nielsen.

The table showing the number of days on which an actress is mentioned allows us to trace a sort of relay race in the effectiveness of cinema publicity. The promotion of Asta Nielsen as a star, a key element in the publicity for her films, is the first example of this process in Spain. The table clearly reveals the precedence of the German system of film promotion. The disappearance of

German films from Spanish programmes following the outbreak of the First World War meant that she had to be replaced by other stars. Obviously, the Italian film industry and its star Francesca Bertini proved the most effective replacement on the Spanish market.

Conclusions

The consolidation of the most modern operating methods, which was based on the system of exclusive hire of feature films, the dominance of the feature-length film (or at least of films of two or more reels over those of just one reel) and of longer programmes in general, together with the increased use of advertising in the promotion of the films and in the development of the star system, met with a number of obstacles in Spain.

Barcelona was very much ahead of the rest of the country in terms of cinematographic development. Here, the atomisation of the business was so great that there was fierce resistance to any innovation which would imply initial outlay and these innovations were met with an enormous amount of distrust.

Thus, the first challenge was to secure the acceptance and subsequent consolidation of feature films in the programmes that were on offer to the public. As we have already seen, Catalan exhibitors (and there is no reason to think that this was any different anywhere else in Spain) tried every means possible to ensure that features did not become part of the schedules, despite the fact that they had already been accepted by the majority of audiences. In spite of this resistance, feature-length films prevailed throughout the period, from 1911 to 1918.

The exhibitors' resistance to the spread of the long-feature film was based on the need to reduce costs in a sector in which intense competition made price increases difficult. However, increases became inevitable and in the summer of 1912, the sector's businessmen agreed to generally raise the price by some 5 centesimos per ticket. Proportionally, the prices of the cheapest tickets went up most (by as much as 50 per cent: from 10 to 15 centesimos). The press attributed this necessary increase to the greater length of the programmes in general, and the increase in the screening of features in particular.[22]

We must highlight the fundamental role played by Asta Nielsen and her films in the spread of the new form of advertising based on the popularity of individual actresses. Asta Nielsen's case is without precedent. In Barcelona, she was the first film star to systematically figure in the promotion of feature-length films. Adverts in the daily press addressing potential cinema-goers based the importance of seeing the films solely on the basis of her participation. The plotlines are hardly ever mentioned. What made those German films stand out was that the Danish actress had a leading role in them. In fact, this system survived, but in new guises. In 1914, with the start of the First World War, the flow of German films into Spain was cut off. They were replaced first by Italian, and later by American films. Advertising continued to focus on promoting the films' respective stars.

"Celebrada artista de fama mundial" Asta Nielsen in Barcelona, 1911–1915

Acknowledgements: This essay was conducted as part of the authors' research activity under the project GR35/10-A in the Complutense research team Historia y estructura de la comunicación y del entretenimiento (History and structure of media and entertainment).

Notes

1. We only know for certain that one of these companies imported films from Nordisk in Copenhagen. Cf. Palmira González López, *El cine en Barcelona, una generación histórica, 1906–1923* (doctoral thesis, Universidad de Barelona 1984), 511. There are no mentions of any German producers or distributors having their own branches in Barcelona.
2. Kristin Thompson, *Exporting Entertainment. America in the World Film Market 1907–34* (London: British Film Institute, 1985), 10.
3. López, *El cine en Barcelona*, 521–524 and 757–761. Conflict over bicycling prints can be followed in *Arte y Cinematografía*, no. 137 (31 July 1916); nos. 105 and 106 (15 and 31 August 1915); no. 69 (15 September 1913); cited by López.
4. The atomisation of the distribution and exhibition sectors continued as much as twenty years later, according to a German report. Cf. Julio Montero and María Antonia Paz, *La larga sombra de Hitler. El cine nazi en España (1933–1945)* (Madrid: Cátedra, 2009), 40–46; 130–140 and 245–256.
5. The films could be hired exclusively for double the normal price. Sometimes another cinema would show the film first. This was known as 'breaking the exclusivity agreement' and involved the existence of copies of a film outside the control of the distributors. At the time, these cases could not be brought to trial in Spanish courts. In November 1917, the distributors agreed to rigorous control of the copies and to freeze relations with anyone who infringed the terms of exclusivity. Cf. López, *El cine en Barcelona*, 761–762, and *Arte y Cinematografía*, 168–169 (November 1917).
6. López, *El cine en Barcelona*, 508. Only Gaumont, Eclair, Pathé, Cines and Cox had branches in Barcelona.
7. According to information published in *Arte y Cinematografía*, no. 74 (30 November 1913), 44, cited by López, *El cine en Barcelona*, 505.
8. López, *El cine en Barcelona*, vol. IV; advertisements in *Arte y Cinematografía* (30 September 1912); (15 January 1913).
9. López, *El cine en Barcelona*, 507 onwards.
10. *La Vanguardia* is available online: www.lavanguardia.com/hemeroteca/.
11. López, *El cine en Barcelona*, 749–750.
12. *La Vanguardia* (23 January 1912).
13. *Arte y Cinematografía* (15 September 1912).
14. *La Vanguardia* (23 May 1913).
15. *La Vanguardia* (13 August 1912).
16. *El Cine* (7 December 1912).
17. *El Cine* (12 April 1913).
18. Trata de blancas was shown in Barcelona in 1911. It must have been a great success with audiences to have merited a reference in this advertisement. Cf. *La Vanguardia* (1 October 1912), and the two following days.
19. *La Vanguardia* (15, 16 and 18 July 1913).
20. *El Cine* (14 September 1912).
21. *La Vanguardia* (19 February 1914).
22. *El Cine* (27 July 1912).

PART V

CENSORSHIP VERSUS ART DISCOURSE

ACCORDED BY UNIVERSAL PUBLIC ACCLAMATION

THE WORLD'S GREATEST PICTURE-PLAY ARTIST.

INCOMPARABLE

ASTA NIELSEN

Miss Asta Nielsen is publicly recognised as the Queen of the Picture Loving Patrons. For fully Illustrated Synopses of her plays, and particulars of Exclusive Rights, apply to

THE WALTURDAW EXCLUSIVE FILM DEPARTMENT,
46 GERRARD STREET, LONDON, W.

Jon Burrows

"The Great Asta Nielsen," "The Shady Exclusive" and the Birth of Film Censorship in Britain, 1911–1914

I will suggest in this essay that Asta Nielsen's films had a highly significant and even transformative impact on British film culture in the early 1910s. But my contention will be that this impact lay not so much in the direction of stimulating the development of a discourse of film stardom, and more in the way that her productions helped to establish the commercial viability of feature length films and the exclusive rental system in the UK. In order to fully appreciate her significance for the British film trade, I think it is necessary to look more broadly at the developing profile within it of imported German films between 1911 and 1914. The British film industry had been largely dominated by French films since the mid-1900s, and then increasingly by American imports after 1909. Its distribution of German *Monopolfilms* and the concomitant promotion of Asta Nielsen as a defining brand identifier for such films had three very significant consequences: (i) a dramatic enhancement of the profile and influence of German product in this commercially very important market; (ii) the stimulation of strong enthusiasm for exclusive feature films amongst hitherto resistant British exhibitors, and – inadvertently – (iii) the introduction of organised film censorship in the UK.

The method of renting films to cinemas at higher than normal prices for the exclusive right to show them in a particular geographical district did not originate in Britain with German imports. Certain newsworthy non-fiction titles, for example, particularly films of major sporting events, had frequently been handled in this way for a number of years.[1] The London branch of the Danish firm Nordisk, which was run by a German managing director called Ludwig Landmann, deserves credit as the first company to regularly release three-reel fiction films on an exclusive basis, a practice they began in March 1911.[2] There was enormous early resistance to the system which Nordisk attempted to establish, however. Throughout the spring and summer of 1911,

Facing page:
Kinematograph Monthly Record (February 1912).

the film industry trade press expressed militant hostility to exclusive rental, decrying it as a "crying evil" on the grounds that:

> Whilst exclusive rights may prove beneficial to the individual who is fortunate to secure them, the principle is one which operates against the interests of the smaller individual exhibitor, who is quite as much entitled to consideration as wealthy companies.[3]

Editorial attitudes towards the exclusive did not soften until the UK's oldest film renting company, Walturdaw, began offering multiple reel feature films on exclusive terms in the autumn of 1911. Walturdaw, who justifiably promoted themselves in their company logo as "The Original Film Renters", had been founded in 1896, and by 1900 had become the first organisation in the UK to offer films for hire rather than outright sale.[4] They would come to play a similarly pioneering role in the development of exclusive film renting, but this was the direct result of an infusion of new blood to their board of directors. In December 1910, a 36 year-old film merchant called Harry Browne acquired a large shareholding in Walturdaw and the position of its managing director. Significantly, Browne was also a director of, and the second largest investor in, a company called A.E. Hubsch and Co., Ltd. The founder of this latter firm, Albert Eberhardt Hübsch, was a German film merchant who had set himself up in 1909 as the UK agent for a number of the leading German production companies. It was clearly as a result of Browne's close connection with Hubsch that Walturdaw began offering multiple-reel German films for hire as exclusives from August 1911 onwards.

It is a more speculative assumption on my part to suggest that the elaborate promotional treatment which Walturdaw lavished on their first German feature films was probably modelled on the recent successful exploitation in Germany, and elsewhere, of Asta Nielsen's first film AFGRUNDEN (THE ABYSS) of 1910. However, it is a curious fact of the events I am documenting that – in contrast to most of the other European case studies presented in this volume – AFGRUNDEN itself played practically no part in establishing the cultural and commercial viability of the exclusive feature film in Britain. This is for the simple reason that it only received a belated and somewhat desultory release in the UK. It did not appear until October 1912, under the same title – WOMAN ALWAYS PAYS – used for its troubled American release six months earlier. The film was placed on the open market, rather than as an exclusive, by a 26 year-old second hand film dealer (originally from Karlsruhe) called Max Baer.[5] Baer's business largely involved selling and re-titling second-hand British prints for the continental market and his hire department was modest.[6] We can only guess why a film that had been so successful throughout the rest of Europe was passed on by all the leading British renters and only surfaced in this low-key fashion: presumably its provocative content rendered it too risky a proposition in the eyes of the principal dealers.[7]

AFGRUNDEN thus made no direct impact in the UK, but the influence of the distinctive exploitation campaign this landmark film received in Germany does seem to be evident in the treatment which Walturdaw lavished upon its first German exclusive feature. This was a now-forgotten (and non-extant) Deutsche Bioscop film called SÜNDIGE LIEBE (Sinful Love) of 1911, to which Walturdaw gave the less provocative title of FOOLS OF SOCIETY. Just like AFGRUNDEN, FOOLS OF SOCIETY was an adult melodrama dealing with transgressive female behaviour. It presented the story of a married middle-class woman who embarks upon a passionate affair with her husband's best friend. When her lover is killed in a riding accident, the husband discovers evidence of the relationship, and offers his wife an escape from the consequences of her dishonour by handing her his pistols; the film ended with her suicide.[8] Walturdaw launched this 3,200 foot film in the UK with what was, for them, unprecedented fanfare in advance of its official release on 16 September 1911.[9] It was thus made available a full week before it was actually released in Germany, and the fact that such treatment was lavished upon a title which represented a type of film that was very unfamiliar for the British film trade, and one which had not yet even been tested in its home market, would seem to suggest that Walturdaw had been emboldened by the success of the pioneering promotional campaign which previously accompanied the release of AFGRUNDEN in Germany and elsewhere.[10] Walturdaw's handling of FOOLS OF SOCIETY duplicated many of the key innovative features of the special treatment of the Danish film documented elsewhere in this volume. Cinemas were encouraged to book the film for two weeks rather than the customary three day engagement period, despite the fact that it cost more than double Walturdaw's normal hiring rates,[11] and the similarly unprecedented step was taken to quote letters from satisfied exhibitors testifying to the record profits they had experienced and the number of extra showings and re-bookings they had arranged to satisfy audience demand.[12]

Given the fact that a very large proportion of cinemas in the UK did not advertise their programmes in local newspapers in this period, it is impossible to generate useful statistical data about the number and length of bookings of FOOLS OF SOCIETY in any particular district. I can only point to indirect and anecdotal evidence concerning the impact of this film, but it does seem to me significant that 15 years later, as part of a series of published recollections of the early years of the British film industry, one of the founders of Walturdaw, E.G. Turner, singled out FOOLS OF SOCIETY as a film which he thought everyone connected with the Edwardian film business would remember both for its enormous commercial success and the role it played in establishing exclusive film hiring as standard practice.[13]

A couple of months after the release of FOOLS OF SOCIETY, Walturdaw had another German exclusive available for bookings which they were very keen to brand as a natural successor, containing a similar combination of controversial adult content and scenes of sensational spectacle. Their "No. 2 Exclusive", THE GREAT MOMENT (IN DEM GROSSEN AUGENBLICK), was the story of a young maidservant who becomes pregnant by her employer's nephew and is only released from a life of misery when she sacrifices herself in a fire to save her illegitimate child from the flames.[14] It was another Deutsche Bioscop film, but, of course, this time Asta Nielsen featured in the leading role. Nielsen also took the principal role in Walturdaw's third German exclusive GYPSY BLOOD (ZIGEUNERBLUT). However, it is important to note that Nielsen's name was not mentioned in any of Walturdaw's advertisements at this time, and emphasis was placed instead on the shared generic qualities of the films – i.e. the degree to which they followed the template set by FOOLS OF SOCIETY: contemporary melodrama delivering sin and sensation. This practice changed with the advertisements for Walturdaw's fourth exclusive, THE TRAITRESS (DIE VERRÄTERIN), which identified Nielsen's involvement as a key selling point.[15] This was another narrative driven by transgressive female desire, but as it was also a costume drama set during the Franco-Prussian war, it is possible that the shift in genre was felt to require the identification of Nielsen as an additional element of brand identity shared across these German exclusives. Nielsen was henceforth consistently foregrounded in Walturdaw's advertisements for her films – though it's interesting to note that, unusually, she shared top billing on THE BETTER WAY (DIE MACHT DES GOLDES) with Marie van Oeser, an actress clearly thought to be worth promoting because of her tangible link to the film which seemingly remained the gold standard for exclusives: she was "of FOOLS OF SOCIETY fame".[16] For Walturdaw's next exclusive release, RETRIBUTION (NACHTFALTER), Nielsen's name was given greater prominence than the film title in promotional materials, and she subsequently became the focal point of the company's attempts to define a brand label guaranteeing the quality and attractiveness of its exclusive releases, and for subsequent releases over the next two years, individual titles were of secondary importance compared with the emphasis placed on the involvement of "The Great Asta Nielsen".[17]

It is important, nonetheless, to note that, as distinct from the emergence of the film star system in Germany and elsewhere, Asta Nielsen was not the first film actress to be promoted as a star performer within the British film trade. American companies began systematically foregrounding the identities of their stock company players for the benefit of British audiences in March 1911.[18] Nielsen was undoubtedly one of the most popular and recognisable film stars in Britain: she was twice made the cover star of the most important fan magazine, *Pictures and the Picturegoer*, in 1914, and in its "Answers to Correspondents" section, this publication responded on a very regular basis to queries from readers desperate to pay tribute to, gain postcards of, or make direct contact with Nielsen.[19] However, the results of the first ever poll measuring the respective popularity of film stars in Britain, conducted by the same magazine in early 1914, was dominated by American performers.[20]

Richard deCordova has very influentially argued that a fully developed film star system only emerged in 1913–14, when the circulation of, and desire for, knowledge of the performer's off-screen existence constituted "the primary focus of discourse".[21] Initially, such knowledge commonly took the form of

Kinematograph Monthly Record (April 1912).

stories about dramatic behind-the-scenes adventures that stars endured during the making of films. He distinguishes this mode of stardom from an earlier type of screen celebrity in which emphasis was placed exclusively upon a performer's acting ability.[22] It could be argued that the constituent features of Asta Nielsen's fame in Britain did not move very much beyond a focus upon her artistic talent and accomplishments. Walturdaw promoted her as "The German Sarah Bernhardt", insisting that she "is acknowledged by picture play experts and dramatic critics to equal Madame Sarah Bernhardt as a tragedienne and emotional actress".[23] In the only personal interview which *Pictures and the*

Picturegoer secured with Asta Nielsen, in April 1914, she actively resisted the dominant line of questioning adopted in the magazine's regular star profiles:

> Adventures? You want my adventures? Why ever do people imagine that cinema actresses are always having hair-raising experiences? I am an actress, not an acrobat! (...) I have never fallen out of a balloon, over a cliff, under a train, out of a motor-car, or anything like that, you know. And, also, I'm not a little bit anxious to undergo any experiences like those one reads about as having happened to some of the American players. I think our Yankee friends seem to make a speciality of having adventures, don't you?[24]

It seems to me that the chief pioneering distinction of Asta Nielsen's prominence in British film culture lies less in her contribution to the development of the star system, and more in the fact that she was the first named actress to appear regularly in exclusive feature films. The way in which Walturdaw handled her films represents the first instance in the UK wherein the presence of a familiar screen performer with an established track record was used to help justify the imposition of higher rental prices. Booking "The Great Asta Nielsen" potentially ameliorated the risk that increased expenditure on a single film entailed for the exhibitor.

Business records for Walturdaw were never preserved, but there is some data accessible which gives us, indirectly, a sense of the commercial significance of these German exclusives in the UK. In a 1919 prospectus which solicited new investment to recapitalise the company, it was revealed that in the 12 months prior to the end of August 1911, Walturdaw's gross turnover was £37,084. In the following 12 months – the period in which the firm first handled German exclusives – turnover rose by 34%. By 1913, it was up by 75%, and Walturdaw had more than doubled the level of business it was doing in 1911 by August 1914.[25] At the outbreak of the First World War, the board of directors were asked by their shareholders to disclose the extent of their dealings with the German film industry, and it was revealed that they handled £80,000 worth of German films a year. Managing director Harry Browne defended this scale of past trading with the 'enemy' on the grounds that "it was only because the public desired them. He assured the company that now he would have nothing more to do with Germany, but would in future support British production by every means in his power."[26] It is clearly significant that during the following 12 months, when Walturdaw stopped buying German exclusives in order to conform with the Trading with the Enemy Act (1914), turnover declined by 37%.

The impact of German feature films on the British market was not purely commercial. In early 1912 a concerned member of the public apparently found the content of FOOLS OF SOCIETY so troubling that he made a complaint to the Home Office asking them to take action about it.[27] In December 1911 the Chief Police Constable of Sheffield ruled that Walturdaw's first Asta Nielsen film THE GREAT MOMENT was "not a fit picture on the score of morality" and prohibited any further screenings in the city.[28] In the same month, an outraged patron asked the Metropolitan Police to take action over Nielsen's "indecent"

GYPSY BLOOD after seeing it at the Electric Pavilion in Brixton. Although he had re-booked the film at the request of other customers, the cinema's manager elected not to screen it again as a result of this minor furore.[29] Around the same time, the trade organisation which represented British filmmakers and the agents of foreign production companies, the Kinematograph Manufacturers' Association (KMA), began to formulate plans for a voluntary form of film censorship to address the problem of what one trade paper called "The Shady Exclusive" – that is to say, continental feature films characterised by "suggestiveness and ultra-sensationalism".[30] Discussions of this topic repeatedly identified Germany as the principal offender. One anonymous commentator explained the perceived problem thus:

> The censor in Germany differs from the critic in this country (who is at present the censor here) in that the former will pass films where the plots deal with modern social questions and the general doings of modern society, as long as the carrying out of the plot is kept decent and inoffensive. And it is just the film plot dealing with such questions to which the strongest objection is found amongst the buyers in this country. The chief reason for this objection is that the audiences of picture palaces consist to a great extent of children and very young people, on whom the moral influence of such films might be injurious (...) As there are no separate picture performances in this country for adults and for children, and the above-mentioned film subjects must rightly be considered as non-suitable for children and young people, such films have to be barred from picture shows altogether. There are separate shows in Germany, and there is therefore a market there for films which are not considered suitable for this country.[31]

When finalised plans for the introduction of the British Board of Film Censors (BBFC) were revealed to the national press in November 1912, one of the most vocal sponsors of the scheme, the British filmmaker Will Barker, declared:

> [I] was led to take this up to protect my business. It is not the crime in cinematographs I fear so much, for "Punch and Judy" is founded upon crime, but I am up against anything which I would not like my children to see – the sexual element that is creeping in more and more every day.
>
> The manufacturers have voluntarily adopted the censorship for the good of the trade.[32]

In evidence presented to the investigation of the cinema's impact on society conducted by the National Council of Public Morals in 1917, the first secretary of the BBFC, Joseph Brooke Wilkinson, explained that the introduction of self-censorship was a direct response to "a certain class of film which was being introduced from Germany".[33] As Nick Hiley has previously established, there was one film in particular that appears to have played a decisive role in provoking action.[34] Reflecting back on the formation of the BBFC 24 years later, Barker was more specific about the catalyst: "One film, imported from Germany and rented out by Walturdaw, named 'Sins of Society' was a very bad example of what could be shown to the public. I and a few others thought we saw the end of our business if such wrapped up filth was to be shown."[35] The intended reference here is obviously to FOOLS OF SOCIETY.

However, it was very probably not just altruistic fears for the general good of the film business in Britain which motivated the formation of the BBFC to clamp down on provocative exclusives.[36] The system of censorship that was adopted in the UK was practically identical to the National Board of Censorship set up by the American film industry in 1909, and the similarities were not accidental. Indeed, although it has previously escaped comment, surviving government records reveal that advocacy of the BBFC proposals to the Home Office was largely orchestrated by representatives of the British branch of the Edison company.[37] This is a very significant detail. Richard Abel has suggested that the American system of film censorship was surreptitiously used to undermine the strong commercial performance in the USA of rival continental firms like Pathé. As he explains,

> As the demands for social control of the cinema converged with those of economic control, the need to deal with Pathé's illegitimacy took on ever greater urgency. This is perhaps no more evident than in the actions of the National Board of Censorship (...). [T]hroughout 1909 and 1910, Pathé films were either rejected or returned for alteration, proportionately, more frequently than were the films from American producers (...). In effect, the early work of the National Board of censorship neatly complemented that of the M[otion] P[icture] P[atents] C[ompany]: the one curbed Pathé's economic power while the other curtailed what was perceived as its undesirable, immoral, "foreign" influence.[38]

When the BBFC was inaugurated in 1912, various sceptics speculated that it had been similarly designed by American interests to help weaken and marginalise their strongest continental competitors in the British market. An anonymous "sufferer" commented thus:

> "The proprietors of picture theatres will be invited to show only those passed by the Board of Censors", says Mr. [George] Redford [the newly-appointed BBFC President]. Ah! now we have it. Does this not mean that certain manufacturers' goods are to be forced upon the showmen because certain individuals in their superior wisdom consider them suitable, and other makers' subjects, which may be far more valuable from an attractive point of view, are to be boycotted and kept out of the programs? Knowing the history of the past, it looks to me (and I hope I am wrong) as if the manufacturers (...) have now arranged another plan of campaign to get the whole business into the hands of a select few. They intend, in other words, to use this new weapon to destroy those who have done much in the past and are still trying to popularise and widen the scope of the business.[39]

A debate on the new censorship scheme held by the Glasgow district branch of the Cinematograph Exhibitors Association gave rise to a comment that it should be recognised that there were now two distinct "camps" of filmmakers in the industry: "one Continental camp, and the other a British and American camp", each seeing the other as a threat to their interests.[40] These conspiracy theories are perhaps lent a greater degree of credibility when considering the fact that – contrary to what has traditionally been understood concerning the relative strengths and weaknesses of the German film industry before the First World War – German feature films were viewed as an extremely significant commodity in the British film trade. W. Lacon Threlford, the managing director of London and Provincial Electric Theatres, Ltd, one of the largest circuits of cinemas in the UK, suggested in April 1913 that, from his perspective as an exhibitor, "The leading film producing companies of the world are France, the United States, and Germany".⁴¹ Despite the crippling problems subsequently presented to the film trade in Europe by the First World War, some commentators felt that the fact that Germany could no longer export their films to the UK would create an enormous hole in the market, and an opportunity to make up acres of lost ground:

> It seems to me that manufacturers will be confronted with the chance of their lifetime. (...) If pictures of the German type are wanted, and the appreciation they have hitherto met with makes it clear that they are, we can make them as well as, if not better than, the Teutons. (...) The difficulties in the way of the British producer have been considerably lessened, if they have not been entirely removed, through this war.⁴²

Similar sentiments were expressed a couple of months later:

> The British manufacturer should not at the present time miss the slightest opportunity of doing all in his power to raise the standard of British productions, so that when this disastrous war is concluded the ubiquitous German may no longer be in a position to monopolise film production to the extent that he has done in the past.⁴³

The idea of the Germans "monopolising" pre-war international film trade is clearly rhetoric coloured by a hostile wartime sensibility, but, as I have hopefully shown, there is a considerable volume of discursive evidence pointing to more extensive levels of success and influence earned by German exclusives overseas than has generally been realised. Perhaps it would not be unreasonable to suggest that the overriding perception of Asta Nielsen in Britain made her the key iconic figurehead for German cinema's successful rebranding as one of the great (albeit controversial) innovating forces in Edwardian film culture.

Notes

1. To take two examples from the early years of permanent film shows, the film of the Burns-Johnson boxing fight was distributed on an exclusive basis in 1908, as was the Summers-Britt fight film the following year. Cf. *Kinematograph and Lantern Weekly* (5 November 1908): 625; (4 March 1909): 1203.
2. Landmann reflected on, defended, and revealed the levels of hostility to this policy in *Kinematograph and Lantern Weekly* (4 May 1911): 1789, 1791.
3. Quotations from, respectively, "Rival Theatres at Variance", *Kinematograph and Lantern Weekly* (23 March 1911): 1423, and "Itala Company to Release Lengthy Films", *Kinematograph and Lantern Weekly* (27 July 1911): 597.
4. See Richard Brown, "War on the home front: the Anglo-Boer War and the growth of rental in Britain. An economic perspective", *Film History* 16:1 (2004): 33.
5. "WOMAN ALWAYS PAYS", *Kinematograph and Lantern Weekly* (7 November 1912): 249.
6. *Kinematograph and Lantern Weekly* (26 May 1910): 143; (27 October 1910): 1653.
7. Walturdaw did acquire the film – possibly in the form of second-hand American prints – at one point, because they provisionally advertised WOMAN ALWAYS PAYS as a forthcoming release in *Kinematograph Monthly Record* (November 1912): 76–77. One must assume that they either had second thoughts and sold the rights to Baer, or bought the film from Baer and then decided against release.
8. "FOOLS OF SOCIETY. Walturdaw's Great Social Drama", *The Bioscope* (5 October 1911): 5, 7.
9. *Kinematograph and Lantern Weekly* (17 August 1911): 818; (24 August 1911): 872.

10. For details concerning the programming and promotion of AFGRUNDEN in Germany, cf. Martin Loiperdinger, "*Afgrunden* in Germany: *monopolfilm*, cinemagoing and the emergence of the film star Asta Nielsen", in Daniel Biltereyst, Richard Maltby and Philippe Meers (eds): *Cinema, Audiences and Modernity. New perspectives on European cinema history* (London: Routledge, 2011), 142–153. The later German release date of SÜNDIGE LIEBE was advertised in *Der Kinematograph*, no. 241 (9 August 1911): 1. (I am grateful to Martin Loiperdinger for providing me with copies of German adverts for this film.)

11. *The Bioscope* (21 September 1911): 600. Details of the cost of hiring FOOLS OF SOCIETY have been drawn from the surviving ledger books of the Cheriton Electric Hall, Kent. This cinema booked the film in the week beginning 30 October 1911 and made a payment to Walturdaw of £39 10s in that week, compared with normal weekly fees paid to Walturdaw for a full programme, including a bi-weekly change of films, which ranged from £8 to £18 during August and September (EK/U193/2, East Kent Archives Centre). This seems to have been an unwise investment for a small 400 seat cinema in a town of 7,577 residents which did not take out any special advertising in its local newspaper to promote this special attraction (cf. *Folkestone, Hythe, Sandgate and Cheriton Herald* (4 November 1911): 8); the week's takings of £28 13s 2d. were the highest of the month, but only better by £4 2s. from the average box office receipts in the other weeks.

12. "Walturdaw's Stupendous Success", *Kinematograph and Lantern Weekly* (28 September 1911): 1204–1205.

13. E.G. Turner, "From 1896 to 1926: Recollections of Thirty Years of Kinematography. No. 3 – Regulations and the 'Exclusive'", *Kinematograph Weekly* (1 July 1926): 18.

14. *Kinematograph and Lantern Weekly* (26 October 1911): 1428.

15. *Kinematograph and Lantern Weekly* (29 February 1912): xxviii–xxix. It is curious to note that the Monpol Film Company did publicise Nielsen's name (albeit misspelled as Nielson) in November 1911, in its distribution campaign for one of her earlier Danish films, THE BALLET DANCER (1911); cf. *The Bioscope* (23 November 1911): 596–597.

16. *Kinematograph and Lantern Weekly* (28 March 1912): xxviii–xxix. The same practice was adopted to promote the involvement of another member of the cast of FOOLS OF SOCIETY, Hugo Flink, in a subsequent Asta Nielsen film, FALSELY ACCUSED (DIE KINDER DES GENERALS); cf. *Kinematograph Monthly Record* (November 1912): 76–77.

17. For example *Kinematograph and Lantern Weekly* (16 January 1913): lxxi; (23 January 1913): lxx.

18. *Kinematograph and Lantern Weekly* (30 March 1911): 57, 69, 70, 73, 81, 83–84, 97.

19. For cover features cf. *Pictures and the Picturegoer* (21 March 1914); (30 May 1914). For readers' queries see (21 March 1914): 120; (4 April 1914): 168; (25 April 1914): 240; (2 May 1914): 264; (9 May 1914): 288; (30 May 1914): 356; (6 June 1914): 380; (20 June 1914): 420; (18 July 1914): 500; (8 August 1914): 560; (15 August 1914): 580; (12 September 1914): 76.

20. "Our 'Favourite Players' Competition Result", *Pictures and the Picturegoer* (30 May 1914): 354. It is possible that Asta Nielsen may have been placed relatively highly in this poll: only the names of the top three male and female stars were revealed.

21. Richard deCordova, *Picture Personalities: The Emergence of the Star System in America* (Urbana and Chicago: University of Illinois Press, 1990): 98.

22. Ibid., 23–46.

23. *Kinematograph Monthly Record* (October 1912): 72–73.

24. "The Girl on the Film No. 7: Miss Asta Nielsen", *Pictures and the Picturegoer* (25 April 1914): 219. It is worth noting here that six other actresses had been profiled in this way before Asta Nielsen.

25. National Archives, BT31/17291/81913.

26. *Kinematograph and Lantern Weekly* (24 September 1914): 3.

27. Letter from Home Office to R. Adkins, 2 May 1912, National Archives, HO 179/1. (This document was discovered by Nicholas Hiley and referenced in his "'No mixed bathing': The creation of the British Board of Film Censors in 1913", *Journal of Popular British Cinema* 3 (2000): 7.)

28. *Kinematograph and Lantern Weekly* (14 December 1911): 321. There is no record of this action being taken in either the local press or the minutes of the Sheffield Watch Committee. Another account of this incident – which simply refers to "the action of a Chief Constable in a large industrial town" rather than identifying Sheffield – reports that he threatened "to report the whole

matter to the licensing authority" if his injunction was flouted. The fact that this appears to have been a spontaneous personal initiative by the Constable presumably explains why there is very limited information that can be found about it. Cf. "A New Form of Censorship. Remarkable Action", *The Bioscope* (14 December 1911): 743.

29. This incident was reported by the police to the London County Council's Theatres and Music Halls Committee, and all the relevant correspondence is preserved in their records: London Metropolitan Archives, LCC/MIN/10,957, meeting of 17 January 1912, agenda item 18 (189).
30. "The 'Shady' Exclusive", *The Bioscope* (13 June 1912): 763.
31. "Censorship and its Difficulties", *The Bioscope* (18 April 1912): 175.
32. "A Censorship of Films", *Morning Post* (6 November 1912): 11.
33. National Council of Public Morals, *The Cinema: Its Present Position and Future Possibilities* (London: Williams and Norgate, 1917), 213.
34. Hiley, "No mixed bathing", 7.
35. Will Barker, Cecil Hepworth and Robert Paul, "Before 1910: Kinematograph Experiences", *Proceedings of the British Kinematograph Society*, 38 (1936): 15.
36. The calculated hypocrisy at stake here is neatly demonstrated by the ironic fact that the same member of the public, Robert Adkins, who complained to the Home Office about FOOLS OF SOCIETY, in the letter discussed above, wrote to them again on 16 July 1912 to protest about a British feature-length exclusive made by the Clarendon Film Company called SAVED BY FIRE. The film's combination of sin and sensational spectacle seems to have been an attempt to emulate the German exclusives which Walturdaw had enjoyed such success with, and a scene in which a married man was seduced by an actress lying provocatively on a sofa led Adkins to exclaim that "It leaves the much discussed FOOLS OF SOCIETY completely in the shade!" London Metropolitan Archives, LCC/MIN/10,961, meeting of 24 July 1912, agenda item 3.
37. National Archives, HO45/10551/163175, File 26. The presentation to the Home Office which took place on 24 February 1912 was delivered exclusively by Edison's Paul H. Cromelin, and it was made abundantly clear that the scheme was modelled on the American system of self-censorship.
38. Richard Abel, *The Red Rooster Scare: Making Cinema American, 1900–1910* (Berkeley and Los Angeles: University of California Press, 1999): 101.
39. "Is a Film Censor Necessary? A Criticism of the New Appointment", *Kinematograph and Lantern Weekly* (14 November 1912): 325. It is interesting to note in this regard that several of Walturdaw's advertisements for Asta Nielsen films in 1913 felt the need to make clear that they had been "Passed by the British Board of Censors". Cf., for example, *Kinematograph and Lantern Weekly* (6 March 1913): 1873; *Kinematograph Monthly Record* (May 1913): 88–89.
40. "Glasgow Exhibitors and Film Censorship", *Kinematograph and Lantern Weekly* (30 January 1913): 1423.
41. *Kinematograph and Lantern Weekly* (17 April 1913): 24–56.
42. *Kinematograph and Lantern Weekly* (10 September 1914): 1–2.
43. *Kinematograph and Lantern Weekly* (19 November 1914): 10.

DAGENS NYHETER.

Nr 14912 Stockholmsupplagan — Tisdagen den 14 November 1911.

Alkoholen och degenerationsformerna.

Norsk nykterhetsledare om alkoholens biologiska verkan.

Ett föredrag af dr Scharffenberg i sällskapet för rashygien.

ÄR BIOGRAFDRAMAT KONST ELLER EJ?

Frågan högaktuell för Stockholm, "de 50 biografernas stad". — Diskussionsmöten utlysta här i dag och i morgon för intresserade

Hotande konflikt mellan Ryssland och Persien.

De diplomatiska förbindelserna afbrutna.

Persiska regeringen afgår. — Interpellation i engelska underhuset.

Anne Bachmann

Vindicating THE GREAT MOMENT against Swedish Censorship: Asta Nielsen's Soulful Eyes as On-Screen Pantomime

When a total ban descended upon I DET STORA ÖGONBLICKET (IN DEM GROSSEN AUGENBLICK, THE GREAT MOMENT) in Sweden in 1911, discourses of respectability and of art in narrative cinema instantly converged. The hot debate that ensued in many newspapers swiftly left the details of censorship criteria or the film's actual frames and synopsis aside, and instead slid onto aesthetic territory. Asta Nielsen's star persona came to play a significant part in providing the hallmark needed for winning the battle of the pages of the daily press, if not on the actual censorship board. Furthermore, the general lines of the debate fed into further censorship disputes in Sweden the following year.

The Swedish Board of Censorship became the first centralised film-censoring body in the world in September 1911, and within a week of its inauguration, it put the clearly debatable ban on the German film I DET STORA ÖGONBLICKET.[1] The censor pointed to the climactic horror scenes in the burning house as a motive for censoring the entire picture. One aspect of the Board's newly legislated authorisation was indeed to eliminate scenes or entire pictures judged by the censors to have a brutalising effect, in addition to those deemed to be contrary to law or morals, to "excite the senses", or to "confuse concepts of justice".[2] Grasping for the reasons for the decision, Asta Nielsen, by then already not only a star but also an adamant, if occasional spokesperson against censorship, fuelled a flammable film culture debate exceeding the scope of this particular case.[3] She initiated this chain of events by defending the film in an open letter to the Board, or rather to its one female member in order to play up the motherhood theme. Referring to the role that the film was at the time playing for the German *Mutterschutz* (maternity protection) movement she stressed how the film concerns itself with moral issues. She went on to acknowledge the irreconcilabilities between art and censorship, and destined

---

Facing page: The front page of *Dagens Nyheter* on 14 November 1911 asks: "Is the film drama an art form or not?" [National Library of Sweden.]

cinema to be the eventual winner: "What you have helped lace up into the most constricted form is a new art that has arisen, an art capable of affecting millions of people all over the globe, a flood so broad and powerful it is at length hopeless to stem it with censorship".[4]

Asta Nielsen's initiative and the debate and events that followed have been described by Jan Olsson as a token of agency in a star in the making, establishing herself firmly in the Swedish public consciousness as articulated in the press.[5] The long-running press story appearing in a number of Stockholm dailies spread and multiplied as journalists cited each other. Rather than merely reflect the debate, it acted on it as a force in itself. Considerably more detailed and extensive than other daily press texts about cinema at the time, the controversy was a significant media event in a Swedish perspective and was also reported abroad.[6] Further contextualising the repercussions of this rich incident is, then, a worthwhile activity.

Attempts to pin down cinema's status in terms of art is an issue more or less obsolete in today's cinema culture, while at the time claiming columns upon columns of press space. Thus marked by historical otherness, aesthetic metadiscourse is easily obscured as a blind spot for the concerns of today's historians. Yet, the art question is interwoven with contemporary narrative strategies and cinema culture in the transition to multiple-reel films in Europe. In the case of Asta Nielsen, it is significant that when the art question is answered in the affirmative, the answer turns out to be an articulation of stardom. By tracing the principal lines of the debate, I will locate the influence of Asta Nielsen's star persona qualities on the film-as-art debate in the Stockholm press, as this is a constellation that brings out how arguments about cinema as art came to be articulated as early musings on what stardom brought to cinema.

During the Swedish transition to multiple-reel films there was a fuzzy line between issues of censorship and issues of cultural and artistic status. It took a mere instant for the press to frame the issue of censorship in the Asta Nielsen case as depending on a query of whether or not cinema should be counted as art. In trying to articulate the question of cinema's level of prestige through the prism of I DET STORA ÖGONBLICKET, the determining factor was the status of art as emotional drama's deliverer from base instincts. The question resounded in headlines in the reporting, sometimes sprawled across the front page, and was addressed in running polls, in letters to the editor, and in responses to two separate special screenings and a big debate meeting. The events took place well within the course of three weeks: Asta Nielsen's open letter was published on 8 November 1911, and was followed by another also penned by Nielsen on 14 November. On the same day, Pathé's representative in Stockholm, Siegmund Popert, took the opportunity to invite the press and interested members of the public to the company's private theatre in Drottninggatan for a screening of carefully chosen films that were to prove the merits of the medium. The controversy reached its apex on a debate meeting organised by the theatre

"All right, we'll have to approve of this film! – Oh, well, this one, too! – No, this one we'll absolutely need to cut!" From left to right Walter Fevrell, Marie Louise Gagner, and Jakob Billström. Drawing by G. Ljunggren in *Puck*.

journal *Thalia* held at Stockholm Y.M.C.A. on 15 November. Finally, it came to a logical conclusion with a private screening of the banned film hosted by

Asta Nielsen at the Brunkebergsteatern cinema on 25 November, where journalists were invited to at last make up their own minds about the ban.

In the news discourse and the debate meeting, the agenda was defined by the at that time not yet hackneyed question whether film was to be considered art. Asta Nielsen herself refused to comment on the question and, with rhetorical flair, considered it long settled anywhere but in Sweden.[7] In fact, the film-as-art question was far from settled, but was to be rephrased in many guises, not least throughout the 1910s. Its stakes lay in contemporary film marketing, which would brand a diversity of films as 'art' or 'quality' films in the wake of the *film d'art* movement proper. In a Scandinavian perspective, such ambitions had brought about historical or literary epics with a national inflection in Sweden and Denmark, and would within the next couple of years produce the so-called author's film in Denmark, catapulting the idea of the (actually, German) author as literal underwriter of cultural value into the burgeoning German filmmaking business.

As the events in Stockholm unfolded in the public eye, the discussions that arose touched upon three now-familiar bones of contention: the essence of cinema and of theatre; the realism of cinema and theatre; and mass culture and elitism. While today's cinema scholars recognise this as ground that has since been heavily inscribed by the ground breakers of classical film theory – be it by Ricciotto Canudo, André Bazin, Jean Epstein, or Walter Benjamin – the debaters then resorted chiefly to their own experience of cinema. It follows that the arguments surfacing on both sides in this debate were often anecdotal, subjective and emotional, and clearly informed by their respective political stances: conservative, liberal, or sometimes socialist.

(Mis)reading I DET STORA ÖGONBLICKET

The three censors at the time had the following backgrounds:[8] Walter Fevrell, who decreed the actual ban (and was soon to be regarded as he who was always unable to let things alone), was an academic specialising in psychology and pedagogy. Marie-Louise Gagner, the addressee of Asta Nielsen's open letter, was a teacher and had as such been committed to the cinema question for several years.[9] Lastly, Jakob Billström was a psychiatrist and was also involved in the influential popular movements in Sweden associated with social reform. A fourth person who was not a regular employee at this time, but who was nevertheless instrumental in setting up the Board and prominent in its later activities and media image, was Gustaf Berg.

Gagner was on many occasions subjected to ridicule as a woman and a spinster, particularly for her image as a pedantic schoolmistress.[10] Even outside Sweden, she was occasionally referred to as a "hysterical woman" devoid of reason.[11] To some degree, in singling out the female board member whom it might be easier to sway than the men with a higher social status, Asta Nielsen unwittingly attached her petition to such contributions. Open letters in the press were a common enough way of debating at the time, and this letter was not the first one addressed to Miss Gagner. Two years previously, when she was still only advocating the idea of protecting the young from the corruptive effects of cinema, a challenging letter in the trade press from Axel Rydin, a photographer and cinema owner, was addressed to her in the trade press.[12] Like the Danish film pioneer Peter Elfelt, Rydin was Purveyor to the Court of photographic services, and using this title, he passed strictures on Gagner's alleged lack of practical knowledge about the cinema business, audience taste and cinema owners' concerns.

In the case of I DET STORA ÖGONBLICKET Gagner was not the only censor who might be accused of occasional deficiencies in their understanding of the workings of the cinema.[13] To the public eye, i.e. at least to those moulders of public opinion who attended the two special screenings, the film did not warrant targeting for betterment and reform. And indeed, it does seem to be possible only with a certain excess of zeal to interpret the Board's somewhat scarce legal guidelines so strictly as to strike down upon I DET STORA ÖGONBLICKET. Rather, the rigour displayed by the Board mirrored what was at stake in their work, and in that light the particularities of film scenes became mere pawns in a game. Jan Olsson has described this agenda: In *Stockholms Dagblad* Fevrell had been the driving force in condemning the sensation-oriented attributes of melodrama as manifestations of lax morals, crime and suicide. These ingredients were firmly associated with the Danish style of filmmaking, and after Fevrell had been appointed censor he and his colleagues were vigilant about such Danish-flavoured melodramas in their ambition to shape the fiction film as screened in Sweden in a certain direction.[14] On the other side of the Sound, the Danish censor P.A. Rosenberg was unappreciative of Fevrell's crusade and in particular pointed to and criticised the idea that a badly made film should in itself give cause for censorship.[15] The disagreement hinged on the respective censors' understanding of their goal. What the Swedes wanted was not so much to weed out bad apples as to shape a future Swedish cinemascape of worthwhile and, preferably, educational film material. Their vision was 'perfectionist' with a pedagogical bias, envisaging better films for betterment in the population.[16] Thus, is that even if the censors' agenda was applauded in the conservative press, it was not exactly a conservative and merely forbidding one, but rather had elements of the progressive.

Even when seen through the lens of this plan of action, Board's dealings with the film nevertheless give an impression of clumsiness and naiveté. To the censors' defence, they were both new to the task and extremely busy. I DET STORA ÖGONBLICKET was examined within the very first week of the Board's activities and is registered as film number 40. Between them, the three censors went through no less than 2000 films that autumn, which would imply around nine films each every day, in a six-day week.[17] By the beginning of December the censors were reported to work much overtime.[18] In January, Fevrell was allowed extra compensation,[19] and around the same time, two temporary employees were taken in.[20]

Walter Fevrell's (1876–1961) gaze may seem piercing, but it could not view I DET STORA ÖGONBLICKET correctly. The educationalist Fevrell headed the Swedish Board of Censorship from its beginning until 1914.
[National Library of Sweden, Maps and Pictures.]

Haste and beginner's mistakes combined might help explaining why Fevrell did not seem to fully grasp the film's narrative codes. As so few had been able to actually see the film, everyone, understandably, demanded to know what it was about, and Fevrell was among those trying to convey the film's storyline to the press. While accounts ranged from the vilifying to the apologetically benign, one of the details that stood out in Fevrell's version was to whom he attributed fatherhood of Asta Nielsen's character's illegitimate child. In his version, the father was not her employer's relative who is socially superior to her and takes advantage of her, but rather the coachman, her suitor and later ally, who is a drunk and violent but loyal character. This somewhat displaces the layout of the moral significance, with mainly two implications: that the young mother is to blame for winding up with a child since she freely got involved with her equal, and, through this close association with the coachman, that she is morally responsible for his actions such as causing the fatal fire.[21] More crucially, Fevrell seems not to have grasped what happens in the ending, i.e. the great sacrifice of Asta Nielsen's character's own life for the child's, as alluded to in the title. Instead, he claims the film is open-ended.

The trouble with the lacking spoken word

The choice to treat the film as sensationalist rather than as a psychologically informed narrative is the backdrop to Fevrell's arguments about the effects of the film medium on putative audiences. His first public reaction to Asta Nielsen's open letter was to describe his views of the difference between the theatre and the cinema as regards harmful effects on the audience. Conveying powerful emotion while sparing the audience brutally harsh effects is easier in the theatre, he claimed, as the stage has other means of stating the mental justification of the actions, meaning dialogue. In the light of his deficiencies in understanding the film plot, one might instead a little spitefully suggest that the actual problem resided in is his own need for dialogue to make the events on the screen meaningful.

Ever which way, the point about dialogue did find resonance. Although quick off the mark, Fevrell had not been the first one to put the matter down to the spoken word. Theatre director Gustaf Linden, known by his nickname Muck, had got there first, and to a degree Fevrell only walked in his footsteps. Linden was openly critical towards cinema after having made several fiction films which he – and others – regarded as failures. In an evening paper on the same day as Asta Nielsen's open letter was published, he argued that the cinema's realism is coarsened and intensified because it is silent and needs visual movement. Realism on stage, he argued, is conversely softened and abstracted by words.[22]

Another writer affirming cinema's speechlessness as the damning piece of evidence was Fredrik Nycander in a conservative paper.[23] Tellingly, however, only a few years later the same Nycander was a contributor to the cinema journal *Biografen*, and all seems to have been forgiven, although he was to remain a technology sceptic. For those appearing on the stage of this cultural debate, positions were easily shifted or switched, though some took longer than others. As film changed fast during the 1910s, reasoning about it sometimes suffered from time lag. The celebrated actor Anders de Wahl, who participated in the *Thalia* debate meeting, remained staunchly anti-cinema for several years before he started acting on the screen. An instructive snapshot from the debate of how the cultural elite conceived of cinema is how de Wahl ridiculed the idea of literary adaptation by claiming he had heard the reason for shooting Strindberg's naturalistic tragedy *The Father* was that the straitjacket scene would make "such a brilliant number".[24]

Gustav Linden, the failed film director, also introduced a second line of argument concerning the possible implications of technical reproduction. He cited, obviously not in cinema's favour, the difference between a renaissance work of art and a cheap print from the marketplace. Art historian Carl Laurin latched onto this idea in his reasoning in the debate meeting.[25] In Laurin's view, realism and artistic value had been confused, and he set out to state the difference between art and expensive equipment, illusion and deftness. Gramophones or cinemas were no more art than wax cabinets were science.

More pragmatically, Laurin pointed out that the entire question about cinema as art hardly sprang from a sudden interest in philosophical aesthetics. Rather, it was brought to the fore by what we might term anxieties in the cultural field: theatres being anxious about competition from the cinemas, and cinemas being anxious about more severe censoring if the films were not regarded as art and enjoyed art's freedom. His comment appears precise, as the previous years had been economically trying for Swedish cinema owners, and the stage theatre business was terrified of being subjected to similar censorship as films. More nonchalantly, Laurin goes on to bring up the clichéd theme of actors' fees, which would cling to Asta Nielsen in Sweden in years to come, indicating that serious actors would never concern themselves with the cinema was it not for the stars' more than generous pay checks.[26]

New art, old world

From Gustav Linden's agenda-setting reasoning, two main themes emerge: absence of the spoken word and technical reproduction. Interestingly, the same concepts are used to vindicate cinema: firstly, the absence of the spoken word differentiates narrative cinema from the stage as an independent fine art and related to the pantomime. Secondly, technical reproduction makes possible the emphasis on Asta Nielsen's face, blown up on the screen.[27]

Among cinema's apologists, the most emotionally high-strung speaker was Asta Nielsen's close friend Daniel Fallström, who was a high-profiled theatre critic and poet, and a character shrouded in myths and anecdotes. Involved in Swedish-Danish cultural relations at the time, Fallström was attached to the famous set of the cross-Scandinavian cultural elite. He was sometimes referred to as the 'Swedish Drachmann' with respect to his romantic view on women and muses, much like the Danish poet Holger Drachmann to whom he, characteristically, was befriended.[28] In this debate, he took on many roles, plausibly taking part in the publication process for Asta Nielsen's open letter in Sweden's largest newspaper *Stockholms-Tidningen* for which he wrote himself. He is even likely to have written the admiring introduction to it anonymously, and reported from the events in pieces both signed and unsigned. At the same time he debated the case publicly. His own reasoning in the case, which he phrased and rephrased, was that 'a woman like Asta Nielsen would not be passionate about an art that is shabby'. From the premise that Asta Nielsen is unfailingly great, he induces that her films must be art.

Although this view of the artist as guarantor may sound trite, it did have impact. Using a cross-media analogy from the printing press, Fallström introduced a metaphor of film acting that trickled down into a number of the newspapers in whose offices it apparently rang a bell, as it stated that silent actors must "italicise their emotions, use extra bold types, where others might make do with bourgeois" – the bourgeois being the diminutive 8-point type.

Coincidentally, bourgeois is certainly a term with which to describe the gallant Fallström himself. His contemporaries labelled him 'the bard of the bourgeoi-

Vindicating *The Great Moment* against Swedish censorship

Asta Nielsen's personal friend Daniel Fallström (1858–1937) portrayed in 1918 by the then fashionable celebrity photographer C.H.B. Goodwin. Fallström was a theatre critic and poet, and a well-known figure of an old-fashioned, chivalrous sort.
[National Library of Sweden, Maps and Pictures.]

sie', 'the last troubadour', and 'the ladies' bard', and his gigantic moustache became a synecdoche for his persona. Being such an old-world type, it seems perhaps an anomaly that he should come to the defence of cinema, and it is clear that his support for I DET STORA ÖGONBLICKET hinges wholly on Asta Nielsen herself. When scrutinised, Fallström comes across as ambiguous about the cinema. For instance, in 1913 he could be counted among those not

On 16 November 1911, the daily *Social-Demokraten* reports from Thalia's discussion meeting and outlines the debating gentlemen Gustaf Linden, Carl Laurin, Siegmund Popert and Daniel Fallström. [National Library of Sweden.]

believing in literary adaptation,[29] although he worked as manager of the literary department at Skandinavisk Filmcentral at a later stage of his career.

Careful not to depreciate the theatre when elevating the cinema, Fallström accepted a solution in praising cinema's silent acting. At Thalia's debate meeting, he is quoted as having said: "The image is silent, but the face, the eyes speak. If the film actor cannot achieve this he is no actor, but if he can, then the film is art".[30] Fallström was to hold steadfastly onto this idea in his cinema career as well. In a 1919 trade-press interview, Fallström dismissed the idea of talking films and embraced the titleless film:

> [True film art] is the art of speaking in images, without words, you see. If we were to exchange the intertitle for audible spoken lines, cinema would become photographed theatre, not the art of silent images (...) the exact opposite of the ideal film. Instead, cinema should develop in the direction of films without intertitles.[31]

Acting without speech seems generally to have been the first thing to come to the debaters' minds when singling out the characteristics of the cinema from those of the theatre.[32] When disparaged, it was often referred to comically in terms of disability, with the code word 'Manilla' after a Stockholm school for deaf and hearing-impaired children.[33] Asta Nielsen, however, rerouted the debate from mere speechlessness to mimicry and pantomime. In a second open letter a few days after the first one, she answered Gustaf Linden's criticisms: "[...] it is certainly surprising to see a man who is much involved in the theatre such as Mr. Linden absolutely reject mimicry as a form of expression – because it has transported itself directly from the old pantomime and ballet to the child of the present, cinema".[34]

In Denmark, *films d'art* were generally associated with stage actors.[35] The logical defence for cinema for Asta Nielsen was to locate a particular space for cinema among the arts as a specifically pantomimic art of acting, finely calibrated for the face. To a Danish journal, she would later say: "On the stage, one can confuse the audience with words. In a film, one has recourse only to one's face. If *that* is lying, the audience will understand nothing. Every fiber trembling with strain, one must live in the present."[36] In the debate about I DET STORA ÖGONBLICKET, she said to a Swedish daily newspaper: "For a mimic artist, cinema is more dangerous and better. There are bigger victories to be had there than in the theatre".[37] Asta Nielsen was a trademark artist of mimicry.[38] She also draws attention to this status as part of her star persona, for instance when she wittily concludes the second open letter: "Hereby I believe I will retire to that expressive silence which is now my vocation".[39]

Locating the ideas of the star and the pantomime in subsequent debate

The next rounds of censorship debate in Sweden may help contextualise these lines of arguing. In 1912 there were three main battles, and in the first one in January, the debate on I DET STORA ÖGONBLICKET repeatedly reared its head, as it again concerned Fevrell. This time, he had slashed a local screening in Norrköping which formed part of a revue, featuring a cross-dressing dance which Fevrell thought unsavoury and consequently struck down upon.[40] The intricacy of the case was that the sequence in question in fact consisted of a take of the first act of that revue, appearing as a screening within the second act, as part of the story. Thus it highlighted the seemingly random legal difference between stage and screen as regards censorship.

Among those reacting strongly to this was Hjalmar Branting, newspaperman, politician and prime minister to be, who labelled Fevrell parochial and exhorted him to step back into his classroom.[41] During a short interval at this time, national politicians and statesmen in Sweden took an acute interest in censorship questions. In April 1912, another special screening was attended by Prime Minister Karl Staaff along with his Minister for Finance and the Minister for the Interior.[42] The latter was ultimately responsible for cinema censorship.

Along came still one more minister, this one without portfolio (let alone such a weighty portfolio as those of the others), and one newspaper ran the headline "With the government to the movies".[43] The film was Swedish Pathé's banned TVÅ BRÖDER (TWO BROTHERS), directed by Georg af Klercker, and the screening was organised in connection with a formal appeal against the ban. In all probability the debate on I DET STORA ÖGONBLICKET and Asta Nielsen's contribution had not only inspired that kind of arrangement but also lent it a sense of both urgency and glamour. Furthermore, Staaff's liberal government would likely have found the question of censorship an interesting question of principle. However, as the film was not thought very good, the excitement dwindled.

What the run-of-the-mill reception of the screening of TVÅ BRÖDER did bring up again was the question of how the quality of the films might influence censorship. One line of arguing from the debate on I DET STORA ÖGONBLICKET was that any film's status of art should be an extenuating circumstance for the censorship authorities. Logically, but conversely, conservative journalists did not hesitate in seconding censorship on the basis of TVÅ BRÖDER being in bad taste.[44] Several debaters attempted to keep the delineation clear between artistic judgement and the judgement of what is not advisable for public screenings.[45] Nevertheless, the 'bad taste' argument gained ground, fitting safely in with the discourse defined by the Censorship Board's 'perfectionist' visions for Swedish cinema.

It was also within this normative discourse about what cinema could and should be that the concept of mimicry resurfaced in the censorship/art debate at this point. Again, it was Fevrell who made a surprising statement: that cinema's true mission was documentary and educational, not fictional, because cinema's renditions of drama was limited to mere pantomime.[46] The concept of mimicry could readily be invested with either an idea of ridicule or an idea of sublimity. A reply piece printed in several papers quoted the Danish writer Sven Lange, who had a few months earlier in the Danish *Biografteaterbladet* echoed Asta Nielsen in this way:

> Since the beginnings of theatre, mimical acting has accompanied the spoken word, at times even pushing it aside. (...) The silent art is only a renewal (...) of that mimicry which has moved millions and millions of spectators. Why should it not be – or have the potential of being – art?[47]

The last censorship debate of the year 1912 concerned TRÄDGÅRDSMÄSTAREN (THE BROKEN SPRING ROSE), directed by Victor Sjöström for Swedish Biograph. Along with two foreign-made films, it was banned, the ban was appealed against, and the now-familiar special screening was arranged. Swedish Biograph published a pamphlet titled *A few words for the Cinema Censorship Board*, whereupon the censorship board promptly published the similar brochure *A few words from the Cinema Censorship Board*.[48] These do not so much concern the art question as questions of how to interpret film matter. In this case censor Gustaf Berg, unlike Fevrell, emerges as an exegete in full control of his subject matter when describing exactly why the protagonist of TRÄDGÅRDSMÄSTAREN is to be conceived of as a prostitute.[49] The stardom angle to the art question resurfaces once more in the section of Swedish Biograph's pamphlet concerning one of the other two banned films, Messter's NATTENS DROTTNING (DIE KÖNIGIN DER NACHT, THE QUEEN OF THE NIGHT) with Henny Porten. Here, the case for letting the reputation of I DET STORA ÖGONBLICKET rest on the performance of Asta Nielsen reappears as a plea that the noble and artistic achievement of Henny Porten be taken into consideration:

> Furthermore we beg that we may call attention to the role of the heroine in the aforementioned drama, performed by the well-known actress Henny Porten, whose acting – the spectator will be able to be convinced of this himself – is characterised throughout by sincerity in her interpretation [*innerlighet i uppfattningen*], by delicacy, noblesse and artistry in the performance, which is doubtlessly at the apex of the achievements in this business in our time.[50]

Gustaf Berg punctures the attempt in the counter-pamphlet by drily referring to it as Swedish Biograph's attempt to keep certain divas off limits for censorship.[51]

Haunting eyes, publicity value, and some strange bedfellows

The argument made about Henny Porten in order to address the art question did not venture beyond acting abilities and artistic renown. By contrast, in the press discourse about I DET STORA ÖGONBLICKET, Asta Nielsen and Daniel Fallström together connected Asta Nielsen's face to the virtues of silence and pantomime. The idea proved contagious. When Asta Nielsen arrived in Stockholm in order to screen the banned film privately and thus vindicate herself, the media reports both of her and the film concerned themselves with her soulful eyes.[52] One writer, who was very different from Fallström, but nevertheless adopted his stance was the feminist Elin Brandell, member of a circle of liberal female journalists linked to the suffrage movement and partaker of forays into filmmaking (along with fellow feminist Elin Wägner, a household name in Sweden). Considering Brandell's background, it comes perhaps slightly unexpected that when covering the STORA ÖGONBLICKET story under the signature "Regan", she would not choose a strategy of either generally defending the new narrative medium or emphasising the film's content of gendered social predicament. Instead, she bought into Fallström's argument when supporting the film in her pieces, stating that an actress of Asta Nielsen's rank uses mimic to convey psychology and thus pardons coarse effects for "the true, touching art that is given us". No words were needed, then; the star's face said it all.[53]

Asta Nielsen got vast publicity effects from the debates.[54] The exhibitors understood this. Already on the very next day after Asta Nielsen's open letter, adverts began appearing on the front pages of the same paper for a Danish-made Asta film, BALETTDANSÖSEN (BALLETDANSERINDEN, THE BALLET DANCER) apparently one week before the Danish premiere. After two weeks the film moved to a different theatre and was again advertised on the front page of the same paper – the media synergies are obvious. Another case in point is that shortly after the private screening of I DET STORA ÖGONBLICKET, the previous success AVGRUNDEN (AFGRUNDEN, THE ABYSS) was taken up for screening again as a re-run. The advert mentions the star's presence in Stockholm and her part in the cinema debate as a reason for catching up on the older film, as her greatest role yet.

For the history of Swedish censorship, an interesting point is that according to the adverts, the film would only run for a few days. The reason is no doubt that just a few days later, censorship was finally obligatory. During the first few months, September through November, submitting the films for censorship preview was voluntary. It had not been mandatory to submit I DET STORA ÖGONBLICKET, a circumstance which is slightly ironic considering the heated debate.[55] After this short run AVGRUNDEN was censored on 1 December 1912, and the infamous cut was made that paradoxically saved the best-preserved version of the gaucho dance to the world at the Swedish Board of Censorship.[56] However, not only the clou in terms of attraction scenes was cut. The very narrative climax, the actual murder, was included in the incisions, too, although it directly motivates the celebrated ending: the few seconds of Asta Nielsen's haunting, dead gaze as she descends the stairs of the house accompanied by a policeman. Thus, knowing that the film ran not only the previous year, but also refreshed audiences' memories in screenings during the days immediately preceding the cut might help understand why the meaning of that film was still not entirely lost to the Stockholm audience when the abbreviated film was eventually back on the repertoire.

With Asta Nielsen's performance penetrating so deeply, it is no wonder that as late as 1918, an author signing "Orvar" was still considering the very same question – "Is cinema art?" – in the very same terms in a Gothenburg daily.[57] Walking once again in Fallström's footsteps, he concluded that a true artist could indeed make film art. The evidence was Norma Talmadge's "silent, desperate" fight for custody of her child in the divorce drama NAOMIS SKILSMÄSSA (FIFTY-FIFTY): "Any dialogue, however cleverly written, would have given a realistic and pronounced illusion to the spiritual struggle of the young mother. But her art consisted in giving her role its worth without any words, and that was truly enviable." Was desperate motherhood the insurmountable peak of quality acting? It was certainly Asta Nielsen's own favourite kind of tragic role.[58] Or was the media event over I DET STORA ÖGONBLICKET still the benchmark for aesthetic discussion about cinema? In a historical Stockholm dominated by its many daily newspapers, it would certainly have produced not only public opinion but also points from which to take one's bearings in the Swedish cultural debate. A small token of this is that three years later, some of the same standpoints still formed the basis of the comedy in a satirical trade-journal questionnaire: "What would you like the most to see on the silver screen?"[59] In the fake answers, the supposedly haughty Anders de Wahl needed to ask what kind of a thing a cinema might be. Fallström, on the other hand, did not particularly care to see anything, except, of course, Asta Nielsen.

Notes

1. For accounts of the motives and methods in the launching of the Board of Censorship, cf. Gunnel Arrbäck, *Statens Biografbyrå 1911–2000* (Stockholm: Statens Biografbyrå, 2001), or Jan Olsson, "Magnified Discourse: Screenplays and Censorship in Swedish Cinema of the 1910s" in John Fullerton (ed.), *Celebrating 1895: The Centenary of Cinema* (Sydney: John Libbey, 1998), 239–252.
2. "Dansk skådespelerska mot vår biografcensur", *Dagens Nyheter* (11 November 1911).
3. No one actually appealed formally against the ban. In the Board's own statistics the case is listed as an appeal (cf. Arrbäck, *Statens Biografbyrå*, 103), but no formal appeal is registered.
4. Asta Nielsen, under the umbrella heading "Uppseendeväckande kritik af den svenska biografcensuren", *Stockholms-Tidningen* (8 November 1911).
5. Jan Olsson, "Dear Miss Gagner: A Star and her Methods" in Tytti Soila (ed.), *Stellar Encounters: Stardom in Popular European Cinema* (Eastleigh: John Libbey, 2009), 217–229, and Jan Olsson, "Asta's Ink: The Stockholm Letters", *Journal of Scandinavian Cinema* 2:1 (2012): 5–11.
6. In Denmark, Asta Nielsen's letter was printed under the title "Svensk Censur", *Biografteaterbladet* 1:6 (1911): 86–87. For an account of the controversy published in Germany cf. "Ein Interview mit Asta Nielsen", *Lichtbild-Theater* 3:48 (30 November 1911).
7. Jaya, "Hos Asta Nielsen i egen person", *Aftonbladet* (22 November 1911).
8. G. Ljunggren, "Biografcensur" (satirical drawing), *Puck*, no. 42 (19 October 1912).
9. Gagner was a member of Stockholm Pedagogical Society's cinema committee; see for instance the reporting in "Biografcensorerna tillsatta", *Svenska Dagbladet* (15 August 1911).
10. The unruly and very short-lived *Biograf-Tidningen* proved the most uninhibited publication when railing at the censors in its first and only issue: "Allow me out of courtesy to dwell on aunt Maria [sic] Louise Gagner, for it would probably delight her ageing maiden heart to be the object of attentions from any gentleman". Bruntus, untitled, *Biograf-Tidningen* 1:1 (1911): 2.
11. The words reportedly fell from the lips of the Danish film censor Rosenberg, although he in the following issue claimed he would never call a woman hysterical "in print". Paul Sarauw, "Et Interview med Censor P.A. Rosenberg", *Filmen* 1:1 (1912): 8–9.
12. Axel Rydin, "Öppna svar", *Nordisk Filmtidning* 1:14–18 (1909): 7–8.
13. Later, even Gustaf Berg admitted that experience may open every censor's eyes: *Några ord från biografcensuren* (Stockholm: Sv. tr.-a-b. 1912): 8.
14. For Jan Olsson's account of this in Swedish, see "Svart på vitt: Film, makt och censur", *Aura* 1:1 (1995): 14–46.
15. "En 'Samtale' med Censor P.A. Rosenberg", signed V. B-n, *Biografteaterbladet* 1:3 (1911): 39.
16. For a more comprehensive, if condensed, account of what this perfectionism entailed, see Björn Harström, *Vad vi inte får se: 100 år av censurpolitik* (PhD thesis in political science, Stockholm University 2009).
17. One year later the censors are reported to be paid for only five hours a day, but implied to work considerably more. "Biografcensorerna ej överbetalda", *Aftontidningen* (20 December 1912).
18. "Biografcensurens forcerade verksamhet", *Stockholms Dagblad* (3 December 1912).
19. RA/1206.01 series E1 vol 4197 (19 January 1912).
20. Ibid., vol 4178 (17 November 1911) and vol 4234 (6 June 1912).
21. Tellingly, Daniel Fallström's very supportive rendition of the storyline needs to omit how the fire came about. "I DET STORA ÖGONBLICKET", *Stockholms-Tidningen* (27 November 1919).
22. Jaya, "Öfverdrift i biografcensuren? Ett inlägg af skådespelerskan Asta Nielsen", *Aftonbladet* (8 November 1911).
23. Fredrik Nycander, "Filmen", *Stockholms Dagblad* (19 November 1911). Nycander was unequivocal: "May cinema be put in its rightful place. Down low."
24. "Dagens stridsfråga: är biografdramat konst eller ej?" *Dagens Nyheter* (16 November 1911). The

film FADEREN (THE FATHER) was in production in Stockholm at the time, directed by Anna Hofmann-Uddgren.

25. Ibid.

26. The money theme was to stay closely with the reporting about Asta Nielsen in Sweden in the years to come, with a tinge of envy not in the same way incident to, for instance, the reporting about Hollywood stars. I see this in line with a sense of cultural and geographical closeness or ownership that can be detected in the writings about the Danish star.

27. Part and parcel of this discourse, on the incriminating side, is what Jan Olsson has described as the "magnified discourse": censors' wariness of close-ups and other close shots depicting undesired behaviour, thought to be excellent manuals for misbehaving or committing crimes. See Jan Olsson, "Magnified Discourse: Screenplays and Censorship in Swedish Cinema of the 1910s" in Fullerton, *Celebrating 1895*, 239–252.

28. Waldeck, "Daniel Fallström inför köpenhamnarne", *Stockholms Dagblad* (30 March 1911).

29. "Filmdramatiken och den modärna litteraturen", *Afton-Tidningen* (6 March 1913).

30. "Biografen som konst eller icke konst. Teatertidningen Thalias diskussionsmöte", *Stockholms Dagblad* (16 November 1911).

31. "Den talande filmen får mothugg", *Filmjournalen* 1:2 (1919): 45.

32. The many comparisons to the theatre in this debate were possibly further fuelled by Asta Nielsen having toured Scandinavia in her youth as a stage actress. Her Danish company, De otte (The Eight), had gained attention. For a testimonial see "Anna Fallström jubilerar och berättar", *Sydsvenska Dagbladet* (30 April 1936).

33. One example is "Filmens Duse" signed Floridor, *Aftonbladet* (11 November 1911).

34. Asta Nielsen, "Konst eller icke konst? Asta Nielsen skrifver på nytt till Stockholms-Tidningen", *Stockholms-Tidningen* (14 November 1911).

35. Casper Tybjerg, "Denmark", in Richard Abel (ed.), *Encyclopedia of Early Cinema* (Abingdon: Routledge, 2005), 173.

36. V.S., "Mellem Film-Slagene. Et Besøg hos Asta Nielsen", *Verden og vi*, no 1 (1915).

37. In Jaya, "Hos Asta Nielsen i egen person".

38. As part of her star image construction, she liked to recount interviews and in her autobiography an anecdote from her audition to Copenhagen's Royal Theatre when very young, where instead of delivering her lines she suddenly found herself miming her scene from Ibsen's *Brand*. Filmatiker (Palle Rosenkrantz), "Hvordan Asta Nielsen blev Filmskuespillerinde", *Masken*, vol 4 (1913), page and issue numbers missing, referencing *Wiener Tageblatt*; or Adolf Langstedt, "Asta Nielsen Bogen", *Filmen* 6:10 (1918): 98–100.

39. Asta Nielsen, "Konst eller icke konst?"

40. Walter Fevrell, "Biografcensuren" (letter to the editor), *Stockholms Dagblad* (9 January 1912).

41. Hjalmar Branting (Hj. B-g), "Biografcensuren", *Socialdemokraten* (8 November 1912).

42. Björnung, "Det censurerade biografdramat", *Aftontidningen* (25 April 1912).

43. Knort, "Med regeringen på biograf", *Aftonbladet* (26 April 1912).

44. As in –r.–n., "Biografcensuren", *Nya Dagligt Allehanda* (26 April 1912), and an untitled piece signed –s. in *Svenska Dagbladet* the same day.

45. Björnung, "Det censurerade biografdramat".

46. He expressed this opinion in public speeches and later defended it in a piece titled "Biografdramatiken och folkbildningen", *Aftontidningen* (24 April 1912).

47. This article was likewise titled "Biografdramatiken och folkbildningen". Lars Bergström in *Nya Dagligt Allehanda* (25 April 1912) and other papers, citing *Biografteaterbladet* (February 1912).

48. C.F. Magnusson, *Några ord till biografcensuren* (Stockholm: Wilhelmsson/Swedish Biograph, 1912), and Gustaf Berg, *Några ord till biografcensuren* (Stockholm: Sv. tr.-a-b., 1912).

49. Berg, *Några ord från biografcensuren*, 21. This precise issue makes for a telling case of how offensive object matter might have been slightly ambiguously presented and received. The film's clues are present, but they are not necessarily intrusive on an innocent viewer.

50. Magnusson, *Några ord till biografcensuren*, 11.
51. Berg, *Några ord från biografcensuren*, 15.
52. Regan, "Filmens Duse i Stockholm", *Dagens Nyheter* (23 November 1911).
53. Brandell's reliance on Asta Nielsen's womanly expressiveness can perhaps be taken to harmonise with the difference feminism associated with, at least, Wägner. Cf. Katarina Leppänen, *Rethinking Civilisation in a European Feminist Context: History, Nature, Women in Elin Wägner's* Väckarklocka (PhD thesis, Gothenburg University 2005, Acta Universitatis Gothoburgensis).
54. A cinema column in the press bears witness to how the debate helped her popularity in Stockholm: "Lately there has been so much talk and so much writing about the little Danish cinema actress Asta Nielsen that she seems to have become the most popular one among them all here in Stockholm at the moment". Maurice, "Asta Nielsen på Röda Kvarn", *Stockholms Dagblad* (5 March 1912).
55. Which the conservative press did not fail to point out. See for instance "Biografförordningens ikraftträdande", *Svenska Dagbladet* (15 November 1911)
56. For one account of this cf. Casper Tybjerg, *An Art of Silence and Light: The Development of the Danish Film Drama to 1920*, PhD thesis, University of Copenhagen, 1998 (however, what is missed by Tybjerg here is the run of the uncut film, preceding Swedish censorship). See also Isak Thorsen, "Afgrunden", entry in John Sundholm et al. (eds), *Historical Dictionary of Scandinavian Cinema* (Lanham: Scarecrow, 2012).
57. Orvar (probably Orvar Andersson), "Är filmen konst?", *Göteborgs Aftonblad* (August 1918, undated copy).
58. Fides Adeltand (unknown), "Publikens gunstlingar: Asta Nielsen berättar om arbetet inför filmkameran", *Vecko-Journalen*, vol 9 (12 December 1918).
59. Iwanowitsch, "Vad vill ni helst se på den vita duken?", *Biografen* 2:30 (1914): 560.

PART VI

THE INTERNATIONAL CINEMA CELEBRITY

Attention !!!

Fra poco il pubblico Italiano

potrà ammirare

Asta Nielsen

la più grande interprete ✽ ✽ ✽

✽ ✽ ✽ dell'Arte Cinematografica

nelle Films che i Signori

Del Sole, Ferrari e C.

per l'Italia Settentrionale

Magliulo e Borrelli

per l'Italia Centrale e Meridionale

lanceranno sul mercato

Dieci grandi soggetti di circa 1000 metri caduno
che verranno ceduti in esclusività per zone

Rappresentanti per l'Italia e Trieste
della Casa fabbricante, Ditta VAY e HUBERT - MILANO

Giovanni Lasi

Italy's First Film Star
Asta Nielsen, 'Polaris'

In October 1910, the Milanese trade journal *La Cinefono* published a lengthy article on a number of films produced in Denmark that were regarded as highly innovative.¹ This was the first hint of that 'northern wind' that would turn the Italian cinema scene upside down a few months later. Starting in January of the following year, the various trade magazines heralded the imminent screening in Italy of new full-length films produced by the Danish company Nordisk Film and then, in February, a column in *La Cinefono* entitled "Le novità del giorno" (news of the day) presented LA TRATTA DELLE SCHIAVE BIANCHE (DEN HVIDE SLAVEHANDEL, THE WHITE SLAVE). Despite the film's intensive advertising campaign, the initial reviews in the Italian trade press were far from being unanimously in favour of the film and some even completely wrote it off. The renowned film critic Gualtiero Fabbri had the following to say about this film drama directed by August Blom:

> Hopefully, the agents and exclusive distributors and, above all, the film production company will forgive us for describing this film with the famous title of a Shakespearean comedy, *Much ado about nothing*. In other words, despite the astonishing advertising and being borderline charlatanic, the actual film has no particular value.²

The stinging article pointed to the harshness and vulgarity of the subject ("violence and grotesque endearments"), some inconsistencies in the script ("contradictions in the plot"), the overuse of explanatory captions ("was there any need for that mess of telegrams?") and the excessive modernism ("We could call it a public transport and service film as it featured one or two trains, a ship, the telegraph office, the police station three times, and an uncountable number of coaches and cars"). However, the aspect that received the roughest treatment was the excessive and unjustified length of the film ("one thousand metres of tedious prolixity").³ Paradoxically, the increased length made it possible to develop realistic characters, modern settings and complex plots, but these were the very elements that Gualtiero Fabbri identified as weaknesses.

Facing page: Announcement of ten Asta Nielsen films to be released. *La Vita Cinematografica* 2:15 (10 September 1911).

Yet, these were ultimately the strengths – both in Italy and in many other countries – that drove the success of DEN HVIDE SLAVEHANDEL and the subsequent films of the 'Danish wave'. The hullabaloo sparked off by Nordisk's films was a mere prelude to the heated debate that would engulf a few months later, the Italian release of L'ABISSO (AFGRUNDEN, THE ABYSS). That film, directed by Urban Gad and starring Asta Nielsen, was released in Italian cinemas in the spring of 1911 and once again had those novel features first seen in DEN HVIDE SLAVEHANDEL.

AFGRUNDEN is set in a city. The camera slowly focuses in on the characters, looks at them, dwells on them and explores their expressions, faces and body language. The camera angle – mimicking real life – changes as the perspective changes. It is against this backdrop of daily life that a girl with a dark complexion, large black eyes and an ease of movement, wafts around the screen. This is Asta Nielsen and she would stir up the souls and minds of viewers. The film measures a whopping 772 metres, which was quite something given that the average Italian film – with but a few exceptions – in 1910 was no longer than 300 metres.[4]

The type of criticism levelled by Gualtiero Fabbri at DEN HVIDE SLAVEHANDEL was what greeted the 'metric bulimia' of AFGRUNDEN and of all of the Danish feature films imported in 1911. On the one hand, critics doubted that viewers would be able to watch a film for in excess of an hour; on the other, they objected to using so much film to play out a plot that could have been covered in much less time: A journalist wrote a very cutting criticism of IL GRAN MOMENTO (IN DEM GROSSEN AUGENBLICK, THE GREAT MOMENT), the second film of the first 'Asta Nielsen series': "Of the 1200 metres of film (...), at least 300 metres are redundant to say the least."[5] However, these misgivings found no support among Italian audiences who, flocking to watch AFGRUNDEN and the other Danish films, applauded the new aspects introduced by the Nordic producers. An article on the premiere of AFGRUNDEN in Naples stated: "For four days and for many hours a constant flow of people, hungry for emotion, poured down the aisles of Salone Margherita".[6] The considerable length made for more elaborate story-telling, making it possible to focus on details and broaden or increase the number of perspectives. It also meant it was possible to spend time on each individual narrative situation, allowing them to become more credible, plausible and natural. Italian audiences loved the extremely long shots, the details of each scene and the long close-ups showing expressions and emotions that are possible with a full-length film. For the first time ever, they could see the timing of real life on screen.

AFGRUNDEN depicts daily life, cities and a modern drama. This genre had been ignored by Italian film producers who, in 1911, continued to base their fortunes on historical films, where characters were dressed in period outfits, scenes were shot in studios with painted backdrops[7] and the average length did not exceed 300 metres.[8] In many cases, these were abridged versions of successful novels or theatrical productions where plot complexity required narrative brevity and

La Vita Cinematografica 2:21 (30 November 1911).

lengthy subtitles were often essential to correctly understanding the story. The style of acting also drew heavily on the theatrical tradition. Indeed, the lack of dialogue and the extremely compact nature of the action forced actors to emphasise gestures and expressions since these needed to convey additional meaning and be easily understood by the audience, especially because of the intricate narratives. The shots of the actors were generally full length, frontal and camera movement was virtually non-existent.

Used to such static, theatrical acting, the Italian cinema audiences who saw Asta Nielsen in AFGRUNDEN were enthused. Film director Urban Gad emphasised the details of the face and the tiniest movements and nuances in facial expression. The Danish actress, with her measured style of acting, filled with showing hints, intentions and suggestions, and her energetic, vibrant, sensual "film presence" – that was never redundant or unnatural – really struck a chord in the imagination of Italian audiences. Despite Italian critics doubting Danish film making, the quality of Asta Nielsen's acting was never in question. The review of IL GRAN MOMENTO, published in *La Vita Cinematografica* in November 1911, was particularly harsh on the film and on its author Urban Gad: "I do not know whether this gentleman Urban Gad, whom the poster defines as the 'German D'Annunzio', is a great poet. It seems to me, though, that he is a poor writer of stories for film, or at least, he looks like a beginner."[9] On the other hand, the article praised the undeniable talent of the Danish actress saying: "Asta Nielsen is a true artist. This is true! Ah! But this true artist (we repeat with pleasure) had the bad luck to come up against a film full of silly technical and implausible details".[10] The admiration for Asta Nielsen's screen presence and versatility was even more explicit in an article on the Danish actress published in May 1912 in *Il Cinema-Teatro*:

> The great actress of the Royal Copenhagen Theatre has so far been the most powerful *interpreter* of the multi-faceted female psyche. She 'lives' all the characters she plays in a wonderful synthesis of reality. She has the most unique form of cinematic expression that enables her to move from joy to pain and hatred to love, without any exaggeration that could betray that she is merely acting. Her beauty is extraordinarily appealing. Her large black eyes dart in all directions. Her pearly irises can convey flashes of sensuality or hatred, but can also sweetly caress with the pure love of motherly tenderness.[11]

While Asta Nielsen's talent for acting and her photogenic face are beyond doubt, it must be noted that her interpretation of characters and her screen presence and image were, in many cases, emphasised by the new way of filming adopted by the director Urban Gad which was really quite striking for Italian audiences. The camera was no longer placed at a fixed, standard distance to show full length shots of the actor. The distance between the actress and the spectator shrank, allowing a closeness never before seen. The close-ups encouraged intimacy, introspection and, thus, identification with her. The screen no longer showed resurrected ghosts of historic films or the caricatured, stylized bodies of the comedians, but real people, with flesh, bones and the feelings and emotions of real life. The realism of Asta Nielsen's acting was definitely a feature that contributed to her success on Italian shores. The closeness to the real world, which can be noted in the films produced by Fotorama and, more generally, in those imported from Denmark, is something that really struck a chord with Italian audiences. It was no coincidence that the adverts and promotional articles for these films emphasised how 'real' the plots were. The events, despite being overtly dramatic, were set in everyday life. A review of DEN HVIDE SLAVEHANDEL in the February 1911 edition of *La Cinefono* stated:

> A compelling, real, natural story full of topical, lively events. I have intentionally used the word topical because these almost unimaginable injustices and horrors are, unfortunately, real and undeniable facts that bring disgrace on modern human society! Horrible and shameful offences that belong to our age![12]

Placing the characters in a contemporary setting – violent, cruel, extreme yet real – became an opportunity for the audience to identify with the film since they found places and situations that, albeit not familiar, were at least plausible. By contrast, the contemporary nature of these northern films took Italians into a technological and modernist world that was, for Italy, still more of an ambition than a reality. Asta Nielsen films were 'modern films'. Italian audiences were able to see the widespread use of modern conveniences that people in other nations could enjoy. In those Danish films, ordinary people travelled by tram, car or train, they sent telegrams and even airplanes were not ignored. Despite the acceleration of industrialisation in the early 20th century, Italy was still lagging behind the technical, cultural and social standards found in the most advanced European nations. The true driver for this modernisation was certainly the middle class, which saw the world they desired to live in when watching those Nordic films. In Asta Nielsen films specifically and in Danish films generally, the Italian middle class watched the drama, the emotions and the intrigues of music teachers, clerks and shop assistants as well as of engineers, jewellers, bankers and even gamblers, loan sharks, prostitutes and policemen. In other words, the middle class, with its own virtues and miseries, had become the protagonist of the cinema. In addition, for those Italians who wanted to be part of that reality, the characters on screen became models, both positive and negative. More specifically, the type of woman played by Asta Nielsen – wilful, independent, full of initiative, in touch with modernity – became a subject for secret (and illusory) transference by Italian women. Despite economic progress, Italy remained a culturally backward country, with illiteracy at nearly 37 per cent in 1911.[13] The shortfalls of the education system, the influence of the Church and the paternalistic and centralized moralism of the political class prevented cultural advances similar to the economic ones. Women were the main victims of such backwardness. In Italy, the female employment rate was one of the lowest in Europe and a woman's social role was basically entirely dependent on male authority.

Vittorio Martinelli correctly noted: "Asta Nielsen provided an image of a clever, beautiful woman, overwhelmed by destiny, but reactive to it nonetheless (…) the actress was able to further the cause of redemption for the weak and the tormented".[14] Asta Nielsen foregrounded an empowered, independent model of women, becoming a harbinger for Italian women of new, daring aspirations that remained unthinkable in 1911 Italy. Despite the extraordinary erotic energy, marked femininity and deeply poignant sensitivity, the female characters played by the famous Danish actress had strong personalities, freed from the tethers of convention and never subdued, unless by themselves or an unavoidable fate they fought to the bitter end. Despite the amazing success of her films, Asta Nielsen would not achieve the extraordinary and lasting popularity she enjoyed in other countries. This was probably due to the transgressive and anti-conventional female model that she represented and that clashed with the male-dominated, moralistic and self-righteous nature of Italian society at the time. However, influenced by the Church's strict phobia for sex and the hypocritical moral righteousness pursued by mainstream culture, the sexual ostentation and the explicitly erotic content of Asta Nielsen films resulted in censorship by the authorities and the press. The attacks against the lack of morality of the Danish films were two pronged. On the one hand, the violence and cruelty of the characters was lamented; on the other, there was fierce criticism of the promiscuous, scandalous, shameless scenes. The 'sensational' films[15] by Nordisk and Asta Nielsen's "erotic melodrama"[16] were strongly opposed because, among other aspects, they were radically against the pedagogical duty that film, in the eyes of many, had to educate the masses. In this regard, the words by the critic in *La Cinefono* are very telling. After watching AFGRUNDEN at Salone Margherita in Naples, he reflected on the influence that

Asta Nielsen's debut film might have on younger and less worldly viewers: "Strolling around, somewhat nervously, I no longer had in front of me the scenes from AFGRUNDEN, but I would have loved to enter the minds of all those young men and ladies who had watched the film, and I would have loved to penetrate the minds of all the young wives".[17]

In Italy, despite the lack of specific legislation in this field,[18] AFGRUNDEN was cut, albeit minimally, by censorship. A serious article with the very grievous and precise title "The criminals of cinematography" read: "I remember that for AFGRUNDEN the public authorities, concerned by that wanton erotic dance that Asta Nielsen made famous, resorted to the deplorable means of cutting it short. However, let's face it, did this make that obscene film less shameful?"[19] On the other hand, the film distributors and agents, when advertising it in the press, highlighted that the film had been authorised by the Prefecture. The attitude of the distributors is, nonetheless, ambiguous. The articles published in the trade press enticed the erotic fantasy of readers to make the movie appealing, while avoiding any mention of the excessively scandalous scenes. In the extremely detailed film synopsis published in *La Vita Cinematografica* the author uses some shocking expressions for that time ("she looks with provocative eyes", "attracted by his masculine beauty", "drops at his feet without any willpower" etc),[20] but no reference is made to the 'gaucho dance', the erotic apex of the film, that was considered far too scandalous to be mentioned by the press. However, it is possible to infer from the trade press that the hot dance between Magda and Rudolph was advertised in the wall posters of the film and was referred to as the "dance of desire".[21] Italian male audiences were clearly enthusiastic about Asta Nielsen films, no doubt because of the elevated erotic content and the sultry scenes. In a country so against sexual freedom, the explicitly carnal passion conveyed by the actress on screen caused a somewhat schizophrenic reaction among Italian men, with an intimate, smug even morbid, attraction being combined with a public moral and clearly hypocritical repulsion.

Despite biased criticism that clearly sought to protect the Italian film industry to the detriment of the Danish competition, despite the dislike for full-length films expressed in most trade media and despite the accusations of low morals, Asta Nielsen films spread like wildfire across the Italian market. On 30 April 1911, *La Vita Cinematografica* published an advert for AFGRUNDEN, indicating that Giuseppe Barattolo, who would become one of Italy's most powerful film producers, was the local agent for the film and specified that it was protected by copyright.[22] The film was presented as a "grand drama produced by Fotorama Copenhagen".[23] On 20 July 1911, as Riccardo Redi reminds us, the name Asta Nielsen appeared for the first time in an Italian trade journal.[24] In a full page advertisement purchased by Magliulo and Borrelli, the distributors for central and southern Italy of LA FALENA (NACHTFALTER, RETRIBUTION),[25] the actress was referred to as "The famous Asta Nielsen (the Duse of Cinematography)".[26] Her increasing success was confirmed in the pages of *La Vita*

Italy's First Film Star – Asta Nielsen, 'Polaris'

From the first page of *Il Cinema-Teatro* 2:26 (19 May 1912).

Cinematografica when an advert, used exclusively to publicise her name in very large letters, stated:

> "Please note!!! Soon, Italian audiences will be able to admire Asta Nielsen, the best actress of the cinematographic art, in the films that Del Sole, Ferrari & C. for northern Italy and Magliulo and Borrelli for central and southern Italy will release.10 great films of about 1000 metres each."[27]

In Italy, there would soon be a real 'Asta Nielsen series' and indeed, in the following months, she became increasingly common in Italian cinemas. In November 1911, Florentia Films from Turin announced among its 14 upcoming films three films from Nordisk and three films starring Asta Nielsen: LA FALENA (NACHTFALTER, RETRIBUTION), IL SOGNO NERO (DEN SORTE DRØM, THE CIRCUS GIRL), and IL GRAN MOMENTO (IN DEM GROSSEN AUGENBLICK, THE GREAT MOMENT). In the years that followed, Italian importers would draw plentifully from films starring Asta Nielsen. There was news of the distribution of additional nine Asta Nielsen films in Italy: SANGUE BOLLENTE (HEISSES BLUT, BURNING BLOOD) and LA ZINGARA (ZIGEUNERBLUT, GYPSY BLOOD)[28] as well as UCCELLO FORESTO (DER FREMDE VOGEL, THE COURSE OF TRUE LOVE), TRADITRICE (DIE VERRÄTERIN, THE TRAITRESS), SANGUE DI ZINGARA (DAS MÄDCHEN OHNE VATERLAND, A GIRL WITHOUT A COUNTRY), GIOVINEZZA E PAZZIA (JUGEND UND TOLLHEIT, IN A FIX), DELITTO DI PADRE (DIE SÜNDEN DER VÄTER, THE TEMPTATIONS OF DRINK), SUFFRAGETTE (DIE SUFFRAGETTE, THE SUFFRAGETTE).[29] Such interest by the distributors was certainly justified by the genuine, loyal affection that Italian audiences had for the Danish actress. The comparison with Duse became common practice and, despite the harsh criticism of the Nordic actress, the trade press certainly paid Nielsen many compliments, lauding not only her indisputable talent and her unusually Mediterranean features that were thus familiar to Italian audiences, but also her magnetic charm, her overflowing sensuality and unique capacity to seduce. A journalist poured all of his deep and unconditional admiration for Nielsen into the article:

> Some moves, looks, and snake-like darts, her eyes and that body of hers that flicks and offers itself ... and then flicks again with pleasure say everything about Asta Nielsen's exquisite art. I would place this wonderful queen of gestures and expressions on the golden throne that the cinematographic art, which is becoming increasingly popular, reserves for its greatest artists. This is the best tribute we can pay to this charmer of crowds.[30]

'Charmer of crowds': this title attributed to Asta Nielsen by the passionate journalist suggests the idea of mass worship, that collective idolatry that would be at the basis of the star phenomenon. The actress is elevated to a heavenly level populated by the protagonists of cinema, still undefined, but that would soon become the unattainable world of female film stars. After all, Asta Nielsen was considered – rightly – the first celebrity star. In Italy she enjoyed great success and the media covered her extensively, in a manner previously unheard of for a foreign actress. Her name was printed in large letters on film adverts, billboards spurted out her name and cinema posters celebrated her extraordinary talent.

When Nielsen came to the fore, Italian cinema already had some well-known and talented actors and actresses that had become popular among audiences after appearing in numerous films. One need merely mention Fernanda Negri Pouget, Ubaldo Maria del Colle or the pair of Mary Cleo Tarlarini and Alberto A. Capozzi. Others, like Vittoria Lepanto, Ermete Zacconi and Ermete Novelli, had achieved fame largely because of earlier theatre careers. Up until that moment, cinema producers had opposed the rise of a phenomenon that we could call stardom, believing that films should be solely identified with the production houses that made them. The names of actors did not appear in advertising campaigns, their photographs did not show up in the glossy pages of magazines and no postcards or leaflets were printed with the faces of the most famous actors. The 'Asta Nielsen phenomenon' radically changed this. Probably, following the popularity that the Danish actress enjoyed all over the world and given the pressure from the readers who increasingly wanted news of their screen heroes, *La Vita Cinematografica* and other trade journals started to write individual articles, with photos, about the most famous Italian actors. A mechanism had been triggered and only a few people actually understood its implications. One of those was Alfredo Morvillo, editor of a magazine entitled *Cinema*. In his columns he stigmatised the innovation of full-length films and, with that, the enormous popularity Asta Nielsen acquired: "What do long films boil down to, if not focusing more on the actor's work? Don't the cases of Asta Nielsen and Madamigella Polaire prove precisely that?"[31]

The 'Asta Nielsen situation' might have led to the increased popularity of Italian actors and a consequent increase in the amount of money production houses had to pay to hire these actors, but it would also cause far more profound structural changes. Indeed, cinema moved out of the world of anonymity and "from that moment on (after Asta Nielsen) films would no longer be identified with the trade mark, but rather with the name of the actors and the directors".[32] Morvillo's lucid, yet retrospective position gives an indication as to why such harsh criticism was levelled at Asta Nielsen and her films by *Cinema*, especially by Aniello Costagliola who wrote the following about AFGRUNDEN:

> The most stale and conventional elements of romantic theatre have been used and reproduced in this film that does not even stand out for the quality of the reproduction. AFGRUNDEN does not and cannot stir any emotion whatsoever in the audience. It does not stir compassion, neither terror or horror. If it stirs any emotion at all, it would be boredom. Magda's fatal passion neither moves nor convinces ...[33]

Of course, Costagliola's caustic judgement would be disproved by what actually happened, as Asta Nielsen became – in Italy too – the first true cult figure of the big screen. In truth, Italy had some experience with the phenomenon behind the popularity of Asta Nielsen. In Italian theatre, some lead actors, such as Adelaide Ristori, Ernesto Rossi and Tommaso Salvini, had achieved extraordinary fame and success, acclaimed and worshipped by audiences.[34] Thus, it was no accident that Asta Nielsen was immediately compared to Eleonora Duse, an enormously famous and celebrated Italian stage actress. In addition, Asta Nielsen would also act as a model for the series of Italian film stars who, a few years down the line, would start with the extraordinary Lyda Borrelli in MA L'AMOR MIO NON MUORE (LOVE EVERLASTING)!

A number of differences distinguish Asta Nielsen's style from that of the great stars of Italian silent films. First, the Danish actress came from an acting, cultural and formal background rooted in the Nordic tradition of the great Scandinavian naturalistic theatre, but the Italian stars were far more tied to D'Annunzio's decadentism, symbolist and crepuscular poetry and to pre-Raphaelite painting.[35] In addition, Nielsen based her charm on the dichotomy between extraordinary and ordinary that merged so perfectly in her. She exalted the characteristics, from sensuality to being natural, of the ordinary woman. By contrast, Italian star actresses all placed a distance between the woman and the world. The model that was proposed was that of an unattainable, unreachable, 'fatal' woman.

However, Nielsen would leave a lasting example in the minds of the great Italian actresses of the age that came immediately after her. Interestingly, this connection can even be given a symbolic date since 1910, when AFGRUNDEN was made, was also the debut year for Francesca Bertini,[36] the Italian film star who could be compared most likely with Asta Nielsen, both because of her experience with naturalistic theatre and her natural, measured acting style. Bertini herself noted the similarities between the two, although at the time, they represented more the Italian's desires than reality: "They showed me AFGRUNDEN starring Asta Nielsen. That film had a major impact on me. I wondered 'Why should I wear these baggy clothes and these wigs? I can do modern stuff!'"[37]

Asta Nielsen films not only set a benchmark for Italian actors, but also helped change, at least partially, the perspective of the entire Italian film landscape. After the success of AFGRUNDEN, Italian production houses, despite maintaining their preference for historical content matter, started experimenting with full-length films and later tried to follow the themes made successful by the Danish production. As such, they took on emotional dramas where the characters were rooted in daily life, albeit with 'sensational' stories. After her 'debut' success, Asta Nielsen's popularity in Italy was somewhat dampened by the growth of home made films. In 1913, legendary peplum films had reached their apex in Italy. The increased length of films made possible productions like SPARTACO (SPARTACUS), GLI ULTIMI GIORNI DI POMPEI (THE LAST DAYS OF POMPEII), QUO VADIS? and finally, in 1914, CABIRIA, which conquered markets across the world, attracting the attention of the trade press, distributors and audiences. In 1913, the enormous success of Lyda Borrelli in MA L'AMOR MIO NON MUORE! marked the beginning of the golden era of Italian film stars who increasingly won over the hearts of Italian audiences, overshadowing the very first star Asta Nielsen. Actresses like Borelli, Francesca Bertini, Pina Menichelli, Diana Karenne, Italia Almirante Manzini, Leda Gys and Hesperia would truly be worshipped, bringing the house down for nearly ten years both in Italy and abroad.

However, the major obstacle to Asta Nielsen being celebrated as a true star in Italy was the First World War and the consequent ban on all films from enemy countries, especially Germany. Starting 1915, all films linked to Germany, including Asta Nielsen films, were not shown in Italian cinemas. The situation only returned to normal five years later. In 1920, some Italian distributors attempted to re-launch Asta Nielsen in style, with the return of the Danish star to Italian screens being planned for March. *La Cinefono* wrote: "An event: Asta Nielsen returns to Italian screens in NEL TURBINE, a film of great passion."[38] And: "Asta Nielsen, the actress our audience loves, makes a come back to our screens in NEL TURBINE, a powerful emotional drama about real life."[39]

NEL TURBINE (RAUSCH, INTOXICATION) of 1919, directed by Ernst Lubitsch would be advertised for many months, focusing on the Danish actress's talent. More specifically, Asta Nielsen's return to Italy was highlighted in a trade magazine article entitled "Asta Nielsen's return – the triumph of the naturalistic film NEL TURBINE".[40] The success of the film was confirmed by the report of a journalist from the premiere in Venice.[41] The same issue of the magazine also announced another three films starring Asta Nielsen, namely DORA BRANDES, L'ABBECEDARIO DELL'AMORE (DAS LIEBES-ABC), and LA BAMBINA

DELL'ORFANOTROFIO (DAS WAISENHAUSKIND). Despite this attempt to relaunch Asta Nielsen, the success enjoyed by AFGRUNDEN and the films starring Asta Nielsen in the 1910s was not repeated. In the following years, other foreign actresses would be successful in Italy, including Pola Negri, and, above all, the upcoming stars of the American star system. As early as 1921, a series of films starring Pearl White was set for release in Italy. In the first half of the 1920s Mary Pickford, Mae Murray and Dorothy Dalton were the new undisputed queens of the Italian screens and the dazzling star of 'la Duse della cinematografia', the first to rise, was no longer discernible in the Italian skies.

An earlier version of this article was published as "Polarstern: In Italien" in Heide Schlüpmann et al. (eds), *Unmögliche Liebe. Asta Nielsen, ihr Kino* (2nd edn) (Vienna: filmarchiv austria, 2010).

Notes

1. Erik, "La cinematografia in Danimarca", *La Cinefono*, no. 127 (1 October 1910): 10, as quoted in Aldo Bernardini, *Cinema muto italiano. Arte, divismo e mercato. 1910–1914*, vol. III (Rome, Bari: Laterza, 1982), 86.
2. Gualtiero Fabbri, "Aristarcheide", *La Cinematografia italiana ed estera*, 5:103 (5 April 1911): 1275.
3. Ibid.
4. There were however some exceptions: in 1909 Cines produced MACBETH (442 metres) and I TRE MOSCHETTIERI (THE THREE MUSKETEERS, 475 metres); in 1910, Film d'Arte Italiana produced IL TROVATORE (THE TROUBADOUR, 473 metres). Between 1910 and 1911, Italian audiences could also watch long imported films from the USA and France, in particular Vitagraph's UNCLE TOM'S CABIN (891 metres, in three episodes shown separately) and Vitagraph's adaption of Victor Hugo's novel *Les Misérables* (in the four episodes THE GALLEY SLAVE, FANTINE, COSETTE, JEAN VALJEAN, which were shown together, adding altogether to 1,173 metres).
5. *La Vita Cinematografica* 2:21 (30 November 1911): 5.
6. *La Cinefono* 5: 169 (10 June 1911): 6. In 1911, only a few films in excess of 1000 metres were made in Italy: Milano produced L'INFERNO (DANTE'S INFERNO), and Cines produced LA GERUSALEMME LIBERATA (THE CRUSADERS) and PINOCCHIO.
7. More specifically, Film d'Arte Italiana successfully turned historical events and literary works into films. It was incorporated on 2 March 1909, with Charles Pathé as the chairman and one of the major shareholders, on the basis of agreements signed with André Lafitte, owner and co-founder of the French Film d'Art. Film d'Arte Italiana would distinguish itself, especially after 1911, for outdoor filming on location.
8. Bernardini, *Cinema muto italiano*, vol. III, 98.
9. *La Vita Cinematografica* 2:21 (30 November 1911): 5.
10. Ibid.
11. "Asta Nielsen la Duse della Cinematografia", *Il cinema-teatro – Notiziario internazionale dell'arte cinematografica*, 2:26 (19 May 1912): 1.
12. A. Checcucci, "Impressioni", *La Cinefono* 5:146 (25 February 1911): 8.
13. A. Giardina, G. Sabbatucci and V. Vidotto, *L'età contemporanea* (Rome, Bari: Laterza, 1999), 424.
14. Vittorio Martinelli, *Le dive del silenzio* (Recco (Ge): Le Mani, 2001), 200.
15. 'Sensational' was used to refer to the Danish films, in particular those produced by Nordisk Film, that developed around a particularly compelling event that amazed and caught the audience's attention. The quest for the "sensational" is primarily attributed to Ole Olsen, the historical founder of Nordisk Film. He infused his films with a passion for special effects, something he had learnt in his previous job as the organizer of the Tivoli amusement park in Malmö. Cf. Barry Salt, "Schiave bianche e tende a strisce. La ricerca del 'sensazionale'", in Paolo Cerchi Usai (ed.), *Schiave bianche allo specchio – Le origini del cinema in Scandinavia (1896–1918)*, Pordenone: Studio tesi, 1986), 63.

16. This definition is by Marguerite Engberg, *The erotic melodrama*, in Riccardo Redi (ed.), *1911... La nascita del lungometraggio* (Roma: CNC Edizioni, 1992), 21.
17. Enzo, "Spunti e appunti. Le prime a Napoli. L'ABISSO al Salone Margherita", *La Cinefono* 5:160 (10 June 1911): 6.
18. The rules in force referred to a circular letter from the Ministry dated 31 March 1908 (no.13,500) that warned the prefectures so that they could ban shows with "sensational and impressive representations". Cf. Bernardini, *Cinema muto italiano*, vol. III, 217.
19. Franz, "I criminali della Cinematografia", *Il cinema-teatro – Notiziario internazionale dell'arte cinematografica*, 2: 26 (19 May 1912).
20. *La Vita cinematografica* 2:7 (30 April 1911): 15 and 16.
21. From the press, it is possible to infer that the hot dance between Magda and Rudolph was, however, advertised in the wall posters of the film and was referred to as the "dance of desire". *Il cinema-teatro – Notiziario internazionale dell'arte cinematografica* 2:26 (19 May 1912): 1.
22. The film's copyright was registered, strangely, with the French title, on 20 April 1911. "We know that *L'Abime* with a letter from the Prefecture of Rome of 20 April, no. 3113, Reg. 1911, was placed under copyright and rights of representation". *La Cinematografia italiana ed estera* 5:105 (1–5 May 1911): 1346.
With the circulation of full-length films and the substantial investment for the production and distribution of these films, the film industry in Italy started to press for specific copyright legislation for films. At first, there were Ministerial circular letters, then a specific law was passed on 4 October 1914, no.1114. Cf. Bernardini, *Cinema muto italiano*, vol. III, 116.
23. *La Vita Cinematografica* 2:7 (30 April 1911): 15.
24. Riccardo Redi, *La nascita del lungometraggio*, in Riccardo Redi (ed.), *1911 ... La nascita del lungometraggio* (Rome: CNC Edizioni, 1992), 13.
25. According to the practice existing in Italy at that time, Italian distributors had exclusive rights to the film in Italy (in the case of AFGRUNDEN the holder of these rights was Giuseppe Barattolo). Then, they would sell rights to some other distributors that distributed the film in one or more regions, acquiring in turn exclusive rights for the areas under their authority.
26. *Cinema* 1:14 (20 July 1911).
27. *La Vita Cinematografica* 2:13–14 (20–25 August): 20.
28. Cf. *Il cinema-teatro – Notiziario internazionale dell'arte cinematografica* 2:26 (19 May 1912): 1.
29. Data courtesy of Riccardo Redi.
30. "Asta Nielsen la Duse della Cinematografia". *Il cinema-teatro – Notiziario internazionale dell'arte cinematografica* 2:26 (19 May 1912): 1.
31. Alfredo Morvillo, "L'argomento principe (La fine della fabbrica)", *Cinema* 1:17 (5 September 1911).
32. Redi, "La nascita del lungometraggio", 14.
33. Aniello Costagliela, *Cinema* 1:11 (5 June 1911).
34. Cristina Jandelli, *I ruoli nel teatro italiano tra Otto e Novecento* (Florence: Le Lettere, 2002), 29.
35. Gian Piero Brunetta, *Cent'anni di cinema italiano*, Vol.I, *Dalle origini alla seconda guerra mondiale* (Rome, Bari: Laterza, 2000), 98.
36. Francesca Bertini made her official film debut in IL TROVATORE (Film d'Arte Italiana, 1910).
37. "Bertini su Bertini", a conversation collected by Ciriaco Tiso and Gianfranco Mingozzi in 1980, in Gianfranco Mingozzi (ed.), *Francesca Bertini* (Recco (Ge): Le Mani, 2002). The actress is referring to the period costumes that she had to wear since most of the productions up till that moment were historical films.
38. *La Cinefono e RFC* 14: 411 (15–25 March 1920): 44.
39. *La Cinefono e RFC* 14: 412 (26 March – 10 April 1920): 2.
40. Snob, "La reentré di Asta Nielsen – Il trionfo del film verista NEL TURBINE", *La Cinefono e RFC* 14: 413 (11–26 April 1920): 51.
41. Carlo Fischer, "NEL TURBINE – Al Cinema Modernissimo di Venezia", *La Cinefono e RFC* 14: 413 (11–26 April 1920), 55.

Lauri Piispa

Asta Nielsen and the Russian Film Trade

When Asta Nielsen's Danish debut film AFGRUNDEN had its premiere in Russia, at the turn of 1911, the Russian public had already grown sensitive to both film stardom and, more generally, to female performing stars. Nielsen was not quite the first film star in Russia – this title should go to Max Linder, whose name began to appear in the trade press advertisements as early as 1909. Already six months before his name ever appeared, an article suggested that film theatres and distributors announce the names of the actors in the films; according to the author, the audience had already found their favourites, actors whom they recognised and liked; to further enhance his demand the author gave an example of such an actor – unmistakably Max Linder of LES DÉBUTS D'UN PATINEUR (THE UNSKILLFUL SKATER, 1907).[1]

Moreover, starring actresses had dominated Russian dramatic stage for the past forty years.[2] Since the 1870s, when the trio of the Imperial Theatres, Maria Ermolova (1853–1928), Glikeriia Fedotova (1846–1925) and Maria Savina (1854–1915), began their careers, the greatest stars of the Russian stage had been women. In the first decade of the 20th century, the 'Golden Age' of Russian actresses was already in its twilight, and it came to an end in February 1910 with the untimely death of the youngest of the female superstars, Vera Komissarzhevskaia, 'the Duse of the Russian Stage'. In Russia, the ground was therefore well prepared for 'the Duse of cinema' to emerge.

AFGRUNDEN in Russia

The film that introduced Asta Nielsen to the Russian audience was, as elsewhere, her Danish debut film AFGRUNDEN (THE ABYSS), known in Russia as BEZDNA. The film's importation and distribution was rather confusing. As elsewhere it was one of the breakthroughs of the so called 'exclusive system' – *monopolnyi film* in Russian – but to be that, it was distributed by surprisingly many companies. The first advertisements of AFGRUNDEN, placed by the Warsaw based company Sfinks, appeared in the trade press on 1 December 1910.[3] Most of the film's marketing in the subsequent months followed the style and content of this first advertisement:

> *For an enormous price we have been able to acquire from Scandinavia*
> EXCLUSIVELY FOR ALL RUSSIA
> a picture which leaves far behind everything that has so far appeared on the film market, a picture that should interest all strata of society.
> The picture is:
> THE ABYSS – 850 metres
> HISTORY OF THE DOWNFALL OF A WOMAN
> A sensational drama by URBAN GOOD [sic]. The price: *1,000* roubles.
> This picture was screened for nine weeks to full houses in the most outstanding foreign film theatres, and we can boldly guarantee everyone a grandiose success.[4]

The words "exclusively for all Russia" were called into question a few pages later in the same issue, where another company, Progress, which was based in Moscow, included the film in their repertoire.[5] To make it even more confusing, a week later a third distributor appeared on the scene: according to the news, the company Globus, also based in Moscow, had bought the film's exclusive rights for a sum of 15,000 roubles (c. 8,000 USD).[6] By this time AFGRUNDEN had disappeared from the advertisements of Progress, and in the end it was the last of the three, Globus, who handled the distribution of Asta Nielsen's debut film in Russia.

The inevitable conclusion of this rather strange evidence is that AFGRUNDEN came to Russia through Poland and was a joint venture between the Polish company Sfinks and the Russian Globus. Most probably Sfinks, which in 1911 was actually just a film theatre in Warsaw,[7] bought the exclusive rights, but was unable to handle the distribution in a vast country like Russia alone and therefore sought a Russian associate with the necessary networks and connections. The company Globus was run by the Muscovite Abram Gechtman, one of the pioneers of Russian film trade, who had started to build his film empire as a theatre owner in 1906. Globus was his new company, founded in the autumn of 1910. It was Gechtman who introduced the exclusive system to Russia that same autumn with DEN HVIDE SLAVEHANDEL (THE WHITE SLAVE), the other most successful long-feature film from Denmark of 1910, and some travelogues that his company produced itself.[8] The third company, Progress, on the other hand, was clearly violating the monopoly. The film business in Russia was at times incredibly dirty, and the exclusive system was often criticised for not working in practice. The many opponents of the system claimed that whoever buys an exclusive ends up paying three or four times the price for it, only to discover that their competitor has the same film anyway.[9] Judging by the evidence in the trade press, this seems to have taken place, though AFGRUNDEN is never specifically mentioned in this context.

AFGRUNDEN opened in the premiere theatres of Moscow and St. Petersburg in early January 1911. Mapping the exhibition of a film like AFGRUNDEN in Russia is an impossible task, since in 1911 Russian film theatres did not advertise regularly in the daily press. The few advertisements that I have been

A Russian poster of the Asta Nielsen film Zatravlennaia – probably Zu Tode gehetzt (Driven Out, 1912).

able to find, suggest that AFGRUNDEN was advertised for the cinemagoers in the same manner as in the advertisements directed towards the cinema owners.[10] The style resembled that of Sfinks's first advertisement: the film was referred to as a "sensational film" about "a moral downfall of a woman" – words that subtly suggested erotic content. The advertisements also appealed to the alleged success that the film had had abroad. Asta Nielsen's name never turned up; instead the film was advertised with Urban Gad's name, often misleadingly stating that AFGRUNDEN was based on a "novel by Urban Good". Gad's name was systematically misspelled 'Good' or 'God', obviously to avoid unpleasant association with the Russian word *gad* (which means a reptile).

Without enough evidence I cannot provide any calculations on the size of AFGRUNDEN's audiences or even the amount of screenings in any of the big cities. What can be said with certainty is that the film became probably the greatest single hit in Russia to that date. It stayed in distribution for nearly six months and earned its distributors a fortune. Throughout the spring of 1911 the trade press was full of news about Globus expanding its business and taking over new regions of Russia, which is largely explained by the success of this one film.[11]

AFGRUNDEN inflamed two debates. The first was a debate about the exclusive system, which had begun already before AFGRUNDEN's release, in the autumn of 1910. The film's phenomenal success seems to have turned the general opinion against the new system. In 1911 it was hard to find anyone to defend it – at least in public. The system was criticised for not working in practice and for being against the spirit of free enterprise. In practice, however, many of those who opposed the system in public did not hesitate to take a lucrative enough offer if one came their way.[12] The second debate was on sexual morality, caused by the infamous 'gaucho dance' scene of the film. The general concern in 1911 was that, at the same time as the authorities were taking more determined measures to root out pornographic pictures from the film theatres, elements of the feared 'Paris genre' were finding their way into the regular programme.[13] In June 1911, the trade journal *Vestnik kinematografii* published an article titled "On a Slippery Path", dedicated to the problem of erotic content in mainstream pictures. The anonymous author singled out AFGRUNDEN as a starting point; although he paid respect to the artistic quality of the film and also appreciated Asta Nielsen's performance (ironically, this was the first ever mention of her name in the trade press, although her first name was mistakenly written 'Ada'), he resented the "cowboy dance" as a "serious mistake", which had started the fashion to include erotic scenes in films in order to appeal to the "lower instincts" of the audience. The article ends: "THE ABYSS is where this bacchanalia began, and the abyss is where it shall end".[14]

The film's title was used in the same fashion eight months later – a full year after the film's release – in a feuilleton titled "The Abyss" that appeared in the trade journal *Sine-fono*. In the story a desperate crowd, a delegation representing "the population" of a small provincial town, appears before the film theatre owner and asks whether it would be possible to see AFGRUNDEN (THE ABYSS) again. The theatre owner explains that it might be difficult to get hold of a print of such an old film, but he promises to do his best. A week later the delegation turns up again and is told that a print has been discovered, but unfortunately one where the "belly dance" is cut out by the authorities of some other town. The representatives of the population, understandably disappointed, resign to their fate and the film is screened. The feuilleton ends: "And so the triumphant population plunged into the abyss".[15]

Autumn 1911 in Russian cinema

No doubt AFGRUNDEN's success was one of the factors that made Russian producers turn to the exclusive system, feature-length and star system. All three innovations were introduced in Russian productions of the autumn 1911 season. In terms of the first two, Aleksandr Khanzhonkov's production company held the key position. Khanzhonkov was initially among the opponents of the exclusive system. He, like many, thought that the system was unfair and that it distorted competition.[16]

In the course of 1911 the most prominent Russian film producer changed his mind completely. In June 1911 AFGRUNDEN's two distributors, Abram Gechtman's Globus and the Polish company Sfinks, merged into a new powerful distribution company, Globus & Sfinks. They commissioned from Khanzhonkov two films which were advertised as "the first Russian exclusive films".[17] The first, and more successful of the two, was KREITSEROVA SONATA (THE KREUTZER SONATA), an adaptation of Leo Tolstoy's novella of the same title. At 570 meters the film was the longest produced in Russia hitherto, and made into a success by Globus & Sfinks. The film is lost, but its choice of subject, Tolstoy's sinister story of a husband murdering his wife out of jealousy, clearly indicates a desire to produce a psychological melodrama on an erotic theme similar to the recent Danish hits. KREITSEROVA SONATA was also Ivan Mozzhukhin's debut in a leading role, but Khanzhonkov made no effort at this point to advertise his films with the names of the actors but left them uncredited.

The rise of feature-length films culminated later that autumn when Khanzhonkov released his famous historical epic OBORONA SEVASTOPOLIA (DEFENCE OF SEVASTOPOL), preserved in fragmentary form, the first Russian feature film whose length reached an impressive 2,000 metres. Right before its release the Russian distributors held a meeting in Moscow where they signed a public announcement not to exploit exclusive films anymore.[18] Khanzhonkov, however, had his back up against the wall: as the new film had seriously exceeded its budget he was in danger of losing his business and had to make profit quickly. He came up with the idea of selling his film to several distributors, all with exclusive rights to distribute in a certain region of Russia. Exclusive distribution was guaranteed with a compensation of 1,000 roubles for any possible violation, and Khanzhonkov included in the deal as many positive prints as the distributor needed for the price of film stock alone.[19]

The ink was not dry on the distributors' ban of exclusive films when practically all those who had signed rushed to take Khanzhonkov's give or take offer. The trade journal *Sine-fono*, the most ardent opponent of the exclusive system, was furious: "What is this – are they deliberately making a joke of themselves, or does the right hand not know what the left is doing?"[20] The accused cried all the way to the bank: OBORONA SEVASTOPOLIA became the first really successful film of Russian origin. Khanzhonkov later recounted that this film actually changed the map of Russian distribution in favour of those who took his offer.[21]

In terms of the star system things did not advance as rapidly. As already said, Asta Nielsen's name was never used in marketing AFGRUNDEN. The same thing occurred when her third film NACHTFALTER (RETRIBUTION) was released in May under the title NOCHNAIA BABOCHKA – the film seems to have gone by without any similar attention.[22] Instead, in September 1911, the first 'Asta Nielsen series', imported by Globus & Sfinks, was released with all the appropriate hype around the female star of the series.[23] At the same time the first attempt to create a star cult around a Russian film artist took place. Behind it was another Russian production company, Thiemann & Reinhardt. Their historical drama KASHIRSKAIA STARINA (THE ANCIENT KASHIRA) starred an ensemble from the Imperial Maly Theatre led by Ekaterina Roscshina-Insarova (1883–1970), one of the leading ladies of the Maly at the time. Roscshina-Insarova's appearance became the main attraction of the film: Thiemann & Reinhardt even offered picture postcards of her and other actors of the film.[24] The film failed commercially and Roscshina-Insarova withdrew from film work very soon.

'Astochka'

In the following three years several such attempts were made by many producers, always with already famous stage actors, but with little success. There were really no stars in Russian cinema before 1915, although Russian films were beginning to find their audience. No doubt the decisive reason for Russian actors' low appeal was that the public fell in love with the foreign stars, and, above all, with Asta Nielsen whom her fans soon came to know under the affectionate diminutive form of her name, 'Astochka'.[25] From the introduction of her first series in 1911 to the summer of 1914, Asta Nielsen was the unrivalled queen of Russian screens. A mere glance at any of the trade journals from the period is sufficient evidence – at times she fills literally half of the advertisement pages. An enormous two-page advertisement of the second 'Asta Nielsen series' from June 1912 gives an impression of the immense commercial value she had for the film trade and of the fierce competition over her films:

> *1,500,000* [roubles] of capital has been invested by our company for the organization and exploitation of the new artistic series of ASTA NIELSEN.
>
> *100,000* a year is what the great actress ASTA NIELSEN receives for her unparalleled performances.
>
> *10,000* grateful letters from all over the world were sent to HER because of her champion performances.
>
> EXCLUSIVELY ONLY we sell the new series of ASTA NIELSEN.
>
> WE ANNOUNCE that the precautions we have taken guarantee a hard *monopoly* of the *new* ASTA NIELSEN series.
>
> WE PAY a thousand roubles to anyone who manages to get a single film from the new series behind our back.
>
> IN GERMANY the NEW artistic series of Asta Nielsen is already booked up to

20 screens by happy theatre owners who have rushed to buy the exclusive right to demonstrate these wonderful pictures.
EVERY foresighted theatre owner should already think about the future and get ready for the forthcoming season.
"You reap what you sow".[26]

One source tells a bit more specifically about the audience's preferences in the pre-war years. A survey was made in 1913 among the customers of the film theatre Modern in the city of Kharkov, Southern Russia (present Ukraine). The theatre received 1313 answers to a multiple choice questionnaire asking, for example, favourite film genres, companies, and artists. There were three categories for artists: dramatic female, dramatic male and comic performers. The results were clear enough: 1206 respondents out of the 1313 ticked Asta Nielsen's name as their favourite actress. The male category was won by 'Garrison', which was Valdemar Psilander's Russian screen name, with 817 votes, and Max Linder won the comic category with an overwhelming 1306 votes. Tellingly, the questionnaire did not offer any Russian alternatives in these categories – although quite a few respondents ticked Russia as their favourite when asked which country's production they liked.[27]

It is also noteworthy that the film theatre that conducted the survey was in favour of the educated audience: more than half of the adult male respondents had a higher education. Generally it seems that Asta Nielsen was a favourite of the educated and her name was always connected to artistic quality in films. The three triumphant actors of the questionnaire, Nielsen, Psilander, and Linder, were seen as equivalent with quality and good film acting for the Russian audience. Around 1913 very serious and at times quite sophisticated articles started to appear in film journals about the nature of film art. From the beginning the Russian discourse centred on the actor; the art of cinema, in the Russian understanding, was in fact synonymous to the art of film acting. Acting was a very topical question in Russia of the 1910s; this was the age of new theatre practices and new ideas about the art of acting put forward by such world-famous figures as Konstantin Stanislavski and Vsevolod Meyerhold. Many of the articles dealing with film acting clearly reflected this interest, and Asta Nielsen's name came up whenever good film acting, and especially the specific technique of silent film acting, was discussed.[28]

This was not only the opinion of the film press writers, but it was shared by quite a few of Asta Nielsen's Russian colleagues as well. Konstantin Varlamov (1848–1915), a living legend of the St. Petersburg stage, was a film buff and a great Asta Nielsen fan. He stated after seeing her in GREKHI OTSOV (DIE SÜNDEN DER VÄTER, TEMPTATIONS OF DRINK): "Here's someone whom actresses should learn mime and expression from!"[29] In another questionnaire, artists of Stanislavski's Moscow Art Theatre were asked of their opinions on cinema. Most of the theatre's artists, Stanislavski himself included, openly despised cinema and film actors, but even some of those did make an exception on Nielsen. Vasili Luzhki was quoted as saying:

> A film artist plays with mime and gesture, but these two techniques have not been studied much, and there are not many actors these days who know how to use them for artistic purposes. Look at Asta Nielsen – she is a great mime, and that is why her performances, *as a film actress*, are always artistic.[30]

One more quote to shed light on Asta Nielsen's reception among the regular audience. Anastasia Tsvetaeva (1894–1993) was a teenager, a daughter of a university professor, later a poetess and the sister of a much more famous poetess, Marina Tsvetaeva. In her memoirs she looked back to the amusements of her youth in pre-revolutionary Moscow:

> "Bored! You too? Let's go to the cinema!" And off we went. Sometimes we would end up in – there were many those days – a romantic, complicated plot of a picture starring Asta Nielsen, an actress of inimitable talent and charm. Her thin, sharp face, enormous dark eyes, always tragic roles, her masterfully created characters, full of grace and grief, courage to stand up until the end, – what a wonderful community we found, after crossing the hostile lobby, filled with people and banality, to a dark hall and the flickering of a moonlit screen. Asta Nielsen! She is impossible to forget.[31]

Typically Tsvetaeva, the daughter of the intelligentsia, is not nostalgic to cinema itself. On the contrary, she describes the film theatre as a "hostile" place full of "banality" – the word *poshlost* she uses is the very typical word a member of the Russian intelligentsia would use of petty-bourgeois bad taste and kitsch. Although written in retrospect, this quote reflects very well the general tone of the intellectual discourse around Asta Nielsen: cinema is a great invention, and although its present state is pitiful, a few exemplary figures like Asta Nielsen show the way to what cinema could be in the future.

Russian Asta Nielsens

As already said, before 1915 no Russian actress or actor could challenge Asta Nielsen or the other foreign favourites in popularity. Nevertheless the Russian producers began to realise that the way to the audience's heart was through charismatic actors. Early on Asta Nielsen became an example for a number of female film actors, most clearly the later director Olga Preobrazhenskaia (1881–1971), who made her film debut in Vladimir Gardin's successful melodrama KLIUCHI SCHASTIA (THE KEYS TO HAPPINESS, 1913). The young Preobrazhenskaia was an astounding Asta Nielsen look-alike who, judging by the few existing fragments of her films, imitated not only Nielsen's outward character, but many aspects of her acting style as well.[32] Like other aspiring Russian Asta Nielsens, however, Preobrazhenskaia found more resonance with the critics than with the audience, and Nielsen was left unrivalled in popularity.

In the spring of 1914 an article titled "Russian Asta Nielsens" in *Sine-fono* started to show signs of frustration over the lack of appeal of Russian actors. The author blamed Russian producers for relying entirely on the celebrities of the dramatic stage and not doing anything to train specifically cinematic actors: "So far our own Asta Nielsens and Garrisons sit at the far corners of the province waiting in vain for an opportunity to bring their young effort, energy,

Actress Olga Preobrazhenskaia (1881–1971), a picture postcard (c. 1914).

and talent for the new line of business – the cinema".³³ So it went until the summer of 1914. In July, despite ominous clouds of the coming war, Russian film trade waited happily for autumn: the new 'Asta Nielsen series', imported by Thiemann & Reinhardt, was already booked for the entire season, and Asta Nielsen was expected to do a guest performance in St. Petersburg in September.³⁴ Then one day Russia and Germany were at war. In the atmosphere of nationalistic enthusiasm following the declaration of war even the films of the neutral Denmark were at times under suspicion, not to mention German products which were entirely banned. Asta Nielsen disappeared practically overnight, and as far as pre-revolutionary film culture is considered, nothing was heard of her ever since.

Before the First World War only around ten per cent of the films that were seen in Russia were of Russian origin. The war closed borders and initially isolated the country from the European film market, which changed the situation to the extreme opposite. "The Klondike was opened",³⁵ as film

A Russian poster of Pola Negri's debut film NIEWOLNICA ZMYSLÓV (1914): "THE GREATEST RUSSIAN HIT! An engaging plot! An incredible production! Starring Pola Negri, The Russian Asta Nielsen! SLAVE OF PASSION, SLAVE OF VICE!"

director Vladimir Gardin put it in his memoirs, and the Russian companies now rushed to fill the gap with domestic productions. The biggest gap was left by Asta Nielsen. No one could replace 'Astochka' of course, but the Russian companies cannot be blamed for not trying, and the search for the Russian Asta Nielsen switched to top gear. Given the circumstances, even a Polish actress was close enough, as the advertisement of the Polish film NIEWOLNICA ZMYSŁÓW (SLAVE OF PASSIONS), produced by Sfinks in Warsaw, testifies: "Sensation! Starring Pola Negri, the Russian Asta Nielsen!"[36]

During 1915, now that Asta Nielsen was gone, one by one the Russian actors were finally able to make their breakthrough, and again all the greatest stars, with the notable exception of Ivan Mozzhukhin, were women – 'Queens of the Screen', as they were called in Russia. Vera Karalli (1889–1972), prima ballerina of The Imperial Ballet, debuted in the autumn of 1914, in the next spring Olga Gzovskaia (1889–1962), a star of the Moscow Art Theatre, began her much appraised film work, and June saw the debut of Vera Kholodnaia (1893–1919), the greatest legend of pre-revolutionary Russian cinema. The next three to four years could well be named the "Golden Age of Russian Film Actresses" – ending perhaps with Kholodnaia's untimely death in 1919.

Finally, although Asta Nielsen disappeared into thin air, she was certainly not forgotten. Lev Kuleshov (1899–1970), the founding father of Soviet cinema, wrote a great deal about film acting. In his writings he famously loathed the whole 'bourgeois' pre-revolutionary tradition with its actors like Mozzhukhin and Kholodnaia, but he also cherished the memory of the few pioneering figures of what he considered real cinema, and more than once mentioned Asta Nielsen in this group. In 1923, in an essay on Conrad Veidt, Kuleshov compared Veidt with Nielsen and wrote: "[Asta Nielsen's] name is as important and precious to us as the names of Mary Pickford, Chaplin, the director Griffith and other great teachers".[37] Kuleshov himself found his ideal 'model actor' in his wife Aleksandra Khokhlova (1897–1985). Maybe it is not too far-fetched to see in this expressive actress a late incarnation of Asta Nielsen on the Soviet screen?

Notes

1. R. Mech, "Liubimtsy publiki", *Sine-fono*, no. 5 (1 December 1908): 4.
2. Cf. Catherine A. Schuler, *Women in the Russian Theatre: The Actress in the Silver Age* (London and New York: Routledge, 1996), 1–18 and passim.
3. All dates in my paper are according to the 'old style' Julian calendar which was used in Russia until 1918. Add thirteen days for corresponding dates in the Gregorian calendar.
4. Sfinks advertisement, *Sine-fono*, no. 5 (1 December 1910): 38.
5. Progress advertisement, ibid., 43.
6. "Khronika", *Kine-zhurnal*, no. 23 (8 December 1910): 11.
7. Cf. Andrzej Dębski's essay in this volume.
8. On Gechtman and Globus cf. for example V.P. Mikhailov, *Rasskazy o kinematografe staroi Moskvy* (Moscow: Maternik, 2003), 78–80.
9. This typical argument appeared around the same time with AFGRUNDEN's first advertisements: cf. editorial, *Sine-fono*, no. 6 (15 December 1910): 5–6.
10. Adverts, *Novoe vremia*, St. Petersburg (29 December 1910), 1; (30 December 1910): 1; (2 January 1911), 1; *Russkiia vedomosti*, Moscow (11 January 1911): 6; (16 January 1911): 6.
11. Cf. for example "Khronika", *Sine-fono*, no. 10 (15 February 1911): 15; "Khronika", *Vestnik kinematografii*, no. 5 (19 February 1911): 18.
12. Editorial, *Kine-zhurnal*, no. 24 (23 December 1910): 5–6; editorial, *Kine-Zhurnal*, no. 2 (22 January

1911): 5–7; Z.L.Sheinbaum, "Gde predel?", *Sine-fono*, no. 11 (1 March 1911): 11; editorial, *Vestnik kinematografii* , no. 14 (1 July 1911), 9–10; S.M. Nikolskii, "Perli 'svobodnoi' konkurentsii", *Sine-fono*, no. 2 (15 October 1911): 11–12.

13. Rashit M. Iangirov, "Censorship and Film distribution in Russia, 1908–1914", in Frank Kessler and Nanna Verhoeff (eds), *Networks of Entertainment: Early Film Distribution 1895–1915* (Eastleigh: John Libbey, 2007), 82–83.

14. "Na skolskom puti", *Vestnik kinematografii*, no. 12 (1 June 1911): 14.

15. "Bezdna (s natury)", *Sine-fono*, no. 7 (1 January 1912): 11

16. In December 1910 Khanzhonkov debated the issue with Globus's Abram Gechtman in a meeting of film entrepreneurs in Moscow. Gechtman defended exclusive films as luxury products, comparable with expensive shoes which some can afford and some not. Khanzhonkov opposed the argument: "It is not the buyer of the exclusive film who is doing injustice, but the seller. Your example with the shoes is out of place here: a shoe store sells fine shoes to everyone, but the seller of exclusive films sells his product to one customer only." "Protokol 2-go soveshaniia sinematograficheskikh deitelei, sostoiavshagosia 20 oktiabria v g. Moskve", *Sine-fono*, no. 5 (1 December 1910): 19.

17. Globus & Sfinks advertisement, *Sine-fono*, no. 23 (1 September 1911): 38–39.

18. *Vestnik kinematografii*, no. 21 (17 October 1911): 10–11.

19. Aleksandr Khanzhonkov, *Pervye gody russkoi kinematografii* (Leningrad: Iskusstvo, 1937), 54–55.

20. Nemonopolist, "Monopolizatsiia kartiny 'Oborona Sevastopolia'", *Sine-fono*, no. 3 (1 November 1911): 11.

21. Khanzhonkov, *Pervye gody*, 55.

22. Mintus advert, *Sine-fono*, no. 15 (1 May 1911): 38.

23. Globus & Sfinks advert, *Vestnik kinematografii*, no. 23 (1 September 1911): 45–46

24. Thiemann & Reinhardt advert, *Sine-fono*, no. 3 (1 November 1911): 2; review of the film ibid., 19.

25. Iurii Tsivian, "Asta Nilsen v zerkale russkoi kultury", *Kinovedcheskie zapiski 40* (1998): 259.

26. Tanagra advert, *Sine-fono*, no. 18 (15 June 1912): 44–45.

27. "Rezultaty ankety priniatoi teatrom 'Modern' v Kharkove", *Sine-fono*, no. 8 (5 January 1913): 31.

28. See for example, "Po tekhnike kinematografa: I: Na scene i na ekrane", *Vestnik kinematografii*, no. 12 (15 June 1913): 6–7; S.G.U. "Sila ekrana", *Vestnik kinematografii*, no. 16 (10 August 1913): 12–14; M. Brailovskii, "Russkie Asty Nilsen", *Sine-fono*, no. 17 (25 May 1914): 26–28.

29. "Peterburg", *Vestnik kinematografii*, no. 6 (23 March 1913): 18.

30. "Artisty khudozhestvennago teatra o kinematografe", *Sine-fono*, no. 16 (10 May 1914): 23.

31. Quoted in N.M. Zorkaia, *Na rubezhe stoletii: U istokov massovogo iskusstva v Rossii, 1900–1910 godov* (Moscow: Iskusstvo, 1976), 48, 50.

32. Four fragments of films with Preobrazheskaia are known to exist. Most recently in 2007 film historian Pyotr Bagrov discovered a one and a half minute fragment of *Kliuchi schastia*, the in many ways water-shed film for Russian cinema. I wish to thank Bagrov for an opportunity to see the fragment.

33. M. Brailovskii, "Russkie Asty Nilsen", *Sine-fono*, no. 17 (25 May 1914): 7.

34. "Khronika", *Sine-fono*, no. 20 (5 July 1914): 38; "Peterburg", *Vestnik kinematografii*, no. 11 (7 June 1914): 25.

35. V.R. Gardin, *Vospominaniia*: Tom I (Moscow: Goskinoizdat, 1949), 88.

36. *Kine-zhurnal*, no. 1–2 (17 January 1915): 12. This misleading advertisement gave birth to the long-lasted legend in Russian film literature according to which Pola Negri debuted in Russia. Cf. Bengt Idestam-Almquist, *Rysk film: En konstart blir till* (Stockholm: Wahlström & Wildstrand, 1962), 125.

37. Lev Kuleshov, "Konrad Feidt", *Sobranie sochinenii v trekh tomakh: 1 Teoriia, kritika, pedagogika* (Moscow: Iskusstvo 1987), 92–93.

Ansje van Beusekom

Distributing, Programming and Recycling Asta Nielsen Films in the Netherlands, 1911–1920

When Asta Nielsen visited the Netherlands as the guest of honour at the International Cinema Exhibition (Internationale Kino Tentoonstelling, IKT) in Amsterdam in the summer of 1920, she received a warm welcome from her fans, who went out into the street to hail her. The press clippings on her reception leave no doubt that Nielsen was still the best-known film celebrity among Dutch cinema audiences in 1920.[1] Which Asta Nielsen films could these audiences have seen where, when and how in Dutch cinemas and other venues before 1920, and who imported, distributed and programmed them? Thanks to *Cinema Context*, a digital encyclopaedia of film culture in the Netherlands from 1896, it is possible to sketch a more detailed answer to these questions.[2] The website tells us:

> *Cinema Context* consists of four data collections that inform us about the fundamentals of film culture: films, cinemas, people and companies. Networks and patterns in film culture may be analysed on the basis of this data. *Cinema Context* offers pure information, while it avoids images.[3]

Since 2006, the digital database *Historische Kranten* of the Koninklijke Bibliotheek is accessible to the public, making research in advertisements and writings in national and regional newspapers less time-consuming.[4] A large part of the data in *Cinema Context* is drawn from reports and advertisements traceable in *Historische Kranten*, but the sources themselves are not in it. *Cinema Context* and *Historische Kranten* are therefore complementary. I will focus firstly on 1911 and the pre-war years, and continue with the creative programming during the First World War and after.

1911: DEN HVIDE SLAVEHANDEL (THE WHITE SLAVE) and AFGRUNDEN (THE ABYSS)

In most countries, Asta Nielsen's road to stardom started with the Danish production AFGRUNDEN, produced in the summer of 1910 by Kosmorama in Copenhagen. Everyone who has read Martin Loiperdinger's article on AFGRUNDEN in Germany knows how decisive this film was in turning over

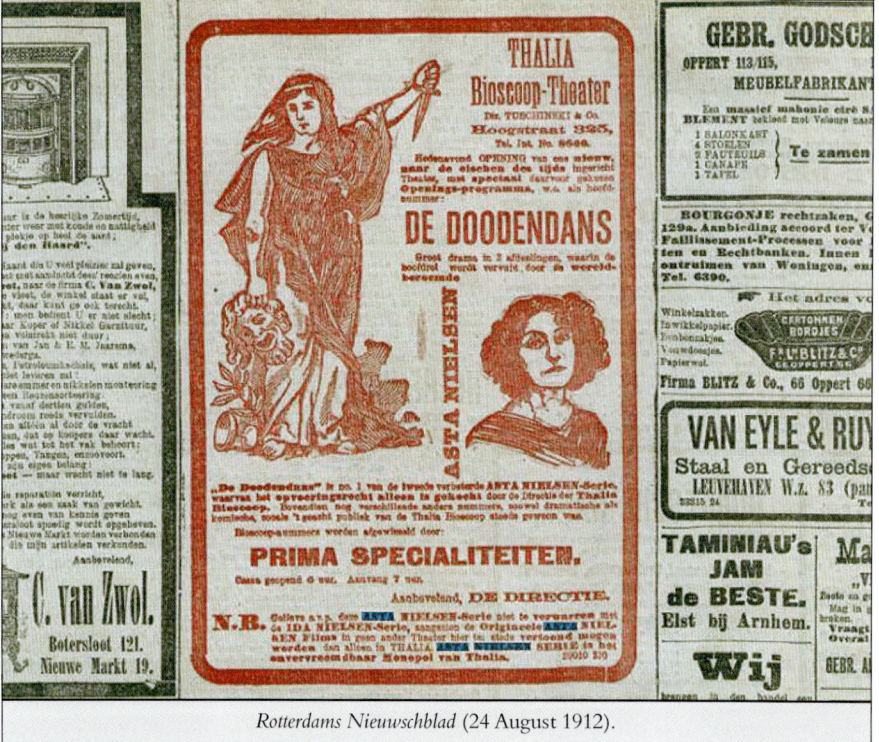

Rotterdams Nieuwschblad (24 August 1912).

the system of cinema exhibition of short film programmes to a system we are still more or less familiar with: the long feature film accompanied by commercials, shorts and until not so long ago, newsreels.[5] Following Corinna Müller's studies from the 1990's, Loiperdinger analyses the crisis in film production and programming that became less and less profitable for producers, distributors and cinema owners alike in Germany. Something had to change. The introduction of the system of exclusive exhibition rights, tied up with a star system, made possible a regular production of feature-length films of one hour or more. It became the solution in providing the large and lavishly furnished cinema theatres in the centres of big cities in Germany with suitable film programmes from October 1911 on. Asta Nielsen's name was treated by the industry as a brand name in order to label the German 'Asta Nielsen series'.[6] The latter were manufactured and distributed in a new financing system based on blind selling and block booking. Exclusivity and seriality were among its main aspects and the name Asta Nielsen guaranteed a continuity in expectations. She played the leading lady in many different roles. In trade as well as newspapers adverts, the name Asta Nielsen would therefore function as a mark of recognition and a certain quality. This strategy would not have worked if there had not been a truly great actress at work, and according to the contemporary critics she was marvellous.[7]

What struck me most in Loiperdinger's article is that all these cinemas, for example, in Hamburg, were already built and in use as cinemas. The situation in the Netherlands was quite different. In 1911 even the few purpose-built cinemas in Amsterdam such as Nöggerath's Bioscope Theater often programmed variety acts and popular theatre next to films. In the Netherlands the boom in cinema theatres started at the end of 1911 and continued in 1912 and 1913.

However, before AFGRUNDEN two other Danish productions, DEN HVIDE SLAVEHANDEL (THE WHITE SLAVE), and DEN HVIDE SLAVEHANDELS SIDSTE OFFER (IN THE HANDS OF IMPOSTORS) produced by Nordisk Film and directed by August Blom, were a major success in Dutch cinemas. Starting screenings of the first film in January 1911 in Rotterdam, it was shown first in the major cities and, in that summer, also in the provinces in all kinds of cinema programmes and travelling shows, from multi-purpose buildings to fairground cinemas.[8] In Rotterdam the film was advertised with the slogan: overwhelming success in all the cities of Europe and America. The second half of March 1911, three cinemas in Amsterdam, Nöggerath's Bioscope theatre, Mullens' Grand Théâtre and Gildemeijer's Union theater (all very near to each other) showed it for two weeks at the same time.[9] Here we encounter a situation that might call for an exclusive system, but for the Netherlands it was a unique situation.[10] The success of this film was much greater than that of any of the Asta Nielsen films; in fact, it was greater than that of any long film exhibited before 1920, according to the hit list drawn form *Cinema Context* (Table 1).

Table 1: Top ten of all popular films shown in The Netherlands before 1920, as measured by the number of weeks on screen. Source: www.cinemacontext.nl

	Original title	Hits
1	*Den Hvide Slavehandels sidste offer* (1911)	54
2	*Quo vadis?* (1912)	54
3	*L'Enfant de Paris* (1913)	42
4	*La Vie et la passion de Jésus Christ* (1903)	41
5	*Klovnen* (1917)	38
6	*Maciste* (1915)	32
7	*Cabiria* (1914)	31
8	*Maciste alpino* (1916)	29
9	*From the manger to the cross* (1912)	29
10	*Heisses Blut* (1911)	29

DEN HVIDE SLAVEHANDELS SIDSTE OFFER and, in its wake, other 'white slave' films prepared Dutch audiences for the long-feature films that would follow. Apart from its high frequency of screenings, there was no mention of exclusivity by any of the cinemas, whereas AFGRUNDEN would be advertised shortly afterwards, mentioning exclusivity and 'monopol'.

AFGRUNDEN was the first Asta Nielsen film shown in the Netherlands,

Het Centrum (24 March 1911).

although the first adverts by the cinemas that showed the film did not mention her name. The earliest advert I was able to trace was that of Bioscoop-Salon Vreeburg in Utrecht, published on 20 March 1911 in the Catholic newspaper *Het Centrum*.[11] It mentioned the title AFGRONDEN as a triumph of the cinema. The film was screened from Monday to Friday and the last day was again advertised, now with the supplement: "with a skilful interpretation by Mr. Louis Hartlooper".[12] The advert mentioned exclusive exhibition rights for Utrecht. Performances were scheduled every hour: from 6.30 to 9.30. On 13 April the Grand Théâtre of Albert Frères (owned by Albert Mullens) in Amsterdam announced a 'Groot Realistisch Drama LEVENS AFGRONDEN' (LIFE'S ABYSS) on the evenings of Saturday, Sunday and Monday, the Easter weekend, starting at 8.15 pm.[13] According to its adverts, cinema Scala in Rotterdam had exclusive exhibition rights for The Netherlands and the colonies for AFGRUNDEN, and in this case the artists of the Royal Theatre of Copenhagen were mentioned, though not by name. *Cinema Context* shows that Scala programmed the film from 1 to 3 April 1911 and from 5 May to 12 June 1911, with a short break from 12 to 19 May, when the film was exhibited in Leeuwarden in cinema Friso. An extension policy such as this, longer than a month in the same cinema, was a new phenomenon in the Netherlands. In Vlissingen AFGRUNDEN was exhibited in the Cinema Pathé in July 1911, in three parts on three different days.[14] In the meantime, Asta Nielsen's second film, HEISSES BLUT (BURNING BLOOD), was also shown in May 1911, starting on 5 May, two weeks after its release in Berlin.[15]

I go into these first performances in such detail because the performances of feature-length films differed from programme to programme. Either the long feature was presented as a single film standing alone, which would then have been a short programme of less than one hour, so that this long film could be screened four times on the same evening, or it was presented as the major attraction in an evening programme, with or without the accompaniment of a lecturer. Moreover, it is worthwhile emphasising how often the notion 'monopol' and its equivalents in Dutch appear in the adverts. In a few months it seemed to have become a synonym for long films. Not only feature films with Asta Nielsen but also Sherlock Holmes adaptations with Viggo Larsen, for instance, were advertised as *Monopolfilms*. However, as long as only one copy of a film circulated, the film was exclusive. This was the case with AFGRUNDEN.

Another announcement that needs special attention is the word 'series'. Before the first 'Asta Nielsen series' was introduced, the word was used by cinema owners to announce a selection of short films, views, 'tableaux' or scenes. The notion '18th Completely New series' by Albert Frères refers to a mode of promotion used by travelling showmen, just like the slogan 'Entirely new programmes!' It refers more to exhibition practices than to particular films.

Distributing AFGRUNDEN and HEISSES BLUT

Who imported AFGRUNDEN and distributed the film for the first screenings is not certain. It could very well have been Franz Anton Nöggerath Jr. since he had imported Nordisk's DEN HVIDE SLAVENHANDEL as well. Nöggerath and, before him, his father were the first film salesmen in the Netherlands from 1898 on. They programmed film in their variety theatre Flora and opened the first purpose-built cinema, Bioscope Theater, in Amsterdam. It was not Jean Desmet because there is no reference this early to AFGRUNDEN found in his archive.[16] Before he went into film distribution, Jean Desmet had a travelling cinema and turned to purpose-built cinemas from 1908 on. It could not have been film tradesman Johan Gildemeijer, either, because he confessed in his *Koningin Kino* of 1914 that he was taken for the first time with Asta Nielsen's performance in the last act of AFGRUNDEN when he saw the film in Amsterdam's Grand Théâtre in April.[17] By mid-July 1911, the Cinema Pathé in Vlissingen hired its copy from Desmet, nonetheless, as is registered in Desmet's customer book that *Cinema Context* uses as archival source.[18] On 19 June, however, the film was shown at the Skating Rink in Rotterdam at the Schiedamsche single.[19]

HEISSES BLUT was distributed by Desmet, who kept all the records of renting it out as *Cinema Context* shows when one searches for the title and performances. The Mullens brothers were among his customers and showed HEISSES BLUT in 1911 as part of their programmes at multi-purpose buildings (Grand Théâtre in Amsterdam and de Haagsche Kunstkring in The Hague), and Albert Frères from Breda presented the film in multi-purpose buildings in cities like Deventer, whereas the travelling cinema of Antoon Wegkamp showed HEISSES BLUT there on the fairground only a week later. *Cinema Context* draws this information from the Desmet customer books, which show that Desmet

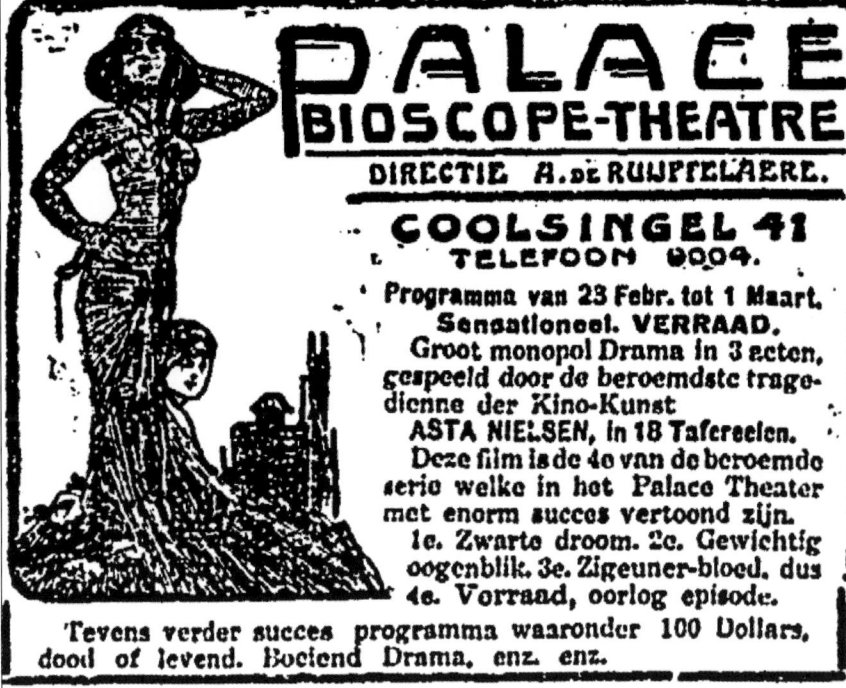

Nieuwe Rotterdamsche Courant (24 February 1912).

sometimes rented out their only copy of the film to all kinds of customers even for just one day.[20] In December 1911, Desmet sent his buyer to Berlin in search of more Asta Nielsen films. The buyer came back only with the Danish Nordisk film BALLETDANSERINDEN (THE BALLET DANCER) and with the Deutsche Bioscop film DER FREMDE VOGEL (THE COURSE OF TRUE LOVE) because Desmet did not want to bind himself to a multi-film contract, as the business model for the 'Asta Nielsen series' required.

In the Netherlands, distribution patterns in 1911 were not neatly organised at all; cinema owners and distributors did their business as they were accustomed to before the exclusive system. They at least did not leave their old practises right away of buying and reselling films from and to each other. Both AFGRUNDEN and HEISSES BLUT were shown in fixed cinemas such as the Pathé theatre in Vlissingen, in multi-purpose venues such as the Grand Théâtre or De Haagsche Kunstkring managed by Albert Frères. HEISSES BLUT was also shown in programmes of travelling cinemas together with short film numbers. Desmet traded films with everybody, even for a single day. In the summer of 1911 at least four travelling cinemas had HEISSES BLUT on their programme, bringing Asta Nielsen to fair grounds deep in the provinces. *Cinema Context* shows that, based on exhibition dates, there were two prints of HEISSES BLUT in circulation at the same time:

Table 2. Asta Nielsen films in the Netherlands to 1914 with simultaneous performances in different locations in the same week. Source: www.cinemacontext.nl

Number of copies	Original title
3	*Engelein* (1914)
2	*Fremde Vogel, Der* (1911)
2	*Heisses Blut* (1911)
2	*Im grossen Augenblick* (1911)
2	*Komödianten* (1912)
2	*Jugend und Tollheit* (1912)
2	*Kinder des Generals, Die* (1912)
2	*Mädchen ohne Vaterland, Das* (1912)
2	*Tod in Sevilla, Der* (1913)
2	*Suffragette, Die* (1913)

As far as I can see there was no competition among the cinemas in the same city or between travelling cinemas on the same fair grounds, so the exclusivity was provided – but this was not a regulated exclusivity as in the German cities, more an exclusivity provided by scarcity. It is quite hard to compete with two copies of the same film circulating in the entire country. Comparing the number of copies of the Asta Nielsen films with that of the 'blockbusters' of the 1910s, we can say that even the incidental four or five copies do not call for a stringent system as the exclusive system.

Table 3. Long-feature hits in the Netherlands to 1914 with simultaneous performances in different locations in the same week. Source: www.cinemacontext.nl

Number of copies	Original title
6	*Padre* (1912)
5	*Le Fils de Lagardère* (1913)
5	*Cabiria* (1914)
4	*Monte Cristo* (1912)
4	*Le Mystère des Roches de Kador* (1912)
4	*From the Manger to the Cross* (1912)
4	*Gli ultimi giorni di Pompei* (1913)
3	*Quo vadis?* (1912)

Asta Nielsen as brand name and then dumped to the colonies

According to his own words, Johan Gildemeijer had exclusivity in September 1911 when he showed DEN SORTE DRØM in his Union cinema in Amsterdam. The Danish and German Nielsen productions entered the Netherlands after AFGRUNDEN through the imports by Jean Desmet and Johan Gildemeijer, who actually fought in 1912 over the rights to show and distribute Nielsen's films, as Ivo Blom points out.[21] Gildemeijer says himself that he was responsible for importing PAGU's *Monopolfilms* from October 1911 on. The first runs of this company were for his affiliated Union theatre and its direct customers, although *Cinema Context* shows that Union was not always the first cinema to show a new Asta Nielsen film. In his opinion, Jean Desmet and his customers were allowed to show re-runs of the PAGU-films after a year or so. Of course,

Nieuwe Rotterdamsche Courant (29 April 1913).

these re-runs were shown in addition to the distribution of other Asta Nielsen titles Desmet had managed to acquire. According to Union's advert in *De Kinematograaf*, announced the season 1913/1914 that contained DIE SUFFRAGETTE (THE SUFFRAGETTE), S1 (A GIRL'S SACRIFICE) and DIE FILMPRIMADONNA (THE FILM PRIMADONNA). "Old movies shown by others are dumped old ones of the season 1911/1912, withdrawn from circulation by us".[22] It was just typical of the Dutch situation that no one seemed to really have the exclusive rights to show Asta Nielsen's films. All Dutch distributors/exhibitors showed and traded them: Nöggerath (FAN), Mullens (Albert Frères), Desmet, Gildemeyer and, from 1912 on, also Abraham Tuschinski. Tuschinski was a Polish immigrant who was on his way to the United States via Rotterdam but stayed in the Netherlands because of his booming businesses. In 1911 he opened his first cinema, Thalia, in Rotterdam and within ten years he would become head of a chain of cinemas in Rotterdam and Amsterdam. A wild story circulating on the Internet mentions a deal between Gildemeijer and Tuschinski: The former would have sold his exclusive rights to the Nielsen films to the latter, but because they were friends they had not made up a written agreement … .[23] Although no other sources confirm the story, Tuschinski would soon become a major exhibitor of Asta Nielsen's films and would stay loyal to her as long as she made films.

Dutch distributors and exhibitors did not tie themselves to the strict 'monopol' regime but adopted particular aspects of the promotion tactics that came along with the 'exclusive' system. From 1912 on, the name Asta Nielsen was much more and much longer advertised in various forms than any other screen or stage star. A browse through the trade weekly *De Kinematograaf* of 1913, the first year of its appearance, shows that Nielsen's name is not mentioned as often as one might expect at the height of her success, but when it happens it is always in a manner of great respect. When Desmet's Apollo theatre in The Hague showed JUGEND UND TOLLHEIT (IN A FIX), "Asta Nielsen's only comedy" [! AvB] it is "Naturally a great success".[24] Except for the French comedians Rigadin, Polidor or Max Linder, who gained success as touring stage personalities before they tried their luck in film, no film star was mentioned by name as early, as often or for so many years as Asta Nielsen was. Next to the trade press, she was also often mentioned in Dutch newspaper adverts: not the film title but her name as most important eye catcher. For a film star this was a new phenomenon in the Netherlands: a privilege reserved for stage stars like Sarah Bernhardt. For the Netherlands one can conclude that Asta Nielsen was by far the best-known and most valued film star in the Netherlands. Not because she performed in the most frequently attended film event of the year, but because she was present in several films all year long, and year after year, as the table drawn from *Cinema Context* shows.

Table 4. Top Ten popular films with Asta Nielsen shown in The Netherlands before 1920, as measured by the number of weeks on screen. Source: www.cinemacontext.nl

Number	Original title	
1	*Heisses Blut* (1911)	29
2	*Engelein* (1914)	20
3	*Das Feuer* (1914)	17
4	*Jugend und Tollheit* (1912)	16
5	*Afgrunden* (1910)	16
6	*Der Tod in Sevilla* (1913)	16
7	*Den sorte Drøm* (1911)	12
8	*Die Sünden der Väter* (1913)	11
9	*In dem großen Augenblick* (1911)	10
10	*Engeleins Hochzeit* (1915)	9

As Martin Loiperdinger has pointed out, the 'monopol' strategy worked out quite well for Germany's larger cities and PAGU's own about 60 cinemas, but it did not work as smoothly in a small country such as the Netherlands because of the small number of copies in circulation. In its capital, Amsterdam, in 1913 the largest number of cinemas was 43 (including every barn or storefront cinema), and hardly any large organisation in film distribution existed. Distributors rather bought films than hired them, a practise Jean Desmet stubbornly persisted in. Gildemeijer managed only the rather small Union 'Elite'-bioscope (300 seats) in the centre of Amsterdam and was foremost an exporter of films to the Dutch Indies after their runs in the Dutch cinemas and could not keep exclusivity on the films he showed. Although Dutch audiences were not always able in later years to see her latest films shortly after their release from the studio, they were able to see them all. Gildemeijer's warning about the last year's series presumably did not have much effect; audiences went to see Asta Nielsen in old or new films alike.

The practice of exporting films to the Dutch Indies that had already had their runs in the Dutch cinemas was common until the First World War. Nine Asta Nielsen films from 1911, 1912, 1913 that had regular showings and re-releases in Dutch cinemas probably were shipped to the colonies. They did not reappear in later years: AFGRUNDEN, HEISSES BLUT, BALLETDANSERINDEN, DER TOTENTANZ, KOMÖDIANTEN, MACHT DES GOLDES, DIE FILMPRIMADONNA, DIE SUFFRAGETTE, DER TOD IN SEVILLA, ZAPATA'S BANDE. Ivo Blom observed that Desmet sometimes very quickly sold his films through to the Dutch Indies, and some of the mentioned copies surely must have suffered this fate.[25] As said before, Johan Gildemeijer started his career in the film business by exporting old films to the Dutch Indies.

Tuschinski's creative Asta Nielsen series during the First World War

Between 1911 and 1914 a building boom in purpose-built cinema can be observed in the Dutch cities, as in any other European city but on a more modest scale. Interesting is that in the most prestigious of these cinemas the opening film often was a Danish feature film or an Asta Nielsen film. This started with Gildemeijer's Union in Amsterdam, Desmet's Apollo in The Hague, Tuschinki's Thalia of 1912 in Rotterdam. Abraham Tuschinski, upcoming cinema chain owner and film distributor in Rotterdam, was one of the loyal theatre owners who showed Asta Nielsen films in his Rotterdam cinemas, Thalia, Royal and Olympia, from 1912 on until the 1920s. Before and during the war he advertised her films in the *Nieuwe Rotterdamsche Courant* and the *Rotterdamsch Nieuwsblad*. In his announcements he regularly juggled with the series and always mentioned Asta Nielsen's name.

During the First World War he managed to present a 'new' Asta Nielsen series every year in September from 1916 on: the Asta Nielsen series 1916/17 containing 14 new titles, while she produced only one new film.[26] Thanks to this sort of creative programming and recycling, Asta Nielsen films never left the film theatres for long. The *Cinema Context* database shows that pre-war films produced in 1914 such as DIE FALSCHE ASTA NIELSEN (THE FALSE ASTA NIELSEN) and ENGELEINS HOCHZEIT (LITTLE ANGEL'S WEDDING) were released in 1916 for the first time, whereas ENGELEIN (UP TO HER TRICKS), after its first release in 1914, had re-runs every year in various programmes until 1918. Many Asta Nielsen films produced in 1915 or 1916 premiered in the Dutch cinemas in 1918.[27] DIE BÖRSENKÖNIGIN (THE QUEEN OF THE STOCK EXCHANGE) of 1916 even had to wait until after the War and was shown in 1919 and 1920.

Cinema Context shows that some early Asta Nielsen films from 1911 to 1914 returned regularly in different programmes throughout the War. At least twelve titles appeared more than once in the cinemas during the war. This mixed programming, often in a double bill format with more recent productions, caused the Asta Nielsen films to compete with more recent productions from various places. IN DEM GROSSEN AUGENBLICK (1911) was re-released in two movie theatres in The Hague in 1916. In one theatre Asta Nielsen had to compete with Italian diva Lyda Borelli in FIOR DI MALE (1916); in the other the film was programmed together with Franz Hofer's DAS ROSA PANTÖFFELCHEN. Asta Nielsen films were programmed together with Danish, Swedish, American, French and German films; she also shared programmes with films by Victor Sjöström, Louis Feuillade, Tom Mix and Charlie Chaplin.

Table 5. Francesca Bertini's top ten films

Number	Original title	
1	La Signora delle Camelie (1915)	28
2	La Tosca (1918)	18
3	Diana, l'affascinatrice (1915)	10
4	Malea (1917)	10
5	Fedora (1916)	9
6	Sangue bleu (1914)	9
7	Ivonne, la bella danzatrice (1915)	9
8	Nel gorgo della vita (1916)	9
9	Nelly la Gigolette (1915)	8
10	Eroismo d'amore (1916)	7

Because of the First World War, film imports were obstructed between 1914 and 1918 or were at least risky, and old stocks of favourites had re-runs more than would have been the case under normal circumstances. Not only were the old Asta Nielsen films cheap, they could also be regarded as Danish, and reckoning with the Netherlands as a neutral state, they brought with them few risks. If we may believe the adverts, Asta Nielsen kept the audience going to the cinema during the difficult years, just as she had before the war. Moreover, she inspired Dutch directors to produce melodramas with Dutch Asta Nielsens: Johan Gildemeijer with Meina Irwen in EEN DANSTRAGEDIE (A DANCE TRAGEDY) and Maurits Binger with Annie Bos, who was the star in various melodramas.[28] Although the production of her films dropped dramatically after 1916, only one film in 1917 and two in 1918, the Dutch cinemas kept on promoting new Asta Nielsen series throughout the War. After the war she was by no means forgotten, but her star-status was no longer beyond criticism.

After the First World War

Nevertheless, the critics kept Asta Nielsen high. Although her lively acting and changes of mood expressed in her face and body were considered of the finest quality, the films she performed in were gradually more disputed. The Dutch critics raised questions such as: Why was she neglected by the industry? Why did no one care to make use of her special skills in good scenarios? The later Asta Nielsen films were not considered better than the early ones, or they did not deserve the predicate 'art' anymore. On the contrary, in 1918, Felix Hageman criticized her more recent productions and favoured her early ones: "If we want to be honest, don't we have to admit that in Asta Nielsen's dramas the line certainly is not going up?"[29] He suggested that the cinemas should re-run her first films and expected that the audience would come running to see them. The Asta Nielsen films were categorized as mainstream 'burgerlijk drama'. From 1916 on, real art was delivered by Italian divas such as Lyda Borelli and Pina Menichelli or the French actress Suzanne Grandais. Those great stage actresses performed in adaptations of famous literary works, whereas Nielsen had to lift up cheap, flimsy melodramas all by herself. When she occasionally performed in films based on famous plays by Strindberg or Ibsen, there were complaints about the dull direction. Moreover, critic Max van Wesel wrote that she had become too old to play little girls. She, like no other, had to be aware of the cruelty of the all-seeing camera in combination with the all-revealing lights.[30]

Table 6. Asta Nielsen's top ten films

Number	Original title	
1	*Heisses Blut* (1911)	29
2	*Engelein* (1914)	21
3	*Das Feuer* (1914)	17
4	*Afgrunden* (1910)	16
5	*Jugend und Tollheit* (1912)	16
6	*Unmögliche Liebe* (1932)	16
7	*Der Tod in Sevilla* (1913)	16
8	*Dirnentragödie* (1927)	15
9	*Die Gesunkenen* (1925)	14
10	*Das Kind ruft* (1914)	13

Table 7. Henny Porten's top ten films

Number	Original title	
1	*Gräfin Donelli* (1924)	16
2	*Das alte Gesetz* (1923)	15
3	*Skandal um Eva* (1930)	14
4	*Die Geierwally* (1921)	14
5	*Krach im Hinterhaus* (1935)	14
6	*Kohlhiesels Töchter* (1920)	13
7	*Ihre Hoheit* (1914)	13
8	*Weh, dass wir scheiden müssen* (1910)	12
9	*Zuflucht* (1928)	11
10	*Die Prinzessin von Neutralien* (1917)	10

The Netherlands had kept her neutrality during the War and, afterwards, considered herself the best place for negotiations and reconciliations between the former belligerent parties. The International Filmexhibition (I.K.T.), organised by Johan Gildemeijer in 1920 in the Amsterdam Concertgebouw was a brave attempt at restoring the broken relations in the international film business after the First World War. Although the event as a whole was considered a flop – the Americans stayed away, the French hardly showed up and the Dutch authorities did not take it seriously – Asta Nielsen's visit was regarded as a success. Critics compared Nielsen's welcoming to that of Sarah Bernhardt, and her performances doubled the number of visitors at the exhibition in the week she was there. The scenes of ENGELEIN (UP TO HER TRICKS) of 1914 and LA DAME AUX CAMELLIAS that she re-enacted live with the Dutch actor Willem van der Veer still stunned her audience.[31] Asta Nielsen surely lived up to the high expectations she had created in her films over the years, but critics were more sceptical. Charlie Chaplin had replaced her as most mentioned name in the newspaper adverts, and during the film contest at the International Cinema Exhibition (Internationale Kino Tentoonstelling, IKT) a jury member said about the 3rd prize winner THE CURE (Chaplin): "I would not dare to say that the acting of Charlie Chaplin is less than that of Asta Nielsen".[32] Still, despite these comments she confirmed that she formed a class by herself. In 1920 publicist Henri Borel emphasised her extraordinary qualities once more as 'electrifying' and 'nervous', angelic as well as devilish. He admits going to the most awful film dramas if only Asta Nielsen starred in it.[33] That she was by no means forgotten after 1920 shows the last top ten list drawn from *Cinema Context*. There are two films of the late 1920s and her very last feature film UNMÖGLICHE LIEBE from 1932 in this list, and Pabst's DIE FREUDLOSE GASSE is not even in it. If we compare the top ten films of Henny Porten, whose fame peaked in the 1920s, Porten and Nielsen changed places.

Notes

1. For a more elaborate report on Asta Nielsen's visits to the Netherlands, see Ansje van Beusekom, "Bühne und Leinwand: Auftritte in den Niederlanden 1911–1920", in Heide Schlüpmann et. al. (eds), *Asta Nielsen. Unmögliche Liebe* (2nd edn) (Vienna: filmarchiv austria, 2010), 396–404.
2. www.cinemacontext.nl, launched in June 2006 is a database designed by Karel Dibbets at the University of Amsterdam. I wish to thank Karel Dibbets for contributing the tables in this article.
3. *Cinema Context*, 'About'.
4. www.HistorischeKranten.kb.nl
5. Martin Loiperdinger, "AFGRUNDEN in Germany: *monopolfilm*, cinemagoing and the emergence of the film star Asta Nielsen", in Daniel Biltereyst, Richard Maltby and Philippe Meers (eds), *Cinema, Audiences and Modernity. New perspectives on European cinema history* (London: Routledge, 2011), 142–153.
6. Corinna Müller, *Frühe deutsche Kinomatographie. Formale, wirtschaftliche und kulturelle Entwicklungen 1907–1912* (Stuttgart and Weimar: Metzler, 1994).
7. Thanks to the work of Karola Gramann and Heide Schlüpmann of the Kinothek Asta Nielsen, we can again today see how marvellous she was!
8. *Rotterdams Nieuwschblad* (20 January 1911).
9. *Algemeen Handelsblad* (16, 18, 20, 21, 24 and 28 March 1911). Adverts by Grand Theatre, Bioscope Theater (Nöggerath) and Union.
10. *Cinema Context*, record F029221

11. Adverts for AFGRUNDEN, *Het Centrum* (20, 22, 24 March 1911).
12. *Het Centrum* (24 March 1911). See also Bert Hogenkamp, "The Impact of Audiovisual Media in the Town of Utrecht. A Research Project at the University of Utrecht", *KINtop 9* (Frankfurt am Main: Stroemfeld, 2000), 117–129.
13. Advert Grand Théâtre, *Algemeen Handelsblad* (13 April 1911).
14. *Cinema Context*, record V078279.
15. Advert Cinema Palace Jean Desmet for HEET BLOED, *Rotterdamsch Nieuwschblad* (8 May 1911).
16. Jean Desmet is notorious for having kept every scrap of paper in his extensive archive. Cf. Ivo Blom, *Jean Desmet and the Early Dutch Film Trade* (Amsterdam: Amsterdam University Press, 2003).
17. Ivo Blom, "Gildemeijer versus Desmet. The Tug-of-War for Asta Nielsen" , ibid., 218–222.
18. *Cinema Context* Archival sources: C026-155, customer book November 1910 – July 1911.
19. *Cinema Context* record V087862.
20. *Cinema Context* record F011494, programmes.
21. Blom, *Jean Desmet*, 218.
22. *De Kinematograaf* 1:46 (1913), 421.
23. Jesse Goossens, "De man die alles voor elkaar krijgt", in Idem, *Tuschinski, droom, legende en werkelijkheid*. www.jessegoossens.nl/tuschinski
24. "Uit de residentie VII", *De Kinematograaf* 1:33 (1913), 226.
25. Blom, *Jean Desmet*, 222.
26. *Nieuwe Rotterdamsche Courant* (31 August 1916).
27. This concerned VORDERTREPPE – HINTERTREPPE, DAS WAISENHAUSKIND, DAS ESKIMOBABY, and DIE ROSE DER WILDNIS.
28. Cf. for the films of Annie Bos: Geoffrey Donaldson, *Of Joy and Sorrow* (Amsterdam: Nederlands Filmmuseum, 1997).
29. Felix Hageman, "Oude films", *De Filmwereld* 1:43 (1918).
30. M.H. van Wesel, "Een praatje over Filmacteurs", *De Filmwereld* 1 (1918), no. 11.
31. "Asta Nielsen op de I.K.T.", *De Filmwereld,* 3:32 (1920).
32. "Filmwedstrijd op I.K.T.", *De Filmwereld* 3:36 (1920).
33. Henri Borel, "Asta Nielsen", *Het Vaderland* (10 November 1920), Avondblad B.

Valdo Kneubühler

Opportunities Gone By
Asta Nielsen Films in France before the First World War

"Over a period of four weeks – a record – L'ABÎME [AFGRUNDEN, THE ABYSS] in the Cinéma Palace,[1] which has purchased exclusive rights to the film for France, has provided for sold-out houses morning and night." This note appeared on 11 March 1911 in the *Ciné-Journal*, one of the first trade journals in France.[2] But neither the actress, nor the director nor the country of origin was mentioned. The actress, however, did not remain anonymous for long. As early as 22 April 1911 her name is mentioned in connection with the film title in an advertisement for the subsequent film LE VERTIGE (HEISSES BLUT, BURNING BLOOD):

> Coming soon
> LE VERTIGE
> The most wonderful drama taken from real life
> that has ever been shown in the cinema,
> interpreted by
> Miss Asta Nielsen
> the famous Danish actress and creator of L'ABÎME[3]

It is obvious that Asta Nielsen had now made her entrance! She started off with a record: four weeks of exclusive screenings with two shows per day in one of the largest Paris cinemas. And that was only the beginning of the sudden interest by the French public for an actress who was to be seen in over 20 films in three years. The trade press adverts designed for the cinema owners must be viewed with a certain amount of scepticism; yet they bear witness to the extraordinary attraction Asta Nielsen exercised on the world of film art. These adverts were also geared at the Balkan countries, Turkey, Romania, Bulgaria, Greece and Serbia. They offer indirect evidence of Asta Nielsen's increasing celebrity in these countries, at least among film traders.

The noteworthy feature of the films from the North is their length: L'ABÎME at 600 metres and LE VERTIGE at 800 metres. "Take advantage of the wave of long-feature films now filling the cinemas!"[4] And it was said of RÊVE NOIR (DEN SORTE DRØM, THE CIRCUS GIRL): "Despite the length of the work, interest did not wane for a second, and the audience – for the most part trade professionals – proved to be impressed by the dramatic plot".[5]

The First Review

The name Urban Gad appeared for the first time in *Le Courrier cinématographique.*, at the end of September 1911, in a whole-page article advertising the release of MATERNITÉ (IN DEM GROSSEN AUGENBLICK, THE GREAT MOMENT). The title – "A Beautiful Film" – is, at first glance, rather mundane. However, after the first section, a real lecture in cinema, the article, framing a photo with a dedication by Asta Nielsen, becomes absolutely effusive:

> [Urban Gad] knows how to surround himself with first-class actors, among whom the famous actress Asta Nielsen, the soul of MATERNITÉ, quite clearly is a cut above the rest. (...) Asta Nielsen (...) is an extraordinary actress who need not shy away from comparison with the greatest dramatic artists of our time such as Eleonora Duse, Réjane or Sarah Bernhardt. Her talent is characterised by a personal touch; she cannot be placed in any school. Above all, she attempts to embody the true life of the character she is portraying, and with such grand simplicity that the theatre no longer exists for the audience. She emits an almost supernatural energy. In the role of the happy mother or wife, she is just as affecting as in the role of the scorned mistress of the small-time gangster. As a sophisticated woman, she is not out of place in any elegant salon. As a dancer or a music-hall artist, on the dance floor or the stage, she remains true to herself. The indefinable and mysterious gaze in her gorgeous eyes is unforgettable. Her acting is distinctive. It overcomes all difficulties. She never exaggerates. That is her strength. She gives everything she must give. Urban Gad can be proud of his actress. Finally, we would like to add that this star in the current artistic heaven shines the brightest, and we are delighted to inform our readers that they will be able to continue applauding her. We are going to provide you with the portrait of the unforgettable artist. *Asta Nielsen* is a unique actress, MATERNITÉ a true masterpiece of film art.[6]

This unsigned article, which was written less than six months after the first screening of an Asta Nielsen film in France, already contains the premises of future commentaries: the comparison with theatre divas, the supernatural and inestimable aspect of her personality, her style of interpretation and, of course, her mysterious gaze. The only thing missing is the analysis of her gestures and body language.

Asta Nielsen in the Headlines

On 14 February 1913, a second lengthy article appeared, signed by a certain Wisby, on the first page of *Le Cinéma et l'Echo du Cinéma réunis*, a large-format trade journal founded the previous year. The article was written on the occasion of the first showing of LES ENFANTS DU GÉNÉRAL (DIE KINDER DES GENERALS, FALSELY ACCUSED) and the announcement of CE QUE FEMME VEUT (JUGEND UND TOLLHEIT, IN A FIX). The article is extremely valuable because it contains a list of the films presented in Paris and explains why the Asta Nielsen films are "well-known in the entire country and famous worldwide". Below a picture of the actress, the author begins his text with the following words: "Asta Nielsen shines brilliantly on the cinema firmament. She is one

Opportunities Gone By – Asta Nielsen Films in France before the First World War

Courrier Cinématographique (30 September 1911).

of the greatest artists in the world." And, after a very naïve biography: "Then she met Urban Gad, director at the Copenhagen Theatre, and they by chance exchanged ideas. They were thirsting for freedom." Her acting is then analysed:

> As she likes to say of herself, *she does not play her roles, she loves them*. To empathise in such a way with her role that she is no longer Asta Nielsen, but the image of the persona she embodies is simply marvellous, unbelievable. You need only to see these two Asta Nielsen films to realise this. The actress is completely reborn

> in each of the two roles, both of which she embodies so vividly and ingeniously and which are so clearly distinguished from each other. (…). And when our readers first learn that Asta Nielsen is an accomplished rider, that she can drive a car and can steer a yacht, then they will understand that she is an outstanding film actress.

The end of the article implies, however, a certain French deficit in comparison with other countries where

> (…) theatres have been built to show people fantastic films. Especially in Germany, in Austria and in the Scandinavian countries. (…) Let us hope, therefore, that we will soon be able to marvel at her in France in the manner she deserves and that other such fantastic films will shortly follow LES ENFANTS DU GÉNÉRAL, whose brilliance and beauty is the admirable performer Asta Nielsen.[7]

All films of the first 'Asta Nielsen series' and several films of the second series, one after the other, were presented in France, between the publication of the two articles, and there was a great amount of advertising in the trade press. Remarkably, the expression "Asta Nielsen, the Duse of the screen", a label Louis Delluc was to take up again in 1919, was used for the first time to announce the film PAUVRE JENNY (DIE ARME JENNY, POOR JENNY).[8] The advertisements for this film gained significance: they now took up a double page and the adverts became more varied. Summaries of the films LES COMÉDIENS (KOMÖDIANTEN, THE HEART OF A PIERROT), LA SUFFRAGETTE (DIE SUFFRAGETTE (THE SUFFRAGETTE), L'AVION S1 (S1, A GIRL'S SACRIFICE), and LA REINE DU CINÉMA (DIE FILMPRIMADONNA, THE PRIMA DONNA) were also printed.

The Silence of the Daily Press and an Homage attributed to Apollinaire

Up to that time, the name Asta Nielsen was mentioned only in the trade press, the only information source about the response to the actress and her films in France. Cinema columns started to appear in some newspapers at regular intervals at the end of 1913. But these were still kept very technical and, appearing only shortly before the war, came too late to communicate the excitement of the world of cinema to the readers. Paradoxically, a brief article in *Comœdia*, a daily newspaper[9] devoted mainly to theatre and poetry, gives us an idea of the admiration the actress enjoyed on both sides of the Rhine:

> Asta Nielsen, the star of Scandinavian film, gave a performance in Frankfurt am Main. She played in a drama by her husband, Urban Gad. If we may believe the newspapers, she was remarkably successful, and the stage was strewn with flowers. The subject of the drama was the perennial but ever new story of Colombina, Harlequin and Pierrot. / The tickets for the following performances are much sought-after. The film prima donnas are triumphing everywhere.[10]

Asta Nielsen, "film prima donna", "triumphs everywhere" – the most well-known French praises in the pre-war period, however, do not stem from the press but can be found in a hagiographical book, written by a certain Pablo Diaz and published by the Lichtbild-Bühne Company in Berlin, in 1920. Diaz had visited Guillaume Apollinaire in Paris in the 1910s and transcribed an extraordinary declaration by the poet:

He pronounced a judgement on the film actress: "She is everything: She is the drunkard's vision and the lonely man's dream. She laughs like a girl who's happy, and her eyes know of things so subtle and shy that no word is ever uttered about them. She has the delicacy of a Japanese woman [from] Utamaros' most infamous prints and the panache of Yvette Guilbert when she sings a night song from Montrouge. When hate speaks from Asta Nielsen's eyes, our hands close into fists, and when she opens her eyes the stars shine down".[11]

Paris artists and literati took up a position with this, if only orally transmitted homage. Diaz describes the incredible effect the entrance of this "satanic black diva with her black-lined eyes looking up at a gaucho", an allusion to AFGRUNDEN, eyes that "bewitched an entire city", had on the Parisian bohemian scene, to which he belonged.[12] Michel Décaudin, Guillaume Apollinaire specialist and scholarly publisher of his works, declares in his essay "Apollinaire" that he could find no trace of this homage.[13]

End of the Play

The First World War was to interrupt Asta Nielsen's French carrier over a long period. The last mention of her name in the pre-war press can be found in a brief article by Wagner, correspondent in Berlin, in the column "Chronique allemande" of the *Courrier cinématographique* from 28 March 1914 announcing the screening of her new film DAS FEUER (VENGEANCE IS MINE) in Germany, a film, however, which seemingly was not screened in France anymore. It was seven years later that there was talk of a new Asta Nielsen film, HAMLET, and eight years later that another was screened, VANINA. For this film, she is described as "the great *Swedish* artist"! But the First World War was not the only reason for this long interruption. In May 1916, Henri Diamant-Berger states in his editorial in the magazine *Le Film*:

> Cinema in France is going through a crisis (…). It is said that solely the war was the single cause; however, I disagree with that energetically. The war has brutally uncovered a situation that was becoming increasingly more difficult. It merely accelerated our problem, which is the truth. (…) It has at least freed us from the German competition, which was becoming ever more serious.[14]

With the same protectionist logic, entrenching themselves behind an ideological façade, the cinema owners, directly after the end of the hostilities, "obligated themselves not to show any films of [their] old enemy for ten years",[15] that is, to boycott German films.

It was not until the summer of 1921 that the German-French film cooperation began to revive, and, starting in March 1922, a few months after the screening of DAS CABINET DES DR. CALIGARI in the Ciné Opéra, relationships were finally normalised.[16] In addition, it was more than unlikely that the film MOD LYSET (TOWARDS THE LIGHT), starring Asta Nielsen and produced by Nordisk in Denmark, and premiered in Copenhagen in July 1919, would be shown in France. As early as 1916, a controversy arose over the alleged cooperation of Nordisk with Germany. Delluc regretted this allegation: "The war robbed us of almost all of Nordisk's films because of the numerous German films they temporarily promoted".[17] Despite the long-lasting caesura in her French carrier, Asta Nielsen was not forgotten:

> Her films are prohibited in France since it is known that they were financed by German funds. It is regrettable that they are not screened for professional audiences, at least, in order to keep them informed. Four years ago, Asta Nielsen dominated the screens of the entire world. The Germans respect her as a great artist. We do as well.[18]

A longer version of this contribution was published as "Verpasste Gelegenheiten. Asta Nielsen und Frankreich" in Heide Schlüpmann et al. (eds), *Unmögliche Liebe. Asta Nielsen, ihr Kino* (2nd edn) (Vienna: filmarchiv austria, 2010).

Notes

1. Opened in 1907, the Cinéma-Palace (42, boulevard Bonne-Nouvelle) was the first Paris film palace. With 350 seats, it offered the exclusive opportunity of projecting films even in lighted screening rooms beginning in 1908. Cf. Jean-Jacques Meusy, *Paris-Palaces ou le temps des cinémas, 1894–1918* (Paris: CNRS Editions, 1995).
2. *Ciné-Journal*, no. 133 (11 March 1911).
3. *Ciné-Journal*, no. 139 (22 April 1911).
4. *Ciné-Journal*, no. 140 (29 April 1911).
5. *Ciné-Journal*, no. 168 (11 November 1911): 41.
6. *Le Courrier Cinématographique*, no. 12 (30 September 1911).
7. Ibid.
8. Louis Delluc, "L'Allemagne, la guerre et le cinéma", *Paris-Midi* (22 February 1919).
9. This essay also was published in *Le Courrier cinématographique*, no. 40 (4 October 1913), as both journals were linked. This version contains more information about the Asta Nielsen films in Germany than in France!
10. *Comœdia* (6 October 1913).
11. Pablo Diaz, *Asta Nielsen. Eine Biographie unserer populären Künstlerin*, Berlin 1920, 6–8.
12. Ibid.
13. Michel Décaudin, "Apollinaire" (Paris: Références, 2002). For this essay, Décaudin received the *Grand Prix de la Critique littéraire* from the French section of the PEN club.
14. *Le Film*, no. 10 (20 May 1916).
15. Cf. "Victoire française" (notice under the heading: 'Information'), *Comœdia*, (2 August 1921).
16. Cf. "Protestation" (notice under the heading: 'Cinemas: Information'), *Comœdia* (14 April 1921).
17. "Le Cinquième Art", *Le Film*, no. 113 (13 May 1918).
18. Louis Delluc, *Cinéma & Cie: confidences d'un spectateur* (Paris: 1919), 314.

Richard Abel

Asta Nielsen's Flickering Stardom in the USA, 1912–1914

"The Bernhardt of the Danish Stage." "The German Bernhardt." "Sweden's Bernhardt." Even "The Bernhardt of Switzerland". In 1912, when a half dozen films starring Asta Nielsen were imported into the USA, these were the epithets or clichés that circulated in the trade press and newspapers. Although these could be seen as cross-border evidence that her status and versatility as an actress in Europe should make her famous in America, I am afraid they actually suggest how difficult it was for Americans to pin down exactly who was Asta Nielsen. More important, I am also afraid they suggest how little impact she and her films had in the USA, especially compared to the celebrity she enjoyed throughout Europe. So let me first survey the range of trade press and newspaper discourse about Asta Nielsen – from distributor and exhibitor ads to articles and reviews – during what Jennifer Bean has called the two "waves" of her films' releases, in early 1912 and again in early 1914.[1] Then I will hazard some reasons for why Nielsen and her films had so little success – why, in effect, she did not 'go over' on the American market – by analyzing the industrial and cultural contexts within which she made her appearances as an actress, persona, and star.

Publicity for the first wave of Asta Nielsen films began in late March 1912 with the two-reel WOMAN ALWAYS PAYS (AFGRUNDEN), released on 18 April by Carl Laemmle's IMP Films. Laemmle promoted this two-reel film rather extensively in the *Motion Picture News*, *New York Dramatic Mirror*, and *New York Morning Telegraph*, once pretending that the "German Bernhardt" was now an IMP, hailing the film as "sensationally strong in plot, acting, and staging", and boasting that "exhibitors and exchanges in several cities (...) have shown the wildest enthusiasm".[2] At the time, most other foreign film imports of multiple reels were distributed through what was called the state rights system, so it is puzzling to find Laemmle buying the rights for a "regular release". It also is unusual that a full-page IMP Films ad in the *Motion Picture News* quoted from an article in its rival trade paper, the *Moving Picture World*: Asta Nielsen's name "stands on a par with that of Julia Marlowe in this country, or with Sarah Bernhardt's name in France" and Mrs. Patrick Campbell's in England".[3] Given this hype, trade press reviews of WOMAN ALWAYS PAYS were mixed. The *New York Morning Telegraph* praised the staging, atmosphere, and photography but was disappointed with Asta Nielsen, due to "the extraordinary amount of [advance] advertising".[4] An exhibitor reported in the *Moving Picture World* that the film's sensational "story is perfectly clear and smooth", "extremely well photographed" (with "most delightful backgrounds"), and "naturally acted, with Nielsen in the leading role".[5] Yet the *New York Dramatic Mirror* found the film "far from perfect" in construction, especially in the first reel: "Situations and scenes are jumped from and glided over, showing little dramatic sequence or logical reason".[6] Highlighting the "great scene" of the gaucho dance that has come to define the film, this review intriguingly noted that "essential points (...) have evidently been cut out by some overscrupulous authority".[7]

WOMAN ALWAYS PAYS was a Danish production, which may explain why Laemmle released only that one film. In fact, just as IMP Films was promoting this Danish import, the *Moving Picture World*, perhaps as part of its campaign to support multiple-reel features, printed a lengthy article introducing Asta Nielsen as a leading stage actress in "Teutonic countries" who recently had made "a series of dramas" for Deutsche Bioscop in Germany.[8] The Walturdaw Company of London was said to have negotiated the North American rights to six of these German films with the Tournament Film Company of Toledo, Ohio, a state rights distributor. The first of these, also released in April 1912, was the three-reel GIPSY BLOOD (ZIGEUNERBLUT) in which Asta Nielsen plays a "gipsy girl" in what the *Moving Picture World* described as a sensational plot with many twists and turns.[9] She has a clandestine love affair with a baron, obeys "her thieving instincts" to steal some of his money, casts blame on her hated father, eventually marries the baron and has a child, is betrayed when he takes up with the countess to whom he was once engaged, leaves the baron with her child under cover of a faked suicide, and years later returns the child secretly to the now married aristocratic couple. The only other Tournament release to receive any notice in the trade press was the three-reel THE TRAITRESS (DIE VERRÄTERIN), in which Asta Nielsen plays an aristocratic French woman caught up in another sensational plot set during the Franco-Prussian war. Despite her patriotic ardor, she falls in love with a German lieutenant who scorns her, so she betrays him to capture and death by firing squad, negotiates with the French officer who loves her for his release (the German refuses), crosses French lines to help plan a German attack and rescue, and eventually expires in the dying French officer's arms. In promoting THE TRAITRESS, the *Moving Picture World* sought to highlight the "possibilities for emotional work by Miss Nielsen", especially praising the "mobility of expression" in her facial features.[10]

How widely these early Asta Nielsen films circulated in exhibition is uncertain, as is a clear sense of their reception. There are few traces of WOMAN ALWAYS PAYS, but one story in the *Iowa City Press* did promote a Friday night screening by reproducing part of the *Moving Picture World* article that had lauded Nielsen

IMP Films ad, *Moving Picture World* (6 April 1912); also in *Motion Picture News* (6 April 1912).

a month before.[11] There are more traces of GIPSY BLOOD, and several small town theater ads are noteworthy for their tactics. The Eagle cinema, in Hamilton, Ohio, lured its audience by describing the scene that sets up the film's plot, and nothing more; the Columbia cinema in Athens, Ohio, highlighted this "most gifted actress" and "her daring and sensational role".[12] There are even more traces of THE TRAITRESS, and the first, by contrast, came in a typically tiny ad for a mid-week screening at the Virginia, a major theater in Washington, D.C.[13] This was but one of a weekly series of screenings that the Virginia must have contracted with Tournament Film, beginning with GIPSY BLOOD on 27 May and THE TRAITRESS on 5 June, followed by two other Asta Nielsen titles not mentioned in the trade press: THE MIGHT OF GOLD (DIE MACHT DES GOLDES) on 12 June and A STRANGE BIRD (DER FREMDE VOGEL) on 18 June.[14] For the latter, the Virginia made a wary promise: "Money refunded if dissatisfied." In the shoe factory town of Lynn, Massachusetts, the Central Square Theatre arranged a similar series featuring only GIPSY BLOOD and THE TRAITRESS: one for the first three days of the Labor Day holiday week, the other for the next three days.[15] That summer Tournament Film turned into U.S. Feature Film to distribute popular "novelty foreign pictures", among them Asta Nielsen films.[16] THE TRAITRESS, for instance, appeared at the Empress cinema in Toledo, Ohio, the Royal in Janesville, Wisconsin, the Palace in Altoona, Pennsylvania, the Bijou in Racine, Wisconsin (the day after Christmas), and the Mozart in Los Angeles, which featured the film for an entire week.[17] Three other titles unmentioned in the trade press also had one-day screenings at the Virginia, in Washington: THE BAREFOOT DANCER (DAS MÄDCHEN OHNE VATERLAND) on 28 October 1912, POOR JENNY (DIE ARME JENNY) on 18 November 1912, and MOTHS (NACHTFALTER) on 12 February 1913.[18]

For the rest of 1913, Asta Nielsen's name vanished from the American trade press, newspapers, and movie screens. Despite all the promotional rhetoric that equated her with Bernhardt and celebrated her acting prowess, her potential stardom flickered out. In December, however, a second wave of new German films emerged, this time as regular releases from Pathé-Frères; a major distributor of French films on the German market before the First World War, Pathé seems not to have reciprocated by importing German films onto the French market. What prompted the French company to import more of Nielsen's films onto the American market? Was it her unusually sustained popularity in Europe (including Great Britain), the growing influx of other imported German films, or the US affiliate's need to fill out or balance its weekly releases through General Film? Whatever, between December 1913 and April 1914, Pathé released more than half a dozen multiple-reel films starring Asta Nielsen. First, FALSELY ACCUSED (DIE KINDER DES GENERALS) and LADY MADCAP'S WAY (JUGEND UND TOLLHEIT), followed by BEHIND COMEDY'S MASK (KOMÖDIANTEN), SPANISH BLOOD (DER TOD IN SEVILLA), THE DEVIL'S ASSISTANT (DIE SÜNDEN DER VÄTER), A ROMANY SPY (DAS MÄDCHEN OHNE VATERLAND), and A MILITANT SUFFRAGETTE (THE SUFFRAGETTE).

At least two points are noteworthy about Pathé's trade press promotion. Several films – BEHIND COMEDY'S MASK and THE DEVIL'S ASSISTANT – had been reduced from three reels in the German release prints to just two reels.[19]

Tournament Films ad, *Moving Picture World* (20 April 1912).

Moreover, although Pathé initially banked on Asta Nielsen's name, as in the cross-dressing comedy of LADY MADCAP'S WAY, beginning with THE DEVIL'S ASSISTANT, trade press ads made no mention of her.[20] One ad for A ROMANY SPY quoted three trade press reviews without including her name.[21] Others for A MILITANT SUFFRAGETTE were illustrated by production stills of Nielsen's recognizable face yet made no reference to her name at all.[22]

Trade press reviews and local newspaper ads did keep Nielsen's name in circulation – for a while. The *Dramatic Mirror* described BEHIND COMEDY'S MASK as "an Asta Nielsen film", adding that "her presence insures a film['s] worth" and, as a suffering mother, "she has a story back of her that is strong in its emotional appeal".[23] The same trade paper was even more enthusiastic about THE DEVIL'S ASSISTANT, calling it a "happy blending of a strong story, suggestive acting in the three dominant parts" – notably Asta Nielsen's "remarkably varied acting" as a betrayed artist's model who destroys the painting for which she posed – and "a fine regard for the details that give tone to an artistic production".[24] Assuming that moviegoers would not remember her, the reviewer went on, "more pictures of this caliber are needed to give Asta Nielsen a thoroughly favorable introduction to Americans". In the *Moving Picture World*, two comments from exhibitors (one was more usual) praised the acting, but one confirmed the *Dramatic Mirror*'s remark by having no memory of her earlier films: "The girl playing this part is possessed of a wonderfully strong and expressive face".[25] Reviews of A ROMANY SPY expressed the same level of enthusiasm. The *Dramatic Mirror* lauded "the versatility of Miss Nielsen" and her portrayal of "a conscienceless gypsy girl" but also the film as a superb example of "foreign" productions that "have a leisurely manner of developing a drama" so that characters "become distinct individuals [and] the story is allowed to grow naturally".[26] Although W. Stephen Bush, in the *Moving Picture World*, praised this "finely finished production" and Asta Nielsen's performance "with an inspiration which amounts to genius", his words lost all specificity when quoted in that Pathé ad in the *New York Morning Telegraph*.[27] The last of these releases, A MILITANT SUFFRAGETTE, was not only the longest at five-reels but also the most unusual. The suffragette is a Mrs. Panburne, the British mother of Nellie (played by Asta Nielsen), who first joins the suffrage campaign but then disavows its violence in order to save Lord Ascue, the man she loves. In the *Moving Picture World*, Bush again cited Nielsen's "verve and daring" in this allegedly "attractive picture".[28] "Anti-suffragists (…) are going to enjoy this film immensely", the *Dramatic Mirror* reviewer wrote and then tried to appease suffragists by naively noting they too might like it: "After all, there is nothing in the film to hurt the feelings of anybody in this country".[29]

Similar patterns of avowal and disavowal surface in newspaper ads and stories. Many either highlighted or at least included Nielsen's name: e.g. the ads for FALSELY ACCUSED in Baltimore and Washington, a rare ad for SPANISH BLOOD in Lebanon, Pennsylvania, and others for THE DEVIL'S ASSISTANT in Chicago, Omaha, and Lebanon.[30] Some also revealed that, in contrast to mid-week screenings of LADY MADCAP'S WAY and BEHIND COMEDY'S MASK,[31] THE DEVIL'S ASSISTANT and A ROMANY SPY often were shown on a Friday or a Saturday – from Chicago and Portland, Oregon, to Atlantic, Iowa, and Ann Arbor, Michigan – or even on Thursday through Saturday, in Los Angeles.[32] In mid-April, Pathé's film story of A ROMANY SPY also made a rare appearance as the first of six printed in the *Washington Times*' "Photoplays and Photoplayers" column.[33] Yet there also were signs that interest in Asta Nielsen across the country was falling off. An exceptional full-page ad for The Old Reliable Rockford Picture Parlor in the small town of that name in Illinois listed some two dozen stars featured in General Film companies; the next to last company was Pathé, and Asta Nielsen was accepted, at least by this theater, as a minor Pathé star.[34] In Los Angeles, Miller's theater cited "Eastern critics unite[d] in giving [A Romany Spy] unstinted praise", but made no mention of Nielsen.[35] Although the Oakland Photo Theater still described Asta Nielsen as "the highly talented and famous European star", the manager gave top billing on his Thursday through Saturday program not to A Romany Spy but to Thanhouser Film Corporation's Cardinal Richelieu's Ward, starring Florence La Badie and James Cruze.[36] Most surprising is the brief story, in early May, of a rare screening of A Militant Suffragette in the textile town of Lowell, Massachusetts. That story claimed that President Woodrow Wilson and other high public officials had seen the film and were so "strong in their words of endorsement" – as were the Women's Clubs of New York – that they hoped it would be shown all over the country.[37] Yet not only did this anti-suffrage film apparently not gain widespread exhibition, Nielsen's name once again went missing.

So what does this survey tell us about why Asta Nielsen failed to 'go over' during either wave of her films' releases in the USA? There were several industry factors, although they differed from one wave to the other. In 1912, Tournament Film was a very small state rights distributor with nothing like the network of branch offices that others had – e.g. Feature & Educational Films, World's Best Films, or Warner's Features.[38] The Toledo company also released her films just as the 'Independent' system of distribution was thrown into turmoil: the Sales Company splintered into two and then three factions, with Film Supply, Universal, and eventually Mutual each maneuvering to establish a stable system of weekly releases that included multiple-reel 'specials' – which forced General Film to do likewise.[39] At the same time, the 'foreign features' making the greatest impact were longer films – e.g. Dante's Inferno, The Crusaders, or Zigomar, none of which had a potential star to promote – or a double program like that of Bernhardt's Camille and Réjane's Madame Sans-Gêne.[40] By early 1914, American as well as European feature-length films – from Quo Vadis? to Les Misérables – were beginning to redefine picture theater programs, especially as Famous Players set out to form a nationwide system of regular weekly feature releases, aided by Mary Pickford's star attraction[41] – a system implemented most successfully later that year by Paramount. Asta Nielsen's two- and three-reel films, by contrast (A Militant Suffragette was an exception), became part of Pathé's contribution to General Film's weekly package for theaters still devoted to variety programs of 'short' films. As Bean points out, Pathé also quickly got caught up in producing and distributing serials, beginning with The Perils of Pauline, released in March 1914;[42] indeed, serials – e.g. Lucille Love and The Million Dollar Mystery – would have an impact rivaling features on exhibition practices that year.

But there were cultural factors bound up with industry practices as well. Perhaps most important was a so-called Americanization – the alleged demand, in the early 20th century, to construct a distinctly American national identity – that came to dominate the cinema's institutionalization as a mass amusement. That certainly framed movie fans' fascination, abetted by the industry, with American stars to such an extent that nearly any others were excluded, however 'big' they may have been in Europe.[43] Bernhardt was an exception because her many American tours had aggrandized her fame and reputation long before she starred in films such as CAMILLE and then QUEEN ELIZABETH – the latter earned her a fan magazine cover that no other non-American movie star enjoyed.[44] Yet, after that film, she too faded on the American market. Critics also tended to praise Nielsen in such a way that her identity seemed too fluid, almost unstable, especially in relation to American stars. It was her versatility – her 'remarkably varied' talents and roles – that proved difficult to assimilate within a star system that favored recurring, recognizable character types, particularly in series and serials. Nielsen may have come across, writes Bean with apt acumen, as "a confusing chimera".[45] Finally, many of her films, during either wave of releases, were pigeonholed as sensational melodramas.[46] Trade press critics and apparently some exhibitors often may have found her films compatible enough with conventional American moral values, despite illicit sexual relations, violence, and occasional gender-bending. Yet the climate of acceptance was changing, provoked by growing trade press attacks on grim, unnaturally morbid "foreign features".[47] Perhaps Pathé realized that, regardless of a rare Presidential endorsement, such a climate ultimately would restrict the circulation and reception of this "Bernhardt of the Photoplay", particularly given the "confusing chimera" of her star persona.

Postscript

The First World War closed off German film imports to the USA, including Asta Nielsen films, although at least one title, THE PRIMA DONNA (DIE FILMPRIMADONNA), probably shipped prior to the war's outbreak, eventually did show up in theaters like the Pastime, in Altoona, Pennsylvania, in October 1915.[48] Quickly usurping her place, however, as a potential star of 'foreign import' in the 1914/15 season, were the Italian divas, Lyda Borelli and Francesca Bertini, in films whose titles were not unlike those of Asta Nielsen. The divas appeared by courtesy of George Kleine, with Borelli starring in THE NAKED TRUTH, LOVE EVERLASTING, and SOULS ENCHAINED, and Bertini in THE WOMAN WHO DARED.[49] In early June, in fact, just as Asta Nielsen's films were ending their runs, THE NAKED TRUTH followed at the Chandler Theatre in New York City.[50] Not only were local theater ads for the Italian divas larger than those had been for Nielsen, at least one heralded Bertini as "the girl who taught the Sultan of Turkey to tango", and others simply switched their praise from Nielsen to Borelli as "the world's foremost emotional actress" and the "Bernhardt of the Photoplay".[51] As for Asta Nielsen herself, if she was remembered at all once the war ended, the "confusing chimera" of her persona vanished to be replaced by a fixed image now ironically aligned with a fading American movie star, as "Denmark's 'Theda Bara'".[52]

Notes

1. Jennifer Bean, "'Übers Meer gebracht': In Amerika, 1912–1914", in Heide Schlüpmann et al. (eds), *Unmögliche Liebe. Asta Nielsen, ihr Kino* (2nd edn) (Vienna: filmarchiv austria, 2010), 337–352.
2. Cf. the IMP Films ads, *New York Dramatic Mirror* (3 April 1912), 30; *Motion Picture News* (6 April 1912): 39 and back cover, and (13 April 1912): 38; and *New York Morning Telegraph* (14 April 1912): 4.2.5.
3. IMP Films ad, *Motion Picture News* (6 April 1912), back cover.
4. "Motion Picture Distributing and Sales Co.", *New York Morning Telegraph* (21 April 1912): 4.2.5.
5. "Comments on the Films", *Moving Picture World* (27 April 1912): 330.
6. "Reviews of Special Feature Subjects", *New York Dramatic Mirror* (24 April 1912): 27.
7. Ibid.
8. "The Asta Nielsen Pictures", *Moving Picture World* (23 March 1912): 1054.
9. "Gypsy Blood", *Moving Picture World* (13 April 1912): 142–143.
10. "The Asta Nielsen Pictures", *Moving Picture World* (23 March 1912): 1054.
11. "Great Feature at the Pastime", *Iowa City Daily Press* (19 April 1912): 1.
12. "Amusements", *Hamilton Evening Journal* (18 May 1912): 3; the Columbia Theatre ad, *Athens Daily Messenger* (8 August 1912): 3.
13. "City Bulletin", *Washington Post* (5 June 1912): 14.
14. "City Bulletin", *Washington Post* (27 May 1912): 12; (12 June 1912):14; (18 June 1912): 16.
15. Central Square Theatre ads, *Lynn Daily Item* (31 August 1912): 2; (4 September 1912): 2.
16. C.J. Ver Halen, "The Film Situation in Chicago", *Billboard* (14 September 1912): 93; "At the Photoplays", *Toledo News-Bee* (14 October 1912): 13.
17. "At the Photoplays", *Toledo News-Bee* (16 October 1912): 13; Royal Theater ad, *Janesville Daily Gazette* (4 November 1912): 4; Palace Theatre ad, *Altoona Mirror* (15 November 1912): 20; the Bijou ad, *Racine Journal-News* (26 December 1912): 9; "Fairyland on Majestic Stage", *Los Angeles Times* (19 January 1913): 3.1
18. "City Bulletins", *Washington Post* (28 October 1912): 12; (18 November 1912): 12; and (12 February 1913): 14.
19. Pathé-Frères ads, *New York Morning Telegraph* (4 January 1914): 5.4; (25 January 1914): 5.4. Apparently the Chicago Censorship Board reduced THE DEVIL'S ASSISTANT even more by cutting out a barroom drinking scene – "Censors Slash Doubtful Film", *Chicago Tribune* (21 February 1914): 3.
20. Cf., for instance, the Pathé-Frères ads for LADY MADCAP'S WAY, *New York Morning Telegraph* (30 November 1913): 5.3, and *Moving Picture World* (13 December 1913): 1250; for BEHIND COMEDY'S MASK, (4 January 1914): 5.4; for THE DEVIL'S ASSISTANT (25 February 1914): 5.4.
21. Cf. the Pathé-Frères ad, *New York Morning Telegraph* (21 March 1914): 5.7.
22. Cf. the Pathé-Frères ads, *Moving Picture World* (11 April 1914): 176–177; (18 April 1914): 324–325; (25 April 1914): 480–481; (2 May 1914): 628–629.
23. "Feature Films of the Week", *New York Dramatic Mirror* (4 February 1914): 37.
24. "Feature Films of the Week", *New York Dramatic Mirror* (25 February 1914): 36.
25. "Comments on the Films", *Moving Picture World* (7 March 1914): 1237; (14 March 1914): 1385.
26. "Feature Films of the Week", *New York Dramatic Mirror* (18 March 1914): 35.
27. W. Stephen Bush, "A ROMANY SPY", *Moving Picture World* (21 March 1914): 1532. Cf. the Pathé-Frères ad, *New York Morning Telegraph* (21 March 1914): 5.7.
28. W. Stephen Bush," A MILITANT SUFFRAGETTE", *Moving Picture World* (25 April 1914): 494.
29. "Feature Films of the Week", *New York Dramatic Mirror* (22 April 1914): 34.

30. Red Moon Theatre ad, *Baltimore Sun* (21 December 1913): 3–4.4; "City Bulletins", *Washington Post* (22 December 1913): 14; Academy of Music ad, *Lebanon Daily News* (30 January 1914): 5; "High-Class Moving Picture Theaters", *Chicago Tribune* (25 February 1914): 9; (25 March 1914): 11; The 'Hip' ad, *Lebanon Daily News* (14 March 1914): 5; "Favorites on the Screen in Omaha This Week", *Omaha World-Herald* (22 March 1914): O.3.

31. Cf., for instance, the Nickel Odeon ad, *Canton Repository* (11 January 1914): 18; 4th Street Theatre ad, *Moberly Morning Monitor* [Missouri] (15 February 1914): 4; Princess ad, *Victoria Daily Advocate* [Texas] (2 March 1914): 3; Star Theatre ad, *Chillicothe Daily Constitution* [Ohio] (4 March 1914): 4; and The Dixie ad, *Brownwood Bulletin* [Texas] (29 April 1914): 8.

32. "High-Class Moving Picture Theaters", *Chicago Tribune* (25 February 1914): 9; (25 March 1914): 11; The 'Hip' ad, *Lebanon Daily News* (14 March 1914): 5; "'Pinochle' New Burbank Show", *Los Angeles Times* (2 April 1914): 2.6; Majestic ad, *Atlantic Daily Constitution* (16 April 1914): 8; "At Local Playhouses", *Oakland Tribune* (23 April 1914): 5; Majestic ad, *Sunday Oregonian* (1 May 1914): 15; Temple ad, *Ann Arbor Daily Times-News* (6 June 1914): 4.

33. Gardner Mack, "Photoplays and Photoplayers", *Washington Times* (14 April 1914): 8.

34. Old Reliable Rockford Picture Parlor ad, *Rockford Republic* (21 March 1914): 3.

35. "'Pinochle' New Burbank Show", *Los Angeles Times* (2 April 1914): 2.6.

36. "At the Local Playhouses", *Oakland Tribune* (23 April 1914): 5.

37. "Amusement Notes", *Lowell Sun* (7 May 1914): 2. Cf. also the Pathé-Frères ad, *Moving Picture World* (25 April 1914): 480–481.

38. Richard Abel, *Americanizing the Movies and 'Movie-Mad' Audiences, 1910–1914* (Berkeley: University of California Press, 2006), 26–27.

39. Ibid., 18–19, 28–29.

40. Ibid., 23–26.

41. Ibid., 37–39.

42. Bean, "'Übers Meer gebracht'", 350.

43. Abel, *Americanizing the Movies*, 237–238.

44. Ibid., 31–32, 237–238.

45. Bean, "'Übers Meer gebracht'", 348.

46. In Germany, according to Heide Schlüpmann, Asta Nielsen films were seen more often as significant social dramas. Cf. Heide Schlüpmann, "Cinema as Anti-Theater: Actresses and Female Audiences in Wilhelminian Germany", in Richard Abel (ed.), *Silent Film* (New Brunswick: Rutgers University Press, 1996), 125–141.

47. Abel, *Americanizing the Movies*, 200–201.

48. Pastime Theatre ad, *Altoona Mirror* (19 October 1915): 8.

49. Cf., for instance, the Strand ad, *Atlanta Constitution* (4 October 1914): 38; the Grand ad, *Massillon Evening Independent* [Ohio] (24 November 1914): 11; the Orpheum ad, *Canton Repository* [Ohio] (26 November 1914): 8; and the Eckel ads, *Syracuse Herald* (19 January 1915): 16; (21 March 1915): 9. Although the war halted Kleine's plan to construct a studio in Italy, to produce and export his own Italian films, he could still import already released Italian productions (now contemporary melodramas rather than historical epics like Quo Vadis?) partly because neither Italy nor the USA initially was engaged in the war.

50. "New Films at the Chandler", *New York Sunday Tribune* (7 June 1914): 3.7. One of three illustrations on this page was a production photo that highlighted Borelli in profile as an artist's model.

51. Orpheum ad, *Canton Repository* (26 November 1914): 8; The Bonita ad, *Columbus Enquirer* [Georgia] (15 April 1915): 2.

52. "Denmark's 'Theda Bara'", *Duluth News Tribune* (14 February 1920): 10.

PART VII

OUTSIDE THE WESTERN WORLD

Rielle Navitski

Asta Nielsen as Import Commodity
International Stardom and Local Film Distribution in Brazil, 1911–1915

The study of early global film stars in the Latin American context faces, in addition to the historiographic obstacles posed by the incomplete preservation and limited accessibility of relevant periodicals, a disciplinary stumbling block. In the face of the abysmal survival rate of Latin American silent cinema, previous research on the period conducted in these countries has overwhelmingly focused on recovering the traces left by local film production. In reconstructing national cinema histories, Latin American scholars implicitly contested the historical and economic circumstances that had required citizens of their nations "to assume the position of spectators and become voyeurs of, rather than participants in, modernity", a dynamic Ana M. López observes in her comments on early film-going practices in the region.[1]

The long-standing dominance of imported (especially Hollywood) cinema in Latin American film markets has been abundantly analyzed by leftist intellectuals as a pernicious form of cultural colonization.[2] Beginning in the mid-1980s, cultural critics began to re-evaluate the economic and symbolic hegemonies exercised by neo-colonial powers in Latin American nations, emphasizing complex processes of cultural "mediation" and "hybridization".[3] Recent Latin American film histories have begun to more fully consider the ways in which local audiences consumed, appropriated and contested the visions of modernity offered by imported cinema, facilitated by the large-scale digitization of newspapers by national libraries in Latin America and abroad.[4] Such investigations do not merely expand the range of transnational perspectives brought to bear on the uniquely global stars of transitional-era silent cinema. Rather, they also illuminate the economic and cultural forces, both local and global, that shaped the horizon of audience expectations regarding films' content and format.

Facing page: An advert for a re-exhibition of BALLETDANSERINDEN in Rio de Janeiro in 1915 highlighted three audience draws – Nordisk, Nielsen, and Valdemar Psilander, who also enjoyed great popularity with local spectators. *Correio da Manhã* (16 January 1915), 12.

Examining the case of Asta Nielsen's stardom in Rio de Janeiro and São Paulo in the early teens, it is clear that her popularity with local audiences was not simply a sign of successful domination of the exhibition market by foreign film producers, but rather signals the conflictual process by which this dominance was consolidated locally. Nielsen's star text was articulated in the context of international distribution patterns inflected by local competition between exhibitors. As well-organized film rental and distribution systems emerged in Brazil's two major cities, exhibitors developed marketing strategies that catered to (and cultivated) audiences' desires for cinematic entertainment that was simultaneously associated with cosmopolitan artistic refinement and with a titillatingly modern sensuality. In the case of Asta Nielsen, these apparent opposites would be reconciled by means of abundant references to her dramatic range, a product of training in the legitimate theater that lent a veneer of respectability to the extreme emotions and situations of her erotically charged melodramas.

In the early teens, the Danish actress's popularity with local audiences was leveraged in disputes between rival film importers/exhibitors, following the attempt of Spanish impresario Francisco Serrador to consolidate a distribution and exhibition monopoly, the Companhia Cinematographica Brasileira, in 1912. Serrador's most powerful rival at the time, the Italian Jacomo Rosário Staffa, had two powerful bargaining chips: Nordisk and Nielsen (for local audiences, these categories of films were often conflated, as I will explore below). The circulation and reception of Asta Nielsen films in Brazil thus highlights the local conflicts that accompanied the consolidation of a foreign-oriented system of film distribution and exhibition. This system, in turn, would soon be disrupted by global shifts in the production and distribution of films. French, Italian and Danish films would quickly be superseded by American cinema, which flooded local markets during the First World War. In retrospective accounts of film culture in early twentieth-century Rio de Janeiro and São Paulo, including both histories and memoirs, the figure of Nielsen is almost invariably invoked as a signifier of a prelapsarian age when European cinema reigned supreme on local screens.[5]

Before proceeding to my analysis of the exhibition and reception of Asta Nielsen films in Brazil's major metropolises, it is important to once again note the structural limits facing the study of film culture of early twentieth-century Latin America. In nations with low literacy rates, where large sections of the population had limited buying power, newspaper columns and magazines dedicated to the cinema were far slower to develop than in the United States and Europe. Rio de Janeiro's first magazine exclusively dedicated to local entertainment culture, *Palcos e Telas* (Stages and screens), would not appear until early 1918; illustrated film magazines on the American model debuted in 1921 with the publication of *A Cena Muda* (The Silent Scene).

Similarly, while the Lumière cinematograph appeared quickly in most of Latin America's largest cities, with exhibitions in Mexico City, Rio de Janeiro,

This advert for AFGRUNDEN (exhibited in Rio de Janeiro as A WOMAN'S FALL) includes a detailed summary of the melodramatic plot and warns that children are not allowed in the audience. *Correio da Manhã* (11 August 1911), 12.

Buenos Aires and Santiago de Chile in 1896,[6] permanent cinemas were comparatively much slower to emerge; the first dedicated venues for film exhibition in Brazil's then-capital, Rio de Janeiro, did not open until August 1907.[7] After the establishment of permanent cinemas in the capital, a number of exhibitors would make successful ventures into film production, exhibiting the products in their own establishments. This precarious form of vertical integration produced great box office successes, such as the 1908 film OS ESTRANGULADORES (THE STRANGLERS, photographed by Antonio Leal), based on a real-life criminal case and exhibited more than 830 times,[8] and the "talking and singing film" PAZ E AMOR (PEACE AND LOVE, photographed by Alberto Botelho), a political satire in the form of a musical revue (with performers providing dialogue and song from behind the screen) that reached more than 900 exhibitions in 1910.[9] Some scholars consider these successful productions to constitute a 'belle époque' of Brazilian cinema whose promise was crushed by the consolidation of distribution and exhibition circuits aligned with foreign film producers after 1911, although this notion has been critiqued in recent years.[10] José Inácio de Melo Souza, for example, highlights the role of imported Pathé films in consolidating a local exhibition market; additionally, he notes the role played by melodramas starring Nielsen in the shift from variety programs to those organized around feature-length films.[11] Examining Nielsen's stardom allows us to chart the complexities of the consolidation of film exhibition and distribution circuits in Brazil in the early teens.

In Rio de Janeiro and São Paulo, Asta Nielsen's films by Urban Gad were initially received in the context of the Danish erotic melodramas that helped catalyze the transition to feature-length film worldwide. Despite the variety of production companies with which Nielsen worked, local exhibitors tended to falsely market them as Nordisk films, which had developed strong connotations of sensuality among local spectators. In August 1912, a scandalous public display of affection by a couple on Botafogo Beach (a favorite spot for wealthy locals to promenade) was described as "a long kiss (…) in the style of Nordisk."[12] Later that same year, a Rio de Janeiro society lady was questioned by a journalist regarding her favorite type of films. Expressing a preference for Nordisk productions, she "excited herself by commenting, 'With what violence the people love in the small, enchanting country that Denmark must be!

And what kisses!'" Apparently flustered by this implicitly sexual "excitement", the journalist comments, "I refused to listen any further, as I was seriously muddled".[13] In Rio de Janeiro, children were forbidden to attend the screenings of Asta Nielsen's first international success, AFGRUNDEN (exhibited both with the literal title O ABISMO, and the alternate title A QUEDA DA MULHER, or A WOMAN'S FALL), which was erroneously advertised as a Nordisk film.[14] Upon O ABISMO's first exhibition in São Paulo a month later, it was held over for three consecutive days, due to its allegedly "sensational and never-before seen success", unusual at a moment when film programs often changed daily.[15] Advertisements for the film also emphasized its exceptional length (announced as 1200 meters), as well as the actress's connection to the Royal Danish Theater.[16]

The (mostly spurious) connection between Nordisk and Nielsen was also cultivated by J.R. Staffa in his campaign against Francisco Serrador's Companhia Cinematographica Brasileira (CCB), waged on the strength of his exclusive distribution rights to both groups of films. Proprietor of one of Rio's oldest cinemas, the Parisiense, Staffa had initially aligned himself with Serrador and the CCB. However, he broke his contract with the company in late May of 1912 in order to open a distribution outlet in São Paulo, which the agreement forbid.[17] In an open letter published in the *Estado de São Paulo* in September 1912, Staffa scoffed at the conglomerate's "pretended monopolization of cinema in Brazil". He specifically protested the CCB's infringement on his exclusive rights by showing A DANÇA DA MORTE (DER TOTENTANZ, THE DANCE TO DEATH), a film "from the series by Asta Nielsen, for whose works I am the only distribution agent in Brazil".[18] He eventually won a court case brought against the CCB for the breach of exclusivity.[19]

Advertisements for Staffa's company, the Grande Empresa Cinematographica, strove to demonstrate that he could reliably supply box-office successes by regularly screening films from the 'Asta Nielsen series'. While the star's films were not shown on a strict schedule, between October 1912 and June 1913, one of her productions premiered in Staffa's exhibition chain approximately once a month.[20] Staffa's advertisements constructed Asta Nielsen films, made for a variety of companies in Germany and Denmark, as a unified brand that delivered audience satisfaction as reliably as companies such as Nordisk and the Italian companies Ambrosio and Itala, which Staffa also distributed exclusively. This is suggested by the consistent appearance of Asta Nielsen's name alongside company emblems, a marketing technique not used in connection with any other actor at the time.[21]

Asta Nielsen's value to Staffa's distribution company stemmed in part from her association with the prestige of European theatrical training, which was frequently mentioned in advertisements for her films. Publicity for QUANDO A MÁSCARA CAI (WENN DIE MASKE FÄLLT, WHEN THE MASK FALLS) described it as a "grand film from the artistic series of the celebrated Danish tragedian Asta Nielsen".[22] Similarly, an announcement for O PODER DO OURO (DIE

An advert for O Grito da Creança (The Child's Cry, Das Kind Ruft, 1914) praises "the inimitable work of the eminent Danish tragedian Asta Nielsen," affirming the position of J.R. Staffa's Cinema Parisiense as the "leader in cinematography." *Correio da Manhã* (2 April 1914): 12.

Macht des Goldes, The Better Way), noted that she was "supported by the most reputable artists of Berlin's Imperial Theatre."[23] In evoking Nielsen's training in the legitimate theater, advertisements attempted to legitimate the actress's rendering of the range of extreme emotions demanded by the melodramatic plots of her films, including passionate eroticism and open violence. For example, the aforementioned advertisement for O poder do ouro declares it is both "sensational and majestic" (two adjectives which respectively evoke the extremes of low and high culture) in part thanks to the "rigorous and magisterial performance of the famous and notable tragic actress *Asta Nielsen*".[24] The thrilling, moving, shocking qualities of her films could be recuperated by the virtuosity of her acting, at once praised as spontaneous and artful. Highlighting her ability to play comic as well as tragic roles, an advertisement for O bando dos Zapatas (Zapatas Bande, Zapata's Gang) describes her as "a consummate artist, having dedicated her whole life to the stage", affirming a few lines later that "her grace is spontaneous".[25]

The contradictory characteristics of Asta Nielsen's acting style were highlighted in a presentation given by Dr. García Redondo in the High-Life Cinema on 26 May 1913, and published the following day in the *Estado de São Paulo*. The critic discusses the range of extreme emotions embodied by the actress, consistent with his characterization of cinema as "the synthesis of life with its tempests and bonanzas, with its love and hate". He writes:

> That Asta Nielsen, all nerves, light and elegant as a bird, whom we have seen so often in this cinema in her sympathetic ugliness, vibrating with emotion and throbbing with reality, laughing and crying, loving and betraying, caressing and killing, full of hate, of love, of tenderness, of abnegation and caring, thanks to the cinematograph, fifty or a hundred years from now, when she no longer exists, she will still be seen, performing her art consciously; passionately, like the great artist she is. And, through the film, her name and her image will come down to posterity in a halo of glory.[26]

Nielsen's "passion" was thus mediated by "consciousness", the "sensational" emotions of her films could thus be aligned with the category of "art". In addition to associating the range of Nielsen's performances with the immortality merited by "true" art and assured by cinematic technology, the text also subtly emphasizes the repeated exhibitions of Asta Nielsen films in the cinema where the conference was delivered, Staffa's High-Life.

Between July 1911 and May 1915, there were 27 Asta Nielsen titles advertised in Rio de Janeiro, with AMOR DE DANSARINA (BALLETDANSERINDEN, THE BALLET DANCER) revived with great success,[27] and seventeen in São Paulo, including reprises of BANDO DOS ZAPATOS, A PRIMA DONNA (DIE FILMPRIMADONNA, THE PRIMA DONNA), and MORTE EM SEVILHA (DER TOD IN SEVILLA, SPANISH BLOOD).[28] In a 1915 contest, 9,325 readers of the Rio de Janeiro newspaper *Correio da Manhã* voted to name her their favorite female star; Asta Nielsen lost narrowly to Francesca Bertini, with 9,371 votes.[29] However, the 'golden age' of European cinema in urban Brazilian cinemas was quickly coming to an end. In May 1915, Universal became the first American studio to establish a local branch office, followed by Fox and Paramount in 1916.[30] A craze for serial films swept Brazil's capital, catalyzed by the enormous success of the Pathé Exchange serial OS MISTÉRIOS DE NOVA YORK.[31] Physically dynamic actresses like Ruth Roland and Pearl White, considered "the synonym of the happiness, health, sportiveness and courage of the American girl",[32] now captured the imaginations of local film fans. The lyrical gestures and sentimental, often pessimistic plots of European cinema were felt to be distinctly outdated, as suggested by the unfavorable comparison made between Sarah Bernhardt (on whom Asta Nielsen arguably modeled aspects of her performance in HAMLET) and Pearl White in the modernist manifesto *Klaxon*: "Sarah is tragedy, sentimental and technical romanticism. Pearl is ratiocination, instruction, sport, rapidity, joy, life".[33] Associations with the legitimate theater no longer signified prestige, but rather obsolescence.

In the 1920s, a moment when Hollywood cinema almost entirely dominated the national exhibition market, Brazilian journalists recalled Nielsen, and the erotic melodramas in which she specialized, with nostalgia. When a film starring Asta Nielsen debuted on Rio de Janeiro's screens in 1920, more than five years after her last film appearance, a journalist recalled her as "the first star to awaken our curiosity about the stars of the cinematograph", evoking "the successes of Asta Nielsen and the brilliant moment initiated by her films in the Parisiense, when the entire cinema continuously filled up [with spectators] to see her". According to the journalist, only when "the European conflagration prevented us from admiring Asta Nielsen" did stars like "Theda Bara, Virginia Pearson, Geraldine Farrar, Gladys Brockwell [and] Elsie Ferguson" begin to gain the public's admiration.[34]

Author Álvaro Moreyra wrote in 1924: "Today, wandering from cinema to cinema on the Avenue, suddenly, reading a program, the fifth I read, I had an unexpected revelation: I'm getting old". Reflecting on his bygone fascination with the Russian dancer and film star Stacia Napierkowska, he exclaims, "How all that evokes *our time*, the time of those American films in which, suddenly, the people reversed themselves to run after each other (…) the time of Asta Nielsen, of Polaire, of Mistinguett (…) of the fatal Psilander (…). Today, the actresses and actors are almost all from the United States, and have difficult names".[35] The offerings of the elegant movie palaces of the central avenue evoked, through contrast, the vanished film culture of the early teens.

Two years later, a journalist in the northeastern city of Recife noted, "For a long time I was an inveterate frequenter of cinemas"; more specifically "[i]n the victorious era of Danish films, of Valdemar Psilander, Ebba Thompson and the great Asta Nielsen". The writer's passion for the cinema, however, was destroyed when "war broke out and the United States took advantage to invade the cinematographic world", flooding the market with "those so-called detective films with an infinity of episodes".[36] The physical dynamism and compulsory happy endings of Hollywood films had superseded the tragic plots and lyrical acting styles of Italian, French, and Danish melodramas. In a similar vein, memoirist Afonso Schmidt noted decades later: "After the conflagration of 1914, North America dominated the film market. But I still remember the antics of Cretinetti, the suffering of Asta Nielsen, the languorous gestures of 'Chica' Bertini."[37] A key figure in the contested process of consolidating local distribution and exhibition circuits supplied by imported films, Asta Nielsen's tarnished stardom became a potent symbol of the battle lost to Hollywood cinema.

Notes

1. Ana M. López. "Early Cinema and Modernity in Latin America", *Cinema Journal* 40:1 (Fall 2000): 53.
2. See especially Paulo Emílio Salles Gomes, "Cinema: A Trajectory Within Underdevelopment", in Michael T. Martin, *New Latin American Cinema*, vol. 2 (Detroit: Wayne State University Press, 1997), 263–271, and Fernando Solanas and Octavio Getino in Michael T. Martin, *New Latin American Cinema*, vol. 1 (Detroit: Wayne State University Press, 1997), 33–58.
3. See Jesús Martín Barbero, *Communication, Culture, Hegemony: From the Media to Mediations*, trans. Elizabeth Fox and Robert A. White (London: Sage Publications, 1993) and Néstor García Canclini, *Hybrid Cultures: Strategies for Entering and Leaving Modernity*, trans. Christopher L. Chiappari and Silvia L. López (Minneapolis: University of Minnesota Press, 1995).
4. Works that address film exhibition in Latin America before 1920 include José Inácio de Melo Souza, *Imagens do passado: São Paulo e Rio de Janeiro nos primórdios do cinema* (São Paulo: Editora Senac, 2003); Aurelio de los Reyes, *Los orígenes del cine en México: 1896–1900* (Mexico City: Secretaría de Educación Pública, 1984); María Luisa Amador and Jorge Ayala Blanco, *Cartelera cinematográfica 1912–1919* (Mexico City: Universidad Nacional Autónoma de México, 2009); Manuel González Casanova, *Por la pantalla: Genesis de la crítica cinematográfica en México* (Mexico City: Universidad Autónoma de la Ciudad de México, 2000) and Ángel Miquel, *Por las pantallas de la ciudad de México: periodistas del cine mudo* (Guadalajara: Universidad de Guadalajara, 1995).
5. See Melo Souza, *Imagens do passado*, 19–66, for an examination of memoirs dealing with the early years of cinema in the two cities.
6. Paulo Antonio Paranaguá, *Cinema na América Latina: Longe de Deus e Perto de Hollywood* (Porto Alegre: L&PM Editores, 1984), 10.
7. Melo Souza, *Imagens do passado*, 119.
8. *Correio da Manhã* (12 November 1908), 5.
9. Vicente Paula de Araújo, *A bela época do cinema brasileiro* (São Paulo: Editora Perspectiva, 1976), 347.
10. See Jean-Claude Bernadet, *Historiografia clássica do cinema brasileiro* (São Paulo: Annablume, 1995), 15–34; Melo Souza, *Imagens do passado*, 87–101.
11. Melo Souza, *Imagens do passado*, 41, 77, 163–190.

12. "Trepador," "Trepações", *Fon-Fon*, no. 31 (3 August 1912), n/p. All translations from the Portuguese are mine.
13. "M.", "Pequenas Enquetes", *Fon-Fon*, no. 43 (26 October 1912): n/p.
14. Advert, *Correio da Manhã* (11 August 1911): 12.
15. Adverts, *O Estado de São Paulo* (4 October 1911): 8; (5 October 1911), 11; (6 October 1911): 10.
16. Adverts, *O Estado de São Paulo* (2 October 1911): 10; (5 October 1911): 11
17. Melo Souza, *Imagens do passado*, 308.
18. J.R. Staffa, "O 'Cinema Parisiense' ao Público", *O Estado de São Paulo* (28 September 1912): 9.
19. Melo Souza, *Imagens do passado*, 310.
20. The exhibitions, based on advertisements in *O Estado de São Paulo*, include O FILHO DO GENERAL (DIE KINDER DES GENERALS, FALSELY ACCUSED) (28 October 1912): 8; QUANDO A MÁSCARA CAI (WENN DIE MASKE FÄLLT, WHEN THE MASK FALLS) (3 December 1912): 12; A RAPARIGA SEM PATRIA (DAS MÄDCHEN OHNE VATERLAND, A GIRL WITHOUT A COUNTRY) (19 January 1913): 15; MOCIDADE E LOUCURA (JUGEND UND TOLLHEIT, IN A FIX), (8 February 1913): 11; COMEDIANTES (KOMÖDIANTEN, THE HEART OF A PIERROT), (13 March 1913): 12; A MORTE EM SEVILHA (DER TOD IN SEVILLA, SPANISH BLOOD), (11 May 1913): 17.
21. Adverts for Staffa's company later used the name of the Australian dancer and actress Saharet in a similar manner.
22. Advert, *O Estado de São Paulo* (3 December 1912): 12.
23. *O Estado de São Paulo* (17 June 1912): 11.
24. Ibid. [emphasis in original].
25. *O Estado de São Paulo* (6 May 1914): 14.
26. Dr. Garcia Redondo, "O Cinematographo", *O Estado de São Paulo* (27 May 1913): 3.
27. In addition to the Asta Nielsen films also shown in São Paulo, those exhibited in Rio which I have been able to identify include O MOMENTO SUPREMO / A MATERNIDADE (IN DEM GROSSEN AUGENBLICK, THE GREAT MOMENT), (27 October 1911); A PHALENA (NACHTFALTER, RETRIBUTION), (4 December 1911); A TRAIDORA (DIE VERRÄTERIN, THE TRAITRESS), (2 April 1912): 12; SONHO NEGRO (DEN SORTE DRØM, THE CIRCUS GIRL), (12 May 1912): 11; O GRITO DA CRIANÇA (DAS KIND RUFT, THE CRY OF A CHILD) and O FOGO E A PALHA (DAS FEUER, VENGEANCE IS MINE), (4 June 1914): 14. AMOR DE DANSARINA was shown from 23 to 25 December 1911 and 14 to 17 January 1915.
28. In addition to those mentioned above, advertisements in the *Estado de São Paulo* refer to the following films: OS ACASOS DA SORTE NA VIDA (The Happenstance of Fortune in Life, not identified), (30 June 1912): 9; A SUFRAGISTA (DIE SUFFRAGETTE, THE SUFFRAGETTE), (27 November 1913): 14; SANGUE DE BOHEMIA (ZIEGEUNERBLUT, GIPSY BLOOD), (19 July 1914): 16; O DIRIGIVEL S1 (S1, A GIRL'S SACRIFICE), (11 January 1914): 18; O VERDADEIRO OU PRIMEIRO AMOR (ENGELEIN, UP TO HER TRICKS), (1 May 1915): 13, A PRIMA DONNA was shown on 9 and 12 February 1914, and on 1 June 1915, while BANDO DE ZAPATAS was exhibited on 6 May 1914 and 24 May 1915.
29. *Correio da Manhã* (18 October 1915), 5.
30. Melo Souza, *Imagens do Passado*, 328.
31. THE MYSTERIES OF NEW YORK was the local exhibition title of the edited-down version of THE EXPLOITS OF ELAINE, THE ROMANCE OF ELAINE and THE NEW EXPLOITS OF ELAINE.
32. Pedro Nava, *Balão cativo: Memórias* (Cotia, SP: Ateliê, 2000), 215.
33. *Klaxon* 1 (May 1922): 3.
34. "Operador n. 3", "Os Films da Semana", *Para Todos* (17 April 1920): n/p.
35. Alvaro Moreyra, "Do Passado…", *Para Todos* (19 April 1924): n/p [emphasis in original].
36. Samuelo Campello, "Fitas de Cinema", *Diário de Pernambuco* (22 March 1924): 4.
37. In Portuguese, "Chica" is a nickname for Francesca. Quoted in Melo Souza, *Imagens do passado*, 36.

Dafna Ruppin

Asta Nielsen, Cinema-going and Film Censorship in the Netherlands Indies, 1912–1918

The earliest screening of an Asta Nielsen film in Batavia, the capital of the Netherlands Indies (present-day Indonesia) found in this research took place in May 1912, when HEISSES BLUT (BURNING BLOOD) was featured on the programme of the Globe Bioscope in Batavia (now Jakarta).[1] Probably the most successful of the five cinema houses offering shows to residents of the multicultural city that evening, the Globe Bioscope had been around since 1910, first as a make-shift cinema constructed of zinc plates and, a few months later, as an impressive purpose-built, spacious and well-lit cinema theatre.[2] Located at Pasar Baru in the Chinese quarter, which was traditionally home to plenty of entertainment, it was one of several Batavian cinemas owned by Loa Soen Yang. One month later, on 15 June 1912, AFGRUNDEN (THE ABYSS) was offered on the programme of the West-Java Bioscope at Flora Theatre.[3] This recently opened cinema house, established just a month earlier, at the nearby Pasar Senen, was expected to appeal to local residents of the neighbourhood who up until then would have usually traveled to Pasar Baru to watch films.[4] Drawing much attention by lighting up the exterior of the cinema with giant arc lamps, the inside was deemed to be spacious, airy, comfortable and capable of accommodating many viewers. It also featured a well-stocked buffet and pleasant seating area for spectators to enjoy before the picture.[5] Both of these venues would have been attended by viewers from all ranks of colonial society.

People in the Netherlands would have been surprised to learn of cinema's popularity and well-developed infrastructure in the Indies at the time, as a 1913 report in the Amsterdam-based trade weekly *De Kinematograaf* claimed.[6] In fact, film-going back in the mother country never really took off on a large scale before the First World War, compared to other European countries.[7] However, the report in *De Kinematograaf* continued:

> To the connoisseur of conditions in the Indies, this fact may seem less strange, since the path of the cinema there was already fully paved in advance. The yonder living Europeans and also the natives had hitherto little pleasure to taste, as the

circumstances linked to the establishment and installation of an entertainment venue always carry with them the danger of not being profitable and usually the enterprise even results in failure. The cinema, however, quickly and easily obtained a foothold, and where once only dull tents stood with the ringing name "Cinema Theatre", it has now elevated itself to proud palaces, which conform to the most modern demands. Europeans and natives have become the loyal visitors of the Photoplay [Lichtbeelden] Theatre, and the Chinese, the Malays and the Javanese are already fanatic about your cinema darlings and "World Stars".[8]

In the light of the last comment, one would only expect to find Asta Nielsen featured on the film programmes in the Netherlands Indies throughout the 1910s. But where did these films come from? According to Ansje van Beusekom's contribution to this volume on the distribution of Asta Nielsen films in the Netherlands, AFGRUNDEN and HEISSES BLUT were two of the nine titles which were most likely shipped off to the Dutch colonies once they finished their runs in the Netherlands in 1911, 1912 and 1913.[9] This may have indeed been the source of these films as there was certainly Dutch involvement on the cinema scene at the time, such as the film rental company Filmverhuurkantoor Union from Amsterdam which offered shipping services to the Dutch colonies, including of Asta Nielsen titles.[10] In addition, as Ivo Blom found, in 1913–14 Jean Desmet was in contact with various buyers trading in the Netherlands Indies, among them Ernemann representative M.B. Neumann who in 1913 bought the Asta Nielsen title BALLETDANSERINDEN (THE BALLET DANCER).[11] Yet by 1914, the sales of Desmet and other Dutch distributors was interrupted by both the outbreak of the First World War, which disrupted the shipping lines, and also due to exhibitors and distributors in the Indies buying films directly from major firms such as Éclair, Bison, Vitagraph and American Biograph for much cheaper prices.[12] Nevertheless, as the above report in *De Kinematograaf* proposed, there was a lively cinema scene in the Netherlands Indies long before it became the dumping ground for films that ended their circulation in the Netherlands.

In my ongoing research on cinema-going in the Netherlands Indies from 1896 to 1918, I have found that the first public screenings of animated photography took place in Batavia already in October 1896, soon to be followed by a host of other independent exhibitors traveling with their machines across the archipelago, with the Netherlands Indies often serving as one stop on a longer tour of the region.[13] During the late nineteenth century and first decade of the twentieth century, cinema companies operated by managers and traveling exhibitors of various ethnicities and nationalities (including: American, British, Chinese and native Indonesian, Dutch, French, German, Indian, Indo-European and Japanese), were offering shows at different venues: from theatres, through tents and bamboo huts, to converted *manèges* (or stables). Their film programmes were often very much up-to-date with the latest films produced and exhibited in Europe and the US, at times taking just a matter of weeks before a film found its way to screens in the Indies. Entrance fees were in the same price range as circus acts, tableaux vivants and komedi stambul

GLOBE BIOSCOPE
PASSAR BAROE -- WELTEVREDEN
Directeur S. Y. LOA

Globe Bioscope, Batavia, constructed in 1910. Picture post card. [*Greetings from Jakarta* © Scott Merrillees and Equinox Publishing Jakarta.]

(popular Malay opera), to name just a few of the contemporary competition, with different ticket prices for "Natives" and sometimes for "Foreign Orientals" (Chinese and Arabs), thus corresponding to the colonial division of population groups in the colony.[14]

For the purpose of this research, I have found newspapers to be the richest source of information, providing advertisements, reviews and other reports on cinema shows. While they are obviously limited because there are no newspapers from some of the smaller towns and since, even in the major cities, not every cinema would have been reviewed or advertised in the newspapers, they still provide an extraordinary impression of the local cinema scene. Most of the Dutch-language colonial newspapers from the period are available – either as hard copies or on microfilm – at the Dutch Royal Library (KB) in The Hague, and some of them have been included in the KB's newspaper digitization project.[15] In order to counter the often biased point of view of the colonial newspapers, I also reviewed Indonesian newspapers in Malay, the vernacular language that pre-dates Indonesian as the national language of Indonesia, as well as Malay-Chinese newspapers. Far from complete and with gaps particularly from the period of the 1910s, the surviving materials are preserved at the Royal Netherlands Institute of Southeast Asian and Caribbean Studies (KITLV) in Leiden and at the National Library of Indonesia (PNRI) in Jakarta.[16]

Due to the fragmentary state of the source materials, it may be the case that there were other earlier screenings of Asta Nielsen films in the Indies which

Elite Bioscope, Batavia. Picture post card, c1915. [*Greetings from Jakarta* © Scott Merrillees and Equinox Publishing Jakarta.]

have yet to resurface: In fact, the earliest screening found in this research of AFGRUNDEN was in Surabaya, the major port city in Eastern Java, already in July 1911.[17] The public in Batavia, in any case, was certainly familiar with her name even before the aforesaid screenings there in 1912, as an article from October 1911 about the handsome earnings of stars of the cinematograph highlighted Asta Nielsen as the highest-paid female film star, receiving 85,000 Mark for appearing in ten films for merely five months of recording work and second only to Max Linder, yet another major name headlining film programmes across the archipelago.[18] By the end of 1912, when the West-Java Bioscope advertised its screening of DIE ARME JENNY on 15 December, the advertisement read: "Asta Nielsen is no stranger to the audience in the Indies. Her appearance on the Norwegian [sic] stage has been the means to get to know this great Danish tragedienne".[19]

Regarding the question of exclusivity over the exhibition of Asta Nielsen films, it appears that there was no clear-cut exclusive system in the Netherlands Indies, at least not during the first couple of years.[20] Nevertheless, from 1914 onwards, whenever an Asta Nielsen film circulated in Batavia, it seems that it was always exhibited in cinema houses under the same ownership. Such was the case of DIE FILMPRIMADONNA (THE PRIMA DONNA), for instance, which was screened at the Globe Bioscope at the end of April 1914, only to be shown again at the Elite Bioscope at the beginning of August 1914.[21] Nevertheless, only at the end of 1916 did the Globe Bioscope include a direct reference in its advertisement to having exclusive rights over exhibition: "It is brought to the public's attention that the 'Globe' has obtained the monopoly over all new 'Asta Nielsen' films".[22]

Asta Nielsen, Cinema-going and Film Censorship in the Netherlands Indies, 1912–1918

West-Java Bioscope at Flora Theatre. Picture post card, postmarked 21 January 1920. [*Greetings from Jakarta* © Scott Merrillees and Equinox Publishing Jakarta.]

It should be noted that Asta Nielsen's fame was not restricted only to Batavia. This research has found advertisements for cinema shows with her films on the programme across various cities and towns in Java, Sumatra and Celebes (Sulawesi) throughout the 1910s and 1920s. One incident at a cinema in Makassar certainly proves the male audience's attraction to and familiarity with the Danish star. Thus, when gentlemen who came to watch an Asta Nielsen film at the Sientje Bioscoop found out that the picture rather featured another actress, they complained to the cinema owner. The latter was subsequently forced to apologize over the pages of the newspaper, explaining that the error was not his but rather of the film traders who, in the note attached to the film, misidentified the picture as featuring Asta Nielsen.[23] Moreover, it appears that her films quickly attracted the attention of the local censors as well. For instance, a screening of her film NACHTFALTER (RETRIBUTION) in August 1912 at the Oranje Bioscoop in the city of Medan sparked the concerns of the recently-instated film censor in Sumatra. Apparently the film's title, which in German and Dutch (NACHTVLINDER means 'moth') could have been interpreted as insinuating unseemly nocturnal activities, aroused suspicion that this might be a spectacle of questionable morality. The film was subsequently "tested, tried, weighed and approved" for screening by the police commissioner.[24]

As mentioned above, native, Eurasian and Chinese Indonesians were frequent visitors to cinema houses, leading to increasingly growing concerns about the kinds of films and topics that these spectators were being exposed to. By 1914 the Senate of the Dutch Parliament in The Hague was discussing the growth of the cinema industry in Java, its popularity among the indigenous population, and the increasing need for supervision "because some of the shows are not only dangerous in terms of public morality, but also with regard to their potential political influence, which should not be underestimated".[25] The authorities in the Indies were moving towards new censorship schemes, showing more sensitivity to potential disruptions in relations between European residents of the colonies and the local populations. This shift can be identified also in the treatment of Asta Nielsen's films by the censors. Thus, when DER SCHWARZE TRAUM (THE CIRCUS GIRL) was screened at the Oranje Bioscoop in Medan in February 1913, assumptions that the film might pose a problem on race or native issues – once again, presumably deriving from the film's title DE ZWARTE DROOM (The Black Dream) – were quickly dismissed when it was revealed that the film was actually "a very interesting drama of high society, which shows circus people, with the famous actress Asta Nielsen in the leading role."[26]

Since newspapers were often fascinated with how Indonesian spectators reacted to films, political anxiety was becoming ever more apparent in this sort of reporting as expressions of Indonesian nationalism were becoming more prevalent and in the lead up to the First World War. For instance, a report from Surabaya in August 1913 referred to the screening of DER TOD IN SEVILLA (SPANISH BLOOD) in the context of Sarekat Islam (Islamic Union, SI). Initially a cooperative of batik traders in Java, as of 1912 the SI began to stress Islam over commercial interests, rapidly becoming "an expression of group solidarity, united and apparently motivated by dislike of the Chinese, the *priyayi* officials, those who did not join SI, and the Dutch, approximately in that order".[27] When in one scene in the film a Spaniard was shown fully-clad in national costume including a headscarf, which was identified in the article as similar to that worn by the Javanese, the journalist reported a conversation in Malay that he allegedly overheard between two audience members, with one saying to the other: "Later he is also going to ask to become a member of Sarekat Islam," to which the other replied: "Let's not get carried away now".[28]

By 1914 it seems the taste of cinema-goers in the Netherlands Indies had changed. While new and reused Asta Nielsen films continued to appear all the way through to the 1920s, local spectators were supposedly no longer interested in the films of actors like Werner Krauss, Valdemar Psilander and Asta Nielsen, and these film stars were now fighting a losing battle against detective films.[29] It was this tension around the veneration of violent films and specifically the detective genre which, in the interest of public safety, drove the Resident of Surabaya to prohibit the screening of all detective films and any film, in which a European person was seen "abused, injured or killed by Natives, Foreign Orientals or Indians", effectively banning most detective, cowboy and war films.[30] These sanctions were soon after adopted by other districts across the archipelago.

Finally, in 1916 the Governor General drafted the Cinema ordinance, which touched on issues of copyright, taxation and film censorship, on both moral and political grounds, placing an emphasis on Batavia, Surabaya, Semarang and Medan as local hubs of the cinema trade.[31] Intended to go into effect in March 1917, by 1918 the police was still struggling to implement it in full and to keep up with the flow of films, which would have required 48 viewing hours per week just for the twelve cinema houses in Batavia, according to a calculation by the local police commissioner.[32] This meant that censorship decisions in some cities were being made based on reviewing film titles alone.[33] As the examples of the Asta Nielsen films above show, this was not a satisfactory solution since some suitable films might have been dismissed out of hand, while others could have simply been re-titled by savvy exhibitors in order to sneak forbidden films through the system.[34] The police was then discussing the possibility of waiving films previously approved by censorship committees in other countries directly to cinemas.[35] Moreover, it was proposed to establish censorship committees based on volunteers, preferably consisting of retired policemen and European women. The latter, having enough free time on their hands and perceived to be strict and meticulous, were particularly expected to benefit the censorship process.[36] Due to the chaotic state of materials in the archives in Jakarta and their limited accessibility, it is difficult to find any documents relating to the exercising of these censorship committees in effect. Nonetheless, we can undoubtedly assume that over the next few years Asta Nielsen continued to feature not only in cinema houses, advertisements and newspaper columns in the Netherlands Indies, but also on the ever-growing list of films to be viewed by the local censors.

Notes

1. *Het Nieuws van den Dag voor Nederlandsch-Indië* (18 May 1912).
2. *Het Nieuws van den Dag voor Nederlandsch-Indië* (2 December 1910) and *Taman Sari* (3 December 1910).
3. *Het Nieuws van den Dag voor Nederlandsch-Indië* (15 June 1912).
4. *Taman Sari* (7 May 1912).
5. *Het Nieuws van den Dag voor Nederlandsch-Indië* (6 May 1912).
6. "Het Bioscooptheater in onzen Oost", *De Kinematograaf*, 1:35 (1913): 254.
7. André van der Velden & Judith Thissen, "Spectacles of Conspicuous Consumption: Picture Palaces, War Profiteers and the Social Dynamics of Moviegoing in the Netherlands, 1914–1922", *Film History*, 22:4 (2010): 453–462.
8. "Het Bioscooptheater in onzen Oost", *De Kinematograaf*, 1:35 (1913): 254. All translations from Dutch and Malay are mine.
9. Cf. Ansje van Beusekom's essay in this volume. Other than BALLETDANSERINDEN and KOMÖDIANTEN, this research has found that all the other titles indicated were indeed screened in the Netherlands Indies. Among the Asta Nielsen films found on film programmes across the archipelago between 1912 and 1918 were: HEISSES BLUT, AFGRUNDEN, DER TOTENTANZ, MACHT DES GOLDES, DIE FILMPRIMADONNA, DIE SUFFRAGETTE, DER TOD IN SEVILLA, ZAPATA'S BANDE, DIE ARME JENNY, DIE VERRÄTERIN, DIE KINDER DES GENERALS, DER SCHWARZE TRAUM, DAS MÄDCHEN OHNE VATERLAND, WENN DIE MASKE FÄLLT, JUGEND UND TOLLHEIT, ZIGEUNERBLUT, IN DEM GROSSEN AUGENBLICK, DIE SÜNDEN DER VÄTER, DAS KIND RUFT, DAS FEUER, NACHTFALTER, ENGELEIN and DORA BRANDES. It is likely to assume that not all of these films were bought as handed-down copies from the Netherlands, but were also obtained through other channels of trade.
10. *De Kinematograaf*, 1:24 (1913): 148.

11. Ivo Blom, *Jean Desmet and the Early Dutch Film Trade* (Amsterdam: Amsterdam University Press, 2003), 214.
12. Ibid.
13. Until recently the history of early cinema distribution and exhibition in the Netherlands Indies has not been the subject of rigorous study. Books on the history of cinema in Indonesia begin in 1900 and only briefly cover the period up to the 1920s, when Indonesians began to be involved in film production themselves. However, recent work on early cinema in the region, such as this present research and the work of Nadi Tofighian, reveals that moving pictures were introduced in colonial Indonesia much earlier. See: Taufik Abdullah, Misbach Yusa Biran and S.M. Ardan, *Film Indonesia. Bagian I (1900–1950)* (Jakarta: Perum Percetakan Negara Ri, 1993); Misbach Yusa Biran, *Sejarah Film 1900–1950: Bikin Film di Jawa* (Jakarta: Kommunitas Bambu, 2009); HM Johan Tjasmadi, *100 tahun sejarah bioskop di Indonesia* (Bandung: Megindo Tunggal Sejahtera, 2008); Nadi Tofighian, *Circuit of Cinema, Colonialism, and Commerce: Turn-of-the-century Transnational Entertainment in Southeast Asia*, PhD Dissertation (Stockholm University, 2013, forthcoming).
14. For more on the system of racial classification in the Netherlands Indies, see: C. Fasseur, "Cornerstone and Stumbling Block; Racial Classification and the Late Colonial State in Indonesia," in Robert Cribb (ed.), *The Late Colonial State in Indonesia: Political and Economic Foundations of the Netherlands Indies 1880–1942* (Leiden: KITLV Press, 1994), 31–56.
15. It should be noted that there are many gaps in the material available on http://kranten.kb.nl, sometimes months but at other times entire years. Moreover, only a fraction of all colonial newspapers published in the Indies has been digitized so far.
16. On top of these, while the locally-published trade press only began to appear in the 1920s, the abovementioned trade weekly *De Kinematograaf* which began publication in Amsterdam in 1913 was also sold in the Indies and seems to have employed a correspondent locally. I have also consulted government documents, photos and other materials at the Sinematek Indonesia and the National Archives of Indonesia (ANRI) in Jakarta, as well as the National Archives of the Netherlands (NA) in The Hague and the EYE Film Institute Netherlands in Amsterdam.
17. *Soerabaiasch-Handelsblad* (14 July 1911).
18. *Het Nieuws van den Dag voor Nederlandsch-Indië* (27 October 1911).
19. *Het Nieuws van den Dag voor Nederlandsch-Indië* (13 December 1912).
20. Interestingly, similarly to the situation Van Beusekom describes in the Netherlands and as opposed to the case Martin Loiperdinger sketches out in Germany, it seems the word 'Monopolfilm' was used in connection with various feature films – in both Dutch and Malay newspapers – and not exclusively ones featuring Asta Nielsen. It did not appear in adverts on a regular basis. Cf. Martin Loiperdinger, "AFGRUNDEN in Germany: *monopolfilm*, cinemagoing and the emergence of the film star Asta Nielsen", in Daniel Biltereyst, Richard Maltby and Philippe Meers (eds), *Cinema, Audiences and Modernity. New perspectives on European cinema history* (London: Routledge, 2011), 142–153.
21. *Het Nieuws van den dag voor Nederlandsch-Indië* (25 April 1914) and (4 August 1914). In March 1912, the Globe Bioscope was handed over to the "Naamlooze Vennootschap Maatschappij tot Exploitatie van Bioscopen en handel in film" directed by J. Frank, who was also the owner of the Elite Bioscope, with F. Still and Loa Soen Yang serving as Members of the Board. *Het Nieuws van den dag voor Nederlandsch-Indië* (30 March 1912).
22. *Het Nieuws van den dag voor Nederlandsch-Indië* (30 December 1916).
23. *Pembrita Makassar* (14 September 1915).
24. *Sumatra Post* (16 August 1912).
25. *Handelingen Eerste Kamer* (The Hague, Staatsdrukkerij, 1914–15), 5.
26. *Sumatra Post* (21 February 1913).
27. M.C. Ricklefs, *A History of Modern Indonesia since c. 1200* (3rd edn) (Houndmills, Basingstoke, Palgrave, 2001), 211.
28. "Uit de Kinowereld", *De Kinematograaf* 1:37 (1913), 274.
29. *Soerabaiasch-Handelsblad* (23 March 1914).
30. Ibid. This development made the headlines also in Malay and Chinese-Malay newspapers in a wide range of towns, including Batavia, Makassar, Padang and Semarang.

31. Besluit van den Gouverneur-Generaal 18 March 1916, no. 47, *Staatsblad van Nederlandsch-Indië 1916* (Batavia: Landsdrukkerij, 1916), nos. 276 and 277. The ordinance was made available in Dutch, Malay and Chinese, in order to avoid any potential misunderstandings.
32. *Sumatra Post* (25 September 1918).
33. *Het Nieuws van den Dag voor Nederlandsch-Indië* (27 February 1918).
34. Cinema operators and film distributors heavily opposed the Cinema ordinance from the beginning because it would have meant a hefty tax on films they had not been able to watch before they were shipped and would not necessarily be allowed to exhibit and profit from. Even after the ordinance was amended in 1917 in an attempt to appease them somewhat, they were still charged quite a significant tax for submitting a film to the censorship committee, therefore placing them at risk. *Sumatra Post* (29 April 1918).
35. Britain was brought up as an example, since it also had indigenous populations under its rule which had to be taken into consideration in its decision-making. This was also believed to potentially solve the problem of exhibitors and distributors, who could then instruct their agents to ship only films which had already received the seal of approval in their respective production countries. *Sumatra Post* (25 September 1918).
36. Ibid. Another report cautioned against employing too many "old spinsters" to perform the task, thus running the risk of ending up with a far too scrupulous censorship system. *Sumatra Post* (29 April 1918).

A CARDINAL'S EDICT   Acted.
UNERRING JUSTICE.
A Detective traces a Fugitive to the Snowbound Fastnesses of the Rocky Mountains and makes a Sensational Capture.

Musical Accompaniments by
DE GROEN'S VICEREGAL ORCHESTRA.

West's Prices,—2/, 1/6, and 1/, and Sixpence. Children Half-price to 2/ and 1/ Seats, 1/ to 1/6 Seats.

Booking Office, Dubst & Biven's.

MONDAY NEXT,
SOLE AND EXCLUSIVE ATTRACTION.

THE CIRCUS GIRL
or
ALL FOR THE MAN I LOVE.

One of the Greatest Pictorial Dramatic Successes ever presented to an Australian Audience.

A STORY OF LOVE, TEMPTATION, AND SACRIFICE.

The leading character is portrayed by Miss Asta Neilson, of the Follies Bergeries, Paris, and other leading Continental Theatres. Miss Neilson is one of the most fascinating ladies on the Continental stage. A woman of remarkable stage presence and exceeding beauty, she has long been the idol of Parisian and Berlin audiences.

WEST'S
SUBURBAN AND COUNTRY TOUR.
TO-NIGHT—Norwood.
Thursday—Gawler.
Friday—Burra.
Saturday—Unley.
Monday—Hindmarsh.
Tuesday—Walkerville.

ENTERTAINMENTS.
THE CIRCUS GIRL.
To-morrow night an exceptionally big attraction in "The Circus Girl," a film 3500ft in length, comprising some 60 different scenes, will be exhibited for a short season. It is a story of love, temptation, and sacrifice, and is considered one of the greatest pictorial dramatic successes ever presented to the New Zealand public. The leading character is pourtrayed by Madame Asta Nielson, considered one of the most fascinating ladies on the Continental stage. Of exceeding beauty and possessed of a remarkably fine stage presence she has long been the idol of Parisian and Berlin audiences. The photography throughout the lengthy film is very highly spoken of and the leading artists appear to fairly live on the screen.

PRICE'S PICTURES.
The construction of the Panama Canal is regarded as one of the great triumphs of the century, and Mr Price of the Drill Hall, with his accustomed enterprise, lost no time in securing the wonderful film depicting this marvellous engineering works in progress. The picture has excited great interest wherever shown, and the large crowd at the Drill Hall last Wednesday night were simply astounded at the extensiveness of the operations in progress and they began to realise for the first time what can be accomplished by modern machinery. The picture is one that should be seen by all to appreciate the Panama undertaking. In addition to this very fine film a varied and most interesting programme of other subjects will be screened to-night. One star dramatic film is "Across the Plains," a stirring story of the Wild West. Another picture is an educational one, entitled "Carrot Caterpillars." Altogether Mr Price, in repeating the programme to-night, again indicates his enterprise as a picture providore. The Panama Canal is alone worth

Stephen Bottomore

"The Great Favorite, Miss Asta Neilson" Asta Nielsen on Australasian Screens

There is virtually nothing in the secondary film history literature about Asta Nielsen films shown in Australasia (Australia and New Zealand) during the early cinema era.[1] In fact, relatively little has been written about any foreign films shown in Australasia at this time, because most film history books and articles about the two countries deal mainly with film *production*, rather than exhibition.[2] Therefore, the only way of finding information on Asta Nielsen 'down under' is to go back to basics and look in trade journals or newspapers of the time. I have had little access to Australasian theatrical and film journals, but have searched newspapers (probably a richer source), through the admirable open-access digitisation projects that have been realised in both countries.

I will present my findings about Asta Nielsen on Australasian screens as follows. Firstly, I will discuss my research methodology. Then, based on details of the many Asta Nielsen film titles I have found on these websites, I will compare release patterns between the two countries. Thirdly, I will question whether she was as much a pioneer of movie stardom and 'feature' films in Australasia as she was in Europe. Finally, I will try to explain why, after Asta Nielsen's swift rise to popularity in Australasia from 1911, her film career ended in both countries by 1915.

Research methodology

For this project I used two main websites for digitised newspapers. The Australian site is called *Trove* and the New Zealand site is called *Papers Past*. *Trove* has (as of 2011) digitised runs of some 200 newspaper titles, of which I estimate almost 50 were going in the run-up to the First World War during the height of Asta Nielsen's worldwide success, and *Papers Past* has digitised nearly 70 newspaper titles of which around 15 were running during the same period (both projects plan further digitisation).[3] Thus, in searching these two coun-

---

Facing page:
Left: *The Advertiser* [Australia] (30 August 1911);
Right: *Feilding Star* [New Zealand] (10 November 1911).

tries' websites, one is accessing some 65 newspapers from the 'Asta era'. Despite this wealth of source material, the high number of 'hits' about Asta Nielsen surprised me.

Initially I simply used the search phrase, 'Asta Nielsen': in the Australian *Trove* site I found 288 results or 'hits', and in the New Zealand *Papers Past* site 185 hits.[4] That was impressive (473 results), but then I thought I might go further. I noticed that a few mentions of Asta Nielsen's name in Asian and American sources of the time had been misspelled.[5] So I tried searching some variations of her name in *Trove* and *Papers Past*, and sure enough the Australasians also had a tendency to misspell her name, often transposing the first two vowels, i and e, or using the English 'son' ending instead of the Danish 'sen'. In Table 1 are my results from these four variations of spelling of Asta Nielsen's surname, with the correct spelling at the top of the list:

Table 1: Number of search 'hits' on the two Australasian digitised newspaper sites using variations of spellings of Asta Nielsen.

Spellings of name	Number of 'hits'	
	Trove (Australia)	*Papers Past* (New Zealand)
'Asta Nielsen'	288	185
'Asta Neilsen'	305	185
'Asta Neilson'	227	191
'Asta Nielson'	74	36
Totals	894	597

So by using all four name variants my totals were now far larger: 894 for *Trove* and 597 for *Papers Past* (a grand total of 1491 hits). Then I found a few more hits using other misspellings and further search permutations.[6] In all I now had about 1,500 references to Asta Nielsen in Australasian newspapers.[7]

My first decision in contemplating this daunting total was that I could not download and look at them all, and I decided that I needed some sampling system to whittle them down. I worked out a methodology and ended up with what I think is a reasonably representative sample. For each of the main four spelling variations in the two websites I selected a sample using the following system. I first sorted the results using the sort option 'most relevant', and selected the top 5% to 10% of each list; then I sorted the results chronologically and selected the first hit, the last, and about every 20th or 25th (*Trove* offers results in batches of 20, whereas *Papers Past* offers them in batches of 25.) Finally I scrolled through the total of each search and selected any particularly interesting-looking hits, using the preview thumbnail view in *Trove* (there is no thumbnail view in *Papers Past*, but one can achieve this through searching on Google 'advanced search'). I took solace in my incompleteness from the following thought: many newspaper pages from the 1910 era were very badly printed, so much so that the optical character recognition (OCR) software of these two databases cannot correctly interpret some of the print into characters (especially in *Trove*). Thus, many references to Asta Nielsen are lost to the historian because of mangled printed characters that will not be found in searches. Therefore, I thought, although I was making a somewhat haphazard selection of the many hits I had found, the OCR software had itself already made a haphazard selection, based on the mangled print of the original printing presses. My final working pool of data consisted of 185 reference hits from *Trove*, and 104 hits from *Papers Past*, which is about 20 percent and 17 percent of the totals. The selected references come from 17 newspapers in Australia and 15 newspapers in New Zealand.

Numbers of films

These references to Asta Nielsen were in a very circumscribed period: for Australia between August 1911 and January 1915, and for New Zealand between March 1912 and July 1915. They were either advertisements for Asta Nielsen films, or articles mentioning them, often in 'what's on' type of columns telling readers what was showing at local cinemas or halls, and sometimes giving a plot synopsis and/or a brief opinion about the films.

I noticed an interesting discrepancy: while I found 35 titles of films attributed to Asta Nielsen (and variants of the spelling), she had in fact only played in 27 films which went into distribution before the First World War.[8] Probably this discrepancy is mainly due to variant and misidentified titles. By analysing the newspaper plot summaries, I expect that more of these Australasian given titles will be properly identified.[9] At least two films can be attributed to the Swedish actress Ida Nielsen: A FALLEN STAR (HJÄLTETENOREN) and THE SNAKE DANCER (ORMEN).[10] Maybe some titles were falsely connected with Asta Nielsen by error or intention. But even if some of the 35 titles are variant titles, I suspect that many are not, and so probably a high proportion of those 27 Asta Nielsen films were seen in Australasia.[11]

Release dates and numbers of prints

I would like at this point to compare release dates for Asta Nielsen films in the two Australasian countries for reasons that will become apparent. In my next table I have taken the previous complete list of 35 titles and eliminated films shown in only one of the two countries, to display (with simplified titles) just 18 films (including one re-release with a new title) which I found were exhibited in *both* countries, with date of release based on the first press mention.

If one compares dates for films in the Australian column with those in the New Zealand column it is clear that the New Zealand release was almost always later. For example, the first mention I have found of THE GREAT MOMENT in Australian papers was December 1911 while the first in New Zealand was March 1912, which is four months later. In general it seems Asta Nielsen films were released in New Zealand between one and five months later than in Australia (the delay was sometimes considerably longer).[12] There is only one case where the releases were in the same month: WHEN THE MASK FALLS was first shown in both countries in January 1913, though it turns out that here too there was a delay, but only of a few days, as the press mention was on 4 January in Australia and 15 January in New Zealand.

Table 2. Titles of 17 Asta Nielsen films exhibited in both Australasian countries, with year and month of first release (year:month), in chronological order of Australian release (last title is re-release of THE TRAITRESS).

Title in Australia and New Zealand, Original title	Australian first release	New Zealand first release
The Circus Girl, Den sorte Drøm	1911:08	1911:11
The Great Moment, In dem großen Augenblick	1911:12	1912:03
Gipsy Blood, Zigeunerblut	1912:01	1912:03
The Course of True Love, Der fremde Vogel	1912:02	1912:06
The Traitress, Die Verräterin	1912:03	1912:11
The Better Way, Die Macht des Goldes	1912:04	1912:08
Retribution, Nachtfalter	1912:06	1912:08
Falsely Accused, Die Kinder des Generals	1912:10	1913:03
The Fatal Dance, Der Totentanz	1912:11	1914:01
The Girl Without a Country, Das Mädchen ohne Vaterland	1913:01	1913:02
When the Mask Falls, Wenn die Maske fällt	1913:01	1913:01
In a Fix, Jugend und Tollheit	1913:03	1913:05
The Heart of a Pierrot, Komödianten	1913:05	1913:10
Spanish Blood, Der Tod in Sevilla	1913:06	1913:07
Temptations of Drink; Die Sünden der Väter	1913:07	1913:10
The Suffragette, Die Suffragette	1914:03	1914:05
Up to Her Tricks, Engelein	1914:05	1914:10
A Woman of the People, Die Verräterin	1914:05	1914:08

Why should there be this consistent delay between first release in Australia and New Zealand? One possibility is that there was only one print sent from Europe to 'down under'; that it was first delivered to Australia, projected for a run in that country and then sent on to New Zealand. To confirm that hypothesis one would have to look at the dates in more detail and work out exactly when each film played in each country. I have compared some booking dates for particular films within each of the two countries, and this initial analysis does seem to show a lack of overlap in bookings, supporting the 'single print' hypothesis.[13]

If there was indeed only one print of Asta Nielsen films for the region, that would have certain consequences. It would mean there would be no need for an 'exclusive bookings' policy to ban concurrent screenings of a particular film in one district (which was done for her films in Britain and Germany),[14] because a single print made that impossible (unless the print was 'bicycled' from one venue to another nearby). However, other kinds of exclusivity were still possible, and it is noticeable that Asta Nielsen films tended always to be shown at the same theatres in particular towns and territories: often at theatres run by West's, for example. A wider significance of having a single-print was that one could never 'flood the market' with Asta Nielsen films: they could only have been seen by a minority of the Australasian public. That would put

Lustige Blätter, 1913.

some limit on her impact or influence on cinema in the region, and there was little chance that a wave of 'Asta-mania' could have developed across these large nations.

However, numbers of spectators reached is only one aspect of the possible influence of Asta Nielsen films on the development of cinema in Australasia.

Let us now look at two other aspects. In Europe (especially Germany) Asta Nielsen and her films are said to have had a major influence on the advent of the *feature film*, and of the *star system*. Was it the same 'down under'?

Star system

The significance of Asta Nielsen for the star system would partly depend on what definition one uses for 'film star' (various definitions have been proposed by scholars), but let us say that it means, fairly neutrally, "a named performer who appears repeatedly in major film roles". I mentioned above that Asta Nielsen first appeared on Australian screens from August 1911 and on New Zealand screens from March 1912. But by that time, according to searches in the same websites I used for my research on her, Australasians had had a chance to see half a dozen other named repeat-appearance film performers.

In first place was André Deed, known as 'Foolshead' in Anglophone countries. Foolshead first appeared 'down under' in 1909 – Australia in May and New Zealand in June – which is more than two years before Asta Nielsen. Max Linder made his Australian debut at the end of that year, and a year later Charles Prince, known as 'Wiffles', first appeared on screens in the two countries. All three comics continued to be seen in further films shown in Australasia over the next few years. It should be noted that these serial comic film actors were only credited on-screen with the name of their characters – 'Foolshead', 'Max', 'Wiffles' – not with their own names, so perhaps a stricter interpretation of 'star', requiring the real name to be acknowledged, would exclude them. Yet even on that basis, Asta Nielsen was not the first. Biograph's Dorothy Nicholson appeared on screens of the two countries from mid-1910 and Vitagraph's Florence Turner in Australia from the end of that year, both actresses still being months ahead of Asta Nielsen.[15] Then there was Australia's own Lottie Lyell, often called the country's first movie star, who made her debut appearance on Australian screens in 1911, the same year as Asta Nielsen. So whatever her other accomplishments, Asta Nielsen was not the first film star 'down under'.

Feature films

As regards the feature film, an argument for Asta Nielsen's priority in Australasia is even weaker than for her priority as film star. Indeed, it would be an almost impossible argument to make. This is because Australia herself was almost certainly the world's pioneer in multi-reel or feature filmmaking. Although long film-based shows had first been seen from 1900, Australia's stronger claim lies in the period 1906 to 1912 when some 93 multi-reel story films were made in the country, of which nearly half were over three reels long.[16] Amazingly, in 1911, the very year when Asta Nielsen arrived on screens 'down under', no fewer than 51 multi-reel narrative films were produced in Australia.[17]

So Asta Nielsen films of three and four reels arriving in the latter half of 1911 would hardly even have been news, in terms of their length anyway. It is true that an Asta Nielsen film would often be promoted as the main film featured on the programme (the "star picture", they called it[18]), but that happened with other long films of this era too. Perhaps the only argument one could legitimately make in this context is that because features were already accepted in Australia and perhaps in New Zealand, Asta Nielsen long-feature films might have found quite a receptive market place in these territories.

Popularity, quality and acting

If Asta Nielsen can claim priority in neither of the respects asserted for her in Europe – stardom and long-features – did she make any mark in Australasia? Indeed she did. For a start, while I cannot say that her films were as popular 'down under' as they were in, say, Germany or Britain,[19] they garnered much praise and considerable success. The large number of Asta Nielsen film titles screened in Australasia surely speaks for itself, because certainly renters and exhibitors would not repeatedly have imported and exhibited films that did not pay. Even more persuasive are the comments in press articles from both countries about her films, which were invariably complimentary.[20] Here are some examples:

Table 3: Samples of press comments from Australian and New Zealand newspapers about Asta Nielsen (often misspelled) and her films.

"Miss Asta Nielson, the famous Danish actress"

"Miss Asta Nielson, the world-famous artist, the Bernhardt of the photo-play"

"…the charming star film actress, Miss Asta Neilson"

"…the ever-popular Asta Neilson"

"…headed by the Incomparable Asta Neilson"

"*Asta Neilson's* art which will make her remembered when nearly all her contemporaries are forgotten"

"See Miss Asta Neilson, the Picture Bernhardt"

"Reappearance of the most popular pictorial artiste in the world, Miss Asta Neilson"

"…the Star of the day, Miss Asta Neilson"

"…the famous Tragedienne"

"…the Great Favorite, Miss *Asta Neilson*"

"The outstanding picture on the programme was THE GREAT MOMENT introducing one of Denmark's most prominent actresses, Miss *Asta Neilson*."

"Miss *Asta Neilson*, Wellington's Favourite Bio-Actress"

"The marvellous versatility of Miss *Asta Nielsen*"

"The Asta Nielsen Boom"

Asta Nielsen films attracted large and enthusiastic audiences. In the west of Australia, at Freemantle Town Hall, a newspaper reported "not a vacant seat" for ASTA NIELSEN IN A FIX.[21] At a programme at the Olympic and Glaciarium Theatres, Melbourne, a reporter noted: "The popularity of Miss Asta Nielsen never seems to wane. Time and again she has been starred on Messrs' West's screens, and each time receives a warmer welcome".[22] A New Zealand reporter wrote that THE SUFFRAGETTE picture "has been going with a big swing at Fuller's King's Picture House. Asta Nielsen, the favourite 'movie' artist, plays the leading part."[23] A Melbourne journalist noted: "the appearance of this lady on the screen is now the signal for an outburst of applause from the audience, so popular has she become".[24] I have found several other reports of her being applauded, and many other statements showing the deep respect and affection for Asta Nielsen across Australasia.

In fact, in all the many press comments I have seen, I have noticed only *one* negative comment, which was about the film THE TRAITRESS (set in the Franco-Prussian War) where the journalist criticised Asta Nielsen's costume, saying "ladies never wore modern hobble skirts in those days". But that was just the costume, and the same writer then went on to praise the performer herself – "that sterling actress, Miss Asta Neilsen" – and also praised aspects of the staging and "beautiful scenic surroundings" of the film.[25] It is worth adding that this and other eulogistic press comments about Asta Nielsen are not necessarily in city newspapers appealing to the middle-classes. The one I have just quoted, for example, was in *The Barrier Miner* newspaper, published in the labour stronghold of Broken Hill, so her appeal clearly seems to have extended to the working people of these southern latitudes.[26]

What was that appeal? Certainly, Asta Nielsen was packaged within quality, multi-reel films, and this production quality was sometimes mentioned in the press, but I would suggest that the main appeal was the performer herself and her acting ability. From her first screen appearances, Asta Nielsen was seen as a classy, talented actress. Initially the Australasian press reported erroneously that she was from the Folies Bergère in Paris, and some kind of European high-class theatrical background was later claimed for her.[27] More usually, the press simply extolled her talents, as quoted above.

Although other talented performers had been seen on screen in the region by this time, in films from companies including Pathé, Biograph and Vitagraph, these were generally shorter films, not of near-feature length. A fairer comparison of Asta Nielsen with her 'rivals' would involve examining screen performances in other multi-reel films of the period. For example, what was the standard of acting in the long films made in Australia that I have mentioned above? That is hard to gauge, because most of these pioneering Australian feature-length films have disappeared, but one of them does partly survive, THUNDERBOLT (1910), of which the NFSA's catalogue states: "the acting in the surviving footage is broad and unconvincing".[28] I have found an equally dismissive comment from 1912 on acting standards, by a frustrated Sydney exhibitor who was receiving Australian-made feature films: he stated that, while the photography was fine, "the acting – ugh – it is awful", adding that the "would be" performers in such films, "are no earthly good for picture work".[29] This lack of quality is scarcely surprising, as some of these Australian films were produced by small, inexperienced and underfunded film units, probably on a 'one-take' basis. Asta Nielsen and her colleagues, on the other hand, had years of experience of stage (and some film) acting, and larger budgets. Perhaps therefore, what Asta Nielsen brought, above all, to the early Australasian cinema was a model of truly great acting in a series of long, high-quality films.[30]

Why she disappeared?

If she was so admired and popular, why did Asta Nielsen disappear from Australasian screens in 1915? I have no one single answer, but I would suggest four factors should be considered.

Censorship: The censorship of films by Australian state governments began to develop in the early teen years, and firm action was sometimes taken against particular films. The New South Wales authorities, for example, in 1912 ordered sexually suggestive scenes – involving couples sitting on beds, etc – to be removed from one Scandinavian and two German films.[31] Though I have seen no evidence that Asta Nielsen films were ever cut by Australian censorship bodies, such action against these other imported films might have given distributors pause for thought about whether it was worth the risk to provoke the censors by screening her films (in which she sometimes portrayed 'daring' characters in dubious situations).

Tax: From December 1914, a tax was imposed by the Australian national government on imported films, at up to 50% of their value (whereas films had hitherto been zero-rated).[32] If Asta Nielsen films were so much more costly for distributors to import, then perhaps they would wonder if they could ever get their money back from exhibition. Perhaps this factor of increased cost contributed to a slump in orders for her films (and if these films failed to come to Australia, then downstream New Zealand would also be cut off).

The First World War: The outbreak of war is probably the predominant factor in the disappearance of Asta Nielsen in Australasia. Hitherto her films had come to Australia from Walturdaw in London,[33] but after the War started, the trade in German items in Britain was banned, including films. E.G. Turner of Walturdaw later recalled: "In August, 1914, the Great War started. We had many thousands of pounds worth of German film just issued, or about to be issued. In two months its value was the price of scrap for melting down to make dope for our aeroplanes."[34] If Asta Nielsen's films were not coming to and from Britain, they could not then be sent from there on to third countries. It is unlikely that Australasian distributors would have sought alternative import routes for films from Germany, because both Australia and New Zealand entered the War on the allied side in 1914, and there was strong sentiment against Germany and in favour of Britain (several leading lights of the early Australian film industry had been born in Britain: notably Spencer Cousins and T.J. West).

US domination: However, by the end of the war, conditions had changed. Most of the above factors which kept Asta Nielsen films out of Australasia had disappeared or dissipated: trading with Germany was again possible, the 50% import tax had been reduced, and a more liberal moral climate was emerging which might have made Asta Nielsen's "frankness" more acceptable. But, while the conditions were right, another barrier now appeared, for during the War America had gained a stranglehold on film distribution in Australasia (and elsewhere), and Hollywood films soon dominated screens 'down under'.[35] By the early 1920s the vast majority of films exhibited in Australia were American – so Asta Nielsen's non-Hollywood films would have had an insurmountable task to penetrate their old Australasian markets.[36]

Asta Nielsen's impact in Australasia

Although Asta Nielsen was neither the first film star to appear on screen in Australasia, nor the pioneer of feature-length films in these countries, my research has shown that her films were very successful in this part of the world in the few years leading up to the First World War. Newspaper advertisements and articles demonstrate that most of her available films were shown in many different towns and cities across the region, although admittedly, the number of prints imported was small, and she only appeared on Australasian screens for very few years. Nevertheless, despite that limited exposure, Asta Nielsen might well have had a degree of influence on the emerging film culture, particularly in terms of demonstrating fine screen acting in quality, longer-length films. Undoubtedly she was held in high esteem by newspaper writers in both Australia and New Zealand who saw her films, for they consistently praised her performances; and certainly she was liked and admired – even applauded – by diverse audiences throughout the region.

Acknowledgement: I would like to thank Ina Bertrand for reading and commenting on an earlier version of this article.

Notes

1. I checked for references to Asta Nielsen in books about Australasian film history by authors such as Eric Reade, Jonathan Dennis and Ina Bertrand using their indexes and also using Google Books.

2. For example, Joan Long and Martin Long, *The Pictures That Moved: a Picture History of the Australian Cinema 1896–1929* (Richmond: Hutchinson, 1982) is mainly about Australian production. There are however a few studies covering film exhibition, including some cited below. Cf. also: Max D. Bell, *Perth: a Cinema History* (Lewes: Book Guild, 1986); Jonathan Dennis, *Aotearoa and the Sentimental Strine: Making Films in Australia and New Zealand in the Silent Period* (Wellington: Moa Films, 1993); and an issue of *Studies in Australasian Cinema* 1:3 (2007).

3. *Papers Past* includes only newspapers, while *Trove* covers other works as well. In some of the citations below I give the newspaper title in shortened form.

4. On *Trove*: 288 hits (1911 to 1915); on *Papers Past*: 185 hits (1912 to 1915).

5. In southeast Asian newspapers her last name sometimes appears as "Neilsen", "Nielson" and even "Nicholson". (Thanks to Nadi Tofighian for this data.) There were similar misspellings in publications in other countries, including "Asta Neilsen" (*Moving Picture World* [US] 23 March 1912, 1054) and "Ada Nielsen" (*Pictures and Pleasures* [UK] 20 April 1914, 24). "Ada Nielsen" may confuse Asta Nielsen with Ida Nielsen, the Swedish actress.

6. Misspellings included "Ada Neilson" and "Nelson", "Astra" and "Istra".

7. My numbers of hits would be even greater if the search were done now or in the future because these two projects continue to digitise other newspapers, which would contain references to Asta

"The Great Favorite, Miss Asta Neilson" Asta Nielsen on Australasian Screens

Nielsen. I excluded a few hits from 1916 and later which were back-references to her, or reports of screenings of her films abroad.

8. Cf. Karola Gramann and Heide Schlüpmann (eds), *Nachtfalter. Asta Nielsen, ihre Filme* (2nd edn) (Vienna: filmarchiv austria, 2010). These films can be found in the filmography at the end of this volume.

9. There might even be further variant titles in these newspapers, which I unknowingly sampled out using my selection system described above. Sampling by its nature would preferentially pick the most reported and advertised films, so I might have missed titles of Asta Nielsen films which were, say, shown briefly at one theatre.

10. Cf. Jan Olsson, *Sensationer från en bakgård. Frans Lundberg som biografägare och filmproducent i Malmö och Köpenhamm* (Stockholm: Symposion, 1988).

11. Those films which could not be positively identified will be dealt with in the database which correlates with this book.

12. All these Australasian release dates are later than the European release dates, though I have not worked out how long was the average delay.

13. In New Zealand I have found THE GIRL WITHOUT A COUNTRY announced in five newspapers, and as my hypothesis predicts, the screenings in each town were not during the same dates; the same applies for four bookings in Australia. Moreover, THE SUFFRAGETTE was announced and advertised in nine New Zealand newspapers, but not for concurrent dates.

14. Probably a similar exclusive system applied to Australasian-produced films in this era within their own countries.

15. For these 'stars' the first mentions I found in *Trove* and *Papers Past* were: 'Foolshead': *Trove* 5 May 1909, *Papers Past* 11 June 1909; Max Linder: *Trove* 6 December 1909, *Papers Past* 5 March 1910; 'Wiffles': *Trove* 22 November 1910, *Papers Past* 1 December 1910; Dorothy Nicholson: *Trove* 16 July 1910, *Papers Past* 23 July 1910; Florence Turner: *Trove* 7 December 1910, *Papers Past* 1 June 1911. I also found first mentions for Florence Lawrence: *Papers Past* 15 June 1911; and John Bunny: *Trove* 28 October 1911.

16. More than half were over two reels long and 46 % over three reels. Cf. Ina Bertrand and Bill Routt, *The Story of the Kelly Gang* (Canberra: NFSA, 2007), 18. This book carefully dissects the claims of THE STORY OF THE KELLY GANG to be the world's first feature film.

17. Andrew Pike and Ross Cooper, *Australian Film 1900–1977: a Guide to Feature Film Production* (Melbourne: Oxford University Press, 1998), 1.

18. The projectionist of the Olympia, Rockhampton, noted that he showed THE CIRCUS GIRL as the "star picture" in late 1911. Incidentally, he had also shown other "star pictures": In THE GRIP OF ALCOHOL (LES VICTIMES DE L'ALCOOL, Pathé) and FOOLS OF SOCIETY (SÜNDIGE LIEBE, Deutsche Bioscop) – a 3500ft sensational society drama. *Kinematograph and Lantern Weekly* (25 April 1912): 3.

19. Asta Nielsen was probably the most popular film actress with German film audiences by 1913. She was also very popular in the UK, to the point that there was an Asta Nielsen "festival" in 1912 (*The Bioscope*, 29 August 1912, 605) and "Asta Nielsen weeks" took place in British towns during 1914 (e.g. in Watford: cf. *The Bioscope* 16 July 1914, 236).

20. Unsurprisingly, advertisements were generally more eulogistic than articles.

21. *The West Australian* (12 May 1913), which noted that there was applause for Asta Nielsen.

22. *Sydney Morning Herald* (3 February 1913).

23. *Observer* (Auckland) (9 May 1914).

24. *The Advertiser* (13 April 1912). The reporter was referring to Asta Nielsen in THE TRAITRESS, the "star film" at West's in Melbourne. The next programme at West's was to include another Asta Nielsen film, THE BETTER WAY.

25. A programme at "Sayers's Pictures", *Barrier Miner* (23 April 1912).

26. Many new cinemas were appearing in working-class areas, for example in Melbourne from 1911. Cf. Daniel Catrice, *Cinemas in Melbourne, 1896–1942*, MA thesis, Monash University (1991), 12–14.

27. As well as this misinformation about French origins, there were sundry other claims in the Australasian press of this period that Asta Nielsen was Norwegian or Swedish.
28. *Keepin' Silent: a Selection of Australian Silent Films Made from 1896 Onwards, Available from the National Collection* (Canberra: NFSA, 1995), 156.
29. Eric Reade, *History and Heartburn: the Saga of Australian Film, 1896–1978* (Sydney: Harper & Row, 1979), 12. This is not to say that fine actors were not available in Australasia at this time, for both countries had long performance traditions and there were many theatres and other venues.
30. A few years after Asta Nielsen's appearances in Australia, one commentator recalled that "Asta Neilson" made the best "features" in the era before 1912. "Early Days in Australia", *Film Daily Year Book* (1922–23), 171.
31. Ina Bertrand, *Film Censorship in Australia* (St. Lucia: University of Queensland Press, 1978), 103. It seems that the issue of most concern regarding films in this era was their alleged effects on young people, and the risk of 'copycat crime' – youngsters copying criminal techniques that they had seen on screen.
32. Ibid., 22. The high tax introduced in late 1914 was reduced in 1917/18.
33. The newspaper databases indicate that at least five of her films were distributed in Australasia by Walturdaw: GIPSY BLOOD, RETRIBUTION, THE FATAL DANCE, UP TO HER TRICKS, and THE GREAT MOMENT. I surmise that Walturdaw also handled most of her other films in these countries.
34. E.G. Turner, "From 1896 to 1926, part 4", *Kinematograph Weekly* (15 July 1926): 30. The banning of German films was under Britain's "Trading with the Enemy" legislation of autumn 1914.
35. Already by 1912 in New Zealand, half of all imported and screened footage was American (ironically, all imported via London: cf. *Daily Consular and Trade Reports* 13 January 1912, 223–24). By 1914 the USA supplied over half (by value) of films imported into Australia, and by 1922/23 the figure was about 94 %. Ruth Megaw, "The American Image: Influence on Australian Cinema Management, 1896–1923", *Journal of the Royal Australian Historical Society* 54:2 (June 1968): 198.
36. Incidentally, in North America Asta Nielsen never achieved the levels of popularity that she commanded in Australasia. This failure was later explained as being because her looks did not appeal to mainstream American audiences: that "the 'hicks' would have none of her" ("Film star's career", *The Observer*, 15 August 1926, 6). But if so, why then did Australasians who were, after all, predominantly a rural people (i.e. 'hicks') appreciate Asta Nielsen so much? In 1911 only a third of the Australian population lived in cities, cf. Graham Shirley and Brian Adams, *Australian Cinema, the First Eighty Years* (North Ryde: Angus & Robertson, 1983), 25.

Sawako Ogawa

Asta Nielsen and *Shimpa* Films in Japan

With her distinctive face and often tragic roles, Asta Nielsen was a highly valued actress in Japan. Her films were particularly popular because her roles of tragic heroines were similar to those in modern Japanese *shimpa* films. Second, Asta Nielsen stimulated artists who tried to transform the Japanese film style into a more westernised, sophisticated one.

German films, including Asta Nielsen films, were imported directly from Germany via L. van Nielop & Co.'s Japan Trading Company in Yokohama. The proprietor of this firm was a German named Richard Werdermann (1870–1931). In 1911, he opened a cinema, Odeon-za (Odeon theatre) in Yokohama, in which he chiefly showed foreign films. Werdermann married a sister of Eizaburo Hirao, who managed a film importing firm, Hirao Shokai, a famous company that released many Italian films in Japan at that time. From the outset, therefore, the Odeon theatre specifically showed Italian films imported by Hirao Shokai and another trading firm, Ugo Masulli. This would be quite natural, since in the years 1911 and 1912 Italian films suddenly appeared on the world market and were highly esteemed. Werdermann, who imported various goods from Germany also conducted the lively activities of film companies in his own country. Therefore, in 1913, he started to add films from Germany to his importing activities.

Of those 27 Asta Nielsen films which were distributed in many countries before the First World War, only five of them were imported into Japan, from 1913 to 1915. After the outbreak of the First World War, the importation of German films ceased almost completely.

Asta Nielsen films in Japan

Kinema-Record, which was the only film magazine in the early 1910s in Japan, promoted Asta Nielsen films and offered used prints of her films for sale. In contemporary criticism, it was said that "her films become great film art through their artistic atmosphere and her natural gift for professional acting. We could not find any actress or actor like her in other countries."[1]

Generally, erotic expression (such as the daring 'gaucho dance' in AFGRUNDEN) and social problems regarding women (such as the portraits of an unwed mother in IN DEM GROSSEN AUGENBLICK or an alcoholic in DORA BRANDES) were criticised in Asta Nielsen films and had problems with the censors; but in Japan, both critics and censors were more troubled by left-wing ideology than by women's issues. Unfortunately, there seem to be no surviving sources on the censorship of Asta Nielsen films in Japan.

Because it was not until 1913 that the first Asta Nielsen film was released in Japan, it would not be true to say that her films helped establish the feature film format in Japan. In 1911, Nippori studio (which belonged to Tabata Kenzo's cinema theatre chain Fukuhodo) made a long *shimpa* film, HOTO-TOGISU, which was over 1,500 metres long, and Umeya Shokichi's studio M. Pathé (which had no connection with the French company of Pathé-Frères) made KOBONNO which was over 900 metres long; i.e. the Japanese feature film began at the same time as on the foreign film markets.[2] Films would also be shown not just with musical accompaniment, but also with a *Benshi*. Each cinema had its own *Benshi*, who commented on the film, explaining the story and providing voices for the characters. *Benshi* were very popular; they even sometimes told the filmmakers to make some scenes longer, such as conversations or dramatic scenes. This meant that Japanese films were getting longer for reasons different from those of foreign films. It had less to do with more complex narratives and more to do with an extension of traditional Japanese arts of narration.

Table 1. Asta Nielsen films in Japan.

Japanese title	Original title English title	Berlin premiere	Tokyo premiere	Tokyo cinema
Hanna Jyo 『ハンナ嬢／父の罪／親の罪』	Die Sünden der Väter Temptations of Drink	28 Feb 1913	Aug 1913	Denki-kan
Tenput'shon [Temptation] 『テムプテーション／夜の蝶』	Nachtfalter Retribution	13 May 1911	Nov 1913	Miyako-Za
Haha 『母』	In dem großen Augenblick The Great Moment	28 Aug 1911	Nov 1913	Miyako-Za
Kuninaki Hito 『国なき人／愛の叫び』	Das Mädchen ohne Vaterland A Girl Without a Country	29 Nov 1912	Jan 1914	Kirin-kan
Katsudosyasin no Syunokagekijyoyu 『活動寫眞の主脳歌劇女優』	Die Filmprimadonna The Prima Donna	25 Nov 1913	Apr 1915	Opera-kan

The five Asta Nielsen films imported into Japan were shown in Tokyo at the Denki-Kan, Kirin-Kan, and Opera-Kan. These were placed in Asakusa, the centre of the entertainment quarter with an amusement park, many cinemas and vaudeville theatres. Denki-Kan was the first fixed-site cinema in Japan, inaugurated in 1903. Opera-Kan had been under the direct management of Nikkatsu since 1912, and, until the great Kanto earthquake in 1923, it projected

Advert for THE PRIMA DONNA, *Kinema-Record*, no. 29 (10 November 1915).

mainly *shimpa* films produced by the Nikkatsu company which was famous for *shimpa* films.

Asta Nielsen played the 'new woman', a figure who becomes independent, fights bravely against male-oriented society, sometimes recklessly, and is defeated. She pursued eroticism, exuded female sexuality, and introduced issues of gender in several cross-dressing roles. By contrast, the Japanese *shimpa* film's heroine was old-fashioned, the sort of woman who sacrificed herself to the traditional customs of patriarchy. Asta Nielsen's 'new woman' might have influenced European film productions, but in Japan this character was criticised. A critic said of RETRIBUTION, "this film, showing a vain woman's last days, is a good lesson for the new type of women in such an era".[3] The 'new woman' played by Nielsen was seen as a 'vain woman' and her film was seen as a moral lesson for modern Japanese women. The critics wrote about this film as an "enlightenment film", warning women not to behave like that and go against the traditional roles of women.

Before the First World War, Asta Nielsen's acting was known by the Japanese audience for its wildness and passion. Many years later, the writer Iwao Mori remembered Asta Nielsen films in his book *Eiga Geijutsu* (The Art of the Motion Picture), published in 1930:

> There were the films in which Asta Nielsen played the leading roles. Born in Denmark, she was regarded as the top passionate actress. Behind the success of her work was the huge support of her husband Urban Gad. TEMPTATIONS OF DRINK, A GIRL WITHOUT A COUNTRY and RETRIBUTION, among others, were highly appreciated. The fascination of Nielsen's gipsy dancer so full of voluptuous stimuli cannot be forgotten from the series of German films released in Japan.[4]

This quotation shows clearly that Asta Nielsen's "voluptuous stimuli" were accepted as insignia of the 'new woman' in Japan. The relationship between the appearance and development of the 'new woman' in Japan, the evolution of the *shimpa* film plot, and the influence of women's representation in foreign countries on Japan is also quite an important topic, but one outside the scope of this article. I point out one example here, Sumako Matsui, one of the first Japanese theatre actresses, an Asta Nielsen-like heroine. She played Nora in Ibsen's *Doll's House* or Katsusha in Tolstoy's *Resurrection* and brought an awareness of the 'new woman' from the theatrical world. In *Resurrection*, Sumako sang a song within a play called *The song of Katsucha*, which was popular throughout Japan, made a big hit as recorded disc, and was placed in a representative *shimpa* film, KATSUSHA (1914). The film was highly popular and several continuations were produced as a serial. Sumako fell in love with Hogetsu Shimamura, a literary man and a dramatizer who had a wife and children. Shimamura deserted his family and his position as university professor and worked with Sumako. When he passed away suddenly, Sumako killed herself soon afterwards, at the end of the 1910s. The aforementioned critic's comment, "a vain woman's last days is a good lesson for the new type of women in such an era", assumed such situations possible with Japanese women.

Sometimes, the critics of the trade journal *Kinema-Record* emphasised the artistic aspects of Asta Nielsen's acting and avoided mentioning the film's content. They said that Nielsen "is good at playing a poor virgin",[5] a role quite unlike most of the characters in her films. They would not specify which film they were referring to, but in the same issue, HANNA JYO (DIE SÜNDEN DER VÄTER, TEMPTATIONS OF DRINK) and KUNINAKI HITO (DAS MÄDCHEN OHNE VATERLAND, A GIRL WITHOUT A COUNTRY) were introduced as German productions. Although Asta Nielsen films and *shimpa* films were contrasted with each other, there were some common points between them. Thematically, Asta Nielsen's tragedies accorded with Japanese taste as *shimpa* films. Her comedies are hardly ever mentioned in the Japanese press. Only ENGELEIN (UP TO HER TRICKS) was once referred to by a reporter in a small article in which

Richard Werdermann's Odeon-za in Yokohama. Photograph taken in 1914.

he announced upcoming films.[6] Whether this film was eventually released to Japanese cinemas cannot be proved. It seems that in Japan tragedies or films based on literary classics were preferred over comedies. A mother has to part with her child and suffer; a woman sinks so low as to become a dancer or singer in a café; a heroine sacrifices herself to alcohol; a woman of low birth cannot get married because of a difference in social standing – such stories appealed to Japanese audiences. Asta Nielsen's image in Japan was that of the suffering heroine, abused by men: "Pitiful Nielsen who sobs in a Nordic evening mist. We cannot even call her name without thinking about that tragic woman, who by harsh destiny falls into the abyss from the world of light."[7]

Asta Nielsen's tragic heroine image is quite similar to the one in *shimpa* films. Japanese films were of two types before the great Kanto earthquake in 1923: the modern *shimpa* films and the classical *Kyugeki* films. *Kyugeki* films became *Jidaigeki,* which means historical films. *Shimpa* films would become modern films. However, *shimpa* films were at first distinct from modern films. They did not use actresses but Onnagata, male actors dressed in elaborate drag and acting in a formalised fashion. Thematically, they dealt with stories of maternal affection; with both admiration and antipathy towards the upper middle class; a mother-in-law's hard treatment of her daughter-in-law, or a step-mother's treatment of her stepchild; hopeless marriages and unrequited love; a daughter or beloved who was sold to a rich man for the sake of money; a woman who lowered herself so far as to become a *Geisha*, then died of an illness such as lung disease etc. This kind of stereotypical sentimental tragedy was repeated over and over in *shimp*a films, where the unfortunate heroine's life moved Japanese female audiences to tears. Under a conservative patriarchy, Japanese women who had a high literacy rate looked forward to seeing these film adaptations and strongly supported *shimpa* films.

THE GREAT MOMENT fitted into the *shimpa* tradition. It was released in Japan with the title HAHA (Mother). The main character of the mother, Asta Nielsen, thinking of her child's future, had sent her to another family as an adopted daughter and was herself reduced to poverty. She wished she could have just one look at her child, but whenever she visited the adoptive family, she was rejected. When the mother saw that the house where her child lived was on fire, she rushed in and saved the child, but she herself was killed in the smoke and flames. In Japan, the image of the mother who sacrificed herself for her children was highly respected. Japanese audiences, especially female audiences, would enjoy such *shimpa*-like foreign films. In Tokyo, Asta Nielsen's literary films were released in Musashino-kan or Hongo-za, near the university students' area, where students or intellectuals went to the cinema or the Kinema-club where cinephiles came together. By contrast, her sentimental tragedies, like *shimpa* films, were released around Asakusa, a place where the general public was accustomed to viewing films.

However, Japanese films faced a dilemma. Stylistically and thematically old-fashioned, *shimpa* films were seen as extensions of the Japanese traditional performing arts such as *Kabuki* rather than as productions peculiar to cinema, the new art. The type of audience for *shimpa* films was almost the same as the one for popular theatre productions. Experimental films which attempted to reform the Japanese cinema were a failure, whereas traditional and outdated *shimpa* films were popular. But the reformers of Japanese films looked down on the conservative *shimpa* films, and the promoters of these films were seen as stubborn traditionalists who curried favour with audiences. Asta Nielsen films bridged the two sorts of cinema. They appealed to the general public because of their *shimpa*-type plots, but were also respected by the more highbrow critics because of their artistic qualities and the power of her acting. Her films pointed to the possibility of a compromise between business and art for the reformers who began to produce westernised film from 1920 onward.

Notes

1. *Kinema-Record*, no. 13 (3 July 1914).
2. There was, however, an unfortunate system in Japan in the 1910s of shooting a film at 8 f.p.s.
3. *Kinema-Record*, no. 5 (1 December 1913).
4. Iwao Mori, *Eiga Geijutsu* (The Art of the Motion Picture) (Tokyo: Shunjusha, 1930), 32.
5. *Kinema-Record*, no. 10 (10 April 1914).
6. *Kinema-Record*, no. 11 (10 May 1914).
7. *Katsudokurabu*, vol. 5 (June 1922). The author remembers the cinematic scene in Japan prior to the First World War.

PART VIII

ASTA NIELSEN – POSITIONING HER STATUS

Caroline Henkes

Asta Nielsen and Her Destitute Female Characters

The year 1911 was an important year for the development of Asta Nielsen's career and her establishment as the first film star of feature-length films in Germany. Slogans like "Der Siegeszug der Asta Nielsen-Serie hat begonnen!" (The triumph of the Asta Nielsen series has started!)[1] or "Asta Nielsen die Duse der Kino-Kunst, die Fortuna für die Theater-Besitzer" (Asta Nielsen, the Duse of the art of cinema, the Fortuna for all theatre owners),[2] published in German trade papers, backed up the signalling effect of her name, which was explicitly mentioned as a unique selling proposition. These large campaigns illustrate Asta Nielsen's emerging stardom and her growing economic importance for the film business.

In a certain way, antithetic to her fame and glamour, this article concentrates on the representation of poverty in Asta Nielsen's early feature films. Generally speaking, Nielsen's films always deal with the female main character's struggle to live an independent life; nevertheless these films simultaneously refer to various social issues, amongst them poverty. Even though Asta Nielsen is not especially known for her interpretation of destitute characters, if we look at the films she featured in in the first 'Asta Nielsen series' 1911/12, it becomes apparent, however, that half of them deal with poverty in distinct variations:[3] Either the female main character is poverty-stricken right from the beginning, as in DIE MACHT DES GOLDES (THE BETTER WAY), or she experiences an only temporary social rise from her vagabond life, as in ZIGEUNERBLUT (GIPSY BLOOD). A further variation of poverty within the first series is the woman's exclusion from her familiar environment because she does not obey common rules, as in DIE ARME JENNY (POOR JENNY) and IN DEM GROSSEN AUGENBLICK (THE GREAT MOMENT).

This article investigates the correlations between the role and representation of poverty within the narrative structure and iconography of Asta Nielsen's feature films in order to evaluate their potential emotional impact on the

Facing page:
POOR JENNY. [Filmarchiv Austria.]

audience. Questions about how poverty was represented and embedded in the films as well as the topic's impact on the films' financial and popular success will be considered. The subsequent case study will concentrate on THE GREAT MOMENT and POOR JENNY as two explicit examples of the representation of poverty in Asta Nielsen's early films. I will point out shared patterns between these two Nielsen-Gad films, which illustrate that the films constitute poverty as a consequence of a woman's action and her moral misbehaviour. But before elaborating on this main point, I will outline some genre characteristics which are of importance to the representation of poverty within the social drama.

The social drama

Emilie Altenloh's frequently cited dissertation *Zur Soziologie des Kino,* published in 1914, is the only contemporary academic piece about early cinematography and its audience.[4] Her results are based on around fifty personal cinema visits, a survey among different social classes and interviews with four cinema owners.[5] Even though Altenloh was not a film scholar but a sociologist – and her results have to be eyed critically – she is a qualified voice from that time and an important source for today's film historians. Altenloh characterises the social drama by emphasising the importance of social questions for the film narratives as well as for the audience. "The social problems of today represent a much more lively presence in people's lives. […] Here [in the films, C.H.] they are dealt with not in abstract form but through real examples and in the most powerful possible form."[6] The social drama's closeness to real life as well as its emphasis on sentiments leads consequently to an emotional impact on the audience, which is in turn deliberate and predetermined by the films' topics. "Films that allow members of an audience to make a connection with their own social environment, whether depicting life as it is or as they wish it could be, are the most popular and allow for greater emotional identification."[7] The social drama more specifically portrays stories that refer particularly to the real-life contexts of women. "These dramas usually describe a woman's struggle between her natural, sensual instincts and the social conditions she faces that contradict these instincts".[8] Thus, they deal with the reality of female life in Wilhelmine Germany. As Andrea Haller points out in her doctoral thesis about female audiences in early German cinema, the social dramas' strong thematic reference to the female real-life context contributed to women's fondness for cinema.[9]

A further key characteristic of the social drama is topicality. Altenloh indicates the close relationship among film, newsreels and newspapers because people are interested in a "portal to the present. Film drama enters and touches people's everyday lives."[10] The range of cinematic topics includes illegitimate children, the loss of social status, female emancipation and the dangers of living in a big city like Berlin – subjects which at that time were part of the general public discourse and part of popular culture in Germany.[11] In addition, a "conformity with national tastes" exists because "dramas made exclusively by

German companies are at the centre of interest".[12] Altenloh used the term 'taste' as self-evident and as a connective element between the genre (social drama) and its success among the audience; 'taste' was being widely used in contemporary sociology at the time, without further definition or categorisation.[13] Asta Nielsen's long feature films, most of them produced by Deutsche Bioscop, Berlin, for Projektions-AG Union (PAGU) and concerned with social questions of the time, fitted perfectly into the general 'taste' of cinema-goers of that day. This is affirmed by Altenloh's reference to Asta Nielsen as the star of social drama: "At the centre of all these films are emotional conflicts experienced by a woman. It therefore goes almost without saying that Asta Nielsen enjoys huge popularity."[14] Nielsen's "passionate temperament, consequent guilt and ultimate destiny"[15] portrayed in her films was enormously successful, for example, because of their potential for identification which derived from the films' closeness to reality. When Altenloh articulates that attitudes of social classes towards cinematography can be distinguished by their attitudes towards the social drama,[16] it becomes evident how influential and important this genre was with regard to cinema's growing success in Germany.

More than seven decades after the publication of Altenloh's dissertation, film scholar Heide Schlüpmann published her *Unheimlichkeit des Blicks* (recently translated into English as *The Uncanny Gaze*).[17] She amplifies Altenloh's genre characterisation, by emphasising the interchange between "mostly 'authentic' reality" and the "staged action": "(...) through their mixture of documentary and staged fiction, these films captured public life: streets, city squares, cafés, places of entertainment, transportation devices, industrial sites – the face of a changing urban environment."[18] This interplay increased the films' reliability and put the stories even closer to the cinema-goers' reality. Moreover, the already mentioned 'changing urban environment' was part of the general discourse among the population of big cities and was of strong interest to them.

Heide Schlüpmann follows Emilie Altenloh's definition of the social drama "insofar as it emphasises the close relationship of social drama to everyday life and its concern with 'women's fight' against social conditions".[19] Yet she extends the definition by amplifying the female impact on these films and by introducing the importance of the female audience and the female narrator for the social drama. In addition, Schlüpmann explains the link and relevance of the interchange between documentary and staged scenes and the important role of the actress for the social drama. "The task of exposing social reality (...) was reserved solely for social drama. (...) To visualize how the actress – a modern woman – was imprisoned in patriarchal structures it was necessary to be aware of that reality that was lying beyond the 'reality' of the presence of the actress in front of the camera."[20] A strong connection between the cinematic reality on the screen and the reality experienced by women in this very period, as well as the examination of these social conditions, was essential for the narrative trustworthiness of the films in which Asta Nielsen played the leading character.

Poverty in POOR JENNY and THE GREAT MOMENT

For the elaboration of this case study, it is crucial to ascertain *who* is affected by poverty; if we look at POOR JENNY and THE GREAT MOMENT, it can be stated that both female main characters are affected. Consequently, poverty was established as a major theme throughout these films, far from being dealt with only marginally. With regard to both social dramas, poverty is not only bound to essential needs such as food and shelter but significantly to the urban milieu and living conditions. Furthermore, poverty is caused by social exclusion which ultimately increases the precarious circumstances of living.[21]

In order to point out the role of poverty, I will take a closer look at the iconography and narrative structure in both films. With the emergence of the long feature film, narratives were being expanded and increased in complexity.[22] In the films examined here, this implied that the character's development is shown in a more differentiated way and that poverty is not only presented as a matter of fact but also established within the broader storyline as a consequence of a woman's moral misbehaviour. By observing at which moments and why the main character descends the social ladder and degrades her social position, I will investigate the narratives' causal links, assuming that poverty adopts a major function of the stories' progression.

The main character's background

The opening scenes of both films illustrate the main character's familial and working environment. The protagonists are ordinary women who lead neither a good nor bad nor an interesting life and thus stand in strong opposition to the film character Asta Nielsen became famous for: the bohemian and the exotic figure of the artist. Annie from THE GREAT MOMENT works in a "preferred position"[23] as a servant at a feudal estate and presumably leads a simple but decent life in the countryside. Even though the first act of THE GREAT MOMENT is lost, one can know from the programme leaflet[24] that she is engaged to the gardener, who, unfortunately, has a drinking problem. The leaflet for THE GREAT MOMENT offers even more information regarding the lost first act of the film: When Annie later meets the squire's nephew, who is staying temporarily at the estate and is looking for a diverting pastime, she ultimately cannot resist the experienced enchanter's advances and becomes pregnant.

In POOR JENNY the eponymous main character is a lower-class girl who grew up in a tenement house within a hard-working lower-class family. This family context is carefully portrayed in the first iconic film scene when Jenny and her father start working early in the morning: They are shown in the poorly furnished kitchen, where the girl helps her father put water into the washing pan. Three other persons run through the kitchen; life is portrayed as bustling in a lower-class household. Nevertheless, Jenny's familial milieu is not poverty-stricken: As film archivist Helmut Regel observes in his instructive essay "Die Welt der Frau von 1914" (Woman's World of 1914), the film's "backyards, stairwells of tenement houses and lower-class dwellings seem realistic in multiple variations. (...) However, stylising them in terms of a picturesque poverty idyll has been avoided. The situation isn't that humble after all."[25] The visual aspects which establish the Asta Nielsen character's background seem realistic: The flat's kitchen is narrow and gloomy, equipped with only the bare necessities, the characters' clothing is simple. These staged scenes increase the film's authenticity and offer a first opportunity to lower-class audiences to identify with the main character and her lower-class living environment.

In the following scene, Jenny fills her bucket at the water pump in the backyard and starts cleaning the front house's stairwell, where Eduard Reinold's flat is located. The building's architectural layout of housing projects juxtaposing a front house and a rear house (or more) was quite common in Wilhelmine Germany. While the middle class lived in the opulent front buildings, the lower-class resided in the gloomy side- and back-flats, where the paths of different social classes necessarily crossed. Thus, while Jenny is cleaning, Eduard, her future seducer, comes home "after a stimulating night" – as the intertitle explains. This scene strikingly establishes the social difference between both characters: Jenny is bending down and brushing the steps, while Eduard is enjoying his leisure time, arriving home in the early hours of the day after a night out. Moreover, this scene presents the young woman as a desirable 'sexual object': Jenny's posture with her buttocks stretched up high while cleaning the steps, deliberately directs the audience's gaze to a highly sexualized body part. Her provocative pose instantly evokes Eduard Reinold's interest and leads him to persuade her to a secret rendezvous.

Despite all the differences which both films evoke in their respective simple familial and working backgrounds, the female main characters, both unmarried young women, do have an attractive appeal to men of a socially higher position. Their later hardship derives exactly from this: The reason for their increasingly precarious position originates from the women's inadequate behaviour when they finally must concede their desire for the socially superior gentlemen. The consequential social decline is thus (at least partly) presented as self-inflicted.

Seduction and exclusion from the familiar environment

After Annie, in THE GREAT MOMENT, has been seduced by the landlord's nephew, Heinz Nelson, "the tragedy's real beginning"[26] starts. When the "slick Don Juan"[27] learns about Annie's pregnancy, he has already left the estate and accepted a job offer in Africa without caring for the pregnant woman at all. Even worse, the landlady expels her from the estate when Annie tells of her sorrow. She moves to a neighbouring city because her pregnancy is out of wedlock. She does not do so of her own free will; ultimately the societal pressure and the lack of alternatives urge her to undertake this step. However, this enforced move also seals her destiny: From the first, the audience suspects that, since she is pregnant, luck will not befall her again in the city and she will have to struggle for her livelihood.[28] Although the unwed mother has the opportunity to find work, earn money and raise her child more or less anonymously, new inclusion into an urban and socially inferior environment is impeded because of her restricted capacity for work.

Looking at POOR JENNY, one recognises that the female protagonist must endure similar consequences of her behaviour. Her father expels her from their flat after she has arrived home, fashionably dressed, the morning after her rendezvous and thereby is excluded from the familial lower-class background. Jenny's reaction to her expulsion is remarkable, however, because she becomes active, manages to become her seducer's mistress and temporarily climbs higher in society. However, Eduard Reinold avoids being seen with Jenny in public at his summer resort, and after a short while he denies her in front of two middle-class women. As Helmut Regel comments:

> The unconsciously entrenched ideas of what is befitting prevent the middle-class man from seeing in the girl from the back house more than an adventure. [...] Behind the film's sympathy for the woman's attempts to release herself from dependencies, the ruling order is confirmed by the plot's construction and the mechanism of fate.[29]

Jenny's hurt pride makes her move back to the big city on her own and finally leads her into most precarious living conditions. Both film narratives closely connect seduction and women's social decline. This is evidenced by the fact that Jenny and Annie lose their home and their income after they have sacrificed themselves to men of socially higher positions. When we look at the role poverty plays in these films, it is particularly striking that poverty is in both cases connected to a woman's desire for a man who guarantees her social advancement. Their social decline originates from a one-time illicit act which causes the exclusion from their familiar social milieu. In both films, the seduction was initiated by the man, whereas the adventure has consequences only for the female characters, suddenly leaving them on their own in the big city.

Anonymity and the Big City

When the two women relocate, they become part of the big city's anonymous mass population as described by Peter Fritzsche:

> In the thirty years before World War I, the population of Greater Berlin doubled from two to nearly four million. [...] Whether they lived up north or out west, most Berliners in 1900 had been born elsewhere, usually in small towns or rural villages. [...] Their very presence in the city represented a sharp discontinuity with their remembered rural past. The city remained strange even to long-time metropolitans. The noise of commerce and bustle of traffic; [...] and, most of all, the restless transformation of the city's physical layout continually augmented the shock and astonishment the newcomers felt upon arrival.[30]

Disorientation and alienation were states of mind closely connected to the general discourse and discussion about 'modernity' in Wilhelmine Germany.[31] This discontinuity is also established in both feature films. Forced to leave their familiar surroundings, the main characters try different ways of surviving on

THE GREAT MOMENT. [Filmarchiv Austria.]

the margins of society. After Jenny has lived a few months on her own, the audience observes poor Jenny as a vaudeville dancer and part of the demi-monde. This precarious community she now belongs to connotes negative moral attributes such as permissiveness, superficiality and restlessness. Nevertheless, although the big city is anonymous, Jenny finds an alternative strategy of belonging here and manages to lead this life while simultaneously forgetting about her past life until the day Eduard Reinold visits this very vaudeville theatre she dances in. This chance meeting between seducer and former mistress provokes, once again, Jenny's further social decline. When she comes across him at her work place, she realises her misery and calls him to account. Since he holds a higher social position, her attempt worsens her situation; she loses her job in the vaudeville, falls into prostitution and seems to have accepted her fate. These scenes illustrate the dangers of a big city's demimonde milieu for a young single woman. Even though it appears that Jenny has found a new, perhaps even satisfying feeling of belonging at the vaudeville, this environment is represented as hostile to a young woman and may cause a further descent at any time.

THE GREAT MOMENT, on the other hand, shows Annie's poor living conditions in a one-room dwelling after she has given birth to her baby. She has fallen from the 'preferred position' of a housekeeper into a low-paying job as a milliner working out of her own flat. The programme leaflet informs cinemagoers: "The care for her child forces Annie to work at home. She works as a milliner for a large clothing store. However, the income is very low, because little Annie doesn't allow her mother a lot of time for work."[32] But the mother seems happy with her child and the anonymity of the city allows her to take care of the baby without being judged.[33] This changes when all of a sudden her former landlady sits next to her in the tramway: Annie immediately feels endangered because her former social environment enters her new life. This intrusion into the main character's new hard-fought-for living space in the city seems, moreover, symptomatic of social dramas with Asta Nielsen playing the lead role, as in, e.g. THE DEVIL'S ASSISTANT (DIE SÜNDEN DER VÄTER) and THE ABYSS (AFGRUNDEN). These mostly coincidental encounters always push the heroine one step further downwards, be it because she realises her misery or because the unambiguous balance of power is in favour of the socially superior intruder who puts the poor heroine in her place. In THE GREAT MOMENT, the landlady quickly proposes to adopt Annie's child, which the mother disapproves of, thereby starting off a power struggle. Or as Heike Klippel writes: "Annie's intimate relationship with her child is threatened by the desire of another woman to have the child, and Annie will not be able to prevent this because her social position is too weak".[34] A few months later, Annie's financial situation worsens and she is confronted with absolute poverty, barely managing to feed herself and her child.[35] When Annie finally forces herself to give the baby away, she despairs at her decision and her defeat. The programme leaflet says that Annie, now that she is "completely abandoned (…), [has] disease and poverty as her companions instead."[36] Nevertheless, after three years without seeing the baby, her financial worries diminish and her social status rises again, which makes her desire for her child even stronger.

These sequences show the women's different reactions once confronted with the exclusion from their familiar surroundings. While Jenny first intends to gain social advancement but fails because of her personal pride and societal pressure, Annie tries to ensure the survival of her little family but experiences a personal defeat because of social and economic circumstances. Both situations negotiate the antagonisms between a socially deprived protagonist and an accepted socially established behaviour. These cases illustrate that the restrictions of the Wilhelmine era did not allow a woman to sustain a life on her own – whichever way she might have chosen. Both characters' misconduct at the beginning of the films is followed by their loss of social status, causing the story lines to end with the protagonists' unstoppable decline. The city's anonymity allows them to live a life on their own, but at the same time implies different dangers: either the decline to the demimonde and prostitution or the workers being exploited. Both films also show the interference of their former lives, which brings about the collapse of their fragile new existences.

The irrevocable social decline

Even though Annie is able to escape poverty after she has given her child to her former landlady, it is her desire for her child that also determines her – this time irrevocable – social decline. When she, together with the gardener, her former fiancé, kidnaps the child, they are arrested by the police. After a one-year prison sentence, Annie has changed; she seems hopeless, without prospects and is now totally excluded from the rest of society. When a fire breaks out in the mansion where her beloved child lives, the adoptive mother escapes and Annie rushes into the flames, determined to save the child. Ultimately she can be relieved from her misery only by sacrificing her own life in the fire.

Jenny suffers a cruel fate as well. After she has left the vaudeville, she seems to have accepted her fate and ekes out a miserable existence. She prostitutes herself, smokes and drinks and finally, on her 30th birthday, which she celebrates in a shabby tavern, Mr. Reinold's wedding announcement in the newspaper causes her to wake up from her lethargy and causes her to commit suicide. Yet again, the woman's fate is sealed by external circumstances, even though her death almost resembles a salvation in this specific case.

The circumstances which cause the main characters' poverty and death, are, in the end, all triggered by seduction. Throughout the narrative structure of both films, the aggravation of the main characters' situations is directly related to their initial moral misbehaviour. The causal argumentation of both films leaves no room for a positive development of the female characters, because each and every small improvement or adaptation to a new environment will be destroyed sooner or later by the next incident. Poverty is represented in direct causal connection with their seduction and implies the women's devotion to the men of higher social position as the source of their hardship.

Selective Viewing by Different Social Classes

Asta Nielsen's film characters were often women who were part of the demimonde, such as artists, dancers or gypsies. These characters were not only very suitable for the representation of poverty because of their status as 'outsiders', but this very fact made it also possible to tell the story of their fall. Alongside restrictions, exclusion and pressure from the social environment prevent the female characters from living a self-determined life. Poverty is used to illustrate the dangers an unmarried woman craving independence was possibly exposed to. Both films, THE GREAT MOMENT and POOR JENNY, concentrate on the contexts in which a woman lives and tell her story by employing concrete personal examples and bringing up topics which were part of a general discourse at the time. Poverty was an integrated element of both the filmic iconography and narrative structure, and drew closely on the woman's behaviour, her position in society and her social mobility.

The case study demonstrates that, for a woman, being impoverished means suffering from the consequences of not being able to successfully enter established society. Since the characters crossed the societal boundaries, they were excluded, had to leave their familiar environment and relocate alone in the city. It was shown that confrontations with the socially superior milieu determined their decline even after they had left their familiar environment. However, Asta

Nielsen's feature films avoid a one-sided answer regarding the reason for a female character's hardship. Even though the seduction by a man causes the decline, the restrictive Wilhelmine society, the naive young woman herself, and often the city's Moloch-like character, do also have a direct and ambivalent influence on the aggravation of the women's situation and the narrative's development.

But not only the narrative elements, also the visual ones in the films, illustrate poverty. These two elements imply aspiring to a semi-documentary and thus contributing to authenticity and consequentially make it more probable that the audience will identify with the main character's lower-class background and her inexorable social decline. According to Helmut Regel, the setting in which they move was "crucial for the characters' attribution to a social class. (…) The audience orientation is based on the 'milieu' which, in turn, determines the character's behaviour. (…) Surprisingly, the poor people's environment avoids a cliché-ridden representation."[37]

In respect to the entertainment value for the audience, Asta Nielsen's feature films established a new kind of interface between the audience and the film industry. With the introduction of the feature-length film, a single film, instead of a variegated short film programme, was to address and please a diverging audience. Emilie Altenloh stated in her dissertation *Zur Soziologie des Kino* that Asta Nielsen films were especially popular among more highly educated female audiences.[38] However, I assume that it was because of the potential of the story line for selective viewing by different audiences that her feature films were also very successful among a lower-class audience.[39] The narrative and visual elements regarding poverty, as exemplified in the case study, offered distinguishing possibilities for an emotional bonding and identification with the protagonist from a lower-class point of view.

I am reminded here of an article in which Ulrich Rauscher described an incident he witnessed in a cinema in a lower-class neighbourhood near the Berlin Alexanderplatz in 1912. The film, the title of which is not given in the article, he characterises as an awfully banal story of a "girl of the common people" who is engaged to a distinguished young gentleman until her depravity is revealed. She flees back to her past lover, a worker, who by now despises her and repudiates her. Certainly not an Asta Nielsen film, but a typical social drama, the likes of which she could also have appeared in on the screen. But what did the film narrator do with this material, according to Rauscher?

> [He] fumed with pure moral indignation. He uttered the words of the scum of big cities, slowly, as if they were delicacies, laying it on thick. He described the inner emotions of those people, and he took even me, or at least all my thoughts, captive, and all of a sudden I realised: the heartless woman, a victim of posh society, the poor worker who they [the bourgeois lovers in the film] thought good enough to raise her up from the filth of the gutter, the poor worker, the cornerstone of proud respectability, who flings this woman back to the murderers up there. This is the *social tragedy* of the entire audience, although the ladies present have not taken

the detour via becoming a high official's mistress but have rather stayed in the gutter from the beginning.[40]

Thus the way the film narrator presented the film to his audience makes clear how large the margin of interpretation actually was: While the film focused on a morally disreputable female protagonist who is ready to leave her working-class lover for the sole purpose of climbing socially, the film narrator transforms her into a victim of established society – obviously catering to the working-class patronage of the cinema that showed the film. Thus the role of the film narrator may not be underestimated with regard to the potential impact of the social drama on audiences: "Indeed, emotional identification really is the crucial factor here, for film representations have a very direct effect, sweeping spectators along with the action and enabling them to experience the hero's predicaments".[41]

In summary, it can be observed that social dramas were a well-known formula to contemporary audiences, offering different possibilities of selective viewing. Besides the social dramas' actuality and reference to a female real-life context, which possibly interested especially the better educated female audience as described by Altenloh, this case study intends to demonstrate the role of poverty within the iconography and narrative structure of feature films from the first 'Asta Nielsen series'. The analysis of the causal chain of events in the main characters' decline reveals that poverty was caused by the women's desire for upward social mobility, an analysis which served as a warning, especially addressed to lower-class women. The social decline that is shown in both films highlights the enormous risk for lower-class women of losing their social position as well as their honour, once they blindly give themselves to socially superior men. We can therefore speak of a clearly conservative world view conveyed in these films, where the commingling of two different social classes does not only not bring about a good ending but also functions as a warning to the audience to remain within their own social classes.

Finally, it can be stated that due to the film narrator's opportunity to change the original story completely in order to adapt the film to the audience – in this context a lower-class audience – the motif of poverty has frequently been used for conveying a collective sense of identity as well as for pointing out potential class conflicts. The success of these long feature films can therefore be described as closely connected to the audience's potential for identification with the characters and its different selective viewing of the single story lines.

Notes

1. *Der Kinematograph*, no. 244 (30 August 1911), 40.
2. *Lichtbild-Bühne* (16 September 1911), 37.
3. Four films of the first 'Asta Nielsen series' 1911/12 are not mentioned here: DEN SORTE DRØM (DER SCHWARZE TRAUM, THE CIRCUS GIRL); DER FREMDE VOGEL (THE COURSE OF TRUE LOVE); DIE VERRÄTERIN (THE TRAITRESS); ZU TODE GEHETZT (DRIVEN OUT).
4. Emilie Altenloh, *Zur Soziologie des Kino. Die Kino-Unternehmung und die sozialen Schichten ihrer Besucher* [1914], edited by Andrea Haller, Martin Loiperdinger and Heide Schlüpmann (Frankfurt

5. Cf. Martin Loiperdinger, "Emilie Altenloh als historische Quelle lesen", in Altenloh, *Zur Soziologie des Kino*, *103–*115.
6. Altenloh, "A Sociology of Cinema", 258.
7. Ibid., 259.
8. Ibid.
9. Andrea Haller, *Weibliches Publikum, Programmgestaltung und Rezeptionshaltung im frühen deutschen Kino (1906–1918)*, doctoral thesis (Trier: University of Trier, 2009), 110–114.
10. Altenloh, "A Sociology of Cinema", 258.
11. Cf. Haller, *Weibliches Publikum*, 222.
12. Altenloh, "A Sociology of Cinema", 259.
13. Cf. Loiperdinger, "Emilie Altenloh als historische Quelle lesen", *109.
14. Altenloh, "A Sociology of Cinema", 283.
15. Ibid.
16. Ibid., 259–260.
17. Heide Schlüpmann, *Unheimlichkeit des Blicks. Das Drama des frühen deutschen Kinos* (Basel and Frankfurt: Stroemfeld, 1990), transl. *The Uncanny Gaze. The Drama of Early German Cinema* (Urbana and Chicago: University of Illinois Press, 2010).
18. Schlüpmann, *The Uncanny Gaze*, 3.
19. Ibid., 14.
20. Ibid., 17.
21. For the purpose of this article, poverty will be defined as a lack of income and thus connected to poor living conditions. In the first decade of the 20th century, urban poverty still was a major problem topic in European cities. Even though living conditions for the lower classes had improved, many people moving from the countryside to the cities suffered from their new environment; especially women, old people and children were threatened by poverty. Besides these physical and financial aspects, poverty also implies the exclusion from reputable social life because of an inability to achieve a minimal economic status or because of questionable moral conduct and life style.
22. Cf. e.g. André Gaudreault, "Showing and Telling. Image and Word in Early Cinema", in Thomas Elsaesser (ed.), *Early Cinema – Space, Frame, Narrative* (London, 1990), 278.
23. Programme leaflet, IN DEM GROSSEN AUGENBLICK, 1.
24. Programme leaflets are an important source regarding lost films. Leaflets are authoritative film interpretations, provided by the production company in order to advertise the film and to provide the audience, cinema owners, distributors as well as the censor with a *detailed* plot description. Leaflets often offer complementary information about the plot and influence the film's interpretation significantly.
25. Helmut Regel, "Die Welt der Frau von 1914", *Filmkritik*, No. 7 (1967), 413.
26. Programme leaflet, IN DEM GROSSEN AUGENBLICK, 5.
27. Ibid., 2.
28. Cf. ibid., 9.
29. Regel, "Die Welt der Frau von 1914", 412.
30. Peter Fritzsche, *Reading Berlin 1900* (Harvard: Harvard University Press, 1996), 30.
31. Cf. Georg Simmel, "Die Großstädte und das Geistesleben", in Georg Simmel, *Aufsätze und Abhandlungen 1901–1908 (Gesamtausgabe*, vol. 7), (Frankfurt: Suhrkamp, 1995), 116–131.
32. Programme leaflet, IN DEM GROSSEN AUGENBLICK, 11.
33. Around that time in Berlin, approximately fifteen percent of the children were born to unmarried women. Cf. Max Marcuse, "Uneheliche Mütter", in Hans Ostwald (ed.), *Großstadt-Dokumente*, vol. 27 (Berlin: Hermann Seeman Verlag, 1906).

34. Heike Klippel, "Roter Rausch: IN DEM GROSSEN AUGENBLICK", in Heide Schlüpmann et al. (eds): *Unmögliche Liebe. Asta Nielsen, ihr Kino* (2nd edn) (Vienna: filmarchiv austria, 2010), 90.
35. This is underpinned by a demonstrative external, and thus visual, aggravation of Annie's situation: She obviously had to move into a smaller dwelling, her clothes resemble rags and she seems emaciated.
36. Programme leaflet, IN DEM GROSSEN AUGENBLICK, 8.
37. Regel, "Die Welt der Frau von 1914", 412–413.
38. Altenloh, "A Sociology of Cinema", 282–285.
39. Most probably, *Monopolfilms* were shown about one to one-and-a-half years later in lower-class, suburban cinemas.
40. Ulrich Rauscher, "Die Welt im Kino", *Frankfurter Zeitung* (31 December 1912), repr. in Jörg Schweinitz (ed.), *Prolog vor dem Film. Nachdenken über ein neues Medium 1909–1914* (Leipzig: Reclam, 1992), 195–201; here 198–199.
41. Altenloh, "A Sociology of Cinema", 259. In order to reliably answer the question about the (lower-class) audience and the social drama, one will have to research local cinema history.

Von Freitag, den 4. April, bis Donnerstag, den 10. April inkl.:

Asta Nielsen

in nachstehenden 6 Theatern:

Waterloo- Dammtorstrasse 14

Elite- Steindamm 32

Palast- Barmbeck

Victoria- Hammerbrookstrasse 76

BelleAlliance- Eimsbüttel

Helios-Theater Altona, Gr. Bergstr. 11

Alleiniges Erstaufführungsrecht!

Der letzte Asta Nielsen-Film der diesjährigen Saison.

Der Tod in Sevilla

Schauspiel in 4 Akten. Ort der Handlung in und um Sevilla

und die weiteren vorzüglichen Programme,

darunter:

Der Stapellauf des Schwesterschiffes des „Imperator": „Vaterland" am 3. April.

Annemone Ligensa

Asta Nielsen in Germany
A Reception-Oriented Approach

In my contribution, I would like to analyse Asta Nielsen's historical status as a star in Germany and hence her theoretical significance for star studies from a reception-oriented point of view. Richard Dyer has defined stars thus: "Stars may be defined as performers in any medium who are highly successful, are widely recognized, and constitute the main attraction of whatever they appear in".[1] Dyer's approach is reception-oriented, because in his view, it is favourable audience response, or popularity, that ultimately makes a star. Similarly, Francesco Alberoni has compared stars with elected politicians in democracies, explaining that the film industry "never creates the star, but it proposes the candidate for 'election', and helps to retain the favour of the 'electors'".[2] The film industry proposes 'candidates' for stardom by choosing actors and actresses whom it regards as promising, casts them in leading roles in expensive films, draws attention to them with publicity etc. However, no amount of effort can force performers upon audiences, especially not in the long term. In fact, failure is more common than success. Asta Nielsen's reception in the USA is a case in point: even though her films were distributed and advertised there, she did not become a success.[3] To this one might add that there have been many performers who have become stars with relatively little build-up (e.g. because their potential was not recognized before the audience communicated its interest). So to extend Alberoni's comparison, sometimes the audience even nominates the candidate – which the industry either picks up, or fails to do. Furthermore, Dyer has pointed out that

> [A] concept of the audience is clearly crucial, and yet in every case I have had to gesture towards this gap in our knowledge and then proceed as if this were *merely* a gap. But how one conceptualises the audience – and the empirical adequacy of one's conceptualisations – is fundamental to every assumption one can make about how stars, and films, work. ... [Other] weaknesses are as nothing compared to our ignorance, theoretical and empirical, of how films work for, on, with audiences.[4]

Even though this assessment was written in 1979, with few exceptions, the situation has not changed much, especially regarding the historical audiences

---

Facing page:
Hamburg, "the last Asta Nielsen film of the season": SPANISH BLOOD in six cinema theatres.
Hamburger Fremden-Blatt (5 April 1913).

of stars.⁵ In what follows, I will try to assess how popular Asta Nielsen was in Germany. I will mainly make use of data from the databases on early cinema in Germany that were compiled by the research projects 'Industrialization of Perception' (University of Siegen, 2002–2009) and 'Visual Communities: Relationships of the Local, National, and Global in Early Cinema' (University of Cologne, 2010–). There are four databases:

1. Film supply database: information on film supply in Germany between 1895 and 1920 (c. 45,000 films offered in Germany, based on data compiled by Herbert Birett);

2. Fairground cinema database: information on c. 7,000 fairground film shows in Germany between 1896 and 1926 (showmen, locations and events);

3. Programme database: a selection of film programmes between 1905 and 1914, compiled from the newspapers of nine German cities of different regions and sizes (c. 1,200 programmes from c. 100 cinemas, containing c. 3,800 different films);

4. Documents database: c. 5,000 contemporary German texts on early cinema from a wide variety of newspapers, magazines and journals published between 1895 and 1914 (non-film publications, compiled by Herbert Birett).⁶

First of all, Asta Nielsen's films are connected with the so-called 'transitional phase' in Germany: the emergence of permanent cinemas and with it the turn towards longer feature films instead of programmes with several short numbers.⁷ As Joseph Garncarz has argued (based on the fairground cinema database), the initial diffusion of fairground cinema has been greatly underestimated, but after being the dominant form of film exhibition in Germany for about fifteen years, it disappeared more quickly than it appeared, most likely due to the spread of permanent cinemas. More specifically, in contrast to early *Ladenkinos* (store front cinemas), which still showed programmes comprised of short films, longer narrative films were usually made for *Kinotheater* (cinema theatres) and *Kinopaläste* (cinema palaces), upscale cinemas that were modelled on dramatic theatre, which particularly appealed to the middle class.⁸ As Emilie Altenloh's study on Mannheim and Heidelberg suggests, Asta Nielsen's films were especially popular with women who attended 'better' cinemas.⁹ Hence, Nielsen's films fit into the general strategy to attract a more sophisticated audience to the cinema.¹⁰

Regrettably, due to the limited sampling of the programme database, it is not possible at this time to compile a 'hit list' of Nielsen's films in Germany based on the number of screenings.¹¹ Nevertheless, due to the relatively large size and the systematic structure of the database sample, it is possible to pose some interesting questions and present some preliminary answers regarding the distribution and, indirectly, the popularity of Nielsen's films.¹² Figure 1 is a list of the programmes with Nielsen films found in the programme database.

Firstly, it is interesting that Asta Nielsen's films reached audiences in smaller places (six programmes in large cities – Hamburg, Leipzig, Munich, three in medium-sized cities – Hagen, Görlitz, Würzburg, six in small towns – Rendsburg, Pirna, Weiden), and a look at the dates reveals that there was not even necessarily a time lag. This is surprising, because the original idea of the exclusive was to ask higher rental prices, which would only have been profitable for exhibitors if the audience was large enough.[13] Perhaps prices were more flexible in practice.[14]

Fig. 1. Programmes with Nielsen films found in the programme database.

Film title	Year	Hamburg	Leipzig	Munich	Hagen	Görlitz	Würzburg	Rendsburg	Pirna	Weiden
Abgründe / *Afgrunden, The Abyss*	1910	1			1	1		1		
Heißes Blut / *Burning Blood*	1911		2		1					
Nachtfalter / *Retribution*	1911			2						
Die arme Jenny / *A Cruel Fate*	1912							2		
Die Macht des Goldes / *The Better Way*	1912						1			
Wenn die Maske fällt / *When the Mask Falls*	1912									1
Die Sünden der Väter / *Temptations of Drink*	1913	1					1			

Since Asta Nielsen's films were very controversial in Germany (more on that below), regional variations in censorship standards may also have been a factor. More research about this aspect in general would be very useful. So far, a systematic study of German censorship only exists for Berlin and Munich.[15] Berlin censorship decisions may often have been adopted elsewhere, but this need not always have been the case, especially for highly controversial films. Asta Nielsen not only addressed an open letter to Berlin censors, in which she complained about their restrictive, arbitrary and often incomprehensible cuts,[16] but Munich censorship was so strict that Urban Gad withdrew DIE SUFFRAGETTE (THE SUFFRAGETTE) from that market entirely.[17] For example, a reviewer of a screening of DER TOTENTANZ (THE DANCE TO DEATH) in Berlin wondered why, in contrast to the description in the programme, there was no 'dance to death' in the film, and assumed that it was cut out by the censor.[18] If these were the prevailing standards in metropolises, Nielsen's films are likely to have met with even more difficulties in provincial places of conservative regions. Even though they may have overestimated the availability of films and the convergence of tastes between city and country, many German contemporaries were extremely worried about this trend:

> We should not be indifferent about the kind of mental fare that is accepted and digested in German and neighbouring metropolises by the social trendsetters, or perhaps just the indiscriminate masses. The connections between these metropolises and our centres are so close, and the traffic is so smooth, that the 'hit' that only yesterday tickled the exhausted imagination of the urbanite already today is greeted with a knowing smile by the provincial, and tomorrow is gawked at as the latest fashion by the farmer's son.[19]

Secondly, the development of screenings over time conveys the impression that Asta Nielsen's popularity in Germany decreased somewhat. I hazard this interpretation despite the small number of screenings covered by the database sample, because Nielsen's strongest competitor, Henny Porten, whom Oskar Messter was initially slow to promote, eventually surpassed her in popularity. As Garncarz has shown, in connection with the turn towards permanent cinemas and longer narrative films, German cinema became more culturally specific.[20] Danish feature films were initially successful and influential in Germany, due to their artistic innovations, the quality of their acting, the sensational subject matter, and the relative degree of cultural compatibility (for example, the so-called social drama was a popular genre in both countries). But in other regards, the exotic Nielsen and her films were hardly even typically Danish, much less German, whereas Porten embodied the archetype of the ideal German woman long before her name was known to audiences.[21]

Fig. 2. 1914 audience survey on film stars in Germany by *Illustrierte Kino-Woche*. The figures are the number of votes received.

"Who is the audience's favourite?"		
1	Waldemar Psilander	382
2	Asta Nielsen	271
3	Henny Porten	258
4	Max Linder	193
5	Suzanne Grandais	152
6	Hanni Weisse	72
7	Carl Clewing	57
8	Viggo Larsen	56
9	Fritz Feher	49
10	Wanda Treumann	43
11	John Bunny	35
12	Anton Ernst Rückert	28
13	Moritz Prince / Toni Sylva	17
14	Moritz Costello / Clara Wieth / Alberto Capozzi	6

Hence, a brief look at other stars is useful. According to what seems to be the first German audience survey on the popularity of film actors and actresses, published by the film magazine *Illustrierte Kino-Woche* in January 1914,[22] Asta Nielsen's and Henny Porten's popularity was about equal at the time. However, the runaway favourite was the Danish actor Waldemar Psilander. Note also that actors such as Max Linder were named, who predated the long feature film, exclusive distribution, extensive promotion and paratextual discourse. In contrast to Richard deCordova, I prefer to call such actors 'stars' as well, because for me, the essence of the phenomenon is popularity (rather than the discourse on private lives, which, as Garncarz has shown, was never as extensive in Germany as it was in the USA).[23] That Linder played a recurring character called Max was a simple, but obviously very effective way of creating a recognisable 'brand'.[24] After all, even though stars are products in themselves, the main function of stars for the film industry is to sell films. A star who plays the same kinds of roles over and over again acquires what today is called a 'marking function': the star's name will communicate to audiences what kind of film they can expect to see and thus contribute to preventing disappointment. Asta Nielsen's roles varied greatly, so one might admire her acting ability, but judging from reviews, it is likely that audiences enjoyed some films more than others. Consequently, she was a relatively 'risky property'.

I find the result of the magazine survey quite credible, because in most audience polls on stars that I have seen (from various countries and periods), whenever there is a forced choice question rather than a differentiation by gender, male stars usually come out on top. Sociologists have explained this phenomenon with the tendency that female viewers not only desire male stars romantically, but are also more likely to identify with them, whereas male viewers are less likely to identify with women.[25] In an industry where most of the decision makers are male, despite the fact that their prime motivation is to make money, the preferences of female viewers are often underexploited (even today, despite improved market research).[26] For example, Andrea Haller mentions that early German fan magazines were slow to report on male stars.[27] Perhaps one reason for this was that female stars were more suitable for advertising other goods besides films, such as cosmetics and fashions. Another reason may have been that just as German editors were very reluctant to provide personal information about stars, they probably looked upon the adulation of male stars by female fans with more disdain, even though this ran against economic interests to some extent. Feeding erotic fantasies would have been a contradiction to the contemporary agenda of making film a respectable art form for the middle classes.[28] Urban Gad himself once claimed that women admire actors merely for their appeal as men, whereas men admire actresses not only for their beauty, but also their acting abilities.[29] Needless to say, one might argue with this opinion. In fact, from the reviews of male writers, one often gets the impression that one of the functions of associating Nielsen with art was to legitimize erotic attraction (more on that below).

Consequently, even though the *Monopolfilm* ('exclusive') was certainly an important development in many regards, I believe that its role in the emergence of film stars has been somewhat overstated.[30] As has been frequently pointed out, the film industry did not invent stardom as such; a star system already existed in theatre.[31] Nor were films with stars necessarily exclusives (Henny Porten, whose films were not distributed as exclusives before the 1913/14 season, is a case in point). In fact, the early *Monopolfilm*'s tendencies towards 'exclusivity' beyond the mere restriction of distribution rights may not even have been optimal for promoting stars. Compared to theatre, the advantage of film was that stars were not limited to personal appearances, but that their (recorded) performances could be made available to a mass audience. However, early advertisements of Asta Nielsen's films not only claimed that she was a renowned stage actress (which was not true), but often called screenings *Gastspiele* (a term from theatre, used almost as if Nielsen were personally appearing at a particular cinema).[32] Furthermore, distributors usually asked higher prices for exclusives and mainly intended them for upscale cinemas. Ironically, all this, together with Asta Nielsen's aloof and avant-garde image ran somewhat counter to mass popularity. By contrast, Henny Porten, even though she was also touted as a great actress and her films were eventually distributed as exclusives, was much more accessible in both a literal and a figurative sense.[33]

Some more data from the programme database is revealing in this regard. Figure 3 below shows the number of films with Asta Nielsen, Henny Porten and Waldemar Psilander that were on offer in Germany between 1910 and 1914 (Psilander's first film was released in 1911), the number of programmes with their films found in the programme database, the number of programmes in which their names were mentioned, the average number of programmes per film (p : f), and the average number of programmes in which a star's name was mentioned (n : p).

Fig. 3. 'Visibility' of Nielsen, Porten and Psilander between 1910 and 1914 according to the supply and programme databases.

Star	Films	Programmes	Mentions	p : f	n : p
Asta Nielsen	27	15	8	0.56	0.53
Henny Porten	65	41	17	0.63	0.41
Waldemar Psilander	52	36	15	0.69	0.42

Even though Porten made over twice as many films, the market absorbed them even better than Nielsen's. Psilander made almost twice as many films, and his films also received a higher number of screenings on average. Hence, I believe that one should not overinterpret the common argument that exclusives were necessary to prevent oversupply. Producers may have made higher profits per film with (successful) exclusives, because rental prices were higher and the secondary trade was eliminated, but this did not necessarily mean that the total profit (with fewer films) was higher. More importantly, 'oversupply' (in the sense of falling prices) did not necessarily mean that supply exceeded audience demand. Even with more comprehensive data one would not be able to answer the question if audiences wanted to see more Asta Nielsen films (or if more people wanted to see them); all one can say is that by all indications, Porten and Psilander were at least as popular, if not more so, and this despite the fact that they were promoted less aggressively.[34]

Especially in the long term, popularity is ultimately due to a star's characteristics rather than hype. The distribution strategy played a role in how much money was made with a star's films and how the profits were allocated among producers, distributors and exhibitors, and thus the exploitation and sustainability, rather than the 'creation' of stardom. The main function of the exclusive was that a greater share of the profits flowed back to the producers, so that more money could be invested in more expensive films. Hence the fact that the exclusive eventually became the norm contributed to the lasting establishment of the long, lavish (and consequently costly) feature film.[35] This had no direct connection with stardom *per se*, but only with the kinds of films that stars appeared in. In contrast to Hollywood, the exclusive, long-term contract between actors and studios (as Nielsen and Porten had) did not even become the typical arrangement in Germany; in Weimar cinema, which had a flourishing star system, actors worked as freelancers.[36]

Finally, the German discourse on Asta Nielsen reveals why Porten would eventually become more successful in Germany. The mere number of mentions is already interesting – in the documents database, there are only 2 of Psilander, 26 of Porten, and 66 of Nielsen. I believe that this is a striking example of the fact that one should not necessarily regard discourses by the cultural elite as representative of popularity with audiences at large. On Psilander, a (male) critic wrote:

> What a man! He takes himself and his task seriously, he does not compromise and works, past all temptations, towards full effects. One often sees him biting his lip while thinking, in a stern and masculine manner, for several minutes, while the expensive film rushes past and conveys nothing but this process of thought, no grimaces, no theatrics. Then one sees him signal with a laboured gesture that he has found what he has been looking for. He walks, talks and acts as if there were no apparatus and no audience. He is governed by strength as well as measure, and beyond his own achievement, his personality leaves its mark upon all who surround him.[37]

There is nothing so elaborate on Henny Porten's acting. Porten was frequently mentioned as appearing in a new film, she was called a great actress and one of the most popular German film actresses, sometimes even the most popular German film actress. Nothing extremely laudatory can be found, but perhaps more significantly, hardly anything negative can be found either. A critic of the socialist press accused her of representing the style of the *Gartenlaube* magazine in the cinema.[38] A particularly apt description of Henny Porten was that her characters conveyed an impression of "amiable and austere chastity".[39] When her characters found themselves in sexual predicaments, they were victims rather than vamps.

By contrast, Nielsen polarised opinion. The most enthusiastic article is one by film critic Josef Aubinger on her and Urban Gad. Aubinger regarded AFGRUNDEN as a revolution in film art and Nielsen as one of the greatest actresses of all time. He did not find Nielsen beautiful, but fascinating nonetheless, due to the very characteristics that others found unattractive (her very slim figure and exotic looks):

> One cannot call Asta Nielsen a beauty, because she lacks the requisite womanly charms. But for what is lacking in this regard, she compensates a hundred times over with hot-bloodedness, temperament, and artistic creativity. It is incredible what this extremely thin person is able to call forth from within herself. If one wanted to forge all of the incarnations of the modern woman with all the deepest abysses of her soul into a single type, like a perpendicular line emerging from a vanishing point, this Danish woman, who is as slim as a gazelle and looks like a genuine Spaniard, would be the most fruitful object for such a daring experiment.[40]

Other positive reviews regarded Nielsen as too good for her films; many reviewers lamented that her films were not much better than average. Finally, many were outraged by the vampish characters that she played, and especially her sensual dancing – or, as Heinrich Auer described it, "Asta Nielsen's dubious manner of exciting the audience's senses with her bodily contortions".[41] Hence, Nielsen's films probably contributed to the stricter and more extensive film censorship that was instated in Germany around 1912.

In sum, the opinions on Nielsen could not have been more extreme – for some she represented the best, for others the worst of cinema, which was regarded either as a new art form or as the epitome of cultural decline. Perceptions of Asta Nielsen as 'exotic and degenerate' and of Henny Porten as 'truly German and healthy' are disturbingly reminiscent of Nazi ideology many years later, but the demure, blond 'good girl' was still the German favourite even in the 1950s, represented by actresses such as Ruth Leuwerik and Maria Schell. In the midst of these controversies, Kurt Tucholsky's assessment from 1913 seems uncharacteristically imperceptive, but characteristically provocative – he simply found Nielsen's films boring.[42]

In sum, if popularity is taken as the measure of stardom, then Asta Nielsen was a star in Germany, but despite extensive and innovative promotion, her appeal had its limits, both temporally as well as regarding the size of her audience. Hence one might regard her as the first film star in longer films in Germany, but stardom as such was hardly invented with Nielsen, and she was neither the first film star nor the most popular one. Rather than the idea of film stardom, what seems to me to have been most novel – and controversial – for contemporaries was the claim that a film actress could be an artist equal to the greatest stage actresses. Together with the image of womanhood that Nielsen represented (emancipated, sensual and exotic), this ambition polarized German audiences.

Acknowledgements: My thanks to Martin Loiperdinger, John Sedgwick, Stephan Michael Schröder and Joseph Garncarz for their comments.

Notes

1. Richard Dyer, "The Star Phenomenon", in *International Encyclopedia of Communications*, Erik Barnouw (ed.) (New York: Oxford University Press: 1989), 176–180, 176.
2. Francesco Alberoni, "The Powerless Elite: Theory and Sociological Research On the Phenomenon of Stars", in Denis McQuail (ed.), *Sociology of Mass Communication* (Baltimore: Penguin, 1972), 75–98.
3. Cf. Richard Abel's essay in this volume.
4. Richard Dyer, *Stars; with a Supplementary Chapter and Bibliography by Paul McDonald*, new edn (London: British Film Institute, 1998 [1979]), 160.
5. For a more extensive discussion, cf. my doctoral dissertation, published as *Stars und ihr Publikum am Beispiel Clint Eastwood* (Hamburg: Kovac, 2011).
6. The databases are publicly accessible at www.earlycinema.uni-koeln.de. Cf. also Joseph Garncarz and Michael Ross, "Die Siegener Datenbanken zum frühen Kino in Deutschland", *KINtop* 14/15 (2006), 151–164.
7. Cf. Martin Loiperdinger, "AFGRUNDEN in Germany: *monopolfilm*, cinema-going and the emergence of the film star Asta Nielsen, 1910–1911", in Daniel Biltereyst et al. (eds), *Cinema Audiences and Modernity: New Perspectives on European Cinema History* (London: Routledge, 2012), 142–153.
8. Joseph Garncarz, *Maßlose Unterhaltung: zur Etablierung des Films in Deutschland 1896–1914* (Frankfurt: Stroemfeld, 2010).
9. Emilie Altenloh, *Zur Soziologie des Kino: Die Kino-Unternehmung und die sozialen Schichten ihrer Besucher* [1914], edited by Heide Schlüpmann, Martin Loiperdinger and Andrea Haller (Frankfurt and Basel: Stroemfeld, 2012); excerpt available in English as "A Sociology of the Cinema and the Audience", *Screen* 42: 3 (2001), 249–293.
10. A few travelling showmen may have shown Nielsen's films (HEISSES BLUT was among the inventory of a travelling showman who appeared at the Munich Oktoberfest, and Ansje van

Beusekom has found examples for this in the Netherlands – cf. her essay in this volume), but this is more likely to have been the exception rather than the rule. In any case, it was not the ultimate trend. Garncarz (*Maßlose Unterhaltung*, 217–228) argues that fairground cinemas only began to show longer films for a short time in response to the competition of permanent cinemas.

11. This is possible for the Netherlands with *Cinema Context* (cf. Ansje van Beusekom's essay in this volume). Due to restrictions of time and manpower, the German programme sample is not only limited geographically (to nine cities from three regions), but also temporally (one month of each year was selected for each region).

12. Compared to the filmographies compiled by others, such as the Danish Film Institute, a handful of titles appear in the film supply database that are questionable. These are either idiosyncratic variations of titles, or mistakes, or deliberately false advertising, which would have to be examined in each case, if it is of interest. Since Nielsen's filmography is well researched, I will not do so here. Note that there are many more questionable entries in Nielsen's filmography at the IMDb. These are more likely to be mistakes by the contributors, rather than by the original sources. Regrettably, the IMDb is not very reliable for early cinema in general (high number of questionable entries, little information etc.). It is a pity that such a widely used Internet database, which is excellent for later periods, is so unreliable for early cinema. It would be very useful if experts on early cinema contributed more to correcting and adding information there, especially because other databases (such as *Cinema Context*) link to it and more might do so in future.

13. As Christina Rönz has argued, based on her study of Trier and Saarbrücken, "'Asta Nielsen Kommt': Der Filmstar und die Kinobetreiber im Deutschen Reich", in Heide Schlüpmann et al. (eds), *Unmögliche Liebe: Asta Nielsen, ihr Kino* (2nd edn) (Vienna: filmarchiv austria, 2010), 187–193. Garncarz (*Maßlose Unterhaltung*, 191) makes the same claim for exclusives in general, but he bases it on films that were *advertised* as exclusives. In small towns with only one cinema, even when a film was shown that was distributed as an exclusive elsewhere, it would not have been necessary for an exhibitor to point out this fact. Conversely, cinema owners in large cities sometimes claimed that they had exclusive rights even when they did not.

14. Thomas Elsaesser and Michael Wedel compare the *Monopolfilm* to Hollywood's later run-zone-clearance system, but this may create the impression that early exclusive distribution was much more organised and strictly controlled than it actually was. Cf. "Distribution", *Encyclopedia of Early Cinema*, Richard Abel (ed.) (London et al.: Routledge, 2005), 390–392.

15. Gabriele Kilchenstein, *Frühe Filmzensur in Deutschland: eine vergleichende Studie zur Prüfungspraxis in Berlin und München 1906–1914* (Munich: Diskurs-Film-Verlag Schaudig und Ledig, 1997). Cf. also my finding that the number of films screened did not simply depend on the size of a place, discussed in "Urban Legend: Early Cinema, Modernization, and Urbanization in Germany, 1895–1914", in Daniel Biltereyst, Richard Maltby and Philippe Meers (eds), *Cinema Audiences and Modernity: New Perspectives on European Cinema History* (London: Routledge, 2012), 117–129.

16. Asta Nielsen, *Die Photographische Industrie* 19 (7 May 1913): 681.

17. Cf. Kilchenstein, *Frühe Filmzensur*, 273.

18. Paul Samuleit, "Der Kinematograph als Volks- und Jugendbildungsmittel", *Die Volksbildung* 42:22 (1912), 423–439.

19. B.H.A. Schmitz, "Kino und Großstadtjugend", *Die Hochwacht* 4:2 (1913).

20. Cf. Garncarz, *Maßlose Unterhaltung*.

21. Cf. Martin Loiperdinger, "German *Tonbilder* of the 1900s: Advanced Technology and National Brand", in Annemone Ligensa and Klaus Kreimeier (eds), *Film 1900: Technology, Perception, Culture* (New Barnet: John Libbey, 2009), 187–200 and "*Des Pfarrers Töchterlein*", in Joseph Garncarz and Annemone Ligensa (eds), *The Cinema of Germany* [24 Frames Series] (London et al.: Wallflower, 2012).

22. "Das Resultat unserer Rundfrage", *Illustrierte Kino-Woche* 2:1 (1914), 7.

23. Richard deCordova, *Picture Personalities: The Emergence of the Star System in America* (Urbana, IL: University of Illinois Press, 1990); Joseph Garncarz, "The Star System in Weimar Cinema", in Christian Rogowski (ed.), *The Many Faces of Weimar Cinema* (New York: Camden House, 2010), 182–206. Cf. also Ian Christie's essay in this volume.

24. Note also that in a Russian survey, where cinemagoers were asked the separate question to name

their favourite comedian, Linder was the most popular actor in that category; cf. Lauri Piispa's essay in this volume.

25. Cf. e.g. Jack Balswick, "Heroes and Heroines Among American Adolescents", *Sex Roles* 8:3 (1994), 243–249. Hence I believe that the initial lack of male stars requires more explanation than the promotion of female stars (cf. Ian Christie's essay in this volume).

26. Cf. e.g. Peter Krämer, "A Powerful Cinemagoing Force? Hollywood and Female Audiences Since the 1960s", in Melvyn Stokes and Richard Maltby (eds), *Identifying Hollywood's Audiences: Cultural Identity and the Movies* (London: bfi Publishing, 1999), 98–112.

27. Haller, "'Nur meine Asta! Und damit basta!'", 335.

28. On the contemporary German discourse on women's sexual desire, cf. my essay "'A Cinematograph of Feminine Thought': *The Dangerous Age*, Cinema and Modern Women", in Annemone Ligensa and Klaus Kreimeier (eds), *Film 1900: Technology, Perception, Culture* (New Barnet: John Libbey, 2009), 225–236.

29. Urban Gad, *Der Film: Seine Mittel – Seine Ziele* (Berlin: Schuster & Loeffler, 1921), 147.

30. Cf. Corinna Müller, *Frühe deutsche Kinematographie: Formale, wirtschaftliche und kulturelle Entwicklungen 1907–1912* (Stuttgart: Metzler, 1994), specif. 143–156 and 170–179 (plus notes). Müller represents a production-oriented view of stardom: 'The structures in the German film industry of the 1910s (…) did not treat the so-called 'fascination' with a star as the decisive factor, but rather created this propensity." (150).

31. Cf. e.g. Knut Hickethier, "Vom Theaterstar zum Filmstar: Merkmale des Starwesens um die Wende vom 19. zum 20. Jahrhundert", in Werner Faulstich and Helmut Korte (eds), *Der Star: Geschichte, Rezeption, Bedeutung* (Munich: Fink, 1997), 29–47.

32. Ludwig Gottschalk's and later Christoph Mülleneisen's role could even be compared to that of a theatrical agent, with the difference that they negotiated the distribution of films rather than personal appearances.

33. Cf. the comments on Porten quoted in Haller, "'Nur meine Asta! Und damit basta!'", 333 (e.g. ("[Porten] steht uns menschlich näher.").

34. My thanks to Isak Thorsen for pointing out to me that Nordisk promoted Psilander in the trade press; but at least in Germany, exhibitors hardly seem to have followed suit. I do not know whether Psilander's films were marketed as exclusives in Germany. One would assume that they were, but in the programme database, there are several instances of his films being shown in more than one cinema in the same city during the same week, sometimes even despite the claim of 'exclusive rights'.

35. One might add that further factors, especially copyright laws and their enforcement, were important for this development. For example, in the beginning, exclusive rights were sometimes circumvented by the production of pirate versions, e.g. a Danish version of Oskar Messter's DAS GEFÄHRLICHE ALTER was made, starring Psilander. Messter successfully sued against its distribution in Germany, which became something of a precedent. Cf. my essay "'A Cinematograph of Feminine Thought'".

36. Cf. Garncarz, "The Star System in Weimar Cinema".

37. Balder Olden, "Dramaturgie des Lichtspiels", *Kölnische Zeitung*, Part 1: no. 1193 (27 October 1912), Part 2: no. 1200 (3 November 1912).

38. Adolf Behne, "Kinokunst", *Sozialistische Monatshefte* 4 (1914), 267–268. *Gartenlaube* was a hugely successful German magazine that was especially popular with middle class women. Among its offerings were sentimental fiction and kitschy artwork.

39. "Die Films der Woche", *Berliner Börsen-Courier* 137 (22 March 1914).

40. Josef Aubinger, "Asta Nielsen – Urban Gad", *Zeit im Bild* 3 (1913), 1992–1993.

41. Heinrich Auer, "Zur Kinofrage", *Soziale Revue* 13, 1 (1913), 19–36.

42. Kurt Tucholsky, "Kinomüdigkeit", *Berliner Volksblatt* 30:8 (5 May 1913), suppl. *Vorwärts*. For a comparison of Porten and Nielsen, cf. also Frank Kessler and Eva Warth, "Early Cinema and Its Audiences", in Tim Bergfelder, Erica Carter and Denis Göktürk (eds), *The German Cinema Book* (London: bfi Publishing, 2002), 121–128, specif. 125 and, of course, Heide Schlüpmann, *The Uncanny Gaze: The Drama of Early German Cinema* (Urbana, IL: University of Illinois Press, 2010).

Ian Christie

From Screen Personalities to Stars
Analysing Early Film Fame in Europe

Is it heretical to suggest that perhaps the major obstacle to understanding what I will call provisionally 'film fame' is the popular field of star studies? Historically, this was one of the first topics within film to attract scholarly study, with several generations of sociologists, anthropologists and early film scholars all fascinated by the star phenomenon, beginning with Hortense Powdermaker and Edgar Morin in the 1950s, and continuing with Alexander Walker in the 1960s and Richard Dyer in the 1970s.[1] Much of this early work focused inevitably on the post-1920s star system operated by the major studios, and naturally therefore has a strong Hollywood bias. We hear routinely about Florence Lawrence and about Mary Pickford becoming the 'first' film stars, but this results from projecting *back* a later and overwhelmingly American conception of studio-based 'stardom'. It is therefore unlikely to shed much light on the Asta Nielsen phenomenon or early screen fame more generally, and may indeed be actively unhelpful in creating a teleological pull towards the studio era as paradigmatic.

So we have to begin by rejecting the routine claims in star studies that there were 'no stars' before around 1908–10.[2] A 'star system' manifestly existed in nineteenth-century performing arts, and established stage and entertainment personalities were prominent in the very first film programmes presented in Britain and the United States by Robert Paul and Thomas Edison. Edison had already filmed such vaudeville stars as the strongman Eugene Sandow and sharpshooter Annie Oakley for the Kinetoscope as early as 1894, before these subjects were projected during 1896; while Paul offered a range of music hall performers, such as the eccentric comedian Chirgwin, the magicians Nevil Maskelyne and David Devant, and the dancing Sisters Hengler. The reasons for filming these are obvious: they were established performers and their presence lent distinction to early animated photography and Vitascope shows. Although they had all begun on stage, their fame was enhanced by the explosion of new media: lantern shows, postcards, cigarette cards, pictures in newspapers and magazines, and now appearances on screen. And with the appearance of sound synchronisation systems in the early 1900s, some of these musical stage

353

stars could extend their existing fame, as with the *Tonbilder* launched by Oskar Messter in 1903, which eventually comprised a repertoire of 500 subjects,[3] or the series of Harry Lauder synchronised films offered by Gaumont through their Chronophone in 1907.[4]

Among the pioneers, Lumière were unique in not offering established entertainers in their earliest films. The first named figures to appear in Lumière films were heads of state – Tsar Nicolas of Russia, the King and Queen of Italy, President Porfirio Diaz of Mexico, Kaiser Wilhelm II, Queen Victoria, all in 1896 and 1897 – who thereby acquired a new kind of celebrity through their frequent appearances on screen. Martin Loiperdinger has shown how the Kaiser's 'star' status in early German cinema derived from and helped reinforce a pre-existing fascination with the Hohenzollern court.[5]

Mutoscope and Biograph also filmed statesmen and, famously, Pope Leo XIII in 1898. British Biograph had a policy of featuring well-known actors, starting with Beerbohm Tree in a scene from his production of Shakespeare's *King John* (1899). Here, as in films starring Herbert Campbell and Dan Leno, the performers' names were an essential part of the films' appeal.[6] However, apart from these 'pre-existing' celebrities it is true that performers in the majority of comic and dramatic films made before 1908 – and many made up to the late 1910s – were effectively anonymous; while by 1920, stars had indeed become desirable, if not essential for the marketing of films.

Argument over how and why this happened is almost as old as writing about the history of cinema, with early accounts provided by Terry Ramsaye and Benjamin Hampton,[7] and these have been analysed, along with additional factors, by Richard deCordova, David P. Marshall and many others.[8] It is not my purpose here to add to this debate about causes and motivations, much of which remains heavily biased towards American companies and their domestic market (again, projecting back from the undeniable importance of American producers and stars after the mid-1910s). My perspective is essentially European; and in this context the obvious starting point is not the celebrated defection of Florence Lawrence from her anonymity at Biograph to being heavily promoted in her own name by Carl Laemmle at IMP in 1909. It is, rather, the trend that began in the previous year towards harnessing theatrical reputations to a new kind of production: the *film d'art*.

The Société Le Film d'art was launched in 1907 with the aim of "making [films] based on scenarios written by contemporary authors, involving recognised artists".[9] Among its leading figures were two actors, Charles Le Bargy of the Comédie Française and André Calmettes, and although the company was not commercially successful, its example was widely noted and continued, both by Pathé (which took it over) and by Pathé's international branches and other companies. 'Film d'art', variously translated, became a recognised genre over the next five years, signifying a level of production values in acting, costume and décor, usually with an historical setting. In Italy and Russia, the genre's impact was decisive: production in both countries began to exploit national-historical traditions, attracting domestic audiences, and producing exportable films. It also brought 'recognised artists' into film more regularly, and an example of this is British Gaumont's announcement in 1908 of "over 40 of London's foremost artistes" appearing in a film based on the Lyceum production of *Romeo and Juliet*.[10] From this point, Jon Burrows has traced a steady progression of what Gaumont called 'celebrity films', with featured actors; and as so-called 'art series' proliferated in France, Italy and Britain, the marketing of these seems to have automatically included the names of their cast. So we can be fairly clear that named actors were a major part of the appeal of the more ambitious new European productions by 1909 – which is of course the tumultuous year when Florence Laurence exchanged her anonymity at Biograph for fame at IMP.

If we look in more detail at the British market, by 1910 and 1911 the names of actors were being noted in trade advertising and reviewing, while famous actor-managers, such as Beerbohm Tree – and soon living legends like Sarah Bernhardt – were also being widely featured in consumer publicity. This, then, is the context in which Asta Nielsen's first films appeared in 1911 and quickly became a major attraction for trade and public alike. By July 1912, perhaps uniquely, her films were being offered to British exhibitors as a 'brand': "'Great Asta Nielsen' Dramas".[11] In Britain, Florence Lawrence and Mary Pickford were the only other actresses regularly recognised by name, although a series of the male film comedians, Max Linder, André Deed and 'Prince', were already established and prolific brands, anticipating the cult of Chaplin that would begin in 1914.[12] But how are we to interpret the fascination that developed around early non-comic and almost exclusively female stars? Before moving on to the anthropological and sociological diagnosis that would become commonplace, we should perhaps try to see it in contemporary terms, since there were observers outside the film industry who noted the emergence of this new form of fascination from contrasting, yet informed, standpoints. Two of these, Hugo Münsterberg and Luigi Pirandello, were both widely known and respected for very different reasons than their interest in film when they published on the subject within the same year, 1916. And in both cases, their positions on the cinema have been subject to dispute.

Münsterberg was a Harvard professor when he published his 'psychological study', *The Photoplay*, in 1916.[13] A distinguished practitioner of experimental psychology in Germany, Münsterberg moved to Harvard in 1897, where he worked in different fields, including forensic and industrial psychology. It was only near the end of his life that he 'discovered' cinema, to which he brought the same enthusiasm that had marked his other work, apparently watching films voraciously for the first time in his life and writing about his reactions for popular magazines as well as preparing a monograph. His fundamental, and still controversial, insight in *The Photoplay* is that the spectator's mind 'moulds' or interprets the scenes in a film "until they appear the embodiment of our feelings",[14] in a kind of projective fantasy relationship. Combining aesthetic and psychological analysis, Münsterberg arrived at "a unified principle": "The photoplay tells us the human story by overcoming the forms of the outer world, namely, space, time, and causality, and by adjusting the events to the forms of the inner world, namely, attention, memory, imagination, and emotion".[15]

Later, he expressed this even more euphorically:

> The massive outer world has lost its weight, it has been freed from space, time, and causality, and it has been clothed in the forms of our own consciousness. The mind has triumphed over matter and the pictures roll on with the ease of musical tones. It is a superb enjoyment which no other art can furnish us.[16]

Immersion in films can produce strange psychological reactions in the audience — neurasthenic symptoms, forms of mass hysteria, and the like. There is also a unique new way of engaging with the actors on the screen, which Münsterberg struggled to articulate:

> The process which leads from the living men to the screen is more complex than a mere reflection in a mirror, but in spite of the complexity in the transmission we do, after all, see the real actor in the picture. The photograph is absolutely different from those pictures which a clever draughtsman has sketched. In the photoplay we see the actors themselves and the decisive factor which makes the impression different from seeing real men is not that we see the living persons through the medium of photographic reproduction but that this reproduction shows them in a flat form. The bodily space has been eliminated.[17]

Screen actors, for Münsterberg, are simultaneously 'real', yet as images, incorporeal. Stars were already a major presence in American cinema when Münsterberg underwent his crash induction into the pleasures of cinema-going, and he refers to going "with the crowd to [see] Anita Stewart and Mary Pickford and Charles Chaplin", while there is also a magazine photograph of an apparently star-struck 'Doctor Münsterberg' meeting Stewart.[18] His discussion of the difference between stage and screen acting, where the former is helped "by the content of the words and the modulation of the voice" to overcome the difficulty of feigning emotion physiologically, produced the observation:

> To the actor of the moving pictures, on the other hand, the temptation offers itself to overcome the deficiency by a heightening of the gestures and of the facial play, with the result that the emotional expression becomes exaggerated. No friend of the photoplay can deny that much of the photoart suffers from this almost unavoidable tendency. The quick marchlike rhythm of the drama of the reel favors this artificial overdoing, too. (…) This undeniable defect is felt with the American actors still more than with the European, especially with the French and Italian ones with whom excited gestures and highly accentuated expressions of the face are natural. A New England temperament forced into Neapolitan expressions of hatred or jealousy or adoration too easily appears a caricature.[19]

As a result, Münsterberg noted, many stage actors were "more or less decided failures on the screen" compared with "the specializing photoactor"; and despite his preference for European actors, Münsterberg contrasts two recent American versions of CARMEN in terms of their editing rate, distinguishing them simply as the "Theda Bara edition" and "the Geraldine Farrar version".[20]

What we find, then, in this first major attempt to apply psychological science – the descendent of Ludwig Fechner's 'psychophysics' – to the developed feature film, is an implicit recognition of the centrality of stars, locating them as 'specialists' within the overall affective apparatus of film.[21]

Münsterberg died shortly after the publication of *The Photoplay*, and this aspect of his work was not carried forward during the period when Hollywood production and stars were conquering the world.[22] Indeed it was largely forgotten during the subsequent seventy years, until experimenters once again sought to investigate 'what psychological factors are involved when we watch the happenings on the screen'. When Münsterberg began to be rediscovered, he was seen by some, especially on the Left, as providing an early rationale for encouraging the consumption of film as 'escape' from the realities of working life; for creating a form of 'pseudo-consumption', which could be regarded as an immaterial equivalent of the consumerism promoted by modern capitalist society.[23] Only more recently, since the rise of experimental psychological approaches to film spectatorship, has his pioneering role begun to be acknowledged.

Almost exactly contemporary with Münsterberg, another account of filmic fascination appeared in Europe, in the form of Luigi Pirandello's novel *Si gira*.[24] The title is a phrase that was used in contemporary filmmaking, meaning literally 'turn over' (referring to the hand-cranked camera), or as it is usually translated, 'shoot'. Pirandello's narrator is an impassive cameraman employed at an Italian studio engaged in making the 'diva' films which had become Italy's most popular genre. Gubbio, the cameraman, observes an off-screen melodrama unfold, which will lead to the tragic death of the leading man while he is being filmed, in an ironic doubling of the 'real' and the fictive that anticipates Pirandello's most famous play, *Six Characters in Search of an Author* (*Sei personaggi in cerca d'autore*, 1921). His cameraman-observer is both fascinated and repelled by the off-screen drama he watches unfolding around him, and especially by the diva star of the Kosmograph studio, La Nesteroff, portrayed as a *femme fatale* who revels in her power "at any moment, whenever the fancy took her, [to] tear from the side of any proud young lady and recapture for herself all the mad young men who threaten tragedies, *pst!*, by holding up a finger, and at once tame them, intoxicate them with the rustle of a silk skirt".[25]

Despite this power, she is also, according to Gubbio, 'a bore', an empty and destructive force, who fatally exerts her influence over the young actor starring in her latest film and brings about his death. Such films, for the alienated cameraman, impassively turning the camera handle, are sadistic spectacles of primitive passion being played out for popular entertainment. And this would seem to have been the position of the Italian Marxist thinker, Antonio Gramsci, who was working as a theatre critic at the climax of the *dive* cult, when *Si gira* appeared. In 1917, Gramsci wrote of the original diva, Lyda Borelli:

> This woman is a primordial relic of prehistoric humanity. They say they admire her for her art. That's not true. No one can explain the art of la Borelli because it

doesn't exist. La Borelli doesn't know how to play anyone but herself. (…) La Borelli is the artist par excellence of the cinema whose language is the human body in its perpetually renewed plasticity.[26]

The background to Gramsci's polemic was his criticism of a society which relegated women to the roles of 'plaything' or 'brood mare', within which the diva film was merely another unwelcome symptom of increased sexualisation, while cinema itself was a debased medium, cynically inflicting kitsch on its vast public.[27]

A more nuanced interpretation of *Si gira* is, however, also possible. Angela Dalle Vacche has argued that the novel does not simply condemn film as mechanical, but attributes this negativity to its protagonist, Gubbio, who "feels insecure about relations between men and women in daily life"[28] and transfers this to his relations with the actors. Furthermore, Dalle Vacche observes, Pirandello is the first author to attempt to portray the inner life of a screen goddess, when he writes of Varia Nesteroff:

> She herself remains speechless and almost terror-stricken at her own image on the screen, so altered and disordered. She sees there one who is herself but whom she does not know. She would not like to recognise herself in this person. (…) She is really tragic: terrified and enthralled …[29]

Whether this was merely inventive speculation on Pirandello's part, or whether it had some basis in his familiarity with the film studios that he visited in Rome while writing *Si gira*, we cannot know. However, it supports Dalle Vacche's claim that we should not too hastily conflate Pirandello's supposedly negative view of cinema with that of his protagonist.[30]

After Pirandello's novel was re-issued in the mid-1920s, Walter Benjamin would build on its diagnosis of the alienation supposedly felt by the diva – "the feeling of strangeness that overcomes the actor before the camera, as Pirandello describes it" – as if this were fact, incorporating it into his essay *The Work of Art in the Age of Mechanical Reproduction*, where "the film responds to the shrivelling of the aura with an artificial build-up of the 'personality' outside the studio".[31] And from Benjamin, it is a short step to the Frankfurt School's familiar critique of popular culture as a debased form of mass-manipulation, which effectively revived the position occupied by Gramsci and many other socialist intellectuals in the 1910s, and is still evident in much hostility to the commercialised culture represented by Hollywood. But if we set aside this familiar judgement, and return to the beginnings of the 'star era', we may discover *structural* reasons for the emergence of the 'human capital' that stars unquestionably came to represent.[32]

Pierre Sorlin has observed, in his study of Italian national cinema, that although it later became fashionable to decry or mock the diva era, in an Italy deprived of state ceremony, "*dive* made up for what was lacking in public life, ostentation, magnificence, theatrical excess – in a word, glamour".[33] Sorlin tries to account for the specific form that early stardom took in Italy; and we can find similarly national characteristics among the earliest star cults in other countries. In

Germany, Henny Porten performed anonymously in at least 22 of short *Tonbilder* between 1906 and 1910, when she made her feature debut. In 1911 she would appear in a short prologue to the dramatic film TRAGÖDIE EINES STREIKS (THE TRAGEDY OF A STRIKE), in which, as Martin Koerber puts it, she "greets the audience like old friends".[34] By the following year, Henny Porten films 'sold themselves', and the star was featured in special trade press supplements "expressing gratitude for all the attention she had been shown",[45] supported by lobby cards and the now widely circulating picture postcards (about which more below). Similar patterns can be found in most of the main producing countries, although there is a striking contrast in between the glamour expected of Italian *dive* and the humility and projection of ordinariness which was the key to stardom in Germany and in Britain, where Chrissie White had been promoted by her producer Cecil Hepworth, and was typically described as "delightful" in reviews that stressed her "genuinely English" qualities.[36]

White and Porten, like all the other 'first wave' stars, owed much of their fame to the explosion of photographic postcards which more or less coincided with the popularisation of cinema. Cigarette cards were the first of these new collectible images, and their manufacturers had traditionally included 'Beauties' and 'Actresses' among the regular subjects. But around 1900, new printing processes made photographic cards significantly cheaper to produce, and output rose steeply in almost all European countries after the introduction of the 'divided back' format spread from Britain in 1902 to France (1904), Germany (1905) and finally the United States (1907), offering a full 14 x 9 cm portrait on the reverse side.[37] Film 'stars' or 'personalities' joined the repertoire of subjects, and producers such as Messter and Hepworth took full advantage of the new craze for sending and collecting such cards to promote their stars, as it reached extraordinary levels by 1914, with up to 20 cards per head of the total population being posted in Britain alone.[38] Looking at these portrait cards today, as displayed on the collectors' website European Film Star Postcards, the transnational dimension of early stardom becomes clear.[39] Portraits of stars could be published in any of the countries where their films were being seen, to satisfy local demand, and indeed their frequency could provide a proxy measure of star 'impact'. Equally clear, iconographically, is how such portraits tended to reinforce a relatively stable star image, with many variations on the same 'type' – except in the case of Asta Nielsen, who perhaps uniquely appears in a wide range of different roles, testifying to *versatility* and *variety* as defining features of her image, rather than repetition.

Female stars became both the expression of national ideals and a transnational phenomenon in the period 1911–15.[40] Similar patterns can be seen recurring across the emergent national industries; and as a step towards trying to understand this phenomenon, I propose here an approach based on the pioneering methodology of George Huaco's *Sociology of Film Art*. Huaco wanted to explore three "stylistically unified waves of film art"[41] – German Expressionism, Soviet expressive realism, and Italian Neorealism – by comparing the social structures that underpinned them, in terms of personnel, industrial capacity and prevailing ideology. This is not the occasion to attempt a similarly comprehensive causal account of the emergence of the film star, but I have borrowed some features of Huaco's methodology to create a preliminary framework for comparison among the early stars. The following table summarises the careers of 22 early female stars – in most cases the earliest in their respective national film industries – and tabulates four main features: whether or not they had previous stage experience; the date and age of their film debuts and the length of their subsequent careers.

Table 1.

Nation	Name	Birth date	Prev. Exp.	Film début	age	Film career
Britain	Gladys Sylvani	1884	Stage	1910	26	Short
	Chrissie White	1895	None	1909	19	Long
France	Sarah Bernhardt	1844	Stage int'l	1912	68★	Short
	Gabrielle Réjane	1856	Stage int'l	1900	44★	Short
	Mistinguett	1875	Stage	1908	38	Long
	Suzanne Grandais	1893	Stage	1909?	16	Long
Denmark	Asta Nielsen	1881	Stage	1910	29	Long
Germany	Henny Porten	1890	None	1906	16	Long
	Lil Dagover	1887	None	1913	25	Long
Italy	Lyda Borelli	1884	Stage	1913	29	Short
	Hesperia	1885		1912	27	Long
	Pina Menichelli	1890	Stage	1913	23	Long
	Francesca Bertini	1892	Stage	1910	18	Long
	Leyda Gys	1892		1912	20	Long
Russia	Vera Karalli	1889	Stage	1914	25	Short
	Vera Kholodnaia	1893	None	1915	22	Short
USA	Anita Stewart	1885?		1911	26	Long
	Florence Turner	1885	Stage	1907	22	Long
	Theda Bara	1885	Stage	1914	29	Short
	Florence Lawrence	1886	Stage	1906	20	Long
	Mary Pickford	1892	Stage	1909	17	Long
	Lillian Gish	1893	Stage	1912	19	Long

★ Both the rivals Bernhardt and Réjane made very early film appearances as theatre celebrities, but their few 'starring' roles came between 1911–16.

The majority of these actresses became 'stars' between 1911 and 1914, benefitting from the rapid structural changes that had transformed the film business in the previous two years, creating a new demand for longer 'headline' films that earned substantial revenues by being shown as 'exclusives' in the new cinema palaces that were appearing in all major cities. Their fame was intricately linked to the new promotional pressures and opportunities that surrounded the programming of these venues. With the notable exception of the three older French actresses (all already famous), the two thirds who had some stage experience did not have major reputations before their rapid rise to screen fame. Indeed, three of the most typically successful of the youngest cohort, those born in the 1890s – Vera Kholodnaia, Henny Porten and Chrissie White – had no stage experience at all before they were 'discovered' by filmmakers, and quickly recognised as favourites of the cinema-going public.

What also stands out in this tabulation is that Asta Nielsen was among the oldest of those who became international film stars, with only Borelli, Hesperia and Bara also gaining fame in their late 20s, and these within a relatively limited range of genre roles. Asta Nielsen, crucially, made her mark before these later 'divas' and 'vamps' appeared, and was already the first transnational European star by the time they emerged. Exceptionally, she continued to be hailed for her 'versatility' and range at a time when star identities were becoming fixed: a 1913 full-page trade advertisement by her British distributor, Walturdaw, featured both the "truly brilliant comedy-drama" IN A FIX (JUGEND UND TOLLHEIT) and THE HEART OF A PIERROT (KOMÖDIANTEN), a "tragedy that will touch the hearts of all".[42] Such comparisons help clarify the uniqueness of Asta Nielsen's reputation and commercial success – and also reveal the significance of its timing. By the beginning of 1914, there were many newer and younger entrants to the screen pantheon, but Asta Nielsen's name and 'brand' was established. However, by the end of that year, the First World War had engulfed Europe, and although it did not immediately damage Nielsen's popularity in other territories, the underlying changes that it would bring about in the structure of the international film business would ensure that in future only American-based stars could enjoy the same global appeal.[43] As the nascent Hollywood majors increasingly controlled distribution after 1916, so the European industries dramatically lost whatever international market share they previously had.[44] Henceforth, film stars would be quintessentially a Hollywood phenomenon, with the qualification 'local' or 'national' attached to all others. Asta Nielsen, meanwhile, continued her independent and innovative career, benefiting from the relative stabilisation of Weimar cinema, and, like Henny Porten and Lil Dagover, a loyal following.

Notes

1. Hortense Powdermaker, *Hollywood the Dream Factory* (New York: Little, Brown, 1950); Edgar Morin, *Les Stars* (Paris: Editions du Seuil, 1957); Alexander Walker, *The Celluloid Sacrifice: Sex in the Movies* (London: Michael Joseph, 1966); Richard Dyer, *Stars* (London: British Film Institute, 1979).

2. Richard deCordova, for instance, writes of "a cinema completely without stars" before 1910, before going on to discuss rival theories of what brought about "a cinema wholly dependent on them" (Richard deCordova, *Picture Personalities: the emergence of the star system in America* (Champaign, Ill.: University of Illinois Press, 1999), 1).

3. On Messter's Biophon system and the *Tonbilder* boom in Germany, cf. Martin Loiperdinger, "German Tonbilder of the 1900s: Advanced Technology and National Brand", in Klaus Kreimeier

and Annemone Ligensa (eds), *Film 1900: Technology, Perception, Culture* (New Barnet: John Libbey, 2009), 187–199.

4. A Gaumont advertisement boasted: "We are fast approaching our 400th consecutive Chronophone performance at the London Hippodrome where Harry Lauder is still going strong". It also invites "offers for the hire of this highly Popular star Comedian's most favourite productions (of which we have the entire rights as Chronophone subjects for Exhibition) in districts not affected by the Moss Stoll circuits" – an indication of the contractual problems being caused the same performer becoming available in two media. *Kinematograph and Lantern Weekly* (16 July 1907): 152.

5. Martin Loiperdinger, "The Kaiser's Cinema: an archaeology of attitudes and audiences", in Thomas Elsaesser and Michael Wedel (eds), *A Second Life: German Cinema's First Decades* (Amsterdam: Amsterdam University Press, 1996), 41–50, here 47; cf. also Martin Loiperdinger, "'Kaiserbilder'. Wilhelm II. als Filmstar", in Uli Jung, Martin Loiperdinger (eds), *Geschichte des dokumentarischen Films in Deutschland.* Vol. 1: *Kaiserreich 1895–1918* (Stuttgart: Philipp Reclam jun., 2005), 253–268.

6. HERBERT CAMPBELL AS 'LITTLE BOBBIE'(1902), DAN LENO AND HERBERT CAMPBELL EDIT "THE SUN" (1904).

7. Terry Ramsaye, *A Million and One Nights* (New York: Simon and Schuster, 1926); Benjamin Hampton, *A History of the Movies* (New York: Covichi-Friede, 1931).

8. deCordova, *Picture Personalities*, 2–7; David P. Marshall, *Celebrity and Power: fame in contemporary culture* (University of Minnesota Press, 1997), 79–81.

9. "La fabrication (...) de scènes établies sur scénarios signés d'auteurs contemporains, avec le concours d'artistes connus", quoted in "Dictionnaire du cinéma français des années vingt", *1895*, no. 33 (2001), 198.

10. Jon Burrows, *Legitimate Cinema: Theatre Stars in Silent British Films 1908–1918* (Exeter: Exeter University Press, 2003), 46.

11. Advertisement by Walturdaw Co., *Kinematograph Weekly* (20 July 1912). The other adjective regularly used in advertisements for Asta Nielsen films was 'incomparable', while adjacent reviews of RETRIBUTION (NACHTFALTER, 1911) and A BEAST AT BAY (Griffith, 1912), refer to "that versatile Norwegian [sic] actress, Miss Asta Nielsen" and "Miss Mary Pickford, the well-known charming actress now with the AB company in America", *Kinematograph Monthly Film Record* (July 1912): 108.

12. Gabriel-Maximilien Leuvielle (1883–1925) made his screen debut as 'Max Linder' in 1907 and was internationally famous by 1911. The French comedian André Chapuis (1879–1940) starred first in numerous Pathé comedies as 'André Deed', before moving to Italy in 1909 to become 'Cretinetti', known as 'Foolshead' in Britain and America. Another French comedian, Charles Prince Seigneur (1872–1933) started working for Pathé in 1909, and also became internationally recognised – as 'Rigadin' in France, 'Moritz' in Germany, 'Whiffles' in Britain and America, 'Tartufini' in Italy, etc .

13. Hugo Münsterberg, *The Photoplay: A Psychological Study* (New York and London: Appleton, 1916). 'Photoplay' had become the accepted term for feature-length filmed drama in the United States by the early 1910s.

14. Münsterberg, *The Photoplay*, references to Project Gutenberg edition online cf. http://www.gutenberg.org/catalog/world/readfile?fk_files=149968: 49

15. Ibid.

16. Ibid., 63.

17. Ibid., 51.

18. Hugo Münsterberg, "Why we go to the movies", *The Cosmopolitan* (December 1915).

19. Münsterberg, *The Photoplay*, 34.

20. Ibid. 31. CARMEN (dir. Raoul Walsh, Fox, 1915) and CARMEN (dir. Cecil B. DeMille, Lasky, 1915).

21. Gustav Fechner (1801–1887) was a German psychologist and philosopher who established 'psychophysics' as the science of measuring mental responses to physical stimuli (*Elemente der Psychophysik*, 1860), and laid the foundations for an experimental approach to aesthetic preferences.

22. Münsterberg's foundational work in forensic and industrial psychology has long been recognised. But an aggressively pro-German stance during the years leading up to the outbreak of World War

23. One made him an unpopular figure within the American academic community, according to Allan Langdale, the editor of *Hugo Münsterberg: The Photoplay – a psychological study and other writings* (New York and London: Routledge, 2002), 5–6.
24. See, for instance, George Mitchell, "The Movies and Münsterberg", *Jump Cut*, no. 27 (July 1982), 57–60, at http://www.ejumpcut.org/archive/onlinessays/JC27folder/Munsterberg.html (accessed 25 January 2012).
25. The first version of the novel, entitled *Si Gira*, appeared in 1916, but this was superseded by a revised edition, known as *The Notebooks of Serafino Gubbio Operator (Quaderni di Serafino Gubbio operatore)* from 1925. The differences between the two do not seem to have been established.
26. Luigi Pirandello, *Shoot!: The Notebooks of Serafino Gubbio*, trans. C. Scott Moncrieff (New York: E.P. Dutton, 1926), 292.
27. "In principio era il sesso", *Avanti* (16 February 1917), quoted in Gian Piero Brunetta, *Storia del cinema italiano 1895–1945* (Rome: Editori Riuniti, 1979), 79–80; also in P. Adams Sitney, "The Autobiography of a Metonymy" (afterword to Chicago University Press reprint of *Shoot!*, 2006), 224.
28. Later, in his influential *Prison Notebooks*, Gramsci would rethink the progressive potential of popular culture and it is this later position that was widely embraced in the 1970s.
29. Angela Dalle Vacche, *Diva: Defiance and Passion in Early Italian Cinema* (Austin: University of Texas Press, 2008), 56.
30. Ibid.
31. Sitney, in "The Autobiography of a Metonymy" (his afterword to *Shoot!*), also attributes some complexity to Pirandello's view of cinema in the novel.
32. Walter Benjamin, *The Work of Art in the Age of Mechanical Reproduction* (1936), in *Illuminations*, ed. Hannah Arendt, trans. Harry Zohn (London: Fontana, 1970), 232–233.
33. "Stars are human capital": so begins John Sedgwick's chapter "Stardom and 'Hits'" in his economic analysis, *Popular Filmgoing in 1930s Britain: A Choice of Pleasures* (Exeter: University of Exeter Press, 2000), 180.
34. Pierre Sorlin, *Italian National Cinema 1896–1996* (London: Routledge, 1996), 32.
35. Martin Koerber, "Oskar Messter, Film Pioneer: Early Cinema between Science, Spectacle and Commerce", in Elsaesser and Wedel, *A Second Life*, 51–61, here 57.
36. Ibid., 58; cf. Henny Porten advert in *Erste Internationale Filmzeitung*, no. 21 (21 May 1912).
37. Review of Drake's Love Story (Hepworth, 1913), *The Bioscope* (27 February 1913): 673.
38. On the history of picture postcards, see Tonie and Valmai Holt, *Picture Postcards of the Golden Age. A Collector's Guide* (London: McGibbon & Kee, 1971); Paul Hammond, *French Undressing: Naughty Postcards from 1900 to 1920* (London: Bloomsbury Books, 1988).
39. Figures of national card postage levels from Hammond, *French Undressing*, 9, who observes that many cards were also being kept in albums. It is impossible to know what proportion of postcards were of film stars, but analysis of current market values among collectors could provide an interesting comparative framework.
40. Cf. http://filmstarpostcards.blogspot.co.uk/p/countries.html (accessed 2 April 2012).
41. There were internationally known early male stars, apart from the comedians already noted, such as 'Broncho Billy' Anderson, René Navarre and Emilio Ghione. But the era of male stars with the same impact as the female stars of 1911–14 began towards the end of the 1910s, with Douglas Fairbanks turning to swashbuckling roles and the emergence of the 'Latin lover', heralded by Rudolf Valentino and Ramon Novarro.
42. George Huaco, *The Sociology of Film Art* (New York: Basic Books, 1965).
43. *Kinematograph Monthly Film Record* (March 1913): 63.
44. Kristin Thompson, *Exporting Entertainment: America in the World Film Market, 1907–1934* (London: BFI Publishing, 1985).
45. Gerben Bakker, "The Economic History of the International Film Industry", at http://eh.net/-encyclopedia/article/bakker.film (accessed 26 January 2012).

FILMOGRAPHY

Asta Nielsen – International Filmography, 1910–1914

This list contains titles of all 27 Asta Nielsen films which were released before the First World War, in chronological order. Most of the titles listed are mentioned in this book. The list is not exhaustive at all. Asta Nielsen's international filmography, 1910–1914, is a work in progress. Further research may evidence many more distribution titles in additional countries which will be added to a full filmography of casts and credits. Cf. the database *Importing Asta Nielsen*.

AFGRUNDEN
Copenhagen premiere 12 September 1910
Abgründe (DE)
The Abyss (international)
Woman Always Pays (GB, US)
All for the Man I Love (AU)
Avgrunden (SE)
Afgrunden (FI)
Kuilu (FI)
Afgronden (NL)
Levens Afgronden (Amsterdam, NL)
Abîmes (FR; Metz, DE)
L'Abîme (FR)
Vers l'abîme (Lausanne, CH)
L'abisso (IT)
Hacia el abismo (ES)
O abismo (BR)
A queda da mulher (BR)
A Woman's Fall (Rio de Janeiro, BR)
Bezdna (RU)
Otchłań (Polish territories)
Al Hawiyà (Alexandria, EG)

Heisses Blut
Berlin premiere 22 April 1911
Großstadtversuchungen (DE)
Burning Blood (GB)
Det hede Blod (DK)
Hartstocht (NL)
Onder sterken wil (NL)
Heet bloed (NL)
Le Vertige (FR)
Sang chaud (FR; Metz, DE))
Sangue bollente (IT)

Nachtfalter
Berlin premiere 13 May 1911
Retribution (GB, AU, NZ)
Moths (Washington D.C., US)
Natsværmeren (DK)
La phalène (FR)
La falena (IT)
A Phalena (BR)
Nochnaia babochka (RU)
Nachtvlinder (Netherlands Indies)
Tenput'shon [Temptation] (JP)

Den sorte Drøm
Der schwarze Traum (DE)
First film of the 'Asta Nielsen series' 1911/12
Berlin premiere on 19 August 1911
The Circus Girl (AU, NZ)
Feigðardraumur (IS)
De Zwarte Droom (NL)
Le Rêve noir (FR; Lausanne, CH; LU)
Il sogno nero (IT)
El sueño negro (ES)
Sonho Negro (BR)

In dem grossen Augenblick
Second film of the 'Asta Nielsen series' 1911/12
Berlin premiere on 28 August 1911
Im grossen Augenblick (DE)
In dem letzen Augenblick (Metz, DE)
The Great Moment (GB, US)
Det store Øjeblik (DK)
Á úrslita stund (IS)

Stundin mikla (IS)
Á síðustu stundu (IS)
Úrslitastundin (IS)
I det stora ögonblicket (SE)
Het Gewichtig oogenblik (NL)
Het Groote oogenblik of de dood van Asta Nielsen (NL)
Maternité (FR)
À l'instant précis (FR)
Au moment décisif (LU)
Puissance maternelle (Lausanne, CH)
Il gran momento (IT)
Momento crítico (ES)
O Momento Supremo (BR)
A Maternidade (BR)
Haha (JP)

Zigeunerblut
Third film of the 'Asta Nielsen series' 1911/12
Berlin premiere on 8 October 1911
Die Vagabundin (DE)
Gipsy Blood (GB, AU, NZ)
Gypsy Blood (GB, US)
Landevejens Pige (DK)
La Tzigane (FR)
Amour tzigane (Lausanne, CH)
Sang de bohémien ou la vagabonde (LU)
Sang de Tzigane (Metz, DE)
Sangue di zingara (IT)
La zingara (IT)
Sangre gitana (ES)
Sangue de Bohemia (BR)

Balletdanserinden
Berlin premiere on 28 October 1911
Brænde Kælighed (DK)
Brennende Triebe (DE)
Ballettänzerin (DE)
The Ballet Dancer (AU)
Balettdansösen (SE)
Brandend verlangen (NL)
Amour de danseuse (FR)
Amor de dansarinda (BR)

Der fremde Vogel
Fourth film of the 'Asta Nielsen series' 1911/12
Berlin premiere on 11 November 1911
The Course of True Love (AU, NZ)
A Strange Bird (Washington D.C., US)
Unge hjerter (DK)
Ung hjörtu (IS)
Een vreemde vogel (NL)
De vreemde vogel in het Spreewald (NL)
L'étrange oiseau (FR)
L'Oiseau étranger (Lausanne, CH)
Uccello foresto (IT)

Die Verräterin
Fifth film of the 'Asta Nielsen series' 1911/12
Berlin premiere on 9 December 1911
The Traitress (GB, AU, NZ, US)
A Woman of the People (GB, AU, NZ)
Den Store Elskov (DK)
De Verraderes (NL)
Verraad (NL)
La Traîtresse (FR)
Trahison (LU)
Traditrice (IT)
La espía francesa (ES)
A Traidora (BR)

Die Macht des Goldes
Seventh film of the 'Asta Nielsen series' 1911/12
Berlin premiere on 3 February 1912
The Better Way (GB, AUS, NZ)
The Might of Gold (Washington D.C., US)
Den vilde Jæger (DK)
De Macht van het goud (NL)
La Force de l'or (FR)
Le Pouvoir de l'argent (FR)
La Puissance de l'or (Lausanne, CH; LU; Metz, DE)
O poder do ouro (BR)

Die arme Jenny
Sixth film of the 'Asta Nielsen series' 1911/12
Berlin premiere on 2 March 1912
Poor Jenny (Washington D.C., US)
Proletarpigen (DK)

Arme Jenny (NL)
Pauvre Jenny (FR)
Jenny la pauvre (LU)

Zu Tode gehetzt
Eighth film of the 'Asta Nielsen series' 1911/12
Berlin premiere on 13 April 1912
Driven Out (AU)
Jaget til døde (DK)
Poussée à la mort (FR)
Jusqu'à la mort (FR)
Tourmentée à mort (Metz, DE)
Persécutée à mort (Metz, DE)

Der Totentanz
First film of the 'Asta Nielsen series' 1912/13
Berlin premiere on 7 September 1912
The Dance to Death (GB)
The Fatal Dance (AU, NZ)
Dødedansen (DK)
Danse funèbre (NL)
La danse de la mort (LU)
Danse macabre (Lausanne, CH)
La danza de la muerte (ES)
Baíle tragico (ES)
Danza macabra (ES)
A dança da morte (BR)

Die Kinder des Generals
Second film of the 'Asta Nielsen series' 1912/13
Berlin premiere on 5 October 1912
Falsely Accused (GB, AU, NZ, US)
For Her Brother's Sake (AU)
Generalens Børn (DK)
Börn hershöfðingjans (IS)
De Kinderen van den generaal (NL)
Les Enfants du général (FR, CH, LU)
Los hijos del general (ES)
O filho do general (BR)

Wenn die Maske fällt
Third film of the 'Asta Nielsen series' 1912/13
Berlin premiere on 1 November 1912
When the Mask Falls (GB, AU, NZ)

Naar Masken falder (DK)
Þegar griman fellur (IS)
Ontmaskerd (NL)
Als het masker valt (NL)
Quand le masque tombe (Metz, DE)
El hipócrita (ES)
Cuando se cae la máscara (ES)
Quando a máscara cai (BR)

DAS MÄDCHEN OHNE VATERLAND
Fourth film of the 'Asta Nielsen series' 1912/13
Berlin premiere on 29 November 1912
A Girl Without a Country (GB, AU, NZ)
A Romany Spy (US)
The Barefoot Dancer (Washington D.C., US)
Pigen uden Fædreland (DK)
Het Meisje zonder vaderland (NL)
Zonder vaderland (NL)
La Fille sans patrie (Metz, DE)
Fusilado por la ley (ES)
Subterfugio (ES)
A rapariga sem patria (BR)
Kuninaki Hito (JP)

JUGEND UND TOLLHEIT
Fifth film of the 'Asta Nielsen series' 1912/13
Berlin premiere on 3 January 1913
In a Fix (GB, AU, NZ)
Lady Madcap's Way (US)
Ungdom og Daarskab (DK)
Æskubrek (IS)
Stormen der jeugd (NL)
Dolle jeugd (NL)
Ce que femme veut (FR)
Jeunesse et folie (Metz, DE)
Giovinezza e pazzia (IT)
Las batallas del amor (ES)
Mocidade e Loucura (BR)

KOMÖDIANTEN
Sixth film of the 'Asta Nielsen series' 1912/13
Berlin premiere on 31 January 1913
The Heart of a Pierrot (GB, AU, NZ)
Behind Comedy's Mask (US)

Komedianter (DK, IS)
De Dood van Pierrot (NL)
Tooneelspelers (NL)
Comedianten (NL)
Les Comédiants (FR)
La muerte de Pierrot (ES)
Comediantes (BR)

Die Sünden der Väter
Seventh film of the 'Asta Nielsen series' 1912/13
Berlin premiere on 28 February 1913
Temptations of Drink (GB, AU, NZ)
The Devil's Assistant (US)
Fædrenes Synd (DK)
Diep gezonken (NL)
De Zonden des vaders (NL)
La Faute d'un père (FR)
Les fautes des pères (Lausanne, CH)
La Faute de nos pères (Metz, DE)
Delitto di padre (IT)
Grekhi otsov (RU)
Grzechy ojców (Polish territories)
Hanna Jyo (JP)

Der Tod in Sevilla
Eighth film of the 'Asta Nielsen series' 1912/13
Berlin premiere on 4 April 1913
Spanish Blood (GB, AU, NZ, US)
The Romance of the Toreadors (AU, NZ)
Spansk Elskov (DK)
Spænsk ást (IS)
Spánversk ást (IS)
Spaansche wraak (NL)
Juanita, de danseres van Sevilla (NL)
Een Liefde in Sevilla (NL)
De Dood in Sevilla (NL)
La Mort à Seville (FR; Metz, DE)
Sangre andaluza (ES)
Morte em Sevilha (BR)

Die Suffragette
First film of the 'Asta Nielsen series' 1913/14
Berlin premiere on 12 September 1913
The Suffragette (GB, AU, NZ)

The Militant Suffragette (US)
Stemmeretsdamen (DK)
Kvenrjettindakonur (IS)
De Suffragette (NL)
La Suffragette (FR; Lausanne, CH; Metz, DE))
Suffragette (IT)
La sufragista (ES)
A Sufragista (BR)

S 1
Second film of the 'Asta Nielsen series' 1913/14
Berlin premiere on 14 November 1913
Militärluftschiff „S1" (DE, AT)
A Girl's Sacrifice (AU)
S. 1. (DK)
S. I. (IS)
L'Avion S 1 (FR)
El aeroplano no. 1 (ES)
O Dirigivel (BR)

DIE FILMPRIMADONNA
Third film of the 'Asta Nielsen series' 1913/14
Berlin premiere on 5 December 1913
The Prima Donna (US)
Filmprimadonnaen (DK)
Kvikmyndadrottningin (IS)
De Film prima-donna (NL)
La Reine du cinéma (FR)
La Reina del Cine (ES)
A Prima Donna (BR)
Katsudosyasin no Syunokagekijyoyu (JP)

ENGELEIN
Fourth film of the 'Asta Nielsen series' 1913/14
Berlin premiere on 3 January 1914
Up to Her Tricks (AU, NZ)
Den lille Engel (DK)
Litli Engillinn (IS)
Engeltje (NL)
Dolle Jesta (NL)
Popje (NL)
El sentir del primer amor (ES)
O Verdadeiro ou Primeiro Amor (BR)

Das Kind ruft

Fifth film of the 'Asta Nielsen series' 1913/14
Berlin premiere on 6 February 1914
The Cry of a Child (AU)
Barnet kalder (DK)
De Stem van het kind (NL)
Het Kind roept (NL)
L'Enfant crie (Metz, DE)
Mater dolorosa (ES)
O Grito da Criança (BR)

Zapatas Bande

Sixth film of the 'Asta Nielsen series' 1913/14
Berlin premiere on 27 February 1914
Zapata's Gang [IMDb]
Zapatas Bande (DK)
De Bende van Zapata (NL)
Zapata (NL)
Bandoleros de los Apeninos (ES)
La novela de la amazona (ES)
O Bando dos Zapatas (BR)

Das Feuer

Seventh film of the 'Asta Nielsen series' 1913/14
Berlin premiere on 7 March 1914
Vengeance is Mine (GB, AU)
Ilden (DK)
Het Vuur als rechter (NL)
Het Vuur (NL)
Le Feu (Metz, DE)
O Fogo e a Palha (BR)

THE CONTRIBUTORS

The Contributors

Richard Abel is Robert Altman Collegiate Professor of Film Studies in Screen Arts & Cultures at the University of Michigan. Most recently he published *Americanizing the Movies and 'Movie-Mad' Audiences, 1910–1914* (2006), co-edited *Early Cinema and the "National"* (2008), and edited a paperback version of the *Encyclopedia of Early Cinema* (2010). His current projects are *Early Cinema*, an edited four-volume set of reprints (Routledge 2013), and *Menus for Movie Land: Newspapers and the Emergence of American Film Culture, 1913-1916*.

Julie K. Allen is Associate Professor of Scandinavian Studies at the University of Wisconsin-Madison. She received her PhD in Germanic Languages and Literatures from Harvard University in 2005. Her research focuses on the cultural phenomena of national, religious, and gender identity constructions in 19th and early 20th century Denmark and Germany. Her book *Icons of Danish Modernity: Georg Brandes and Asta Nielsen* (2012) examines the role of these two celebrities and their use of mass media in shaping German and Danish perceptions of modern Danish national and cultural identity. Other recent publications include "Tea with Goebbels and Hitler: Asta Nielsen in Germany" (*Journal of Scandinavian Cinema*, 2013), "Where does 'die Asta' belong? The role of national identity in Asta Nielsen's German and Danish reception in the early 1920s" (*Journal of Scandinavian Cinema*, 2012), and "Denmark's Ugly Ducklings: Georg Brandes and Asta Nielsen's Metacultural Contributions to Constructions of Danish National Identity" (*Scandinavian Studies*, 2011).

Anne Bachmann is a PhD student in the field of transnational film history at the Department of Media Studies, Section for Cinema Studies at Stockholm University. Her PhD project concerns different aspects of the trans-Scandinavian cinema and cinema culture in the silent era; more specifically interactions, influences, and modes of co-production between Swedish, Danish and Norwegian early narrative cinema and on the discourses surrounding such transnational practices. Other research interests are visual culture, media history, fashion studies, and relations between film and other media.

Ansje van Beusekom teaches film history at the Department of Media and Culture Studies at Utrecht University. In addition to her dissertation *Kunst en Amusement. Reacties op de komst van de film in Nederland, 1895–1940* (2001), she published numerous articles on film and art history in encyclopaedias, journals and edited volumes. Her publications focus on early and silent cinema and cinemagoing, the lecturer and intertitles, cinema and the other arts as well as film represented in the other arts and media. The history of ideas on film as art beyond the Dutch Film Liga and classical film theories is another topic of her research. On Asta Nielsen in the Netherlands she published "Bühne und Leinwand: Auftritte in den Niederlanden 1911–1920" (in *Unmögliche Liebe. Asta Nielsen, ihr Kino*, 2009), and "Asta Nielsen in the Netherlands: 1920" (in *Not so Silent. Women in Cinema before Sound*, 2010).

Patric Blaser is a Senior Scholar at the Theatre, Film and Media Studies Department at the University of Vienna. His research focus is on the archaeology of cinema, pictorial narrative in the 19th century, and intermediality in early cinema.

Stephen Bottomore graduated from Cambridge University and film school, and worked as a film editor and producer at the BBC, and then spent two decades directing broadcast and corporate documentaries in Europe, Africa, Asia and the Americas, completing his television career as executive producer of two series for Channel 4 educational television. He is the author of many articles on silent and pre-cinema in such journals as *Sight and Sound*, *History Today*, *Historical Journal of Film, Radio and Television*, and *KINtop*. He also published *The Titanic and Silent Cinema* (2000) and *I Want to See this Annie Mattygraph* (1995), a history of early cinema based on satirical magazine cartoons. He was awarded a doctorate at Utrecht University in 2007 for his thesis on early cinema and warfare. He has been an associate editor of *Film History* since 1998, editing issues on non-fiction, silent cinema, war films, fiction about the cinema, and the First World War. He lives in Thailand and the UK.

Jon Burrows is Associate Professor in the Department of Film and Television Studies, University of Warwick. He is the author of *Legitimate Cinema: Theatre Stars in Silent British Films, 1908-1918* (2003) and of numerous essays and articles on different aspects of silent film culture in Britain.

Ian Christie is a film historian, curator and broadcaster. He has written and edited books on Powell and Pressburger, Russian cinema, Scorsese and Gilliam; worked on exhibitions, including *Spellbound: Art and Film* (Hayward Gallery, 1996) and *Modernism: Designing a New World* (V&A, 2006); and co-produced the 1994 BBC television series on early cinema *The Last Machine: Early Cinema and the Birth of the Modern World*, as well as writing the accompanying book. His most recent book is *Audiences* (2012). A Fellow of the British Academy, he is currently Professor of Film and Media History at Birkbeck College, Director of the London Screen Study Collection, and President of Europa Cinemas.

Andrzej Dębski is a film historian at the Willy Brandt Center for German and European Studies of Wrocław University where he conducts the research project "Polish and German Cinema between two Cultures". Regional cinema history, early cinema, and the history of Polish and German film embrace the focus of his research. He was awarded his doctorate at the University of Silesia in Katowice for his *Historia kina we Wrocławiu w latach 1896–1918* (Cinema History of Wrocław 1896 to 1918, published 2009). With Marek Zybura he co-edited *Wrocław będzie miastem filmowym … Z dziejów kina w stolicy Dolnego Śląska* (Wrocław becomes a film city… Cinema Histories from the capital of Lower Silesia, 2008); with Rafał Bubnicki he co-edited *Stanisław Lenartowicz. Twórca osobny* (Stanisław Lenartowicz. Independent Artist, 2011); and with Andrzej Gwóźdź he co-edited *W drodze do sąsiada. Polsko-niemieckie spotkania filmowe* (On the way to the neighbour. Polish-German film contacts, 2013).

Adrian Gerber is currently working on his doctoral dissertation on film reception in Switzerland during the First World War at the Film Studies Department at the University of Zurich. He is the author of *Katholische Filmarbeit in der Schweiz 1908–1972: Eine gediegene Aufklärung und Führung in dieser Materie* (2010), a book on cinema and Catholicism in Switzerland.

Andrea Haller is a film historian and curator at the German Film Institute (DIF) in Frankfurt. In 2009, she earned her doctorate from the University of Trier with her dissertation on programming strategies and female cinema audiences in Imperial Germany. She has published various articles on local film history, the history of cinema programming and of cinema audiences, and the relations between cinema, fashion and modernity. Her recent publications include "Film, Fashion and Female Movie Fandom in Imperial Germany" (in *Not so Silent. Women in Cinema before Sound*, 2010), "'Nur meine Asta! Und damit basta!'" (in *Unmögliche Liebe. Asta Nielsen, ihr Kino*, 2009), and "Diagnosis: 'Flimmeritis': female cinemagoing in Imperial Germany, 1910-11" (in *Cinema, Audiences and Modernity*, 2012).

Caroline Henkes studied Media Studies at the University of Trier and at the University Carlos III (Madrid). She graduated with a MA thesis on documentary films about 'new living' in the Weimar Republic. Within the research focus *Screen1900* at the University of Trier, she is currently working on her doctoral dissertation about the representation of poverty in early cinema.

Outi Hupaniittu is a researcher at the Department of Finnish History at Turku University, where she concludes her dissertation in 2013 on cinema entrepreneurship in Finland in the 1900–1920s. As postdoctoral projects she will research for example Finnish stardom and the status of actors in the film companies in the 1920s and 1930s. She has published articles on Finnish film culture, actors and cinema business. Her recent publications include "*Industrial Spotlight: The economics of Finnish cinema: 1910–1930*" and "*The emergence of the star system*" (both in *Directory of World Cinema: Finland*, 2012), "Leskirouva Larissan avioliitto eli kuinka Gustaf Molinin elämäntyö katosi" (Dowager Larissa's marriage or How the legacy of Gustaf Molin disappeared, in *Historian aikakoneessa*, 2011); *"Näihin näytäntöihin ei myydä lasten pilettejä. Asta Nielsenin Kuilu-elokuva Helsingissä vuonna 1911" (No tickets for children. Asta Nielsen's Afgrunden in Helsinki in 1911, in Samanaikaisuuksia. Kansainvälisiä näköaloja vuoden 1911 maailmaan, 2010)*, and *"Nuori Apollo"*, vanhan mamsellin ystävä.

Helsinkiläisten suosikkinäyttelijä Valdemar Psilander ja 1910-luvun elokuvakulttuuri" (Young Apollo, friend of an old lady. Valdemar Psilander, the favourite actor in Helsinki and the cinema culture of the 1910s, in: *Elokuva historiassa, historia elokuvassa*, 2009).

Pierre-Emmanuel Jaques is a researcher at the Section d'histoire et esthétique du cinema, University of Lausanne. He is involved in a joint project dedicated to the expertise and valorisation of the collections of the Cinémathèque suisse, the Swiss Film Archive. He published numerous articles on documentary film and on film criticism, and he contributed to *Schaufenster Schweiz. Dokumentarische Gebrauchsfilme 1896-1964* (2011) and to *Le spectacle cinématographique en Suisse (1895-1945)*, with Gianni Haver (2003).

Uli Jung teaches American literature and film at the University of Trier. He earned his doctorate with a dissertation on Dracula as a motive of popular film between 1922 and 1992 (1997). He works free lance for the Cinémathèque de la Ville de Luxembourg and, as of 1994, he has been general editor of its scholarly book series *Filmgeschichte International*. He published widely on German film history, especially on Early and Weimar Cinema, but also on genre film. Among his book publications are *Filmkultur zur Zeit der Weimarer Republik* (1992, co-editor with Walter Schatzberg), *Der deutsche Film: Aspekte seiner Geschichte von den Anfängen bis zu Gegenwart* (1993), and the monograph *Beyond Caligari: The Films of Robert Wiene* (1999, with Walter Schatzberg). With Martin Loiperdinger, he co-edited *Geschichte des dokumentarischen Films in Deutschland*, vol. 1 (2005 – Willy Haas Award for the Best Book-length Publication on German Cinema 2006).

Valdo Kneubühler is archivist at the Cinémathèque française.

Giovanni Lasi has been working since 2005 as educational consultant of the audiovisual and multimedia laboratory for the cinema, television and multimedia production course held at the Music and Performance Department, University of Bologna. In 2006, he was appointed by the Cineteca di Bologna as a curator for the film festival *Il Cinema Ritrovato*, in charge of the origins of Italian cinema. He is consultant of the Cineteca di Bologna on historical studies and a member of a research group on silent films at the DAMS (Drama, Art and Music Studies), University of Bologna. His publications include "La ripresa di Roma" (in *1905. La presa di Roma*, 2006), "L'immagine della nazione" (in *Da La presa di Roma a Il piccolo garibaldino*, 2007), "La 'revolution' du Film d'Art" (*1895*, vol. 56, 2008), "Polarstern: In Italien" (in *Unmögliche Liebe. Asta Nielsen, ihr Kino,* 2009), and *Il Risorgimento nel cinema italiano* (2011).

Mattia Lento studied Film and Theatre Studies at the University of Milan and Italian Studies at the University of Strathclyde, Glasgow. He received his MA for his thesis on the Italian diva Lyda Borelli. He is currently doing research for his dissertation on the emergence of film stars in Italian cinema during the 1910s.

Paul Lesch (Dr. phil.) teaches film and history at the University of Luxembourg and at the Miami University John E. Dolibois European Center in Luxembourg. He is the director of the documentary film *Call Her Madam* (Samsa Film, 1997) on the American diplomat and party-giver Perle Mesta. He is also the author of *Heim ins Ufa-Reich? NS-Filmpolitik und die Rezeption deutscher Filme in Luxemburg 1933-1944* (2002) and *In the Name of Public Order and Morality. Cinema Control and Film Censorship in Luxembourg 1895-2005* (2005). He is a Council member of IAMHIST (International Association for Media and History) and has written for journals such as *Historical Journal of Film, Radio and Television, Film History* and *Cinema & Cie*. He recently co-curated an exhibition on Hugo Gernsback, the 'father of modern science fiction'.

Annemone Ligensa (Dr. phil.) is currently employed in the research project "Visual Communities: Relationships of the Local, National, and Global in Early Cinema" at the University of Cologne. Her research interests include stardom, psychoanalytic film theory, narratology, and media audiences. Recent publications are *Film 1900: Technology, Perception, Culture* (edited with Klaus Kreimeier, 2009) and "Urban Legend: Early Cinema, Modernization, and Urbanization in Germany, 1895-1914" (in *Cinema, Audiences and Modernity*, 2011).

Martin Loiperdinger is Professor of Media Studies at the University of Trier. From 1993 to 1997 he was Deputy Director of the German Film Institute (DIF). His contributions to film and cinema studies include articles, books, exhibitions, DVDs, and television features. With Frank Kessler and Sabine Lenk, he co-edited *KINtop*, the German yearbook of early cinema, from 1992 to 2006. With them, he has been co-editor of the series *KINtop Schriften* since 1992, and of the series *KINtop. Studies in Early Cinema* since 2011. He co-curated the DVDs *Crazy Cinématographe 1896-1916* (2007) and *Screening the Poor 1888-1914* (2011). He edited *Celluloid Goes Digital* (2003), *Travelling Cinema in Europe* (2008), and *Early Cinema Today. The Art of Programming and Live Performance* (2011). With Uli Jung, he co-edited *Geschichte des dokumentarischen Films in Deutschland*, vol. 1 (2005 – Willy Haas Award for the Best Booklength Publication on German Cinema 2006). Since 2005, he has been conducting the research focus *Screen1900* at the University of Trier.

Ouissal Mejri earned her doctorate from the University of Bologna with her dissertation on foreign influences on the cinema in Maghreb countries from 1896 till 1930. Topics of her current research include Arabic cinema and its relationships with European and particularly Italian cinema from the beginnings till nowadays. Her studies embrace the dual correlation between Africa and the cinema, with a focus on the history of African cinema, and on the representation of the African continent and particularly of Sub-Saharan Africa in European and American films. Another focus of her research are female pioneers in the cinema of Arabic countries.

Julio Montero is a full Professor at the Complutense University of Madrid. His main research topics are history and social history of audiovisual media and broadcasting, and the history of non-fiction film. From 1996 to 2006, he set up and managed the postgraduate course on the history of documentary film production at the Complutense University. He has written numerous books and articles, many of them co-authored with María Antonia Paz. He has also directed documentaries, several of them about the Spanish Civil War: SOMBRAS DEL 36 (2003), LOS AÑOS ROBADOS (2004, Barbara Anson Award for Historical and Cultural Documentaries 2006), and BUSCANDO EL PARAÍSO (2012).

Rielle Navitski is a PhD candidate in the Department of Film and Media at the University of California, Berkeley. Her research examines Latin American cinema in transnational perspective, focusing on the silent and early sound eras. She is currently completing her dissertation entitled *Sensationalism, Cinema and the Popular Press in Mexico and Brazil, 1905–1930*. Her scholarly writing has appeared in *Screen*, *Cinema Journal*, and *The Moving Image*.

Sawako Ogawa is Assistant Professor of Film History at the Institute for Research in Humanities at Kyoto University. She holds a PhD degree in Film Studies from Waseda University with the dissertation on comparative styles in 1910s Japanese and European films. Her articles in Japanese on the history of silent cinema include "The confrontation between Japanese film and foreign film in the 1910s" (in Japanese Cinema is Alive II, 2010), "Onnagata's femininity and actress's modernization in early Japanese film" (Bulletin of the Graduate Division of Literature of Waseda University, 2010), and "The development of the style in the films of Evgenii Bauer" (Studies on Theatre and Film Arts, 2009).

María Antonia Paz is a full Professor in the Faculty of Communication at the Complutense University of Madrid. In the last years, with Julio Montero she has published the monographs *Creando la Realidad. El Cine Informativo, 1895–1945* (1999), *La Imagen Pública de la Monarquía. Alfonso XIII en la Prensa y en los noticiarios cinematográficos de su época* (2001), *La larga sombra de Hitler. El cine nazi en España (1933–1945)* (2009); *Lo que el viento no se llevó. El cine en la memoria de los españoles: 1931–1982* (2012). She also published "The Spanish Remember: movie attendance during the Franco dictatorship, 1942–1975" (*Historical Journal of Film, Radio and Television*, 2003). Since 1995, she has been organising *Las Jornadas Internacionales de Historia y Cine*, the international biennial meetings on history and film at the Complutense.

Lauri Piispa is a PhD student at the Cultural History Department of the University of Turku. He is currently finishing his dissertation on *Actors and Acting in Russian Cinema, 1908–1918*. He teaches the history of Russian cinema at the University of Helsinki and has worked as a researcher for the Finnish National Filmography project at the National Audiovisual Archive. With Heta Mulari he co-edited *Elokuva historiassa, historia elokuvassa* ("Cinema in History, History in Cinema", 2009). His recent articles include "Tolstoy Film Adaptations in Russia, 1909–17" (in *Tolstoy Studies Journal* XXIII, 2011) and several essays in Finnish in *Lähikuva*, *Idäntutkimus*, *Filmihullu* and other journals.

The Contributors

Dafna Ruppin is a PhD candidate in Media and Performance Studies at the Research Institute for History and Culture at Utrecht University, in the research project "The Nation and Its Other" funded by the Netherlands Organisation for Scientific Research (NWO). Her research on the history of cinemagoing in colonial Indonesia focuses on the production, distribution and exhibition of early cinema from 1896 to 1918.

Agnes Schindler was awarded her doctorate at the University of Trier in 2012 for her dissertation on Icelandic national cinema and the negotiation of national identity in Icelandic feature films. She studied Media Studies, Japanese Studies and Teaching German as a Foreign Language at the University of Trier, and Film Studies, Icelandic Language and Culture at the University of Iceland. She has been working on national and transnational cinema, small national cinema and postcolonial cinema. Currently she is employed as Study Abroad Coordinator for Asia and Latin America at the University of Trier.

Pierre Stotzky, a high school teacher of history and geography and a doctoral candidate at the University of Lorraine (2L2S), currently works on the history of cinema in region Lorraine between 1895 and 1930. He previously wrote his BA thesis on cinema in Metz as a new form of leisure between 1908 and 1914 (2004), and his MA thesis on cinema in the Département Moselle from 1908 to 1939 (2005). He is especially interested in the role played by cinema managers and local audiences in developing cinema as leisure time entertainment.

Isak Thorsen holds a PhD degree in Film Studies from the University of Copenhagen with the dissertation *Isbjørnens anatomi - Nordisk Films Kompagni som erhvervsvirksomhed i perioden 1906-1928*. He contributed to the anthology *100 Years of Nordisk Film* (2006) and has written for journals such as: *Film History*, *Scandinavian-Canadian Studies* and *Kosmorama*. He is the editor and author of the Danish entries in the *Historical Dictionary of Scandinavian Cinema* (The Scarecrow Press, 2012).

Casper Tybjerg is Associate Professor of Film Studies at the Department of Media, Cognition, and Communication at the University of Copenhagen. He has published extensively on Danish silent cinema and the films of Carl Th. Dreyer. He is completing a book on the historiography of filmmaking focused on Dreyer's work. He has worked on the restoration of Dreyer's films ONCE UPON A TIME and DIE GEZEICHNETEN and recorded audio commentaries for DVD editions of LA PASSION DE JEANNE D'ARC, MICHAEL, and DAY OF WRATH as well as for Benjamin Christensen's HÄXAN and Victor Sjöström's THE PHANTOM CARRIAGE. He is co-editor of the *Journal of Scandinavian Cinema*.

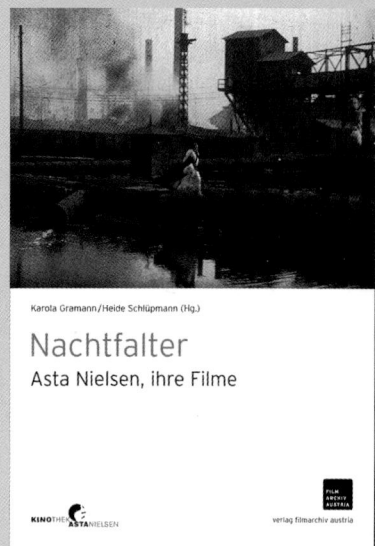

ASTA NIELSEN

Volume 1 (ed.: Eric de Kuyper/Karola Gramann/Sabine Nessel/ Heide Schlüpmann/Michael Wedel)

Unmögliche Liebe. Asta Nielsen, ihr Kino is dedicated to the traces of the phenomenon Asta Nielsen in her films, as well as their contemporary and present reception. International authors confront their movie experiences and screen encounters and perceive topicality and echo of a unique artist individually and scientifically.

Volume 2 (ed.: Karola Gramann/Heide Schlüpmann)

Nachtfalter. Asta Nielsen, ihre Filme traces her films as elusive and fickle structures which only deploy their full glamour in darkness – also or especially the lost ones. They are presented according to the chronology of their release to visualize them as a mirror of historical developments. In addition to the so far most extensive filmography and the reprint of contemporary recensions priority is given to photos, stills, frame enlargements, posters and film leaflets in this unique documentation. Thus what is in large part lost movie history becomes present again.

Both volumes in slipcase
ISBN 987-3-902531-84-1

EUR 39,90

www.filmarchiv.at